MATHEMATICS OF BIOINFORMATICS

Wiley Series on

Bioinformatics: Computational Techniques and Engineering

A complete list of the titles in this series appears at the end of this volume.

MATHEMATICS OF BIOINFORMATICS

Theory, Practice, and Applications

Matthew He

Sergey Petoukhov

WILEY

A JOHN WILEY & SONS, INC., PUBLICATION

Published by John Wiley & Sons, Inc., Hoboken, New Jersey.
Published simultaneously in Canada.

For general information on our other products and services or for technical support, please
contact our Customer Care Department within the United States at (800) 762-2974, outside
the United States at (317) 572-3993 or fax (317) 572-4002.

Wiley also publishes its books in a variety of electronic formats. Some content that appears in
print may not be available in electronic formats. For more information about Wiley products,
visit our web site at www.wiley.com.

Library of Congress Cataloging-in-Publication Data Is Available

He, Matthew
   Mathematics of bioinformatics: theory, practice, and applications / Matthew He,
   Sergey Petoukhov

   Includes bibliographical references and index.

   ISBN 978-0-470-40443-0 (cloth)

10 9 8 7 6 5 4 3 2 1

CONTENTS

PREFACE

Recent progress in the determination of genomic sequences has yielded many millions of gene sequences. But what do these sequences tell us, and what generalities and rules are governed by them? There is more to life than the genomic blueprint of each organism. Life functions within the natural laws that we know and those we do not know. It appears that we understand very little about genetic contexts required to "read" these sequences. Mathematics can be used to understand life from the molecular level to the level of the biosphere. This book is intended to further integrate the mathematics and biological sciences. The reader will gain valuable knowledge about mathematical methods and tools, phenomenological results, and interdisciplinary connections in the fields of molecular genetics, bioinformatics, and informatics.

Historically, mathematics, probability, and statistics have been widely used in the biological sciences. Science is challenged to understand the system organization of the molecular genetics ensemble, with its unique properties of reliability and productivity. Disclosing key aspects of this organization constitutes a big step in science about nature as a whole and in creating the most productive biotechnologies. Knowledge of this structural organization should become a part of mathematical natural science.

Advances in mathematical methods and techniques in bioinformatics have been growing rapidly. Mathematics has a fundamental role in describing the complexities of biological structures, patterns, and processes. Mathematical analysis of structures of molecular systems has essential meaning for bioinformatics, biomathematics, and biotechnology. Mathematics is used to elucidate trends, patterns, connections, and relationships in a quantitative manner that can lead to important discoveries in biology. This book is devoted to drawing a closer connection and better integration between mathematical methods and biological codes, sequences, structures, networks, and systems biology. It is intended for researchers and graduate students who want an overview of the field and who want information on the possibilities (and challenges) of the interface between mathematics and bioinformatics. In short, the book provides a broad overview of the interfaces between mathematics and bioinformatics.

ORGANIZATION OF THE BOOK

To reach a broad spectrum of readers, this book does not require a deep knowledge of mathematics or biology. The reader will learn fundamental concepts and methods from mathematics and biology. The book is organized into 10 chapters covering mathematical topics in relation to genetic code systems, biological sequences, structures and functions, networks and biological systems, matrix genetics, cognitive informatics, and the central dogma of informatics. Three appendixes, on bioinformatics notations, a historical time line of bioinformatics, and a bioinformatics glossary, are included for easy reference.

Chapter 1 provides an overview of bioinformatics history, genetic code and mathematics, background mathematics for bioinformatics, and the big picture of bioinformatics–informatics.

Chapter 2 is devoted to symmetrical analysis for genetic systems. Genetic coding possesses noise immunity. Mathematical theories of noise-immunity coding and discrete signal processing are based on matrix methods of representation and analysis of information. These matrix methods, which are connected closely to relations of symmetry, are borrowed for a matrix analysis of ensembles of molecular elements of the genetic code. A uniform representation of ensembles of genetic multiplets in the form of matrices of a cumulative Kronecker family is described. The analysis of molecular peculiarities of the system of nitrogenous bases reveals the first significant relations of symmetry in these genetic matrices. It permits one to introduce a natural numbering of the multiplets in each of the genetic matrices and to provide a basis for further analysis of genetic structures. Connections of the numerated genetic matrices with famous matrices of dyadic shifts and with the golden section are demonstrated.

In Chapter 3 we define biological, mathematical, and binary sequences in theoretical computer science. We describe pairwise, multiple, and optimal sequence alignment. We discuss the scoring system used to rank alignments, the algorithms used to find optimal (or good) scoring alignments, and statistical methods used to evaluate the significance of an alignment score.

Chapter 4 provides an introduction to the structures of DNA, key elements of knot theory, such as links, tangles, and knot polynomials, and applications of knot theory to the study of closed circular DNA. The physical and chemical properties of this type of DNA can be explained in terms of basic characteristics of a linking number which is invariant under continuous deformation of the DNA structure and is the sum of two geometric quantities, twist and writhing.

In Chapter 5 we introduce protein primary, secondary, tertiary, and quaternary structure by geometric means. We also discuss the classification of proteins, physical forces in proteins, protein motion (folding and unfolding), and basic methods for secondary and tertiary structure prediction.

Chapter 6 covers the topics of network approaches in biological systems. These approaches offer the tools to analyze and understand a host of biological systems. In particular, within the cell the variety of interactions among genes, proteins, and metabolites are captured by network representations. In this chapter we focus our discussion on biological applications of the theory of graphs and networks.

Chapter 7 covers the topics of biological systems and genetic code systems. We explain how the presence of fractal geometry can be used in an analytical way to study genetic code systems and predict outcomes in systems, to generate hypotheses, and to help design experiments. At the end of the chapter we discuss the emerging field of systems biology, as well as challenges and perspectives in biological systems.

Chapter 8 continues the discussion introduced in Chapter 2 on genetic matrices and their symmetries and algebraic properties. The algebraic theory of coding is one of the modern fields of applications of algebra and uses matrix algebra intensively. This chapter is devoted to matrix forms of presentations of the genetic code for algebraic analysis of a basic scheme of degeneracy of the genetic code. Similar matrix forms are utilized in the theory of signal processing and encoding. The Kronecker family of the genetic matrices is investigated, which is based on the genetic matrix [C A; U G], where C, A, U, and G are the letters of the genetic alphabet. This matrix in the third Kronecker power is the 8×8 matrix, which contains all 64 genetic triplets in a strict order with a natural binary numeration of the triplets by numbers from 0 to 63. Peculiarities of the basic scheme of the genetic code degeneracy are reflected in the symmetrical black-and-white mosaic of this genetic 8×8 matrix. Unexpectedly, this mosaic matrix is connected algorithmically with Hadamard matrices, which are well known in the theory of signal processing and encoding, spectral analysis, quantum mechanics, and quantum computers. Furthermore, many types of cyclic permutations of genetic elements lead unexpectedly to reconstruction of initial Hadamard matrices into new Hadamard matrices. This demonstrates that matrix algebra is a promising instrument and adequate language in bioinformatics and algebraic biology.

In Chapter 9 we review briefly the intersections and connections between the two emerging fields of bioinformatics and cognitive informatics through a systems view of emerging pattern, dissipative structure, and evolving cognition of living systems. A new type of math-denotational mathematics for cognitive informatics is introduced. It is hoped that this brief review will encourage further exploration of our understanding of the biological basis of cognition, perception, learning, memory, thought, and mind.

In Chapter 10 we return to the big picture of informatics introduced in Chapter 1. We propose a general concept of data, information, and knowledge and then place the main focus on the process and transition from data to information and then to knowledge. We present the concept of the central dogma of informatics, in analogy to the central dogma of molecular biology.

Each chapter finishes with a summary of challenges and perspectives of corresponding topics. These summaries are structured to bridge the gaps among the interdisciplinary areas, which involve concepts and ideas from a variety of sciences, including biology, biochemistry, physics, computer science, and mathematics.

THE CHALLENGES

The interface between mathematics and bioinformatics and computational biology presents challenges and opportunities for both mathematicians and biologists. Unique opportunities for research have surfaced within the last 10 to 20 years, both because of the explosion of biological data with the advent of new technologies and because of the availability of advanced and powerful computers that can organize the plethora of data. For biology, the possibilities range from the level of the cell and molecule to the level of the biosphere. For mathematics, the potential is great in traditional applied areas such as statistics and differential equations, as well as in such nontraditional areas as knot theory.

The primary purpose of encouraging biologists and mathematicians to work together is to investigate fundamental problems that cannot only be approached by biologists or by mathematicians. If this effort is successful, the future may produce individuals with both biological skills and mathematical insight and facility. At this time such people are rare; it is clear, however, that a greater percentage of the training of future biologists must be mathematically oriented. Both disciplines can expect to gain by this effort. Mathematics is the "lens through which to view the universe" and serves to identify important details of the biological data and suggest the next series of experiments. Mathematicians, on the other hand, can be challenged to develop new mathematics in order to perform this function.

In this book we explore some of the development and opportunities at the interface between biology and mathematics. To mathematicians, the book demonstrates that the stimulation of biological data and applications will enrich the discipline of mathematics for decades to come, as did applications in the past from the physical sciences. To biologists, the book presents the use of mathematical approaches to provide insights available for bioinformatics. To both communities, the book demonstrates the ferment and excitement of a rapidly evolving field—bioinformatics.

Acknowledgments

This book is part of the Wiley Series on Bioinformatics: Computational Techniques and Engineering. The authors would like to express our gratitude to the series editors, Yi Pan and Albert Zomaya, for giving us the opportunity to present our research interest as a book in this series. We would also like to thank many of our colleagues who worked with us in exploring topics relevant to this book. Their names can be found in the chapter references. Only literature closely related to our work is included in the references, and due to the wide extent of subjects in the studies, the references cited are incomplete. The authors apologize deeply for any relevant omission.

We want to thank the Mechanical Engineering Institute of the Russian Academy of Sciences, Moscow, Russia and the Farquhar College of Arts and Sciences of Nova Southeastern University, Fort Lauderdale, Florida for their support. We are deeply indebted to our colleagues Diego Castano, Emily Schmitt, and Robin Sherman of Nova Southeastern University for offering suggestions and for reviewing the final version of the manuscript.

Special thanks also go to the publishing team at Wiley, whose contributions throughout the entire process from initial proposal to final publication have been invaluable: particular to the Wiley assistant development editing team, who continuously provided prompt guidance and support throughout the book editing process.

Finally, we would like to give our special thanks to our families for their patient love, which enabled us to complete this work.

Nova Southeastern University   Matthew He
Fort Lauderdale, Florida

Russian Academy of Sciences   Sergey Petoukhov
Moscow, Russia

March 16, 2010

ABOUT THE AUTHORS

Matthew He, Ph.D., is a full professor and director of the Division of Mathematics, Science, and Technology of Nova Southeastern University in Florida. He has been a full professor and grand Ph.D. of the World Information Distributed University since 2004, as well as an academician of the European Academy of Informatization. He received a Ph.D. in mathematics from the University of South Florida in 1991. He was a research associate at the Department of Mathematics, Eldgenossische Technische Hochschule, Zurich, Switzerland, and the Department of Mathematics and Theoretical Physics, Cambridge University, Cambridge, England. He was also a visiting professor at the National Key Research Lab of Computational Mathematics of the Chinese Academy of Science and the University of Rome, Italy.

Dr. He has authored and edited eight books and published over 100 research papers in the areas of mathematics, bioinformatics, computer vision, information theory, mathematics, and engineering techniques in the medical and biological sciences. He is an editor of *International Journal of Software Science and Computational Intelligence, International Journal of Cognitive Informatics and Natural Intelligence, International Journal of Biological Systems, and International Journal of Integrative Biology*. He is an invited series editor of Henry Stewart Talk "Using Bioinformatics in Exploration in Genetic Diversity" in Biomedical and Life Sciences Series. He received the World Academy of Sciences Achievement Award in recognition of his research contributions in the field of computing in 2003. He is chairman of the International Society of Symmetry in Bioinformatics and a member of International Advisory Board of the International Symmetry Association. He is a member of the American Mathematical Society, the Association of Computing Machinery, the IEEE Computer Society, the World Association of Science Engineering, and an international advisory board member of the bioinformatics group of the International Federation for Information Processing. He was an international scientific committee co-chair of the International Conference of Bioinformatics and Its Applications in 2004 and a general co-chair of the International Conference of Bioinformatics Research and Applications in 2009, and has been a keynote speaker at many international conferences in the areas of mathematics, bioinformatics, and information science and engineering.

Sergey Petoukhov, Ph.D., is a chief scientist of the Department of Biomechanics, Mechanical Engineering Research Institute of the Russian Academy of

Sciences in Moscow. He has been a full professor and grand Ph.D. of the World Information Distributed University since 2004, as well as an academician of the European Academy of Informatizátion. He is a laureate of the state prize of the USSR (1986) for his achievements in biomechanics. Dr. Petoukhov graduated from the Moscow Physical-Technical Institute in 1970 and received a postgraduated from the institute in 1973 with a specialty in biophysics. He received a Golden Medal of the National Exhibition of Scientific Achievements in Moscow in 1973 for his physical model of human vestibular apparatus. He received his first scientific degree in the USSR in 1973: a Candidate of Biological Sciences degree with a in specialty in biophysics. He received his second scientific degree in the USSR in 1988: Doctor of Physical-Mathematical Sciences in two specialties, biomechanics and crystallography and crystallophysics. He was an academic foreign stager of the Technical University of Nova Scotia, Halifax, Canada in 1988. He was elected an academician of Academy of Quality Problems (Russia) in 2000. Dr. Petoukhov is a director of the Department of Biophysics and chairman of the Scientific-Technical Council at the Scientific-Technical Center of Information Technologies and Systems in Moscow. He was vice-president of the International Society for the Interdisciplinary Study of Symmetry from 1989 to 2000 and chairman of the international advisory board of the International Symmetry Association (with headquarters in Budapest, Hungary; http://symmetry.hu/) from 2000 to the present. Dr. Petoukhov has been honorary chairman of the board of directors of the International Society of Symmetry in Bioinformatics since 2000 and vice-president and academician of the National Academy of Intellectual and Social Technologies of Russia since 2003. Dr. Petoukhov is academician of the International Diplomatic Academy (Belgium; www.bridgeworld.org). He is Russian chairman (chief) of an official scientific cooperative body of the Russian and Hungarian Academies of Sciences on the theme "Nonlinear Models in Biomechanics, Bioinformatics, and the Theory of Self-organizing Systems."

Dr. Petoukhov has published over 150 research papers (including seven books) in biomechanics, bioinformatics, mathematical and theoretical biology, theory of symmetries and its applications, and mathematics. He is a member of the editorial board of two international journals: *Journal of Biological Systems* and *Symmetry: Culture and Science*. He was a guest editor of special issues (on bioinformatics) of the international journal *Journal of Biological Systems* in 2004. Dr. Petoukhov is the book editor of *Symmetries in Genetic Informatics* (2001), *Advances in Bioinformatics and Its Applications* (2004), and a Russian edition (2006) of a book by Canadian professor R. V. Jean, *Phyllotaxis: A Systemic Study in Plant Morphogenesis* (Cambridge University Press, Cambridge, UK, 1994). He is a co-organizer of international conferences on the theory of symmetries and its applications (Budapest, Hungary, 1989; Hirosima, Japan, 1992; Washington, D.C., 1995; Haifa, Izrael, 1998; Budapest, Hungary, 2003, 2006, and 2009; Moscow, Russia, 2006). He was chairman of the international program committee of the International Conference on

Bioinformatics and Its Applications in Fort Lauderdale, Florida, in 2004. He was co-chairman of the organizing committees of international conferences on "Modern Science and Ancient Chinese 'The Book of Changes' (*I Ching*)" in Moscow in 2003, 2004, 2005, and 2006. He teaches a course on biophysics and bioinformatics at the Moscow Physical-Technical Institute and a course in architectural bionics at the Peoples' Friendship University of Russia. He is actively involved in promoting science, education, and technology.

1 Bioinformatics and Mathematics

Traditionally, the study of biology is from morphology to cytology and then to the atomic and molecular level, from physiology to microscopic regulation, and from phenotype to genotype. The recent development of bioinformatics begins with research on genes and moves to the molecular sequence, then to molecular conformation, from structure to function, from systems biology to network biology, and further investigates the interactions and relationships among, genes, proteins, and structures. This new reverse paradigm sets a theoretical starting point for a biological investigation. It sets a new line of investigation with a unifying principle and uses mathematical tools extensively to clarify the ever-changing phenomena of life quantitatively and analytically.

It is well known that there is more to life than the genomic blueprint of each organism. Life functions within the natural laws that we know and those that we do not know. Life is founded on mathematical patterns of the physical world. Genetics exploits and organizes these patterns. Mathematical regularities are exploited by the organic world at every level of form, structure, pattern, behavior, interaction, and evolution. Essentially all knowledge is intrinsically unified and relies on a small number of natural laws. Mathematics helps us understand how monomers become polymers necessary for the assembly of cells. Mathematics can be used to understand life from the molecular to the biosphere levels, including the origin and evolution of organisms, the nature of genomic blueprints, and the universal genetic code as well as ecological relationships.

Mathematics and biological data have a synergistic relationship. Biological information creates interesting problems, mathematical theory and methods provide models for understanding them, and biology validates the mathematical models. A model is a representation of a real system. Real systems are too complicated, and observation may change the real system. A good system model should be simple, yet powerful enough to capture the behavior of the real system. Models are especially useful in bioinformatics. In this chapter we provide an overview of bioinformatics history, genetic code and mathematics, background mathematics for bioinformatics, and the big picture of bioinformatics–informatics.

Mathematics of Bioinformatics: Theory, Practice, and Applications, By Matthew He and Sergey Petoukhov
Copyright © 2011 John Wiley & Sons, Inc.

1.1 INTRODUCTION

Mendel's Genetic Experiments and Laws of Heredity   The discovery of genetic inheritance by Gregor Mendel back in 1865 was considered as the start of bioinformatics history. He did experiments on the cross-fertilization of different colors of the same species. Mendel's genetic experiments with pea plants took him eight years (1856–1863). During this time, Mendel grew over 10,000 pea plants, keeping track of progeny number and type. He recorded the data carefully and performed mathematical analysis of the data. Mendel illustrated that the process of inheritance of traits could be explained more easily if it was controlled by factors passed down from generation to generation. He concluded that genes come in pairs. Genes are inherited as distinct units, one from each parent. He also recorded the segregation of parental genes and their appearance in the offspring as dominant or recessive traits. He published his results in 1865. He recognized the mathematical patterns of inheritance from one generation to the next. Mendel's laws of heredity are usually stated as follows:

- *The law of segregation.* A gene pair defines each inherited trait. Parental genes are randomly separated by the sex cells, so that sex cells contain only one gene of the pair. Offspring therefore inherit one genetic allele from each parent.
- *The law of independent assortment.* Genes for different traits are sorted from one another in such a way that the inheritance of one trait is not dependent on the inheritance of another.
- *The law of dominance.* An organism with alternate forms of a gene will express the form that is dominant.

In 1900, Mendel's work was rediscovered independently by DeVries, Correns, and Tschermak, each of whom confirmed Mendel's discoveries. Mendel's own method of research is based on the identification of significant variables, isolating their effects, measuring these meticulously, and eventually subjecting the resulting data to mathematical analysis. Thus, his work is connected directly to contemporary theories of mathematics, statistics, and physics.

Origin of Species   Charles Darwin published *On the Origin of Species by Means of Natural Selection* (Darwin, 1859) or "The Preservation of Favored Races in the Struggle for Life." His key work was that evolution occurs through the selection of inheritance and involves transmissible rather than acquired characteristics between individual members of a species. Darwin's landmark theory did not specify the means by which characteristics are inherited. The mechanism of heredity had not been determined at that time.

First Genetic Map   In 1910, after the rediscovery of Mendel's work, Thomas Hunt Morgan at Columbia University carried out crossing experiments with the fruit fly (*Drosophila melanogaster*). He proved that the genes responsible for the appearance of a specific phenotype were located on chromosomes. He also found that genes on the same chromosome do not always assort independently. Furthermore, he suggested that the strength of linkage between genes depended on the distance between them on the chromosome. That is, the closer two genes lie to each other on a chromosome, the greater the chance that they will be inherited together. Similarly, the farther away they are from each other, the greater the chance of that they will be separated in the process of crossing over. The genes are separated when a crossover takes place in the distance between the two genes during cell division. Morgan's experiments also lead to *Drosophila*'s unusual position as, to this day, one of the best studied organisms and most useful tools in genetic research. In 1911, Alfred Sturtevant, then an undergraduate researcher in the laboratory of Thomas Hunt Morgan, mapped the locations of the fruit fly genes, creating the first genetic map ever made.

Transposable Genetic Elements In 1944, Barbara McClintock discovered that genes can move on a chromosome and can jump from one chromosome to another. She studied the inheritance of color and pigment distribution in corn kernels at the Carnegie Institution Department of Genetics in Cold Spring Harbor, New York. At age 81 she was awarded a Nobel prize. It is believed that transposons may be linked to such genetic disorders as hemophilia, leukemia, and breast cancer; and transposons may have played a crucial role in evolution.

DNA Double Helix In 1953, James Watson and Francis Crick proposed a double-helix model of DNA. DNA is made of three basic components: a sugar, an acid, and an organic "base." The base was always one of the four nucleotides: adenine (A), cytosine (C), guanine (G), or thymine (T). These four different bases are categorized in two groups: purines (adenine and guanine) and pyrimidines (thymine and cytosine). In 1950, Erwin Chargaff found that the amounts of adenine (A) and thymine (T) in DNA are about the same, as are the amounts of guanine (G) and cytosine (C). These relationships later became known as "Chargaff's rules" and led to much speculation about the three-dimensional structure that DNA would have. Rosalind Franklin, a British chemist, used the x-ray diffraction technique to capture the first high-quality images of the DNA molecule. Franklin's colleague Maurice Wilkins showed the pictures to James Watson, an American zoologist, who had been working with Francis Crick, a British biophysicist, on the structure of the DNA molecule. These pictures gave Watson and Crick enough information to propose in 1953 a double-stranded, helical, complementary, antiparallel model for DNA. Crick, Watson, and Wilkins shared the 1962 Nobel Prize in Physiology or Medicine for the discovery that the DNA molecule has a double-helical structure. Rosalind Franklin, whose images of DNA helped lead to the discovery, died of cancer in 1958 and, under Nobel rules, was not eligible for the prize.

In 1957, Francis Crick and George Gamov worked out the "central dogma," explaining how DNA functions to make protein. Their *sequence hypothesis* posited that the DNA sequence specifies the amino acid sequence in a protein. They also suggested that genetic information flows only in one direction, from DNA to messenger RNA to protein, the central concept of the central dogma.

Genetic Code *(see Appendix A)*   The genetic code was finally "cracked" in 1966. Marshall Nirenberg, Heinrich Mathaei, and Severo Ochoa demonstrated that a sequence of three nucleotide bases, a codon or triplet, determines each of the 20 amino acids found in nature. This means that there are 64 possible combinations ($4^3 = 64$) for 20 amino acids. They formed synthetic messenger ribonucleic acid (mRNA) by mixing the nucleotides of RNA with a special enzyme called polynucleotide phosphorylase. This resulted in the formation of a single-stranded RNA in this reaction. The question was how these 64 genetic codes could code for 20 different amino acids. Nirenberg and Matthaei synthesized poly(U) by reacting only uracil nucleotides with the RNA-synthesizing enzyme, producing –UUUU–. They mixed this poly(U) with the protein-synthesizing machinery of *Escherichia coli* in vitro and observed the formation of a protein. This protein turned out to be a polypeptide of phenylalanine. They showed that a triplet of uracil must code for phenylalanine. Philip Leder and Nirenberg found an even better experimental protocol to solve this fundamental problem. By 1965 the genetic code was solved almost completely. They found that the "extra" codons are merely redundant: Some amino acids have one or two codons, some have four, and some have six. Three codons (called *stop codons*) serve as stop signs for RNA-synthesizing proteins.

First Recombinant DNA Molecules   In 1972, Paul Berg of Stanford University created the first recombinant DNA molecules by combining the DNA of two different organisms. He used a restriction enzyme to isolate a gene from a human-cancer-causing monkey virus. Then he used lipase to join the section of virus DNA with a molecule of DNA from the bacterial virus lambda, creating the first recombinant DNA molecule. He realized the risks of his experiment and terminated it temporarily before the recombinant DNA molecule was added to *E. coli*, where it would have quickly been reproduced. He proposed a one-year moratorium on recombinant DNA studies while safety issues were addressed. Berg later resumed his studies of recombinant DNA techniques and was awarded the 1980 Nobel Prize in Chemistry. His experiments paved the road for the field of genetic engineering and the modern biotechnology industry.

DNA Sequencing and Database   In early 1974, Frederick Sanger from the UK Medical Research Council was first to invent DNA-sequencing techniques. During his experiments to uncover the amino acids in bovine insulin, he developed the basics of modern sequencing methods. Sanger's approach

involved copying DNA strands, which would show the location of the nucleotides in the strands. To apply Sanger's approach, scientists had to analyze the
composite collections of DNA pieces detected from four test tubes, one for
each of the nucleotides found in DNA (adenosine, cytosine, thymidine,
guanine). Then they needed to be arranged in the correct order. This technique
is very slow and tedious. It takes many years to sequence only a few million
letters in a string of DNA. Almost simultaneously, the American scientists
Alan Maxam and Walter Gilbert were creating a different method called the
cleavage method. The base for virtually all DNA sequencing was the dideoxy-
chain-terminating reaction developed by Sanger.

In 1978, David Botstein developed restriction-fragment-length polymorphisms. Individual human beings differ one base pair in every 500 nucleotides
or so. The most interesting variations for geneticists are those that are recognized by certain enzymes called *restriction enzymes*. Each of these enzymes
cuts DNA only in the presence of a specific sequence (e.g., GAATTC in the
case of the restriction enzyme EcoR1). This sequence is called a *restriction site*.
The enzyme will bypass the region if it has mutated to GACTTC. Thus, when
a specific restriction enzyme cuts the DNA of different people, it may produce
fragments of different lengths. These DNA fragments can be separated according to size by making them move through a porous gel in an electric field.
Since the smaller fragments move more rapidly than the larger ones, their sizes
can be determined by examining their positions in the gel. Variations in their
lengths are called *restriction-fragment-length polymorphisms*.

In 1980, Kary Mullis invented polymerase chain reaction (PCR), a method
for multiplying DNA sequences in vitro. The purpose of PCR is to make a
huge number of copies of a specific DNA fragment, such as a gene. Use of
thermostable polymerase allows the dissociation of newly formed complementary DNA and subsequent annealing or hybridization of the primers to the
target sequence with a minimal loss of enzymatic activity. PCR may be necessary to receive enough starting template for instance sequencing.

In 1986, scientists presented a means of detecting ddNTPs with fluorescent
tags, which required only a single test tube instead of four. As a result of this
discovery, the time required to process a given batch of DNA was reduced
by one-fourth. The amount of sequenced base pairs increased rapidly from
there on.

Established in 1988 as a national resource for molecular biology information, the National Center for Biotechnology Information (NCBI) carries out
diverse responsibilities. NCBI creates public databases, conducts research in
computational biology, develops software tools for analyzing genome data,
and disseminates biomedical information: all for a better understanding of
molecular processes affecting human health and disease. NCBI conducts
research on fundamental biomedical problems at the molecular level using
mathematical and computational methods.

The European Bioinformatics Institute (EBI) is a nonprofit academic organization that forms part of the European Molecular Biology Laboratory

·(EMBL). The roots of the EBI lie in the EMBL Nucleotide Sequence Data Library, which was established in 1980 at the EMBL laboratories in Heidelberg, Germany and was the world's first nucleotide sequence database. The original goal was to establish a central computer database of DNA sequences rather than having scientists submit sequences to journals. What began as a modest task of abstracting information from literature soon became a major database activity with direct electronic submissions of data and the need for a highly skilled informatics staff. The task grew in scale with the start of the genome projects, and grew in visibility as the data became relevant to research in the commercial sector. It became apparent that the EMBL Nucleotide Sequence Data Library needed better financial security to ensure its long-term viability and to cope with the sheer scale of the task.

Human Genome Project   In 1990, the U.S. Human Genome Project started as a 15-year effort coordinated by the U.S. Department of Energy and the National Institutes of Health. The project originally was planned to last 15 years, but rapid technological advances accelerated the expected completion date to 2003. Project goals were to:

- Identify all the genes in human DNA
- Determine the sequences of the 3 billion chemical base pairs that make up human DNA
- Store this information in databases
- Improve tools for data analysis
- Transfer related technologies to the private sector
- Address the ethical, legal, and social issues (ELSIs) that may arise from the project

In 1991, working with Nobel laureate Hamilton Smith, Venter's genomic research project (TIGR) created the *shotgunning method*. At first the method was controversial among Venter's colleagues, who called it crude and inaccurate. However, Venter cross-checked his results by sequencing the genes in both directions, achieving a level of accuracy that greatly impressed his initial sceptical rivals. Within a year, TIGR published the entire genome of *Haemophilus influenzae*, a bacterium with nearly 2 million nucleotides.

The draft human genome sequence was published on February 15, 2001, in the journals *Nature* (publically funded Human Genome Project) and *Science* (Craig Venter's firm Celera).

1.2   GENETIC CODE AND MATHEMATICS

It is known that the secrets of life are more complex than DNA and the genetic code. One secret of life is the self-assembly of the first cell with a genetic blueprint that allowed it to grow and divide. Another secret of life may be the mathematical control of life as we know it and the logical organization of the genetic code and the use of math in understanding life.

Mathematics has a fundamental role in understanding the complexities of living organisms. For example, the genetic code triplets of three bases in messenger ribonucleic acid (mRNA) that encode for specific amino acids during the translation process (synthesis of proteins using the genetic code in mRNA as the template) have some interesting mathematical logic in their organization (Cullman and Labouygues, 1984). An examination of this logical organization may allow us to better understand the logical assembly of the genetic code and life.

The genetic code in mRNA is composed of U for uracil, C for cytosine, A for adenine, and G for guanine. The genetic code triplets of three bases in messenger ribonucleic acid (mRNA) that encode for specific amino acids during the translation process (synthesis of proteins using the genetic code in mRNA as the template) have some interesting and mathematical logic in their organization.

In the first stage there was an investigation of the *standard genetic code*. In the past few decades, some other variants of the genetic code were revealed, which are described at the Web site http://www.ncbi.nlm.nih.gov/Taxonomy/Utils/wprintgc.cgi and which differ from the standard genetic code in some correspondences among 64 triplets, 20 amino acids, and stop codons. One noticeable feature of the genetic code is that some amino acids are encoded by several different but related base codons or triplets. There are 64 triplets or codons. In the case of the standard genetic code, three triplets (UAA, UAG, and UGA) are nonsense codons—no amino acid corresponds to their code. The remaining 61 codons represent 20 different amino acids. The genetic code is encoded in combinations of the four nucleotides found in DNA and then RNA. There are 16 possible combinations (4^2) of the four nucleotides of nucleotide pairs. This would not be sufficient to code for 20 amino acids (Prescott et al., 1993). The solution is mathematically simple. During the self-assembly and evolution of life, a code word (codon or triplet) evolved that provides for 64 (4^3) possible combinations. This simple code determines all the proteins necessary for life.

The genetic code is also degenerate. For example, up to six different codons are available for some amino acid. Another noteworthy aspect of biological messages is that minimal information is necessary to encode the messages (Peusner, 1974), and the messages can be encoded and decoded and put to work in amazingly short periods of time. A bacterial *E. coli* cell can grow and divide in half an hour, depending on the growth conditions. Mathematically, it could not be simpler.

Selenocysteine (twenty-first amino acid encoded by the genetic code) codon is UGA, normally a stop codon. Selenocysteine is a derivative of cysteine in which the sulfur atom is replaced by a selenium atom that is an essential atom in a small number of proteins, notably glutathione peroxidase. These proteins are found in prokaryotes and eukaryotes, ranging from *E. coli* to humans. The selenocysteine is incorporated into proteins during translation in response to the UGA codon. This amino acid is readily oxidized by oxygen. Enzymes containing this amino acid must be protected from oxygen. As the oxygen concentration increased, the selenocysteine may gradually have been replaced by cysteine with the codons UGU and UGC (Madigan et al., 1997). The three-base code sometimes differs only in the third base position. For example, the genetic code for glycine is GGU, GGC, GGA, or GGG. Only the third base is variable. A similar third-base-change pattern exists for the amino acids lysine, asparagine, proline, leucine, and phenylalanine. These relationships are not random. For example, UUU codes for the same amino acid (phenylalanine) as UUC. In some codons the third base determines the amino acid. The second base is also important. For example, when the second base is C, the amino acid specified comes from a family of four codons for one amino acid, except for valine. Biological expression is in the form of coded messages—messages that contain the information on shapes of bimolecular structure and biochemical reactions necessary for life function. The coded message determines the protein, which folds into a shape that requires the minimal amount of energy. Therefore, the total energy of attraction and repulsion between atoms is minimal. How did this genetic code come to be the code of life as we know it? Nature had billions of years to experiment with different coding schemes, and eventually adopted the genetic code we have today.

It is simple in terms of mathematics. It is also conserved but can be mutated at the DNA level and also repaired. The code is thermodynamically possible and consistent with the origin, evolution, and diversity of life. Math as applied to understanding biology has countless uses. It is used to elucidate trends, patterns, connections, and relationships in a quantitative manner that can lead to important discoveries in biology. How can math be used to understand living organisms? One way to explore this relationship is to use examples from the bacterial world. The reader is also referred to an excellent text by Stewart (1998) that illustrates how math can be used to elucidate a fuller understanding of the natural world. For example, the exponential growth of bacterial cells (1 cell → 2 cells → 4 cells → 8 cells → 16 cells, and so on) is essential information that is one of the foundations of microbiology research. Exponential growth over known periods of time is essential in the understanding of bacterial growth in countless areas of research. The ability to use math to describe growth per unit of time is an excellent example of the interrelationship between math and the capability to understand this aspect of life. For example, the basic unit of life is the cell, an entity of 1. Bacteria also multiply by dividing. Remember that life is composed of matter, and matter is composed of atoms, and that atoms, especially in solids, are arranged in an efficient manner into molecules that minimize the energy needed to take on specific configurations. Often, these arrangements or configurations are repeating units of monomers that make up polymers. Stewart (1998) described it very well in his excellent book when he posed the question: "What could be more mathematical than

DNA?" The ability of DNA to replicate itself exactly and at the same time change ever so slightly allows evolutionary changes to occur. The mathematical sequences of four different bases (adenine, thymine, guanine, and cytosine) in DNA are the blueprint of life. Again, the order of the four bases determines the mRNA sequence, and then the protein that is synthesized. DNA in a cell is also capable of replicating itself precisely in a cell. The replicated DNA can then partition into each new cell when one cell divides and becomes two cells. The DNA can only replicate with the assistance of enzymes that unwind the DNA and allow the DNA strands to act as templates for synthesis of the second strand. The ability of a cell to unwind its DNA, replicate or copy new strands, and then partition them between two new cells has a mathematical basis. The four bases are paired in a specific manner: A (adenine) with T (thymine), C (cytosine) with G (guanine) on the opposite strands along a sugar phosphate backbone. Each strand can contain all four bases in any order. However, A must bond with T and C with G on opposite strands. This precise mathematical pairing must be obeyed.

Living organisms also have amazing mathematical order and symmetry. The repeating units of fatty acids, glycerol, and phosphate that make up a phospholipid membrane bilayer are one example. An excellent example of mathematical symmetry is the S-layer in many Archaea bacterial (prokaryotes consisting of methanogens, most extreme halophiles and hyperthermophiles, and *Thermoplasma*) cell walls that exhibit a hexagonal configuration. A cell that can assemble the same repeating units countless times is efficient and reduces the numbers of errors incorporated into the assembly. This is exactly the characteristic that is needed for a living cell to grow and divide. Yet a little bit of change can occur over time.

Biochemical reactions in cells are accompanied by gains or losses in energy during the reactions. Some of the energy is lost as heat and is not available to do work. In humans, heat is used to maintain a normal body temperature. The energy available to the cell is expressed as free energy and can be expressed as kJ/mol. Without the use of math and units of measurement, it would be impossible to describe energy metabolism in cells. Nor would we be able to describe the rates of enzyme reactions necessary for the self-assembly and functioning of life. Without units of temperature, we would not be able to describe the lower, upper, and optimum growth temperatures of specific microorganisms. The pH ranges for bacterial growth and the optimum pH values for enzyme reactions would be unknown without math to describe the values. Water availability values and oxygen concentrations would not be able to be described for growth of specific organisms. The examples are numerous. Without the use of math and scientific units to express values, our understanding of life would be minimal, and biology would not have made the great advances that it has made in the past decades. One central characteristic of living organisms is reproduction. From nutrients in their environment, they can self-assemble new cells in virtually exact copies. Second, living organisms are interdependent on each other and their activities. The Earth's biosphere, with its abundance of oxygen and living organisms, was self-assembled by living organisms.

From a chaotic lifeless environment on the early Earth, life self-assembled with the cell as the basic unit, with mathematically precise order, symmetry, and base pairing in DNA as the genetic blueprint and with triplet codons as the genetic code for protein synthesis.

It is well known that all knowledge is intrinsically unified and lies in a small number of natural laws. Math can be used to understand life from the molecular level to the level of the biosphere. For example, this includes the origin and evolution of organisms, the nature of the genomic blueprints, and the universal genetic code as well as ecological relationships. Math helps us look for trends, patterns, and relationships that may or may not be obvious to scientists. Math allows us to describe the dimensions of genes and the sizes of organelles, cells, organs, and whole organisms. Without this knowledge, a paucity of information would still exist on many aspects of life.

1.3   MATHEMATICAL BACKGROUND

In this section we provide a general background of major branches of mathematics that we discuss in relation to bioinformatics throughout the book.

Algebra   Algebra is the study of structure, relation, and quantity through symbolic operations for the systematic solution of equations and inequalities. In addition to working directly with numbers, algebra works with symbols, variables, and set elements. Addition and multiplication are viewed as general operations, and their precise definitions lead to advance structures such as groups, rings, and fields in which algebraic structures are defined and investigated axiomatically. Linear algebra studies the specific properties of vector spaces, including matrices. The properties common to all algebraic structures are studied in universal algebra. Axiomatic algebraic systems such as groups, rings, fields, and algebras over a field are investigated in the presence of a geometric structure (a metric or a topology) which is compatible with the algebraic structure. In recent years, algebraic structures have been discovered within the genetic codes, biological sequences, and biological structures. Matrices, polynomials, and other algebraic elements have been applied to studies of sequence alignments and protein structures and classifications.

Abstract Algebra   Abstract algebra extends the familiar concepts from basic algebra to more general concepts. *Abstract algebra* deals with the more general concept of *sets*: a collection of all objects selected by property, specific for the set under binary operations. Binary operations are the keystone of algebraic structures studied in abstract algebra: They form a part of groups, rings, fields, and more. A *binary operation* is a rule for combining two objects of a given type to obtain another object of that type. More precisely, a binary operation on a set S is a binary relation that maps elements of the Cartesian product $S \times S$ to S:

$$f: S \times S \to S$$

Addition (+), subtraction (−), multiplication (×), and division (÷) can be binary operations when defined on different sets, as is addition and multiplication of matrices, vectors, and polynomials. Groups, rings, and fields are fundamental structures in abstract algebra.

A *group* is a combination of a set S and a single binary operation "∗" with the following properties:

- An *identity* element e exists such that for every member a of S, $e \ast a$ and $a \ast e$ are both identical to a.
- Every element has an *inverse*: For every member a of S, there exists a member a^{-1} such that $a \ast a^{-1}$ and $a^{-1} \ast a$ are both identical to the identity element.
- The operation is *associative*: If a, b, and c are members of S, then $(a \ast b) \ast c$ is identical to $a \ast (b \ast c)$.
- The set S is *closed* under the binary operation ∗.

For example, the set of integers under the operation of addition is a group. In this group, the identity element is 0 and the inverse of any element a is its negation, $-a$. The associativity requirement is met because for any integers a, b, and c, $(a + b) + c = a + (b + c)$. The integers under the multiplication operation, however, do not form a group. This is because, in general, the multiplicative inverse of an integer is not an integer. For example, 4 is an integer, but its multiplicative inverse is 1/4, which is not an integer.

The structures and classifications of groups are studied in group theory. A major result in this theory is the classification of finite simple groups, which is thought to classify all of the finite simple groups into roughly 30 basic types.

Semigroups, monoids, and quasigroups are structures similar to groups, but more general. They comprise a set and a closed binary operation, but do not necessarily satisfy the other conditions. A *semigroup* has an *associative* binary operation but might not have an identity element. A *monoid* is a semigroup that does have an identity but might not have an inverse for every element. A *quasigroup* satisfies a requirement that any element can be turned into any other by a unique pre- or postoperation; however, the binary operation might not be associative. All are instances of *groupoids*, structures with a binary operation upon which no further conditions are imposed. All groups are monoids, and all monoids are semigroups.

Groups have only one binary operation. Rings and fields explain the behavior of the various types of numbers; they are structures with two operators. A *ring* has two binary operations, + and ×, with × distributive over +.

Distributive property generalized the *distributive law* for numbers and specifies the order in which the operators should be applied. For the integers $(a + b) \times c = a \times c + b \times c$ and $c \times (a + b) = c \times a + c \times b$, and $\times$ is said to be *distributive* over +. Under the first operator (+), it is commutative (i.e., $a + b = b + a$). Under the second operator ($\times$) it is associative, but it does not need to have the identity or inverse property, so division is not allowed. The additive (+) identity element is written as 0 and the additive inverse of a is written as $-a$. Integers with both binary operations + and $\times$ are an example of a ring.

A *field* is a ring with the additional property that all the elements, excluding 0, form an *Abelian group* (have a commutative property) under $\times$. The multiplicative ($\times$) identity is written as 1, and the multiplicative inverse of a is written as a^{-1}. The rational numbers, the real numbers, and the complex numbers are all examples of fields.

These algebraic structures have been used in the study of genetic codes. Group theory has many applications in physics and chemistry, and it is potentially applicable in any situation characterized by symmetry. In chemistry, groups are used to classify crystal structures, regular polyhedrals, and the symmetries of molecules. The assigned point groups can then be used to determine physical properties (such as polarity and chirality) and spectroscopic properties (particularly useful for Raman spectroscopy and infrared spectroscopy), and to construct molecular orbitals.

Probability   *Probability* is the language of uncertainty. It is the likelihood or chance that something is the case or will happen. Probability theory is used extensively in areas such as statistics, mathematics, science, philosophy, psychology, and in the financial markets to draw conclusions about the likelihood of potential events and the underlying mechanics of complex systems. The probability of an event E is represented by a real number in the range 0 to 1 and is denoted by $P(E), p(E)$, or $\Pr(E)$. An impossible event has a probability of 0, and a certain event has a probability of 1.

Statistics   *Statistics* is a mathematical science pertaining to the collection, analysis, interpretation or explanation, and presentation of data. Statistical methods can be used to summarize or describe a collection of data; this is called *descriptive statistics*. Descriptive statistics can be used to summarize the data, either numerically or graphically, to describe the sample. Basic examples of numerical descriptors include the mean and standard deviation. Graphical summarizations include various types of charts and graphs. In addition, patterns in the data may be modeled in a way that accounts for randomness and uncertainty in the observations, and then used to draw inferences about the process or population being studied; this is called *inferential statistics*. Inferential statistics is used to model patterns in the data, accounting for randomness and drawing inferences about the larger population. These inferences may take the form of answers to yes/no questions (hypothesis testing), estimates of numerical characteristics (estimation), descriptions of association (correlation), or modeling of relationships (regression). Other modeling techniques include ANOVA, time series, and data mining. Both descriptive and inferential statistics comprise applied statistics.

Probability and statistics have been used successfully to investigate sequence analysis, alignments, profile searches and phylogenetic trees, and many problems in bioinformatics.

Differential Geometry   *Differential geometry* is a mathematical discipline that uses the methods of differential and integral calculus to study problems in geometry. The theory of plane and space curves and of surfaces in three-dimensional Euclidean space formed the basis for its initial development. Differential geometry has grown into a field concerned more generally with geometric structures on differentiable manifolds. It is closely related to differential topology and to the geometric aspects of the theory of differential equations. In physics, differential geometry is the language in which Einstein's general theory of relativity is expressed. According to the theory, the universe is a smooth manifold equipped with a pseudo-Riemannian metric, which describes the curvature of space–time. Understanding this curvature is essential for the positioning of satellites into orbit around the Earth. In the biological and medical sciences, differential geometry has been used to study protein confirmation and the elasticity of nonrigid objects such as human hearts and human faces.

Topology   *Topology* is the mathematical study of the properties that are preserved through deformations, twistings, and stretchings of objects; however, tearing is not allowed. A circle is topologically equivalent to an ellipse (into which it can be deformed by stretching), and a sphere is equivalent to an ellipsoid. Similarly, the set of all possible positions of the hour hand of a clock is topologically equivalent to a circle (i.e., a one-dimensional closed curve with no intersections that can be embedded in two-dimensional space), the set of all possible positions of the hour and minute hands taken together is topologically equivalent to the surface of a torus (i.e., a two-dimensional surface that can be embedded in three-dimensional space), and the set of all possible positions of the hour, minute, and second hands taken together are topologically equivalent to a three-dimensional object. Topology can be used to abstract the inherent connectivity of objects while ignoring their detailed form. The mathematical definition of topology is described here briefly.

Let X be any set and let T be a family of subsets of X. Then T is a topology on X if:

- Both the empty set and X are elements of T.
- Any union of arbitrarily many elements of T is an element of T.
- Any intersection of finitely many elements of T is an element of T.

If T is a topology on X, then X together with T is called a *topological space*.

All sets in T are called *open*; note that, in general, not all subsets of X need be in T. A subset of X is said to be *closed* if its complement is in T (i.e., it is open). A subset of X may be open, closed, both, or neither.

A function or map from one topological space to another is called *continuous* if the inverse image of any open set is open. If the function maps the real numbers to the real numbers (both spaces with the standard topology), this definition of continuous is equivalent to the definition of continuous in calculus. If a continuous function is one-to-one and onto and if the inverse of the function is also continuous, the function is called a *homeomorphism*, and the domain of the function is said to be homeomorphic to the range. Another way of saying this is that the function has a natural extension to the topology. If two spaces are homeomorphic, they have identical topological properties and are considered to be topologically the same. The cube and the sphere are homeomorphic, as are the coffee cup and the doughnut. But the circle is not homeomorphic to the doughnut. DNA topology and protein topology are active research areas.

Knot Theory   *Knot theory* is the mathematical branch of topology that studies mathematical *knots*, which are defined as embeddings of a circle in three-dimensional Euclidean space, R^3. This is basically equivalent to a conventional knotted string with the ends joined together to prevent it from becoming undone. Two mathematical knots are equivalent if one can be transformed into the other via a deformation of R^3 upon itself (known as an *ambient isotopy*); these transformations correspond to manipulations of a knotted string that do not involve cutting the string or passing the string through itself.

Knots can be described in various ways. Given a method of description, however, there may be more than one description that represents the same knot. For example, a common method of describing a knot is a planar diagram. But any given knot can be drawn in many different ways using a planar diagram. Therefore, a fundamental problem in knot theory is determining when two descriptions represent the same knot. One way of distinguishing knots is by using a *knot invariant*, a "quantity" that remains the same even with different descriptions of a knot. The concept of a knot has been extended to higher dimensions by considering n-dimensional spheres in m-dimensional Euclidean space.

The discovery of the Jones polynomial by Vaughan Jones in 1984 revealed deep connections between knot theory and mathematical methods in statistical mechanics and quantum field theory. In the last 30 years, knot theory has also become a tool in applied mathematics. Chemists and biologists use knot theory to understand, for example, the chirality of molecules and the actions of enzymes on DNA. In the last several decades of the twentieth century, scientists and mathematicians began finding applications of knot theory to problems in biology and chemistry. Knot theory can be used to determine whether or not a molecule is *chiral* (has "handedness"). Chemical compounds of different handedness can have drastically differing properties, thalidomide being a notable example. More generally, knot theoretic methods have been used in studying *topoisomers*, topologically different arrangements of the same chemical formula. The closely related theory of *tangles* has been used effectively in studying the action of certain enzymes on DNA.

Graph Theory   *Graph theory* is the study of *graphs*, mathematical structures used to model pairwise relations between objects from a certain collection. In this context a graph is a collection of vertices or *nodes* and a collection of *edges* that connect pairs of vertices. A graph may be *undirected*, meaning that there is no distinction between the two vertices associated with each edge, or its edges may be *directed* from one vertex to another. A graph structure can be extended by assigning a weight to each edge of the graph. Graphs with weights, *weighted graphs*, are used to represent structures in which pairwise connections have some numerical values. For example, if a graph represents a road network, the weights could represent the length of each road. A digraph with weighted edges in the context of graph theory is called a *network*.

Many applications of graph theory exist in the form of network analysis. These split broadly into three categories:

1. Analysis to determine structural properties of a network, such as the distribution of vertex degrees and the diameter of the graph. A vast number of graph measures exist, and the production of useful ones for various domains remains an active area of research.
2. Analysis to find a measurable quantity within the network: for example, for a transportation network, the level of vehicular flow within any portion of it.
3. Analysis of dynamical properties of networks.

Graph theory is also used to study molecules in chemistry and biology. In chemistry a graph makes a natural model for a molecule, where vertices represent atoms and edge bonds. This approach is used especially in computer processing of molecular structures, ranging from chemical editors to database searching.

Fractals   A *fractal* is generally "a rough or fragmented geometric shape that can be split into parts, each of which is (at least approximately) a reduced-size copy of the whole," a property called *self-similarity*. Because they appear similar at all levels of magnification, fractals are often considered to be infinitely complex (in informal terms). Natural objects that approximate fractals to a degree include clouds, mountain ranges, lightning bolts, coastlines, and snowflakes.

Fractals can also be classified according to their self-similarity. Three types of self-similarity are found in fractals:

1. *Exact self-similarity.* This is the strongest type of self-similarity; the fractal appears identical at different scales. Fractals defined by iterated function systems often display exact self-similarity.

2. *Quasi-self-similarity.* This is a loose form of self-similarity; the fractal appears approximately (but not exactly) identical at different scales. Quasi-self-similar fractals contain small copies of the entire fractal in distorted and degenerate forms. Fractals defined by recurrence relations are usually quasi-self-similar but not exactly self-similar.

3. *Statistical self-similarity.* This is the weakest type of self-similarity; the fractal has numerical or statistical measures that are preserved across scales. Most reasonable definitions of *fractal* trivially imply some form of statistical self-similarity. (A fractal dimension itself is a numerical measure that is preserved across scales.) Random fractals are examples of fractals that are statistically self-similar, but neither exactly self-similar nor quasi-self-similar.

Approximate fractals are easily found in nature. These objects display a self-similar structure over an extended but finite scale range. Examples include clouds, snowflakes, crystals, mountain ranges, lightning, river networks, cauliflower and broccoli, and systems of blood vessels and pulmonary vessels. Coastlines may be loosely considered fractal in nature.

Complexities   *Complexity theory* and *chaos theory* study systems that are too complex to predict their future accurately, but nevertheless, exhibit underlying patterns that can help us cope in an increasingly complex world. Science usually examines the world by breaking it into smaller and smaller pieces until the pieces can be understood. When we use this approach, we often miss the bigger picture. Knowing all we can about an individual ant will not teach us about how an entire ant colony works. Dissecting a rat will never tell us all that we need to know about living rats. Sometimes the way that the parts interact is critical to how the entire system works. This is what complexity studies. Complexity is relevant to an enormous range of areas of study, including traffic flows, earthquakes, the stock market, and systems biology.

Rademacher and Walsh Functions   Digital communication uses nonsinusoidal orthogonal functions, Rademacher and Walsh functions being among the best known. They are described extentively in the literature (Ahmed and Rao, 1975; Geadah and Corinthios, 1977; Goldberg, 1989a,b; Peterson and Weldon, 1972; Sklar, 2001; Trahtman and Trahtman, 1975; Vose and Wright, 1998; Waterman, 1999; Yarlagadda and Hershey, 1997; Zalmanzon, 1989).

Rademacher functions are an incomplete set of orthogonal functions introduced by Rademacher in 1922. A Rademacher function of index m, denoted by $\mathrm{rad}(m, t)$, is a train of rectangular pulses with 2^{m-1} cycles in the half-open interval $[0, 1)$, taking the values $+1$ or -1 (Figure 1.1). The exception is

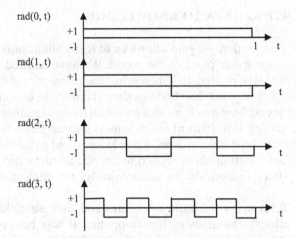

FIGURE 1.1   Rademacher functions.

$rad(0, t)$, which is equal to $+1$ along the entire interval. Rademacher functions can be generated using the recurrence relation:

$$rad(m, t) = rad(1, 2^{m-1}t)$$

$$rad(1, t) = +1 \quad \text{if } t \text{ from } \left[0, \frac{1}{2}\right) \quad \text{and} \quad rad(1, t) = -1 \quad \text{if } t \text{ from } \left[\frac{1}{2}, 1\right)$$

The incomplete set of Rademacher functions was completed by Walsh in 1923 to form a complete orthogonal set of rectangular functions now known as *Walsh functions*. In the field of digital communication, sets of Walsh functions are generally classified into three groups, which differ from one another by the order in which individual functions appear:

1. Walsh ordering
2. Dyadic or Paley ordering
3. Natural or Hadamard ordering

All these variants of the sets of Walsh functions can be presented in connection with relevant Hadamard matrices (see Chapter 8). Peculiarities of these variants are related closely to the famous Gray code (Ahmed and Rao, 1975, pp. 88–93).

The complete set of Walsh functions defined on the unit interval $[0, 1)$ can be divided into two groups of even and odd functions about the point $t = 0.5$. These even and odd functions are analogous to the sine and cosine functions, respectively. The class of nonsinusoidal orthogonal functions described plays an important role in the spectral analysis of signals and in relevant transforms of digital signals to provide effective transfer of information.

1.4   CONVERTING DATA TO KNOWLEDGE

The biological information we gain allows us to learn about ourselves, about our origins, and about our place in the world. We have learned that we are quantitatively strongly related to other primates, mice, zebrafish, fruit flies, roundworms, and even yeast. The findings should induce in us some modesty: in learning and seeing how much we share with all living organisms. The information we are gaining is not just of philosophical interest but is also intended to help humanity to lead healthy lives. Knowledge about primitive organisms provides much information about shared metabolic features and hints about diseases that affect humans in an economically and ethically acceptable manner.

Knowledge from many scientific disciplines and their subfields has to be integrated to achieve the goals of bioinformatics. It was believed (Wilson, 1998) that all knowledge is intrinsically unified, and that behind disciplines as diverse as physics and biology, and anthropology and the arts, lie a small number of natural laws. Applying the knowledge can lead to new scientific methods, new diagnostics, and new therapeutics.

At the beginning of the "genomic revolution," a bioinformatics concern was the creation and maintenance of a database to store biological information, such as nucleotide, amino acid, and protein sequences. Development of this type of database involved not only design issues but also the development of complex interfaces whereby researchers could both access existing data and submit new or revised data. Ultimately, all of this information must be combined to form a comprehensive picture of normal cellular activities. Therefore, the field of bioinformatics has evolved such that the most pressing task now involves the analysis and interpretation of various types of data, including nucleotide, amino acid sequences, protein domains, and protein structures and interactions. Important research branches within bioinformatics include the development and implementation of tools that enable efficient access to, and use and management of, various types of information and new algorithms and statistics with which to assess relationships among members of large data sets, such as methods to locate a gene within a sequence, predict protein structure and/or function, and cluster protein sequences into families of related sequences. The process of converting data to knowledge may be illustrated as shown in Figure 1.2.

1.5   THE BIG PICTURE: INFORMATICS

Informatics is the study of the structure, behaviors, and interactions of natural and artificial computational systems. Informatics studies the representation, processing, and communication of information in natural and artificial systems. It has computational, cognitive, and social aspects. The central notion is the transformation of information: whether by computation or communication,

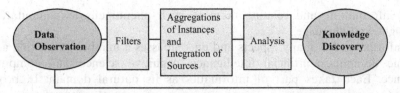

FIGURE 1.2   Process of converting data to knowledge.

TABLE 1.1   Information Building Blocks (Monomer to Polymer)

Monomer	Polymer
Nucleotides	DNA:
Adenine (A)	ACTGGTAGCCTTAGA ...
Cytosine (C)	RNA:
Guanine (G)	ACUGGUAGCCUUAGA ...
Thymine/	
uracil (T/U)	
Amino acids	Protein:
Cysteine (Cys)	Met–Cys–Gly–Pro–Pro–Arg ...
Alanine (Ala)	
Proline (Pro)	
Letters: A, B, C, ...	Words: CAT, GO, FRIEND, ...
Symbols: 0, 1	Binary code: 1001011100101 ...
Monomial: $1, x, x^2, ...$	Polynomial: $P(x), ...$
Line: $l_1, l_2, l_3, ...$	Polygons: triangle, rectangle, ...

whether by organisms or artifacts. Information building blocks are illustrated conceptually in Table 1.1.

Understanding informational phenomena such as computation, cognition, and communication enables technological advances. In turn, technological progress prompts scientific enquiry. The science of information and the engineering of information systems develop hand-in-hand. Informatics is the emerging discipline that combines the two. In natural and artificial systems, information is carried at many levels, ranging, for example, from biological molecules and electronic devices, through nervous systems and computers, and on to societies and large-scale distributed systems. It is characteristic that information carried at higher levels is represented by informational processes at lower levels. Each of these levels is the proper object of study for some discipline of science or engineering. Informatics aims to develop and apply firm theoretical and mathematical foundations for the features that are common to all computational systems.

In its attempts to account for phenomena, science progresses by defining, developing, criticizing, and refining new concepts. Informatics is developing its own fundamental concepts of communication, knowledge, data, interaction, and information, and relating them to such phenomena as computation, thought, and language.

Informatics has many aspects and encompasses a number of existing academic disciplines: artificial intelligence, cognitive science, and computer science. Each takes part of informatics as its natural domain: In broad terms, cognitive science concerns the study of natural systems; computer science concerns the analysis of computation and the design of computing systems; and artificial intelligence plays a connecting role, designing systems that emulate those found in nature. Informatics also informs and is informed by other disciplines, such as mathematics, electronics, biology, linguistics, and psychology. Thus, informatics provides a link between disciplines with their own methodologies and perspectives, bringing together a common scientific paradigm, common engineering methods, and a pervasive stimulus from technological development and practical application.

Computational Systems   Computational systems, whether natural or artificial, are distinguished by their great complexity with regard to both their internal structure and behavior, and their rich interaction with the environment. Informatics seeks to understand and to construct (or reconstruct) such systems using analytic, experimental, and engineering methodologies. The mixture of observation, theory, and practice will vary between natural and artificial systems.

In natural systems, the object is to understand the structure and behavior of a given computational system. Ultimately, the theoretical concepts underlying natural systems are built on observation and are themselves used to predict new observations. For artificial systems, the object is to build a system that performs a given informational function. The theoretical concepts underlying artificial systems are intended to secure their correct and efficient design and operation. Computer language systems have been evolving and communicating with biological data as part of computational systems. The computer languages and their interfaces with various data types are illustrated in Table 1.2.

TABLE 1.2   Communications Between Computer Languages and Data Types and BioModules[a]

Computer Languages	Design Goals
FORTRAN	Numerical analysis
LISP	Symbolic computation
C	System programming
C++	Objects, speed, compatibility with C
Java	Objects, Internet
Perl	System administration
Python	General programming

[a]BioModules = bio + languages.

Informatics provides an enormous range of problems and opportunities. One challenge is to determine how far, and in what circumstances, theories of information processing in artificial devices can be applied to natural systems. A second challenge is to determine how far principles derived from natural systems are applicable to the development of new types of artificial systems. A third challenge is to explore the many ways in which artificial information systems can help to solve problems facing humankind and help to improve the quality of life for all living things. One can also consider systems of mixed character; a question of longer-term interest may be to what extent it is helpful to maintain the distinction between natural and artificial systems. In Chapter 10 we present the evolution, future trends, and the central dogma of informatics.

1.6 CHALLENGES AND PERSPECTIVES

The interaction between biology and mathematics has been a rich area of research for more than a century. The interface between them presents challenges and opportunities for both mathematicians and biologists. Due to the explosion of biological data with the advent of new technologies that can organize the plethora of data, unique opportunities for research and new challenges have surfaced within the last 10 to 20 years. For biology, the possibilities range from the level of the cell and molecule to the level of the biosphere. For mathematics, the potential is great in traditional and nontraditional areas such as statistics and differential equations, knot theory, and topology. Stochastic processes and Markov chains in statistics have their origins in biological questions. Galton invented the correlation method based on questions in evolutionary biology. The analysis of variance was derived from R. A. Fisher's work in agriculture. Modeling the success (survival) over many generations of a family name led to the development of the subject of branching processes. The compilation of DNA sequence data led to Kingman's coalescence model and Ewens' sampling formula. Furthermore, biological applications have stimulated the study of ordinary and partial differential equations, especially regarding problems in chaos, fractal geometry, and bifurcation theory. Further interactions between mathematics and biology have presented new opportunities and challenges. A number of fundamental mathematical and biological issues cut across all these challenges.

- How do we incorporate variation among individual units in nonlinear systems and biological systems?
- How do we explain the interactions among phenomena that occur on a wide range of scales and molecular levels, of space, time, and organizational complexity?
- What is the relation between pattern and process both in mathematical and biological systems?

It is in the analysis of these issues that mathematics is most essential and holds the greatest potential. These challenges, such as aggregation of components to elucidate the behavior of ensembles, integration across scales, and inverse problems, are basic to all sciences, in particular to biological sciences, and a variety of techniques exist to deal with them and to begin to solve the biological problems that generate them. However, the uniqueness of biological systems shaped by evolutionary forces will pose new difficulties, mandate new perspectives, and lead to the development of new mathematics. Algebraic biology and matrix genetics for genetic language are presented in Chapters 2 and 8, and a denotational mathematics for cognitive informatics is introduced in Chapter 9. The excitement of this area of science is already evident, and is sure to grow in the years to come.

REFERENCES

Ahmed, N., and Rao, K. (1975). *Orthogonal Transforms for Digital Signal Processing*. New York: Springer-Verlag.

Cullman, G., and Labouygues, J. M. (1984). The mathematical logic of life. In: K. Dose, A. W. Schwartz, and W. H.-P. Thiemann (Eds.), *Proceedings of the 7th International Conference on the Origins of Life*. Dordrecht, The Netherlands: D. Reidel.

Darwin, C. (1859). *On the Origin of Species by Means of Natural Selection*. London: John Murray.

Geadah, Y. A., and Corinthios, M. J. (1977). Natural, dyadic and sequency order algorithms and processors for the Walsh–Hadamard transform. *IEEE Trans. Comput.*, C-26, 435–442.

Goldberg, D. E. (1989a). Genetic algorithms and Walsh functions: I. A gentle introduction. *Complex Syst.*, 2(2), 129–152.

Goldberg, D. E. (1989b). Genetic algorithms and Walsh functions: II. Deception and its analysis. *Complex Syst.*, 3(2), 153–171.

Madigan, M. T., Martinko, J. M., and Parker, J. (1997). *Brock Biology of Microorganisms*. Upper Saddle River, NJ: Prentice Hall.

Peterson, W. W., and Weldon, E. J. (1972). *Error-Correcting Codes*. Cambridge, MA: MIT Press.

Peusner, L. (1974). *Concepts in Bioenergetics*. Englewood Cliffs, NJ: Prentice-Hall.

Prescott, L. M., Harley, J. P., and Klein, D. A. (1993). *Microbiology*. Dubuque, IA: Wm. C. Brown.

Sklar, B. (2001). *Digital Communication: Fundamentals and Applications*. Upper Saddle River, NJ: Prentice Hall.

Stewart, I. (1998). *Life's Other Secret*. New York: Wiley.

Trahtman, A. M., and Trahtman, V. A. (1975). *The Foundations of the Theory of Discrete Signals on Finite Intervals*. Moscow: Sovetskoie Radio (in Russian).

Vose, M., and Wright, A. (1998). The simple genetic algorithm and the Walsh transform: I. Theory. *J. Evol. Comput.*, 6(3), 253–274.

Waterman, M. S. (Ed.) (1999). *Mathematical Methods for DNA Sequences*. Boca Raton, FL: CRC Press.

Wilson, E. (1998). *Consilience: The Unity of Knowledge*. New York: Random House.

Yarlagadda, R., and Hershey, J. (1997). *Hadamard Matrix Analysis and Synthesis with Applications to Communications and Signal/Image Processing*. New York: Kluwer Academic.

Zalmanzon, L. A. (1989). *Fourier, Walsh and Haar Transformations and Their Application in Control, Communication and Other Systems*. Moscow: Nauka (in Russian).

2 Genetic Codes, Matrices, and Symmetrical Techniques

The genetic code is a key to bioinformatics and to a science of biological self-organizing on the whole. Modern science faces the necessity of understanding and systematically explaining mysterious features of ensembles of molecular structures of the genetic code. Why does the genetic alphabet consist of four letters? Why does the genetic code encode 20 amino acids? How is the system structure of the molecular genetic code connected with known principles of quantum mechanics, which were developed to explain phenomena on the atomic and molecular levels? Why has nature chosen the special code conformity between 64 genetic triplets and 20 amino acids? Can knowledge about the structural essence of the genetic code be useful for mathematical natural sciences as a whole? What type of mathematical approach should be chosen among many possible approaches to represent and model structuralized ensembles of molecules of the genetic code?

What direction is chosen to investigate such questions and what types of answers it hopes to obtain are important for a science. Achieving deep understanding of the genetic code should promote the inclusion of an associated science into the field of the existing, developed mathematical natural sciences. To provide it, the direction of search should be based on fundamental mathematical methods and concepts. Methods and principles of symmetry, and matrix analysis, are some of the bases of modern mathematical natural sciences. Apart from structures inherited genetically, morphological structures of biological bodies are characterized by many types of symmetry. It is known from the history of molecular genetics that investigations of symmetry in genetic molecules have produced essential results. Revelations of new symmetric structures in molecular-genetic systems produce a set of useful heuristic associations due to analogies with known symmetric structures in other scientific fields, such as quantum mechanics, the theory of digital communication and noise-immunity coding, and geometry.

Genetic coding possesses noise immunity, which allows descendants to be similar to their parents despite strong disturbances and noise in the environment of biological molecules. It reminds one of the effective noise immunity

Mathematics of Bioinformatics: Theory, Practice, and Applications, By Matthew He and Sergey Petoukhov
Copyright © 2011 John Wiley & Sons, Inc.

of modern systems of digital communication and signal processing, which is achieved by means of special mathematics. The mathematics is based on matrix and symmetric methods of representation and analysis of information signals. Is it possible that these mathematical methods, which were developed for digital techniques, could be applied adequately to studies of the genetic code?

This chapter is devoted to symmetrical analysis for genetic systems. Mathematical theories of noise-immunity coding and discrete signal processing are based on matrix methods of representation and analysis of information. These matrix methods, which are connected closely with relations of symmetry, are borrowed for a matrix analysis of ensembles of molecular elements of the genetic code. In this chapter we describe a uniform representation of ensembles of genetic multiplets in the form of matrixes of a cumulative Kronecker family. The analysis of molecular peculiarities of the system of nitrogenous bases reveals the first significant relations of symmetry in these genetic matrices. It permits one to introduce a natural numbering of the multiplets in each of the genetic matrices and to provide a basis for further analysis of genetic structures. Connections of the numerated genetic matrices with famous matrices of dyadic shifts and with the golden section are demonstrated.

2.1 INTRODUCTION

Due to the wonderful work of many researchers, modern science knows basic phenomenological facts about molecular structures of the genetic code, including the four-letter genetic alphabet, 64 triplets, and 20 amino acids. The history of molecular genetics chronicles attempts to understand and explain these phenomenological data from various viewpoints. For example, one can mention the famous hypothesis by George Gamow (Ycas, 1969) about the reason for the existence of 20 amino acids. By this hypothesis, the reason lies in the special configuration of the DNA molecule. Other hypotheses, which have only historical meanings, are also considered in a wealth of literature in the field of molecular genetics (e.g., Cantor and Schimmel, 1980; Chapevillle and Haenni, 1974; Karasev, 2003; Ratner, 2002; Roller, 1974; Shults and Schirmer, 1979; Stent, 1971; Watson, 1968; Ycas, 1969).

All living organisms are unified by nature. All of them have identical molecular bases of the system of genetic coding. These bases are amazingly simple. For realization of the genetic messages which encode sequences of amino acids in proteins, all types of organisms utilize in their molecules of heredity, DNA and RNA (ribonucleic acid), an "alphabet" consisting of four "letters" or nitrogenous bases: adenine (A), cytosine (C), guanine (G), and thymine (T) [or uracil (U) in RNA] (Figure 2.1). Linear sequences of these four letters on strings of DNA and RNA contain the genetic information for protein synthesis in all living bodies: from bacteria up to a whale or from a worm up to a bird and even humans. One often hears the figurative expression that the encyclopedia of life is written in four letters.

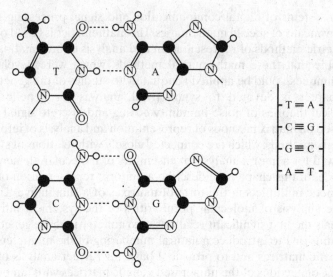

FIGURE 2.1 Complementary pairs of the four nitrogenous bases in DNA: A–T (adenine and thymine) and C–G (cytosine and guanine). Hydrogen bonds in these pairs are shown by dotted lines. Filled circles are atoms of carbon; small open circles are atoms of hydrogen; circles with the letter N are atoms of nitrogen; circles with the letter O are atoms of oxygen.

This set of four letters is usually considered the elementary alphabet of a genetic code. The letters form complementary pairs, C–G and A–U (or A–T), because they stand opposite each other in molecules of heredity. The complementary letters C and G are connected by three hydrogen bonds; the complementary letters A and U (or A and T) are connected by two hydrogen bonds.

Genetic information, which is transferred by DNA and RNA, defines the primary structure of proteins of biological organisms. Each coded protein exists in the form of a chain of 20 amino acids. A sequence of amino acids in a protein chain is defined by an appropriate sequence of genetic triplets. A *triplet* (or a *codon*) is a block of three neighboring nitrogenous bases which are disposed along a filament of DNA or RNA. A sequence of amino acids in any protein is coded by an appropriate sequence of triplets (such a sequence of n triplets is termed a *3n-multiplet*).

The number of types of triplets that can be constructed from the four-letter alphabet is equal to $4^3 = 64$. Each triplet has its code meaning: It encodes one of 20 amino acids or plays the role of a stop or start signal for a process of protein synthesis. Each codon has an *anticodon*, which consists of the appropriate complementary letters; for example, the triplet CUG has the anticodon GAC.

The genetic code is termed the *degeneracy code* because its 64 letters encode 20 amino acids, and different amino acids are encoded by different quantities of triplets. Hypotheses about a connection between this degeneracy and the noise immunity of genetic information have existed since the time of the discovery of the genetic code. Symmetries in the structures of degeneracy of the genetic code are one of the main objects of investigation in this chapter. Many dialects of the genetic code exist in biological organisms and their subsystems, which differ from each other by some differences in correspondences between triplets and objects encoded by them (see details at the NCBI's Web site: http://www.ncbi.nlm.nih.gov/Taxonomy/Utils/wprintgc.cgi).

Proteins are the main dense component of biological organisms. Many thousands of types of proteins exist, each possessing its own individual function. In particular, all biological ferments, which provide phenomenal speeds of many biochemical reactions in organisms, are proteins. The entire harmonic system of metabolism depends on proteins. All amino acids in proteins are connected by the same type of chemical bond, the *peptide bond*.

The correspondence between triplets and objects encoded by them is usually illustrated by a table of size 4×16, which was proposed by Francis Crick half a century ago and which is reproduced in many textbooks and historical reviews in the field of molecular genetics (e.g., Cantor and Schimmel, 1980; Frank-Kamenetskiy, 1988; Roller, 1974; Stent, 1971; Watson, 1968). Each of its 64 tabular cells contains one triplet and an appropriate object (an amino acid or stop codon) encoded by this triplet. However, nobody has insisted that all the possibilities of the analytical and heuristic representation of systems of elements of the genetic code in tabular forms are exhausted by this table. The 20 amino acids which are encoded genetically and their traditional abbreviations are: Ala, alanine; Arg, arginine; Asn, asparagine; Asp, aspartic acid; Cys, cysteine; Gln, glutamine; Glu, glutamic acid; Gly, glycine; His, histidine; Ile, isoleucine; Leu, leucine; Lys, lysine; Met, methionine; Phe, phenylalanine; Pro, proline; Ser, serine; Thr, threonine; Trp, tryptophan; Tyr, tyrosine; and Val, valine.

Modern science does not know why the alphabet of the genetic language has four letters (it could have any other number of letters, in principle), nor why just these four nitrogenous bases were chosen by nature as the elements of the genetic alphabet from billions of possible chemical compounds. Equally unknown is why the quantity of amino acids encoded by the triplets is equal to 20. In our opinion, this choice has a deep meaning. Investigations of symmetries in structures of the genetic code can help us answer these and other important and to understand this meaning.

The problem of heritable noise immunity is a general one for all multichannel systems of informatics of each organism. Many applied tasks of nanotechnology and biotechnology are connected with ensembles of genetic molecules: for example, the task of creating DNA computers and DNA robotics (Paun et al., 2006; Seeman, 2004; Shapiro and Benenson, 2007). It is necessary to study those peculiarities of ensembles of genetic molecules that possess formal analogies with formalisms of digital informatics and its matrix mathematics.

Do these mathematical methods give us the ability to enumerate each genetic multiplet in a binary manner, taking into account the natural characteristics of the genetic letters A, C, G, U/T? The main thrust of the present chapter is primary consideration and substantiation of this effective transfer of these methods into the field of molecular genetics. Some initial constructions of matrix genetics with elements of symmetry are introduced below.

2.2 MATRIX THEORY AND SYMMETRY PRELIMINARIES

A *matrix* (plural: *matrices*) is a rectangular table of *elements* (or *entries*), which may be numbers or, more generally, any abstract quantities that can be added and multiplied. Matrices are used to describe linear equations, to keep track of the coefficients of linear transformations, and to record data that depend on multiple parameters. Matrices are described by the field of matrix theory. They can be added, multiplied, and decomposed in various ways, which also makes them a key concept in the field of linear algebra. Initially, a subbranch of linear algebra, matrix algebra has grown to cover subjects related to graph theory, algebra, combinatorics, and statistics.

The entry that lies in the ith row and the jth column of a matrix is typically referred to as the i,j, (i, j), or (i, j)th entry of the matrix. Matrices are usually denoted using uppercase letters, while the corresponding lowercase letters, with two subscript indices, represent the entries. For example, the (i, j)th entry of a matrix $\mathbf{A}$ is most commonly written $a_{i,j}$. Alternative notations for that entry are $\mathbf{A}[i, j]$ or $\mathbf{A}_{i,j}$.

A number of operations can be used to modify matrices: *matrix addition*, *scalar multiplication*, and *transposition* (Table 2.1). These are the basic techniques employed to deal with matrices.

Familiar properties of numbers extend to these operations of matrices: for example, addition is *commutative*; that is, the matrix sum does not depend on the order of the summands: $\mathbf{A} + \mathbf{B} = \mathbf{B} + \mathbf{A}$. The transpose, which does not exist for numbers, is also very compatible with addition and scalar multiplication, as expressed by $(c\mathbf{A})^{\mathrm{T}} = c(\mathbf{A}^{\mathrm{T}})$, as well as $(\mathbf{A} + \mathbf{B})^{\mathrm{T}} = \mathbf{A}^{\mathrm{T}} + \mathbf{B}^{\mathrm{T}}$. Finally, $(\mathbf{A}^{\mathrm{T}})^{\mathrm{T}} = \mathbf{A}$.

Symmetry plays an important role in nature. Many structural features of molecules are governed by consideration of symmetry. In formal terms, we say that an object is *symmetric* with respect to a given mathematical operation if, when applied to the object, this operation does not change the object or its appearance. Two objects are symmetric to each other with respect to a given group of operations if one is obtained from the other by some of the operations (and vice versa).

Symmetries may also be found in living organisms, including humans and other animals (see Section 2.5). In two-dimensional geometry the main types of symmetry of interest are with respect to the basic Euclidean plane isometries: translations, rotations, reflections, and glide reflections.

TABLE 2.1 Matrix Operations

Operation	Definition
Addition	Given $m \times n$ matrices $\mathbf{A}$ and $\mathbf{B}$, their *sum* $\mathbf{A} + \mathbf{B}$ is calculated entrywise; i.e., $$(\mathbf{A} + \mathbf{B})_{i,j} = \mathbf{A}_{i,j} + \mathbf{B}_{i,j}, \quad \text{where } 1 \leq i \leq m \text{ and } 1 \leq j \leq n$$
Scalar multiplication	Given a matrix $\mathbf{A}$ and a number (also called a *scalar* in the parlance of abstract algebra) c, the *scalar multiplication* $c\mathbf{A}$ is given by multiplying every entry of $\mathbf{A}$ by c: $$(c\mathbf{A})_{i,j} = c \cdot \mathbf{A}_{i,j}$$
Transpose	The *transpose* of an $m \times n$ matrix $\mathbf{A}$ is the $n \times m$ matrix $\mathbf{A}^{\mathrm{T}}$ (also denoted by $\mathbf{A}^{\mathrm{tr}}$ or $^{\mathrm{t}}\mathbf{A}$) formed by turning rows into columns and columns into rows: $$(\mathbf{A}^{\mathrm{T}})_{i,j} = \mathbf{A}_{j,i}$$
Kronecker (or tensor) multiplication	Given $m \times m$ matrix $\mathbf{A} = (a_{ij})$ and $n \times n$ matrix $\mathbf{B} = (b_{ij})$, their Kronecker multiplication is $mn \times mn$ matrix $\mathbf{A} \otimes \mathbf{B}$: $$\mathbf{A} \otimes \mathbf{B} = \begin{bmatrix} a_{11}\mathbf{B} & a_{12}\mathbf{B} & \cdots & a_{1m}\mathbf{B} \\ \hline a_{1m}\mathbf{B} & a_{2m}\mathbf{B} & \cdots & a_{mm}\mathbf{B} \end{bmatrix}$$

2.3 GENETIC CODES AND MATRICES

The mechanisms of genetic coding provide the high noise immunity of transfer of hereditary information from one generation to the next, despite disturbances and noise that exist in biological environments. From the very beginning of the discovery of the genetic code, scientists thought that the structures of the code were connected with the noise immunity (noise-proof features) of genetic systems (see the review by Ycas, 1969). However, when discussing the noise immunity of genetic coding, one is usually limited to citing the high degree of degeneracy in the code, which is capable of reducing the quantity of lethal mutations.

But studies have already been done which suppose that the requirement for the influence of noise immunity on structures of the genetic code is much deeper. This area of research uses the developments of the mathematical theory of noise-immunity coding, which are applied in the techniques of digital communication, in an attempt to understand bioinformatics phenomena. In this area the suppositional influence of noise immunity can be studied by different methods and in different directions of thought (see, e.g., MacDonaill, 2003). Our own research, presented in this chapter, which is based on the idea of a deep connection between structures of the genetic code and the requirement for noise immunity of genetic information, is quite original in the research methods used and in the new facts obtained.

Let us discuss the noise-immunity property of genetic systems more deeply. It seems fantastic, but descendants grow similar to their ancestors due to genetic information, despite enormous disturbances and noise in trillions of biological molecules. How is it possible to approach this problem of such fantastic noise immunity in molecular genetics? Does modern science have any precedents from similar problems of noise immunity?

Yes; science has successfully solved a similar task recently: the noise-immunity transfer of photos from surfaces of other planets to the Earth. In this task, electromagnetic signals, which carry data, should pass through millions of kilometers of cosmic space full of electromagnetic disturbances. These disturbances transform signals tremendously, but modern mathematical technology permits one to restore a transferred photo qualitatively.

The solution to this problem became possible due to the theory of noise-immunity coding created by mathematicians. This theory has appeared rather recently; initial basic work in this field was published by Hamming in 1950 (Hamming, 1980). The theory of such coding utilizes intensive matrix mathematics, including the representation of sets of signals and codes in the form of matrices and their Kronecker powers. Our book describes many interesting results in the field of molecular genetics and bioinformatics which were obtained by its authors on the basis of such matrix mathematics. The investigation of the genetic code from the viewpoint of the theory of discrete signals is natural because of the discrete character of the code.

Coding in modern digital techniques is generally utilized not to prevent reading of text by unauthorized users but to provide technical ease of transfer of discrete information with high noise immunity, speed, and reliability. The most famous example of codes is the Morse code, but of course modern codes are much more effective than the Morse code. These codes allow us to transfer capacious amounts of information across great distances qualitatively. Orthogonal codes, which use Hadamard matrices, is one such code (Ahmed and Rao, 1975; Blahut, 1985; Geadah and Corinthios, 1977; Lee and Kaveh, 1986; Peterson and Weldon, 1972; Petoukhov, 2008a,b; Sklar, 2001; Trahtman, 1972; Trahtman and Trahtman, 1975; Yarlagadda and Hershey, 1997). Any signal transmitted consists of a set of elementary signals (a component of a signal vector of an appropriate dimension). The task of the receiver in conditions of noise is the approximate definition of a concrete vector signal which has been sent from a known set of vector signals (Sklar, 2001). Application of Hadamard matrices allows us to solve similar problems by means of the spectral decomposition of vector signals and the transfer of their spectra, on the basis of which the receiver restores an initial signal. This decomposition utilizes orthogonal functions of rows of Hadamard matrices (Ahmed and Rao, 1975).

One should emphasize important differences in circumstances: Unlike digital techniques, biological organisms solve the task not only to provide noise immunity simply, but to provide it in a way that is suitable for transfer of the noise-immunity property along a chain of biological generations.

In this chapter we pay significant attention to the matrix approach to the genetic code, which forms the special investigatory field of matrix genetics. Investigations in this field reveal an important role for symmetries in the structural organization of molecular ensembles of the genetic code. But why have we chosen the matrix approach to studying the genetic system among the many other possible approaches? The following six reasons explain this matrix choice for studying the genetic code and developing matrix genetics:

1. Information is usually stored in computers in the form of matrices.
2. Noise-immunity codes are constructed on the basis of matrices.
3. Quantum mechanics utilizes matrix operators whose connections can be detected in matrix forms of presentation of the genetic code. The significance of the matrix approach is emphasized by the fact that quantum mechanics arose in a form of matrix mechanics by Werner Heisenberg.
4. Complex and hypercomplex numbers, which are utilized in physics and mathematics, possess matrix forms of presentation. The notion of number is the main notion of mathematics and the mathematical natural sciences. In view of this, investigation of a possible connection of the genetic code to multidimensional numbers in their matrix presentations can lead to very significant results.
5. Matrix analysis is one of the main investigatory tools in mathematical natural sciences. The study of possible analogies between matrices, which are specific for the genetic code, and famous matrices from other branches of sciences can be heuristic and useful.
6. Matrices, which are a union of many components in a single whole, are subordinated to certain mathematical operations which determine substantial connections between collectives of many components. Such connections can be essential for collectives of genetic elements of different levels as well.

A pioneer work in the field of matrix genetics is the article by Konopelchenko and Rumer (1975). Let us recall the basic facts about the elements of the genetic code, the integral ensemble of which is first investigated in matrix genetics.

Genetic Alphabet and Multiplets in Genetic Matrices

Is it possible to propose a matrix approach to represent all sets of genetic multiplets in a well-ordered general form and with an individual binary number for each multiplet on the basis of the molecular features of the four letters A,

C, G, and U/T of the genetic alphabet? Will such a general form be connected with important principles and methods of computer informatics and of noise immunity in digital techniques?

Positive answers to these questions will be useful in analyzing structural properties and symmetries of the genetic system and to reveal analogies between principles of the genetic code and computer informatics for many theoretical and applied tasks.

To get such positive answers, we demonstrate, first, that symmetries in the molecular characteristics of the genetic alphabet provide the existence of binary subalphabets. The four letters (or the four nitrogenous bases) of the genetic alphabet represent specific polynuclear constructions with special bio-chemical properties. The set of these four constructions is not absolutely heterogeneous, but it bears a substantial symmetric system of distinctive-uniting attributes (or, more precisely, *attribute–antiattribute* pairs).

The system of such attributes divides the genetic four-letter alphabet into various pairs of three letters, which are equivalent from the viewpoint of one of these attributes or its absence: (1) $C = U$ and $A = G$ (according to the binary-opposite attributes "pyrimidine" or "nonpyrimidine," that is, purine); (2) $A = C$ and $G = U$ (according to the attributes amino-mutating or non-amino-mutating, under the action of nitrous acid, HNO_2 (Wittmann, 1961; Ycas, 1969), or as given by the attributes "keto" or "amino" (Waterman, 1999); (3) $C = G$ and $A = U$ (according to the attributes, three or two hydrogen bonds are materialized in these complementary pairs). The possibility of such division of the genetic alphabet into three binary subalphabets is known from the book by Waterman (1999). We will utilize these known subalphabets by means of a new method in the field of matrix genetics. We will attach appropriate binary symbols "0" or "1" to each of the genetic letters from the viewpoint of each of these subalphabets. Then we will use these binary symbols for binary numbering of the columns and rows of the genetic matrices of the Kronecker family.

Let us assign the numbers $N = 1$, 2, and 3 to the three types of binary-opposite attributes, and let us ascribe to each of the four genetic letters the symbol 0_N (the symbol 1_N) in the presence (or absence, correspondingly) of the attribute under the number N at this letter. As a result, we obtain a representation of the genetic four-letter alphabet in the system of its three binary subalphabets to attributes (Table 2.2). The table shows that on the basis of each type of attribute, each of the letters A, C, G, and U/T possesses three "faces" or meanings in the three binary subalphabets. On the basis of each type of attribute, the genetic four-letter alphabet is curtailed into a two-letter alphabet. For example, on the basis of the first type of binary-opposite attribute, we have (instead of the four-letter alphabet) an alphabet from the two letters 0_1 and 1_1, which one can term the *binary subalphabet to the first type of binary attributes*.

Accordingly, any genetic message as a sequence of the four letters C, A, G, and U consists of three parallel and various binary texts or three different

TABLE 2.2 Three Binary Subalphabets According to Three Types of Binary-Opposite Attributes in a Set of Nitrogenous Bases C, A, G, U[a]

N	Symbol of a Genetic Letter	C	A	G	U/T
1	0_1, pyrimidines (one ring in a molecule) 1_1, purines (two rings in a molecule)	0_1	1_1	1_1	0_1
2	0_2, a letter with amino-mutating property (amino) 1_2, a letter without it (keto)	0_2	0_2	1_2	1_2
3	0_3, a letter with three hydrogen bonds 1_3, a letter with two hydrogen bonds	0_3	1_3	0_3	1_3

[a]The following scheme explains graphically the symmetric relations of equivalence between the pairs of letters from the viewpoint of the separate attributes 1, 2, and 3:

$$
\begin{array}{c}
C \overset{2}{=\!=} A \\
1 \, \Big\| \, \underset{3}{\overset{3}{\times}} \, \Big\| \, 1 \\
U \underset{2}{=\!=} G
\end{array}
$$

sequences of zero and unity (such binary sequences are used for storage and transfer of the information in computers). Each of these parallel binary texts, based on objective biochemical attributes, can provide its own genetic function in organisms. According to our data, the genetic system uses the possibility of reading triplets from the viewpoint of different binary subalphabets. This possibility participates in construction of genetic octet bipolar algebra (or yin–yang algebra), which serves as the algebraic model of the genetic code in Chapter 8.

Natural System of Numbering the Genetic Multiplets

Genetic information is transferred by means of discrete elements: four letters of the genetic alphabet, 64 amino acids, and so on. The general theory of processing discrete signals encodes the signals by means of special mathematical matrices and spectral representation of the signals, with the principal aim of increasing the reliability and efficiency of information transfer (e.g., Ahmed and Rao, 1975; Sklar, 2001). A typical example of such matrices with appropriate properties is the Kronecker family of Hadamard matrices:

$$H_{n+1} = [1 \ 1; \ -1 \ 1]^{(n)}, \quad \text{where } (n) \text{ indicates an integer Kronecker power}$$
(2.1)

The simplest Hadamard matrix $H_2 = [1 \ 1; \ -1 \ 1]$ is termed the *kernel* of this Kronecker family. Rows of Hadamard matrices (2.1) form an orthogonal system of Walsh functions (see Chapter 1), which is used for a spectral presentation and transfer of discrete signals (Ahmed and Rao, 1975; Yarlagadda and Hershey, 1997). Quantum computers use normalized Hadamard matrixes in the role of logic gates in connection with the important role of these matrixes in quantum mechanics (Nielsen and Chuang, 2001). In Chapter 8 we describe deep connections between Hadamard matrices and ensembles of elements of the genetic code.

On the basis of the idea of a possible analogy between discrete signal processing in computers and in a genetic code system, one can present the genetic four-letter alphabet in the following matrix form: $P = [C \ A; \ U \ G]$. It is obvious that this form is analogous to kernel (2.1) of the Kronecker family of Hadamard matrices. Then the Kronecker family of matrices with such an alphabetical kernel can be considered:

$$P^{(n)} = [C \ A; \ U \ G]^{(n)}, \qquad \text{where } (n) \text{ indicates an integer Kronecker power}$$
$$(2.2)$$

Figure 2.2 shows the first matrices of such a family. One can see in this figure that each matrix contains all genetic multiplets of equal length: $[C \ A; \ U \ G]^{(1)}$ contains all four monoplets; $[C \ A; \ U \ G]^{(2)}$ contains all 16 duplets; $[C \ A; \ U \ G]^{(3)}$ contains all 64 triplets; and so on. It should be emphasized that in this chapter we pay the greatest attention to the genetic alphabet: we consider the alphabetical matrices $[C \ A; \ U \ G]^{(n)}$ from different viewpoints persistently, and we construct algorithms of matrix transformations on the basis of features of the letters A, C, G, and U/T. The genetic alphabet serves as the key structure to investigate system properties of the genetic code and its dialects.

Such a presentation of ensembles of elements of the genetic code in the form of Kronecker families of genetic matrices (*genomatrices* in short) has proved to be a useful tool in investigating structures of the genetic code from the viewpoint of their analogy with the theory of discrete signal processing and noise-immunity coding. The results of matrix genetics reveal hidden interconnections, symmetries, and evolutionary invariants in genetic code systems (He, 2001; He and Petoukhov, 2007, 2009; He et al., 2004; Kappraff and Petoukhov, 2009; Petoukhov, 1999b, 2001a,b, 2003, 2003–2004, 2005, 2006, 2008a,b; Petoukhov and He, 2009). Simultaneously, they testify that genetic molecules are the important part of the specific maintenance of the noise immunity and efficiency of a discrete information transfer.

The Kronecker family of genetic matrices $[C \ A; \ G \ U]^{(n)}$ (2.2) represents all genetic multiplets if the value of n is large enough. This family includes the genomatrix of the genetic alphabet; the genomatrix of triplets, which encode

---

FIGURE 2.2   The first genetic matrices of the Kronecker family $P^{(n)} = [C \ A; \ U \ G]^{(n)}$ with the binary numbering of their columns and rows on the base of the binary subalphabets 1 and 2 from Table 2.2. The lower matrix is the genomatrix $P^{(3)} = [C \ A; \ U \ G]^{(3)}$. Each matrix cell contains a symbol of a multiplet, a binary number of this multiplet, and its expression in decimal notation. Decimal numbers of columns, rows, and multiplets are shown in parentheses.

$$P^{(1)}=$$

	0	1
0	C 00 (0)	A 01 (1)
1	U 10 (2)	G 11 (3)

$$P^{(2)}=$$

	00(0)	01(1)	10(2)	11(3)
00 (0)	CC 0000 (0)	CA 0001 (1)	AC 0010 (2)	AA 0011 (3)
01 (1)	CU 0100 (4)	CG 0101 (5)	AU 0110 (6)	AG 0111 (7)
10 (2)	UC 1000 (8)	UA 1001 (9)	GC 1010 (10)	GA 1011 (11)
11 (3)	UU 1100 (12)	UG 1101 (13)	GU 1110 (14)	GG 1111 (15)

	000 (0)	001 (1)	010 (2)	011 (3)	100 (4)	101 (5)	110 (6)	111 (7)
<u>000</u> <u>(0)</u>	CCC 000000 (0)	CCA 000001 (1)	CAC 000010 (2)	CAA 000011 (3)	ACC 000100 (4)	ACA 000101 (5)	AAC 000110 (6)	AAA 000111 (7)
<u>001</u> <u>(1)</u>	CCU 001000 (8)	CCG 001001 (9)	CAU 001010 (10)	CAG 001011 (11)	ACU 001100 (12)	ACG 001101 (13)	AAU 001110 (14)	AAG 001111 (15)
<u>010</u> <u>(2)</u>	CUC 010000 (16)	CUA 010001 (17)	CGC 010010 (18)	CGA 010011 (19)	AUC 010100 (20)	AUA 010101 (21)	AGC 010110 (22)	AGA 010111 (23)
<u>011</u> <u>(3)</u>	CUU 011000 (24)	CUG 011001 (25)	CGU 011010 (26)	CGG 011011 (27)	AUU 011100 (28)	AUG 011101 (29)	AGU 011110 (30)	AGG 011111 (31)
<u>100</u> <u>(4)</u>	UCC 100000 (32)	UCA 100001 (33)	UAC 100010 (34)	UAA 100011 (35)	GCC 100100 (36)	GCA 100101 (37)	GAC 100110 (38)	GAA 100111 (39)
<u>101</u> <u>(5)</u>	UCU 101000 (40)	UCG 101001 (41)	UAU 101010 (42)	UAG 101011 (43)	GCU 101100 (44)	GCG 101101 (45)	GAU 101110 (46)	GAG 101111 (47)
<u>110</u> <u>(6)</u>	UUC 110000 (48)	UUA 110001 (49)	UGC 110010 (50)	UGA 110011 (51)	GUC 001100 (52)	GUA 110101 (53)	GGC 110110 (54)	GGA 110111 (55)
<u>111</u> <u>(7)</u>	UUU 111000 (56)	UUG 111001 (57)	UGU 111010 (58)	UGG 111011 (59)	GUU 111100 (60)	GUG 111101 (61)	GGU 111110 (62)	GGG 111111 (63)

the amino acids; and the genomatrices of long multiplets, which encode proteins. All of this natural set of genetic multiplets, which have various coding functions in the genetic system, appears coordinated with this simple Kronecker family of matrices $[C \ A; \ G \ U]^{(n)}$ (2.2).

All n-plets, which begin with one of the four letters C, A, U, and G, are assigned to one of the four quadrants of an appropriate genomatrix $[C \ A; \ G \ U]^{(n)}$ because of the specifics of Kronecker multiplication. If one does not pay attention to this first letter in the n-plets of each matrix quadrant, one can see that each quadrant reproduces a previous matrix $P^{(n-1)}$ of this Kronecker family. So, speaking figuratively, each genomatrix of such a family possesses information (or "memory") about all previous genomatrices of this family.

It should be noted that each column of the formally constructed genomatrix $[C \ A; \ G \ U]^{(3)}$ (Figure 2.2) corresponds to one of the eight classical octets by Wittmann (1961), which are famous in the history of molecular genetics and which reflect real biochemical properties of elements of the genetic code (Ycas, 1969). This fact is the first indirect confirmation of the adequacy of the given matrix approach, which reflects a natural orderliness inside the genetic system.

Let us demonstrate now that all 64 triplets can be enumerated binarily in a natural manner by means of the binary subalphabets (Table 2.2), which are based on the real structural and biochemical features of the genetic molecules. As a result of such natural numbering, all triplets appear arrayed in the genomatrix $[C \ A; \ G \ U]^{(3)}$ in monotonical order on increase of their binary numbers.

Really, all columns and rows of the matrices in Figure 2.2 are enumerated binarily by the following algorithm. Their numbers are formed automatically if one interprets multiplets of each column from the viewpoint of the first binary subalphabet (Table 2.2) and if one interprets multiplets of each row from the viewpoint of the second binary subalphabet. For example, from the viewpoint of the first subalphabet, the triplet CAU possesses the binary number 010 (all triplets of the same column possess the same binary number, which is utilized correspondingly as the general number of this column). But from the viewpoint of the second subalphabet, the triplet CAU possesses the binary number 001 (all triplets of the same row possess the same binary number, which is utilized as the general number of this row). One can see in Figure 2.2, that in such a way, all columns and all rows in the genomatrix $[C \ A; \ G \ U]^{(3)}$ appear renumbered and arrayed in monotonic order.

Each genetic multiplet obtains its own individual binary number in the natural system of numbering the multiplets in matrices $[C \ A; \ G \ U]^{(n)}$ that we have described. This multiplet also obtains its own disposition in the appropriate genetic matrix of the Kronecker family. It is obvious that the length of the individual binary number for a n-plet, which contains n letters, is equal to $2n$. The first half of this number is the interpretation of letters of the multiplet from the viewpoint of the second binary subalphabet (Table 2.2), and the second part is the interpretation from the viewpoint of the first binary subalphabet. For example, the sequence GACUUCACGGUG, which contains nine letters, obtains the individual binary number with $9 \times 2 = 18$ binary symbols: 100110001111/110000101101. If one wishes to construct a catalog of genetic sequences of various lengths and composition, it can be done on the basis of the natural system of numbering the sequences as multiplets.

In the genomatrix $[C \ A; \ G \ U]^{(3)}$, each of 64 triplets has its own number, which consists of the association of binary numbers of its row and column (e.g., the triplet CAU has the binary number 001010, which is equal to 10 in decimal notation). This genomatrix reflects real interrelations of elements in the set of triplets: any codon and its anticodon are disposed in inversion-symmetrical manner relative to the center of the genomatrix (Figure 2.2).

Each codon–anticodon pair (and only such a pair) has the sum of its decimal numbers, which is to equal 63 (in binary notation it is equal to 111111). For example, the triplet CAU has the decimal number 10, and the complementary triplet GUA has the decimal number 53; the sum of these numbers is 63. Each sequence of triplets can be presented in the genomatrix $P^{(3)}$ in the form of an appropriate trajectory passing through matrix cells with these triplets in series. It is obvious that the complementary sequences on the two filaments of the double helix of DNA correspond to two appropriate trajectories in the genomatrix $[C \ A; \ G \ U]^{(3)}$, which are inversion symmetrical to each other relative to the center.

The genomatrix $[C \ A; \ G \ U]^{(3)}$ (Figure 2.2) coincides with the famous table of 64 hexagrams in Fu-Xi's order from the ancient Chinese "The Book of Changes" (*I Ching*), which was written a few thousand years ago. This matrix amazed the creator of one of the first computers, Gottfried Leibniz (1646–1716), who considered himself the creator of the system of binary notation, but in one moment he suddenly found ancient predecessors relative to this system. Leibniz saw in features of the ancient table of 64 hexagrams many features similar to his ideas regarding binary systems and universal language. "*Leibniz has seen in this similarity ... evidence of the preestablished harmony and unity of the divine plan for all times and people*" (Schutskiy, 1997, p. 12). Modern physics and other branches of science pay attention to *I Ching* and other ancient Oriental teachings (see, e.g., Capra, 2000; Gell-Mann and Ne'eman, 2000). A possible connection between the genetic code and the symbolic system of *I Ching* has been noted in the literature (e.g., Jacob, 1974, 1977; Stent, 1969). Our results in the field of matrix genetics confirm this guesswork.

So the natural system of numbering the genetic triplets and their cells in the genomatrix $[C \ A; \ G \ U]^{(3)}$ has already been known for thousands of years. From a historical viewpoint it can be called an ancient Chinese system. The matrix approach to the genetic code, in addition to being an object of research and matrix mathematics, leads unexpectedly to historical analogies and connections.

Genetic Multiplets and Matrices of Diadic Shifts

Next we describe the connection between numerated genomatrices $P^{(n)}$ (Figure 2.2) and the matrices of dyadic shifts long known in the theory of discrete signal processing. The theory of discrete signal processing utilizes broadly the special mathematical operation of modulo-2 addition for binary numbers. Modulo-2 addition is a fundamental operation for binary variables. By definition, the modulo-2 addition of two numbers written in binary notation is made in a bitwise manner in accordance with the following rules:

$$0+0=0, \quad 0+1=1, \quad 1+0=1, \quad 1+1=0 \tag{2.3}$$

For example, modulo-2 addition of two binary numbers 110 and 101, which are equal to 6 and 5, respectively, in decimal notation, gives the result $110 \oplus 101 = 011$, which is equal to 3 in decimal notation ($\oplus$ is the symbol for modulo-2 addition). The series of binary numbers

$$000, 001, 010, 011, 100, 101, 110, 111 \tag{2.4}$$

forms a *diadic group*, in which modulo-2 addition serves as the group operation (Harmut, 1989). The distance in this symmetry group is known as the *Hamming distance*. Since the Hamming distance satisfies the conditions of a metric group, the diadic group is a metric group. The modulo-2 addition of any two binary numbers from (2.4) always results in a new number from the same series. The number 000 serves as the unit element of this group: for example, $010 \oplus 000 = 010$. The reverse element for any number in this group is the number itself: for example, $010 \oplus 010 = 000$.

The series (2.4) is transformed by modulo-2 addition with the binary number 001 into a new series with a new sequence of the same numbers:

$$001, 000, 011, 010, 101, 100, 111, 110 \tag{2.5}$$

Such changes in the initial binary sequence, produced by modulo-2 addition of its members with any binary numbers (2.4), are termed *diadic shifts* (Ahmed and Rao, 1975; Harmut, 1989). If any system of elements demonstrates its connection with diadic shifts, it indicates that the structural organization of its system is related to the logic of modulo-2 addition.

Let us use modulo-2 addition to create the binary numbers of columns and rows for all cells in the genomatrix $P^{(3)}$ in Figure 2.2. For example, the cell disposed in column 110 and row 101 obtains the binary number 011 by means of such addition. As a result, a numeric matrix $P^{(3)}_{\text{DIAD}}$ arises (Figure 2.3).

The 8×8 matrix $P^{(3)}_{\text{DIAD}}$ is bisymmetrical because it is symmetrical relative to both diagonals. This matrix contains only eight binary numbers, which are equal to 0, 1, 2, 3, 4, 5, 6, and 7 in decimal notation. Each of these numbers occupies eight matrix cells from 64 numerated cells (see Figure 2.2). The sum of the numbers of these eight matrix cells is equal to 252 in decimal notation

	000 (0)	001 (1)	010 (2)	011 (3)	100 (4)	101 (5)	110 (6)	111 (7)
000 (0)	000 (0)	001 (1)	010 (2)	011 (3)	100 (4)	101 (5)	110 (6)	111 (7)
001 (1)	001 (1)	000 (0)	011 (3)	010 (2)	101 (5)	100 (4)	111 (7)	110 (6)
010 (2)	010 (2)	011 (3)	000 (0)	001 (1)	110 (6)	111 (7)	100 (4)	101 (5)
011 (3)	011 (3)	010 (2)	001 (1)	000 (0)	111 (7)	110 (6)	101 (5)	100 (4)
100 (4)	100 (4)	101 (5)	110 (6)	111 (7)	000 (0)	001 (1)	010 (2)	011 (3)
101 (5)	101 (5)	100 (4)	111 (7)	110 (6)	001 (1)	000 (0)	011 (3)	010 (2)
110 (6)	110 (6)	111 (7)	100 (4)	101 (5)	010 (2)	011 (3)	000 (0)	001 (1)
111 (7)	111 (7)	110 (6)	101 (5)	100 (4)	011 (3)	010 (2)	001 (1)	000 (0)

FIGURE 2.3   Bisymmetrical matrix $P_{DIAD}^{(3)}$ of dyadic shifts. Parentheses contain expressions of numbers in decimal notation.

for each case. For example, the number 5 occupies those eight matrix cells on Figure 2.3, which are numerated individually on Figure 2.2 by the numbers 5, 12, 23, 30, 33, 40, 51, and 58. The sum of these eight numbers is equal to 252. The left and right halves (and the upper and lower halves) of this matrix $P_{DIAD}^{(3)}$ are inversion-symmetrical to each other in the sense of the binary inversion relative to their three-digit numbers in matrix cells (by definition, the binary inversion interchanges the binary symbols 1 and 0 with each other). For this reason, the modulo-2 addition of such binary numbers, which exist in any two mirror-symmetrical cells of this matrix, gives the binary number 111. For example, a cell with the number 001 in the left half of the matrix has a mirror-symmetrical cell in its right half with the number 110 always. Their sum in the sense of modulo-2 addition is equal to $001 \oplus 110 = 111$.

By an analogical algorithm of modulo-2 addition, the entire family of matrices of dyadic shifts $P_{DIAD}^{(n)}$, where $n = 2, 4, 5, \ldots$, can be constructed from the genomatrices $P^{(n)}$ (Figure 2.2). All such matrices $P_{DIAD}^{(n)}$ are bisymmetrical as well. Each of matrices $P_{DIAD}^{(n)}$ is the matrix form of presentation of a particular case of special hypercomplex numbers, termed *hyperbolic matrions* (Petoukhov, 2008a; Petoukhov and He, 2009).

Do such matrices $P_{DIAD}^{(n)}$ have any connection with the theory of discrete signal processing? Yes, they have. The matrix $P_{DIAD}^{(3)}$ and other analogical matrices $P_{DIAD}^{(n)}$ have long been known in information theory under the name *matrices of dyadic shifts* (see, e.g., Ahmed and Rao, 1975). They are fundamentals of some special methods of analysis and synthesis of signals as vectors. In computer informatics, matrices of dyadic shifts are constructed by means of modulo-2 addition without utilizing Kronecker multiplication of matrices, which we have used to obtain the Kronecker family of the genomatrices $P^{(n)}$

of all multiplets from the 2×2 matrix of the genetic alphabet (Figure 2.2). One can note that the analogical 8×8 matrix of diadic shifts is constructed from the table of 64 hexagrams of *I Ching* (Petoukhov, 2008a; Petoukhov and He, 2009).

It should be emphasized especially that dyadic shifts are one of the elements of an interesting theory, which is described in a book about applications of methods of information theory in physics (Harmut, 1989). This theory utilizes the notions of dyadic spaces, dyadic metrics, and dyadic coordinates in connection with special codes. The relation of the genetic code to this theory is one of the prospective topics in the field of matrix genetics for investigations in the future.

Now let us pay attention to the block character of the matrices of dyadic shifts $P_{\text{DIAD}}^{(n)}$. Each $2^n \times 2^n$ matrix $P_{\text{DIAD}}^{(n)}$ is a system of fractal kind. It contains four block matrices, each of which has the size 2×2. Two such block matrices, which are disposed along each diagonal, are identical to each other always. For this reason, the lower half of each $2^n \times 2^n$ matrix $P_{\text{DIAD}}^{(n)}$ can be produced from its upper half algorithmically by a cyclic shift. In this sense, each block matrix $P_{\text{DIAD}}^{(n)}$ is a matrix of the cyclic shift of its 2×2 blocks and is crosswise in character.

Two quadrants along the main diagonal contain identical block elements, which are $2^{n-1} \times 2^{n-1}$ matrices of a dyadic shift. Matrix cells along the second diagonal contain identical block elements in a form of $2^{n-1} \times 2^{n-1}$ matrices also, elements of which are changed only by addition of the number 2^{n-1} relative to elements of the $2^{n-1} \times 2^{n-1}$ matrices along the main diagonal. In turn, these $2^{n-1} \times 2^{n-1}$ matrices are the block matrices of the cyclic shift, which are crosswise in character; and so on.

For example, the $2^3 \times 2^3$ matrix $P_{\text{DIAD}}^{(3)}$ in Figure 2.3 is the block matrix of the cyclic shift relative to its 2×2 quadrants. Identical quadrants, which are disposed along the main diagonal, are $2^2 \times 2^2$ matrices of the dyadic shift with the elements $0, 1, 2,$ and 3. Another type of identical block in the form of the $2^2 \times 2^2$ quadrants with elements $4, 5, 6,$ and 7 are disposed along the second diagonal. They differ from the first $2^2 \times 2^2$ quadrants by addition of the number 2^2 to their elements only. In turn, each of these $2^2 \times 2^2$ quadrants of the matrix $P_{\text{DIAD}}^{(3)}$ in Figure 2.3 is the block matrix of the cyclic shift of its 2×2 blocks.

In connection with cyclic shifts in the genetic matrices described, one can mention *cyclic codes*, which are based on cyclic shifts (Peterson and Weldon, 1972; Sklar, 2001). Cyclic codes are usually considered to be one of the most interesting codes in the field of digital techniques due to their mathematical properties. Some modern publications in the field of molecular genetics analyze the question of a possible important participation of cyclic codes in systems of genetic coding (Arques and Michel, 1996, 1997; Frey and Michel, 2003, 2006; Stambuk, 1999).

Returning to the crosswise character of genetic matrices of diadic shifts $P_{\text{DIAD}}^{(n)}$ (Figure 2.3), which reminds one of the crosswise character of chromosomes to some extent, we note that genetic inherited constructions of physi-

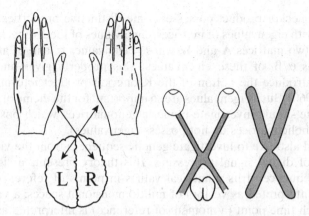

FIGURE 2.4 Crosswise schemes of some morpho-functional structures in the human organism. *Left:* crosswise connections of brain hemispheres with the left and right halves of a human body. *Middle:* crosswise structure of optic nerves from eyes to brain. *Right:* a chromosome.

ological systems (including sensory-motion systems) demonstrate similar crosswise structures for unknown reasons. For example, the connection between the hemispheres of the human brain and the halves of the human body possesses a similar crosswise character: The left hemisphere serves the right half of the body and the right hemisphere serves the left half (Figure 2.4) (Annett, 1985, 1992; Gazzaniga, 1995; Hellige, 1993). The system of optic cranial nerves from two eyes possesses crosswise structures as well: The optic nerves transfer information about the right half of the field of vision into the left hemisphere of brain, and transfer information about the left half of the field of vision into the right hemisphere. The same is true for the hearing system (Penrose, 1989, Chap. 9). One can suppose that these inherited physiological phenomena are connected with genetic crosswise structures, which include, in particular, crosswise matrices of dyadic shifts and octet bipolar matrices (see Chapter 8) to provide noise-immunity properties of genetic systems.

2.4 GENETIC MATRICES, HYDROGEN BONDS, AND THE GOLDEN SECTION

Until this moment we analyzed the symbolic genetic matrices. In this paragraph we analyze numeric genetic matrices, which are produced from the symbolic genomatrices. What are some reasons to consider numeric genomatrices?

Many materials demonstrate that the Kronecker product of matrices is useful for analysis of the genetic code and is adequate for its structure.

But the Kronecker product possesses some distinctive properties, which are connected with eigenvalues of matrices: eigenvalues of the Kronecker product $\mathbf{A} \otimes \mathbf{B}$ for two matrices $\mathbf{A}$ and $\mathbf{B}$, whose eigenvalues α_i and β_k are equal to the products $\alpha_i^* \beta_k$ of these eigenvalues. This property gives an additional reason to introduce the notion of the Kronecker product into mathematics (Bellman, 1960). But if eigenvalues are so important for the theme of Kronecker products, one should investigate numeric genomatrices, which possess eigenvalues (symbolic matrices do not possess eigenvalues).

We would also like to investigate genetic sequences from the viewpoint of the theory of digital signal processing. This theory presents a signal in the form of a sequence of its numerical values in points of reference. Discrete signals are interpreted as vectors of multidimensional spaces: a value of the signal at each time point (a moment of reference) is interpreted as the value of one of the coordinates of multidimensional space of signals (Trahtman, 1972). The theory of discrete signal processing is the geometrical science of multidimensional spaces to some extent. The number of dimensions of such a space is equal to the quantity of moments of references for the signal. Appropriate metric notions and other necessary things for providing the reliability, velocity, and economy of information transfer are introduced in these multidimensional vector spaces. For example, important information notions of the energy and power of a discrete signal are correspondingly the square of the length of the vector signal and the same square of the length of the vector signal, which is divided by the number of dimensions. Various signals and their ensembles are compared as geometrical objects of such metric multidimensional spaces.

These methods underlie technologies of signal intelligence and pattern recognition, detections and corrections of information mistakes, artificial intelligence and robotic learning, and so on. If we wish to use the methods of the theory of discrete signal processing to analyze genetic structures, we should learn to turn from the symbolic genetic matrices and genetic sequences to their numerical analogies.

The method, which is utilized in this chapter for such a turn, replaces the letter symbols A, C, G, and U(T) of the genetic alphabet by quantitative parameters of these nitrogenous bases, which determine their physical–chemical role (Petoukhov, 2001a). First, these symbols are replaced in this chapter by numbers of the hydrogen bonds, which have long been thought to be important participants in the transfer of genetic information. Each molecular element of the genetic code is a component of a harmonic system of genetic coding. Its molecular parameters are coordinated with quantitative parameters of other elements of this system. Quantitative characteristics of separate elements should be investigated as part of the set of quantitative characteristics of a system ensemble of elements. The matrix approach has long been known to be very effective for system investigations: for example, in the fields of quantum mechanics and the physics of elementary particles. In the field of matrix genetics, this approach unites parameters of a set of separate elements not only in a general matrix, but in the entire family of genetic matrices, which embraces sets of multiplets of different lengths (Figure 2.2). In this way, hidden connections between parameters of separate parts of the united genetic system can be revealed, together with their relations to famous physical and mathematical constants and other objects.

Let us consider the numerical genomatrices of hydrogen bonds of the nitrogenous bases. The hydrogen bonds of complementary letters of the genetic alphabet have long been recognized for their important information. In addition, hydrogen plays the main role in the composition of the universe, where of each 100 atoms, 93 are atoms of hydrogen and where the *chemical influence of omnipresent hydrogen is the defining factor* (Ponnamperuma, 1972). Thus, investigation of a possible meaning for hydrogen bonds in genetic information is of special interest.

The complementary letters C and G have three hydrogen bonds (C = G = 3), and the complementary letters A and U have two hydrogen bonds (A = U = 2). Let us replace each multiplet in the Kronecker family of the genomatrices $P^{(n)} = [C \ A; \ U \ G]^{(3)}$ by the product of these numbers of its hydrogen bonds. In this case we get the Kronecker family of the multiplicative matrices marked as $P_{MULT}^{(n)} = [3 \ 2; \ 2 \ 3]^{(n)}$ conditionally. For example, the triplet CAU will be replaced by the number 12 (= 3 × 2 × 2) in the genomatrix $P_{MULT}^{(3)}$. Figure 2.5 demonstrates the three initial genomatrices from the Kronecker family of genomatrices $[3 \ 2; \ 2 \ 3]^{(n)}$ constructed in this way. The numerical characteristics of each genomatrix $[3 \ 2; \ 2 \ 3]^{(n)}$ are connected with the quint ratio 3:2; for this reason we call such genomatrices *quint genomatrices*.

All matrices $P_{MULT}^{(n)}$ are nonsingular. They are symmetrical relative to both diagonals and can be termed *bisymmetric matrices*. All rows and all columns of this matrix differ from each other by the sequences of their numbers. But the sums of all numbers in the cells of each row and each column in any matrix $P_{MULT}^{(n)}$ are identical. For example, in the case of the matrix $P_{MULT}^{(3)}$, these

$$
P_{MULT}{}^{(1)} = \begin{vmatrix} 3 \ 2 \\ 2 \ 3 \end{vmatrix}; \ P_{MULT}{}^{(2)} = \begin{vmatrix} 9\ 6\ 6\ 4 \\ 6\ 9\ 4\ 6 \\ 6\ 4\ 9\ 6 \\ 4\ 6\ 6\ 9 \end{vmatrix}; \ P_{MULT}{}^{(3)} = \begin{vmatrix} 27\ 18\ 18\ 12\ 18\ 12\ 12\ \ 8 \\ 18\ 27\ 12\ 18\ 12\ 18\ \ 8\ 12 \\ 18\ 12\ 27\ 18\ 12\ \ 8\ 18\ 12 \\ 12\ 18\ 18\ \ 27\ \ 8\ 12\ 12\ 18 \\ 18\ 12\ 12\ \ 8\ 27\ 18\ 18\ 12 \\ 12\ 18\ \ 8\ 12\ 18\ 27\ 12\ 18 \\ 12\ \ 8\ 18\ 12\ 18\ 12\ 27\ 18 \\ \ 8\ 12\ 12\ 18\ 12\ 18\ 18\ 27 \end{vmatrix}
$$

FIGURE 2.5 Beginning of the family of quint multiplicative genomatrices $P_{MULT}^{(n)} = [3 \ 2; \ 2 \ 3]^{(n)}$, which are based on the product of the numbers of hydrogen bonds (C = G = 3, A = U = 2).

sums are $125 = 5^3$, and the total sum of numbers inside the matrix is 1000. The rank of this matrix is 8. Its determinant is 5^{12}. Eigenvalues of $P_{\text{MULT}}^{(3)}$ are 1, 5, 5, 5, 5^2, 5^2, 5^2, and 5^3. The matrix $P_{\text{MULT}}^{(3)}$ has four types of numbers only: 8, 12, 18, and 27. Certain laws are observed in their disposition, which are connected with a few interesting properties of this matrix, including the property of invariance of its numerical mosaic under many mathematical operations (see below).

Numerical Genomatrices and the Golden Section

In biology, a genetic system provides the self-reproduction of biological organisms in their generations. In mathematics, the *golden section* (or *divine proportion*) and its properties were a mathematical symbol of self-reproduction from the Renaissance and have been studied by Leonardo da Vinci, Johannes Kepler, and many other prominent thinkers (see the details at the Web site "Museum of Harmony and Golden Section," http://www.goldenmuseum.com). Is there any connection between these two systems? Yes, and we demonstrate here such an unexpected connection.

The golden section has the value $\varphi = (1 + 5^{0.5})/2 = 1.618. \ldots$ (Sometimes the *inverse* of this value is called the golden section in the literature.) If the simplest genetic matrix, $P_{\text{MULT}}^{(1)}$, is raised to the power $\frac{1}{2}$ in the ordinary sense (i.e., if we take the square root), the result is the bisymmetric matrix $\Phi = \left(P_{\text{MULT}}^{(1)}\right)^{1/2}$, the matrix elements of which are equal to the golden section and to its inverse value. And if any other genomatrix $P_{\text{MULT}}^{(n)} = [3\ 2;\ 2\ 3]^{(n)}$ is raised to the power $\frac{1}{2}$ in the ordinary sense, the result is the bisymmetric matrix $\Phi^{(n)} = \left(P_{\text{MULT}}^{(n)}\right)^{1/2}$, the matrix elements of which are equal to the golden section in various integer powers with elements of symmetry among these powers (Figure 2.6). For example, the matrix $\Phi_{\text{MULT}}^{(3)} = \left(P_{\text{MULT}}^{(n)}\right)^{1/2}$ has only two pairs of inverse numbers: φ^1 and φ^{-1}, φ^3 and φ^{-3} (Figure 2.6). Matrices with matrix elements, all of which are equal to golden section φ in different powers only, can be referred to as *golden matrices*. Figuratively speaking, the quint genomatrices have a secret substrate from the golden matrices. The product of all numbers in any row and any column of these golden matrices is 1. The matrices $P_{\text{MULT}}^{(n)}$ and $\Phi^{(n)}$ are connected with matrices of diadic shifts by means of the character of the disposition of their elements.

The matrix elements of the matrix $\Phi^{(n)} = \left(P_{\text{MULT}}^{(n)}\right)^{1/2}$ can be constructed directly from a combination of φ and φ^{-1} using the following algorithm. We take a corresponding multiplet of the matrix $P^{(n)} = [C\ A;\ U\ G]^{(n)}$ and change its letters C and G to φ. Then we take the letters A and U in this multiplet and change each of them to φ^{-1}. As a result, we obtain a chain with n links, where each link is φ or φ^{-1}. The product of all such links gives the value of corresponding matrix elements in the matrix $\Phi^{(n)}$. For example, for the matrix $\Phi^{(3)} = \left(P_{\text{MULT}}^{(3)}\right)^{1/2}$, let us calculate a matrix element which is disposed at the same place as the triplet CAU in the matrix $[C\ A;\ U\ G]^{(3)} = P^{(3)}$. According to the algorithm described, one should change the letter C to φ and the letters

$$(P_{MULT})^{1/2} = \phi = \begin{vmatrix} \varphi & \varphi^{-1} \\ \varphi^{-1} & \varphi \end{vmatrix} ; \quad (P_{MULT}^{(2)})^{1/2} = \phi^{(2)} = \begin{vmatrix} \varphi^2 & \varphi^0 & \varphi^0 & \varphi^{-2} \\ \varphi^0 & \varphi^2 & \varphi^{-2} & \varphi^0 \\ \varphi^0 & \varphi^{-2} & \varphi^2 & \varphi^0 \\ \varphi^{-2} & \varphi^0 & \varphi^0 & \varphi^2 \end{vmatrix}$$

$$(P_{MULT}^{(3)})^{1/2} = \phi^{(3)} = \begin{vmatrix} \varphi^3 & \varphi^1 & \varphi^1 & \varphi^{-1} & \varphi^1 & \varphi^{-1} & \varphi^{-1} & \varphi^{-3} \\ \varphi^1 & \varphi^3 & \varphi^{-1} & \varphi^1 & \varphi^{-1} & \varphi^1 & \varphi^{-3} & \varphi^{-1} \\ \varphi^1 & \varphi^{-1} & \varphi^3 & \varphi^1 & \varphi^{-1} & \varphi^{-3} & \varphi^1 & \varphi^{-1} \\ \varphi^{-1} & \varphi^1 & \varphi^1 & \varphi^3 & \varphi^{-3} & \varphi^{-1} & \varphi^{-1} & \varphi^1 \\ \varphi^1 & \varphi^{-1} & \varphi^{-1} & \varphi^{-3} & \varphi^3 & \varphi^1 & \varphi^1 & \varphi^{-1} \\ \varphi^{-1} & \varphi^1 & \varphi^{-3} & \varphi^{-1} & \varphi^1 & \varphi^3 & \varphi^{-1} & \varphi^1 \\ \varphi^{-1} & \varphi^{-3} & \varphi^1 & \varphi^{-1} & \varphi^1 & \varphi^{-1} & \varphi^3 & \varphi^1 \\ \varphi^{-3} & \varphi^{-1} & \varphi^{-1} & \varphi^1 & \varphi^{-1} & \varphi^1 & \varphi^1 & \varphi^3 \end{vmatrix}$$

FIGURE 2.6 Beginning of the Kronecker family of the golden matrices $\Phi^{(n)} = (P_{MULT}^{(n)})^{1/2}$, where $\varphi = (1 + 5^{0.5})/2 = 1.618\ldots$ is the golden section.

A and U to φ^{-1}. In the example considered, we obtain the following product: $(\varphi \times \varphi^{-1} \times \varphi^{-1}) = \varphi^{-1}$. This is the desired value of the matrix element considered for the matrix $\Phi^{(3)}$ in Figure 2.6.

A ratio between adjacent numbers in numerical sequences inside each such matrix $\Phi^{(n)}$ (e.g., $\ldots \varphi^{-3}, \varphi^{-1}, \varphi^1, \varphi^3, \ldots$) is equal to φ^2 always. The same ratio φ^2 exists in regular 5-stars as a ratio between sides of the adjacent stars entered in each other (this pentagram is the ancient symbol of health).

The golden section is presented in five-symmetrical objects of biological bodies (e.g., flowers), which are present widely in living nature but are forbidden in classical crystallography. It exists as well in many figures of modern generalized crystallography: quasicrystals by Shechtman, Penrose's mosaics (Penrose, 1989), dodecahedrons of ensembles of water molecules, icosahedron figures of viruses, and biological phyllotaxis laws, for example.

One can propose a new principal *matrix-genetic* definition of the golden section on the basis of the matrix specifics of genetic code systems: The golden section φ and its inverse value φ^{-1} are single matrix elements of a bisymmetrical matrix Φ_{MULT}, which is the square root of such a bisymmetrical 2×2 matrix P_{MULT}, the elements of which are genetic numbers of hydrogen bonds $(C = G = 3, A = U = 2)$ and which has a positive determinant.

This matrix-genetic definition does not use traditional elements of definition of the golden section: line segments, their proportions, and so on. Probably, many realizations of the golden section in nature are related to its matrix essence and its matrix representation. It should be investigated specially and systematically, where in natural systems and phenomena we have the bisymmetric matrix P_{MULT} with its matrix elements 3 and 2 in a direct or masked form (e.g., in the form of such pairs of numbers as 6 and 4, or 9 and 6, or 12 and 8, with the same 3:2 proportion which is so frequent for ratios of elements in genetic codes). One can, in this way, hope to discover many new system phenomena and connections between them in nature.

The new theme of the golden section in genetic matrices seems to be important because many inherited physiological systems and processes are connected with it. It is known that proportions of a golden section characterize many physiological processes: cardiovascular processes, respiratory processes, electric activities of brain, locomotion activity, and so on. The golden section has long been described and investigated as a phenomenon of aesthetic perception as well. Taking these facts into account, the golden section should be considered as a candidate for the role of one of the base elements in an inherited interlinking of the physiological subsystems, which provides unity of an organism. The matrix relation between the golden section φ and significant parameters of genetic codes testifies in favor of a molecular genetics that provides such physiological phenomena. One can hope that the algebra of bisymmetric genetic matrices, which are connected with the theme of the golden section, will be useful for explanation and in the numerical forecasting of separate parameters in different physiological subsystems of biological organisms with their cooperative essence and golden section phenomena.

The Kronecker families of the golden and quint genomatrices are connected with the famous Pascal triangle by means of quantities of equal numbers, which are presented in sequences of matrices of increasing size. As is evident from Figure 2.2, the golden 2×2 matrix contains one number φ^1 and one number φ^{-1}; the $2^2 \times 2^2$ matrix contains one number φ^2, one number φ^{-2}, and two numbers φ^0; the $2^3 \times 2^3$ matrix contains one number φ^3, one number φ^{-3}, three numbers φ, three numbers φ^{-1}, and so on. With the appropriate arrangement, which is shown in Table 2.3, Pascal's triangle is formed.

The molecular system of the genetic alphabet is constructed by nature such that other genetic matrices play the role of quint and golden matrices for other parameters. An example is that of the quantities of atoms in the molecular rings of pyrimidines and purines: The ring of purine contains six atoms, and the ring of pyrimidine contains nine atoms (Figure 2.1). From the viewpoint of these types of parameters, $C = U = 6$ and $A = G = 9$. The ratio $9:6 = 3:2$ is equal to the quint. Thus, the symbolic matrices $[A\ \ C;\ U\ \ G]^{(n)}$, $[G\ \ C;\ U\ \ A]^{(n)}$,

TABLE 2.3   Pascal's Triangle for Quantities of Iterative Types of Numbers in the Kronecker Family of the Golden Matrices from Figure 2.6

Matrix Size	Pascal's Triangle[a]				
$2^1 \times 2^1$	$1(\varphi^1)$	$1(\varphi^{-1})$			
$2^2 \times 2^2$	$1(\varphi^2)$	$2(\varphi^0)$	$1(\varphi^{-2})$		
$2^3 \times 2^3$	$1(\varphi^3)$	$3(\varphi^1)$	$3(\varphi^{-1})$	$1(\varphi^{-3})$	
$2^4 \times 2^4$	$1(\varphi^4)$	$4(\varphi^2)$	$6(\varphi^0)$	$4(\varphi^{-2})$	$1(\varphi^{-4})$
......					

[a]The parentheses contain iterative numbers in the matrix of corresponding size.

[A U; C G]$^{(n)}$, and [G U; A C]$^{(n)}$ become the threefold quint matrixes in the Kronecker power n in case of the replacement of their symbolic elements by the numbers 9 and 6. The square root of such numeric matrices is obviously connected with the golden matrices.

A biological organism is the master in the use of a set of parallel information channels. It is enough to point out the many sensory channels by means of which we obtain sensory information simultaneously: visual, acoustical, tactile, and so on. It is probable that many types of genetic matrices are used by an organism in parallel information channels as well.

The theory of discrete signal processing utilizes the important notions of the energy and power of signals (details of which were provided earlier in the chapter). If one interprets any row of the quint genomatrix $P_{MULT}^{(n)} = [3\ 2;\ 2\ 3]^{(n)}$ as a vector signal, the energy of such a vector signal is equal to 13^n and its power is equal to $(13/2)^n$. If one interprets any row of the golden genomatrix $\Phi^{(n)} = ([C\ A;\ U\ G]^{(n)})^{0.5}$ as a vector signal, the energy of the vector signal would equal 3^n and its power would be $(3/2)^n$, where the quint ratio participates. The family of the quint genomatrices is connected with the Pythagorean musical scale (Petoukhov, 2006, 2008a; Petoukhov and He, 2009).

The bisymmetric genomatrices $\Phi^{(n)}$ and $P_{MULT}^{(n)}$ have an unexpected group-invariant property, which is connected with multiplications of matrices and can be termed the *mosaic-invariant property*. We will explain this property using the matrix $P_{MULT}^{(3)}$ from Figure 2.5 as an example. This matrix consists of only four numbers: 8, 12, 18, and 27, with their special disposition. The numbers 8 and 27 are disposed separately at matrix diagonals in the form of a diagonal cross. The number 12 is disposed in matrix cells, a set of which produces a special mosaic. Such a mosaic can be referred to conditionally as the *symbol 69* (note that the numbers 6 and 9 are famous in *I Ching* as traditional symbols of yin and yang, respectively, but such a coincidence can be accidental.) The number 18 is disposed in matrix cells, a set of which produces a mirror-symmetrical mosaic in comparison with a 69-mosaic of the previous case. Figure 2.7 demonstrates these two cases by means of the set of dark matrix cells with the number 12 (left matrix) and with the number 18 (right matrix).

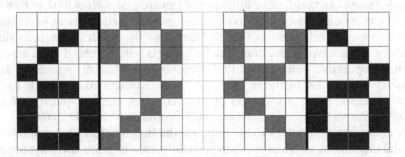

FIGURE 2.7 Mosaic of cells with number 12 (*left*, the dark cells) and number 18 (*right*) from the multiplicative matrix $P_{MULT}^{(3)}$ (Figure 2.5).

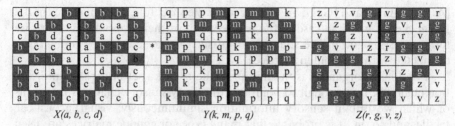

$$X(a, b, c, d) \qquad Y(k, m, p, q) \qquad Z(r, g, v, z)$$

FIGURE 2.8 Multiplication of mosaic-invariant matrices X and Y gives a new matrix Z with the same mosaic of the disposition of its four types of numbers. Cells with the numbers b, m, and s in the matrices X, Y, and Z are shaded.

It is known that if an arbitrary octet matrix with four types of numbers as its matrix elements is raised to the power n, the resulting matrix will usually have many more types of numbers with very different dispositions (up to 64 types of numbers for 64 matrix cells). But our bisymmetrical genetic matrices have the unexpected property of invariance of their numerical mosaic after the operation of raising to the power n. For example, if the octet matrix $P_{MULT}^{(3)}$ is raised to the power of 2, the resulting octet matrix $\left(P_{MULT}^{(3)}\right)^2$ will have a new set of four numbers 2197, 2028, 1872, and 1728 (instead of the initial four numbers 27, 18, 12, and 8) with the same disposition inside the octet matrix.

It is essential that this beautiful property of invariance of the numeric mosaic of the genetic matrix is independent of values of numbers. This property is realized for such matrices with the arbitrary set of four numbers a, b, c, and d if they are located in the same manner inside a matrix. Moreover, if we have one matrix X with a set of four numbers a, b, c, and d, and another matrix Y with another set of four numbers k, m, p, and q, the product of these matrices will be the matrix $Z = XY$ with a set of four numbers r, g, v, and z and with the same mosaic of their disposition (Figure 2.8).

It is obvious that the four symbols (e.g., a, b, c, d) in such matrices can be not only ordinary numbers, but also such arbitrary mathematical objects as complex numbers, matrices, or functions of time (e.g., $a = R\cos wt, b = T\sin wt$, ...). The mosaic-invariant property of these genetic matrices is an expression of the cooperative behavior of its elements, not the result of the individual behavior of each type of element. This property is reminiscent of some aspects of the cooperative behavior of the elements of biological organisms. This property is explained by the fact that the matrices described are matrix forms of presentation of a special type of hypercomplex number, the *hyperbolic matrions* (for details, see Petoukhov, 2008a; Petoukhov and He, 2009).

A mathematical analogy exists between the bisymmetric 2×2 genomatrices and the famous matrices of the hyperbolic turn, which are also bisymmetrical: $[\mathrm{sh}(x) \ \mathrm{ch}(x); \ \mathrm{ch}(x) \ \mathrm{sh}(x)]$, where $\mathrm{sh}(x)$ and $\mathrm{ch}(x)$ are the hyperbolic sine and cosine. This analogy gives us the opportunity to interpret normalized bisymmetric genomatrices in connection with hyperbolic turns, which have the following applications in physics and mathematics:

- The rotation of pseudo-Euclidean space
- The special theory of relativity
- The geometric theory of logarithms, where properties of logarithms are introduced by hyperbolic turns (Shervatov, 1954)
- The theory of solitons of the sine-Gordon equation

In particular, this coincidence of the genomatrices with the matrices of hyperbolic turns reflects the structural connections of the genetic code with the famous psychophysical Weber–Fechner law.

2.5   SYMMETRICAL PATTERNS, MOLECULAR GENETICS, AND BIOINFORMATICS

Symmetry in biological systems, in particular in the form of biological bodies, caused continuing interest to be expressed by thinkers for centuries as one of the most remarkable and mysterious phenomena of nature (e.g., Thompson d'Arcy, 1942; Weyl, 1952), and the work of many modern scientists is devoted to it as well. Problems of biological symmetries at a macromolecular level were considered in a special Nobel symposium (Engstrom and Strandberg, 1968), in which the important role of symmetry in biological research was emphasized. School programs in biology include consideration of numerous examples: rotary, transmitting, and mirror symmetries, symmetries of scale similarity in biological bodies such as flowers and sprouts of plants, and support-motion systems of animals.

Principles of symmetry have played an important role in the x-ray analysis of genetic molecules, as a result of which the concept of the double helix of DNA was developed in the famous work by Crick and Watson (Roller, 1974; Watson and Crick, 1953). Also, living substances are traditionally compared with crystals to reveal similarities and differences between them. For example, Schrödinger (1955) considered a living substance to be an aperiodic crystal. But all crystallography is based on principles of symmetry; crystallography has given a powerful impulse to the development and application of methods of symmetry in the mathematical natural sciences, including mathematical biology. New discoveries in crystallography frequently generate new hypotheses and discussions regarding the role of symmetry in crystals and living substances. The discovery of quasicrystals (Shechtman et al., 1984), which were connected to mosaics by Penrose (1989, 2004), with pentagrams (penta-symmetry) and with the golden section, can serve as an example here. This discovery has drawn the attention of researchers again to five-symmetries, which exist widely in biological bodies (e.g., colors, starfish) and which are forbidden in classical crystallography, with its principles of dense packing, one type of configuration unit.

The development of biological knowledge is accompanied by revealing new facts of subordination of very different biological objects to principles of symmetry on very different levels of their organization. Many biological concepts that have been affirmed in science or that sometimes cause critical discussions are connected to some extent with the question of biological symmetry: the law of homologous series (Vavilov, 1922); theories of morphogenetic fields; the hypothesis by Vernadsky (1965) regarding the non-Euclidean geometry of living matter; and conceptions about the morphogenetic conditionality of many psychological phenomena, including the phenomenon of aesthetic preference of the golden section, which is connected with Fibonacci numbers and morphogenetic laws of phyllotaxis (see the reviews of phyllotaxis in books by Jean, 1994 and Jean and Barabe, 2001).

Molecular biology has discovered the existence of fundamental problems of symmetry and of left–right dissymmetry on the level of biological molecules. On the other hand, development of the theory of symmetry has raised questions about new types of symmetry: for example, of non-Euclidean symmetry in biological bodies (see reviews by Petoukhov, 1981, 1989). Modeling biological phenomena on the basis of modern theories of nonlinear dynamics enters into the biological models at the highest levels of symmetry, which were known earlier in the fields of mathematics and physics. For example, the solitonic model of the macrobiological phenomena involves symmetries of Lorentz transformations from the special theory of relativity (Petoukhov, 1999a). It is no doubt that principles of symmetry were, are, and will continue to be a major component in the development of biology. They will play an increasing role in theoretical biology because of their status as one of the fundamentals of modern natural mathematical sciences as a whole (Bernal et al., 1972; Birss, 1964; Darvas, 2007; Fujita, 1991; Gardner, 1991; Hahn, 1989, 1998; Hargittai, 1986, 1989; Hargittai and Hargittai, 1994; Kappraff, 2002; Leyton, 1992; Loeb, 1971, 1993; Mainzer, 1988; Mandelbrot, 1983; Marcus, 1990, 2006; Miller, 1972; Moller and Swaddle, 1997; Ne'eman, 1999, 2002; Ne'eman and Kirsh, 1986; Petoukhov, 1981; Rosen, 1983, 1995; Shubnikov and Koptsik, 1974; Stewart and Golubitsky, 1992; Weyl, 1931, 1946, 1952; Wigner, 1965, 1967, 1970). Such a fundamental status for the principles of symmetry is connected with the famous Erlangen program by Klein and with the process of geometrization of physics (Lochak, 1994; Weyl, 1952). This process of geometrization has led to the interpretation of many basic theories of physics as theories of symmetry: The special theory of relativity, quantum mechanics, the theory of conservation laws, theories of elementary particles, and some other parts of modern physics are examples.

Investigations of symmetries are most relevant when science does not know how to create a theory of a concrete natural system. Biological organisms belong to a category of very complex natural systems. The variety of organisms is very numerous. They differ from each other vastly in many aspects: by their size, appearance, types of motions, and so on. But to humanity's surprise, molecular genetics has discovered that from a molecular-genetic viewpoint, all organisms are equivalent to each other by their basic genetic structure. Due to this revolutionary discovery, a great unification of all biological organisms has taken place in science, and information-genetic lines of investigation have become one of the most effective not only in biology, but in science as a whole. It is essential that a basic system of genetic coding is strikingly simple. Its simplicities and its orderliness throw down a challenge to specialists in many scientific fields, including specialists in the theory of symmetry and antisymmetry.

It should be noted that the fantastic successes of molecular genetics have been defined in particular by the disclosure of phenomenological facts of symmetry in molecular constructions of the genetic code and by a skillful use of these facts in theoretical modeling. An outstanding example is the discovery of a symmetrological fact, reflected in the famous rule by Chargaff, of an equality of quantities of nitrogenous bases in their appropriate pairs (adenine–thymine and cytosine–guanine) in molecules of DNA in a variety of organisms. This phenomenological rule was used skillfully in the theoretic modeling of the double helix of DNA by Crick and Watson using additional symmetrological principles (Roller, 1974). Many specialists from many countries around the world now work in this very attractive field of investigation of symmetries in the genetic code and bioinformatics (Arques and Michel, 1994, 1996, 1997; Bakhtiarov, 2001; Chernavskiy, 2000; Dragovich and Dragovich, 2007; Frank-Kamenetskiy, 1988; Hargittai, 2001; He, 2001; He and Petoukhov, 2007; He et al., 2004, 2005; Jimenes-Montano, 2005; Karasev, 2003; Karasev et al., 2005; Kargupta, 2001; Khrennikov and Kozyrev, 2007; Konopelchenko and Rumer, 1975; MacDonaill, 2003, 2005; Makovskiy, 1992; Marcus, 2001, 2007; Negadi, 2001, 2005, 2006; Petoukhov, 1990, 2001a,b, 2003, 2003–2004, 2005, 2006, 2008a,b; Ratner, 2002; Shcherbak, 1988; Stambuk, 1999; Stambuk et al., 2005; Szabo and He, 2006; Szabo et al., 2005; Waterman, 1999; Yang, 2001, 2005).

From an information viewpoint, biological organisms are informational essences. They obtain genetic information from their ancestors and transmit it to their descendants. In the biological literature we often come across the statement that living organisms are the texts of a molecular level of their organization. Just from an information-hereditary point of view, all living organisms are wonderfully unified: All have identical bases of genetic coding. A conception of the informational nature of living organisms is reflected in the words: "If you want to understand life, don't think about vibrant, throbbing gels and oozes, think about information technology" (Dawkins, 1991). Or another citation, which presents a similar direction of thought: "Notions of 'information' or 'valuable information' are not utilized in the physics of non-biological nature because they are not needed there. On the contrary, in biology the notions of 'information' and especially 'valuable information' are main ones; understanding and description of phenomena in biological nature are impossible without these notions. A specificity of 'living substance' lies in these notions" (Chernavskiy, 2000).

In the attempt to reveal the genetic code, the theoretical problem of a "bioinformation evolution" has arisen. This problem exists alongside ideas about chemical evolution and is very significant for understanding biological life. Informatics began to be used in concepts of the origin of life and in theoretical biology only in the past few decades. Now modern science hopes to obtain a deeper and more substantive understanding of life and its origin from the viewpoint of bioinformatics. In our opinion, modern investigations in the field of bioinformatics form the foundation of future theoretical biology. Therefore, the problem of the maximum union of molecular-genetic knowledge with the mathematics of the theory of discrete signal processing is especially relevant.

Bioinformatics can lead to deeper knowledge regarding the questions of what life is and why life exists. An investigation of symmetrical and structural analogies between computer informatics and genetic informatics is one of the important tasks of modern science in connection with the creation of DNA computers and with the development of bioinformatics. The development of bioinformatics and its applications requires an appropriate mathematical model of structural ensembles of genetic elements. The methods of symmetry can be one of the most useful in creating such a model. In this chapter we demonstrate the usefulness of methods of symmetry to study the genetic code and to develop effective matrix approaches in the field of genetic coding.

We should note that many attempts have been made to construct mathematical models or biochemical explanations of separate features of the genetic code. One of the most historically famous attempts to answer questions regarding the 20 amino acids was made by George Gamow more than 50 years ago (Gamow, 1954; Gamow and Metropolis, 1954). He proposed an explanation based on morphological character: that this quantity of amino acids is defined by the molecular configuration of the double helix of DNA, which possesses the appropriate quantity of hollows along the double helix. A few initial attempts at an explanation of features of the genetic code have been presented (Stent, 1971; Ycas, 1969).

Some mathematical, and other approaches to the genetic code have been proposed in the literature (Cristea, 2002, 2004, 2005; Dragovich and Dragovich, 2007; He, 2001; Jimenes-Montano, 2005; Karasev, 2003; Khrennikov and Kozyrev, 2007; Konopelchenko and Rumer, 1975; MacDonaill, 2003, 2005; Negadi, 2005, 2006; Petoukhov, 2001a,b, 2003, 2003–2004, 2005, 2006, 2008a,b; Ratner, 2002; Shcherbak, 1988; Stambuk, 1999; Waterman, 1999; Yang, 2001, 2005; etc.). Each of these attempts was important for the general advancement of the science leading to understanding the genetic code. This work was very useful because it has shown the specificity of the code and its differences from many other natural systems, the difficulties in modeling its features to obtain a fruitful model, the multiplicity of approaches in attempts at such modeling, the importance of the decision to perform this task, and so on. These publications have drawn the attention of many young researchers to this fundamental problem. Despite many interesting publications, the general situation in understanding the genetic code is characterized by the following words, which are also cited in the preface: "What do we have now in the 10 million nucleotide of sequence data determined to date? ... We have the program that runs the cellular machinery, but we know very little about how to read it. Bench biologists, by experiment and by close association with the data, have found meaningful patterns. Theoreticians, by careful reasoning and use of collections of data, have found others, but we still understand frustratingly little" (Fickett and Burks, 1989). It is clear that new efforts should be made to study the structural organization of the genetic code from the viewpoint of informatics and the mathematical natural sciences.

There is one more consequence as a result of revealing the connection between the genetic matrices $P^{(n)}$ and the matrices of diadic shifts $P_{\text{DIAD}}^{(n)}$ (Figure 2.3). This consequence concerns utilizing the notions and formalisms of diadic spaces, diadic metrics, and so on (Harmut, 1989), which are known in the field of computer informatics and in the new fields of matrix genetics and bioinformatics. Speculation by Stent (1969) and Jacob (1974) of a possible relation between the genetic code and the symbolic system of the ancient Chinese *I Ching* has resulted in new material for further examination.

Investigations of ensembles of elements of the genetic code with their symmetrical features have led to the construction of the Kronecker family of genetic matrices. This matrix family presents all sets of genetic multiplets in a well-ordered general form, where each multiplet obtains its own individual number in binary notation on the basis of the molecular characteristics of the genetic letters A, C, G, and U/T. Such a general form is connected with important principles and methods of computer informatics and of noise immunity in digital techniques. It gives new mathematical insight into the study of genetic systems and their connections with computer informatics and the algebraic theory of coding. For example, incipient indications were obtained that the logics of structures of the genetic code are related to logical modulo-2 addition.

2.6 CHALLENGES AND PERSPECTIVES

An understanding of the genetic code and the origin and evolution of all life-forms is critically dependent on our ability to analyze the historical data and to reconstruct phylogenetic relationships and connections among species at various levels of organization. The current status of the field offers limited methods for this reconstruction, and only one method provides a measure of uncertainty in the final tree structure. The difficulty of reconstruction grows exponentially with the number of initial data points, and efforts at resolution pose challenging problems in mathematics and computation. Mathematics can play a crucial role in connecting different levels of organization. Computational and algorithmic advances can speed up development of the subject immeasurably. Biologists seek explanations of supramolecular phenomena at the

molecular level. For example, embryogenesis involves the coordinated movement and differentiation of cell populations in terms of chemistry and genetics.
To understand organismal biology, it is important that we understand how
high-level coherent organization results from mechanisms operating at the
molecular level. The fundamental question is to build from one level to another.
What mechanisms could bridge this gap?

Modeling developmental and dynamic processes are challenging and exciting. Nonlinear systems of partial differential equations have been employed
to model these processes. For example, reaction diffusion equations have
stimulated the creation of new mathematics to study the wide spectrum of
solution behaviors exhibited by these equations. The Navier–Stokes equations
on fluid flows possess a rich solution behavior. The methods developed for
Navier–Stokes equations quite often are not adequate to cope with the new
models that arise in biology, but bifurcation theory, linear analysis, and singular
perturbation methods have already revealed new phenomena. Numerical
simulation techniques related to these processes are valuable and need further
refinement. Mechanochemical models for biological quantities concerning
pattern formation have been developed. Murray (1989) provided a general
survey of these and other pattern formation models. Numerical simulation,
particularly with mechanochemical models, is challenging even in two dimensions. Biological applications require solutions in three-dimensional domains
whose sizes change in time. We need to develop new analytical and numerical
simulation techniques and visualization methods to explore the solution
behaviors of such models. Recent advances in experimental biology such as
recombinant DNA technology and computer-enhanced imaging have created
new databases. These data sets are so extensive and complex that mathematical approaches are essential to understand these data sets and make
sense of them.

Biologists use the confocal scanning laser microscope and gene sequencers
to gather data into a database. The modern computer graphics technology
allows us to display the dynamic behavior of a mathematical model in the
same form as that in which experimental data are stored. The graphical visualization of models makes it possible to compare the behavior of a quantitative model with the data sets and yields the most compelling medium of
communication between mathematical modelers and biologists. One may
now obtain three-dimensional stereo reconstructions of the temporal evolution and spatial expression pattern of genes. Similarly, it is possible to observe
intracellular and intercellular events. A model of early pattern formation and/
or morphogenesis (Edgar et al., 1989) in the *Drosophila* embryo could
produce the same output that confocal microscopy gathered as input. The
challenge is to understand how the gene network results in a globally coherent spatial pattern as a consequence of temporal biochemical dynamics. In
recent years, recombinant DNA technology advances have produced
molecular-level databases documenting a complex network of genes that
code for proteins that control the expression of other genes. Given the com-

plexity of genetic networks, mathematical analysis may be the only way to synthesize the global picture from molecular-level parts. Mathematics can compute the macroscopic pattern formation consequences of this molecular-level information. Along with mathematical models, computer graphics are used to visualize data and dynamic behavior. For example, it has been shown that a network of cross-regulating genes regulates early development in *Drosophila*. The cell motility is driven by the cellular cytoskeleton, whose mechanochemical regulation is controlled by a network of regulatory molecules. Mathematics provides a framework for connecting information at the micro level to macro-level observations. According to the classical local activation lateral inhibition mechanism (Keller and Segel, 1970; Oster and Murray, 1989), spatial patterns can be created. Turing (1952) proposed a chemical mechanism for pattern formation (but not morphogenesis). In this model, activator and inhibitor morphogens diffuse at different rates and react with one another. Mathematical analysis shows how spatially heterogeneous patterns of morphogen concentration can arise. Another grand challenge is that of molecular evolution.

Many challenging and important problems remain to be solved in the application of population genetic theory to molecular evolution. The existing methods of population genetics, such as the neutral theory, which were developed to describe variations at single loci, require restructuring to address questions that arise in the analysis of DNA sequence data. Advances in computing power have revolutionized measurement techniques, which generate an abundance of biological data and a need for concomitant advances in quantitative methods of analysis. The interface between experimentation, mathematics, and computations is manifested at every stage of scientific investigation. A biological investigation often results in a proposal for a class of mathematical models. Such models may provide insight into the molecular processes (which need not be observable experimentally) and may also suggest new experiments. Collaborations between biologists and statisticians are essential in developing statistical and other modeling methods for research in biology.

REFERENCES

Ahmed, N., and Rao, K. (1975). *Orthogonal Transforms for Digital Signal Processing.* New York: Springer-Verlag.

Annett, M. (1985). *Left, Right, Hand and Brain: The Right Shift Theory.* Hillsdale, NJ: Lawrence Erlbaum.

Annett, M. (1992). Spatial ability in subgroups of left- and right-handers. *Br. J. Psychol.,* **83**, 493–962.

Arques, D., and Michel, C. J. (1994). Analytic expression of the purine/pyrimidine autocorrelation function after and before random mutations. *Math. Biosci.,* **123**, 103–125.

Arques, D., and Michel, C. (1996). A complementary circular code in the protein coding genes. *J. Theor. Biol.*, **182**, 45–56.

Arques, D., and Michel, C. (1997). A circular code in the protein coding genes of mitochondria. *J. Theor. Biol.*, **189**, 45–58.

Bakhtiarov, K. I. (2001). Logical structure of genetic code. *Symmetry: Cult. Sci.*, **12**(3–2), 401–406.

Bellman, R. (1960). *Introduction to Matrix Analysis*. New York: McGraw-Hill.

Bernal, I., Hamilton, W. C., and Ricci, J. S. (1972). *Symmetry: A Stereoscopic Guide for Chemists*. San Francisco: W.H. Freeman.

Birss, R. R. (1964). *Symmetry and Magnetism*. Amsterdam: North-Holland.

Blahut, R. E. (1985). *Fast Algorithms for Digital Signal Processing*. Reading, MA: Addison-Wesley.

Cantor, C. R., and Schimmel P. R. (1980). *Biophysical Chemistry*. San Francisco: W.H. Freeman.

Capra, F. (2000). *The Tao of Physics: An Exploration of the Parallels Between Modern Physics and Eastern Mysticism*. Boston: Shambhala Publications.

Chapevillle, F., and Haenni, A.-L. (1974). *Biosynthèse des proteins*. Paris: Hermann.

Chernavskiy, D. S. (2000) The problem of origin of life and thought from the viewpoint of modern physics. *Usp. Fiz. Nauk*, **170**(2), 157–183 (in Russian).

Cristea, P. D. (2002). Conversion of nucleotides sequences into genomic signals. *J. Cell. Mol. Med.*, **6**(2), 279–303.

Cristea, P. D. (2004). Genomic signals of re-oriented ORFs, EURASIP. *J. Appl. Signal Process.*, (Special Issue on Genomic Signal Processing), **2004**(1), 132–137.

Cristea, P. D. (2005). Representation and analysis of DNA sequences. In: E. R. Dougherty, I. Shmulevich, J. Chen, and Z. J. Wang. (Eds.), *Genomic Signal Processing and Statistics*. EURASIP Book Series on Signal Processing and Communications, Vol. **2**. New York: Hindawi Publishing, pp. 15–66.

Darvas, G. (2007). *Symmetry*. Basel, Switzerland: Birkhäuser.

Dawkins, R. (1991). *The Blind Watchmaker*. New York: Longman.

Dragovich, B., and Dragovich, A. (2007). *p*-Adic modelling of the genome and the genetic code. Retrieved July 2007, from http://arXiv:0707.3043.

Edgar, B. A., Odell, G. M., and Schubiger, G. (1989). A genetic switch, based on negative regulation, sharpens stripes in *Drosophila* embryos. *Dev. Genet.*, **10**, 124–142.

Engstrom, A., and Strandberg, B. (Eds.) (1968). *Nobel Symposium: Symmetry and Function of Biological Systems at the Macromolecular Level*, Oslo, Norway. New York: Plenum Press.

Fickett, J., and Burks, C. (1989). Development of a database for nucleotide sequences. In: M. S. Waterman (Ed.), *Mathematical Methods in DNA Sequences*, Boca Raton, FL: CRC Press, pp. 1–34.

Frank-Kamenetskiy, M. D. (1988). *The Most Principal Molecule*. Moscow: Nauka (in Russian).

Frey, G., and Michel, C. (2003). Circular codes in archaeal genomes. *J. Theor. Biol.*, **223**, 413–431.

Frey, G., and Michel, C. J. (2006). Identification of circular codes in bacterial genomes and their use in a factorization method for retrieving the reading frames of genes. *Comput. Biol. Chem.*, **30**, 87–101.

Fujita, S. (1991). *Symmetry and Combinatorial Enumeration in Chemistry*. Berlin: Springer-Verlag.

Gamow, G. (1954). Possible relation between deoxyribonucleic acid and protein structures. *Nature*, **173**, 318.

Gamow, G., and Metropolis, N. (1954). Numerology of polypeptide chains. *Science*, **120**, 779–780.

Gardner, M. (1991). *The New Ambidextrous Universe: Symmetry and Asymmetry, from Mirror Reflections to Superstrings*. New York: W.H. Freeman.

Gazzaniga, M. S. (1995). Principles of human brain organization derived from split brain studies. *Neuron*, **14**, 217–228.

Geadah Y. A., and Corinthios, M. J. (1977). Natural, dyadic and sequency order algorithms and processors for the Walsh–Hadamard transform. *IEEE Trans. Comput.*, **C-26**, 435–442.

Gell-Mann, M., and Ne'eman, Y. (2000). *The Eightfold Way*. New York: Westview Press.

Hahn, W. (1989). *Symmetrie als Entwicklungsprinzip in Natur und Kunst*. Königstein, Germany: Langewiesche.

Hahn, W. (1998). *Symmetry, as a Developmental Principle in Nature and Art*. Singapore: World Scientific.

Hamming, R. W. (1980). *Coding and Information Theory*. Englewood Cliffs, NJ: Prentice-Hall.

Hargittai, I. (Ed.) (1986). *Symmetry: Unifying Human Understanding*, Vol. **1**. New York: Pergamon Press.

Hargittai, I. (Ed.) (1989). *Symmetry: Unifying Human Understanding*, Vol. **2**. Oxford, UK: Pergamon Press.

Hargittai, I. (2001). Double symmetry of the double helix. *Symmetry: Cult. Sci.*, **12**(3–4), 247–254.

Hargittai, I., and Hargittai, M. (1994). *Symmetry: A Unifying Concept*. Bolinas, CA: Shelter Publications.

Harmut, H. F. (1989). *Information Theory Applied to Space–Time Physics*. Washington, DC: Catholic University of America.

He, M. (2001). On double helical sequences and doubly stochastic matrices. *Symmetry: Cult. Sci.*, **12**(3–4), 307–330.

He, M., and Petoukhov, S. V. (2007). Harmony of living nature, symmetries of genetic systems and matrix genetics. *Int. J. Integr. Biol.*, **1**(1), 41–43.

He, M., and Petoukhov, S. (2009). Symmetries in matrix genetics and Hadamard matrices of the genetic code. *Symmetry: Cult. Sci.*, **20**(1–4), 77–98.

He, M., Petoukhov, S., and Ricci, P. (2004). Genetic code, Hamming distance and stochastic matrices. *Bull. Math. Biol.*, **66**, 1405–1421.

He, M., Narasimhan, G., and Petoukhov, S. (Eds.) (2005). *Advances in Bioinformatics and Its Applications*. Series in Mathematical Biology and Medicine, Vol. **8**. Hackensack, NJ: World Scientific.

Hellige, J. B. (1993). *Hemispheric Asymmetry: What's Right and What's Left*. Cambridge, MA: Harvard University Press.

Jacob, F. (1974). Le modèle linguistique en biologie. *Critique, Mars*, **30**(322), 197–205.

Jacob, F. (1977). The linguistic model in biology. In: D. Armstrong and C. H. van Schooneveld (Eds.), *Roman Jakobson: Echoes of His Scholarship*. Lisse, The Netherlands: Peter de Ridder, pp. 185–192.

Jean, R. V. (1994). *Phyllotaxis: A Systematic Study in Plant Morphogenesis*. Cambridge, UK: Cambridge University Press.

Jean, R. V. and Barabe, D. (Eds.) (2001). *Symmetry in Plants*. Hackensack, NJ: World Scientific.

Jimenes-Montano, M. A. (2005). Applications of hyper genetic code to bioinformatics. In: M. He, G. Narasimhan, and S. Petoukhov (Eds.), *Advances in Bioinformatics and Its Applications*. Series in Mathematical Biology and Medicine, Vol. **8**. Hackensack, NJ: World Scientific, pp. 473–481.

Kappraff, J. (2002). *Beyond Measure: Essays in Nature, Myth, and Number*. Singapore: World Scientific.

Kappraff, J., and Petoukhov, S. (2009). Symmetries, generalized numbers and harmonic laws in matrix genetics. *Symmetry: Cult. Sci.*, **20**(1–4), 23–50.

Karasev, V. A. (2003). *The Genetic Code: New Horizons*. St. Petersburg, Russia: Tessa (in Russian).

Karasev, V. A., Luchinin, V. V., and Stefanov, V. E. (2005). A dodecahedron-based model of spatial representation of the canonical set of amino acids. In: M. He, G. Narasimhan, and S. Petoukhov (Eds.), *Advances in Bioinformatics and Its Applications*. Series in Mathematical Biology and Medicine, Vol. **8**. Hackensack, NJ: World Scientific, pp. 482–493.

Kargupta, H. (2001). A striking property of genetic code-like transformations. *Complex Syst.*, **11**, 43–50.

Keller, E. F., and Segel, L. A. (1970). The initiation of slime mold aggregation viewed as an instability. *J. Theor. Biol.*, **26**, 399–415.

Khrennikov, A. Y., and Kozyrev S. V. (2007). Genetic code on the dyadic plane. Retrieved Jan. 2007, from http://arXiv:q-bio/0701007.

Konopelchenko, B. G., and Rumer, Y. B. (1975). Classification of the codons in the genetic code. *Dokl. Akad. Nauk. SSSR*, **223**(2), 145–153 (in Russian).

Lee, M. H., and Kaveh, M. (1986). Fast Hadamard transform based on a simple matrix factorization. *IEEE Trans. Acoust. Speech Signal Process.*, **ASSSP-34**(6), 1666–1667.

Leyton, M. (1992). *Symmetry, Causality, Mind*. Cambridge, MA: MIT Press.

Lochak, G. (1994). *La geometrisation de la physique*. Paris: Flammarion.

Loeb, A. L. (1971). *Color and Symmetry*. New York: Wiley.

Loeb, A. L. (1993). *Concepts and Images: Visual Mathematics*. Boston: Birkhäuser.

MacDonaill, D. A. (2003). Why nature chose A, C, G and U/T: an error-coding perspective of nucleotide alphabet composition. *Origins Life Evol. Biosph.*, **33**, 433–455.

MacDonaill, D. A. (2005). Molecular mappings: group theory, coding theory, and the emergence of replication. In: M. He, G. Narasimhan, and S. Petoukhov (Eds.), *Advances in Bioinformatics and Its Applications*. Series in Mathematical Biology and Medicine, Vol. **8**. Hackensack, NJ: World Scientific, pp. 494–501.

Mainzer, K. (1988). *Symmetrien der Natur: Ein Handbuch zur Natur- und Wissenschaftsphilosophie*. Berlin: de Gruyter.

Makovskiy, M. M. (1992). *Linquistic Genetics*. Moscow: Nauka (in Russian).

Mandelbrot, B. B. (1983). *The Fractal Geometry of Nature*. New York: W.H. Freeman.

Marcus, S. (1990). *Algebraic Linguistics: Analytical Models*. Bucharest, Romania: Academic.

Marcus, S. (2001). Internal and external symmetry in genetic information. *Symmetry: Cult. Sci.*, **12**(3–2), 395–400.

Marcus, S. (2006). At the roots of the symmetry phenomena. *Symmetry: Cult. Sci.*, **17**(1–2), 89–90.

Marcus, S. (2007). *Words and Languages Everywhere*. Bucharest, Romania: Polimetrica.

Miller, W., Jr. (1972). *Symmetry Groups and Their Applications*. New York: Academic Press.

Moller, A. P., and Swaddle, J. P. (1997). *Asymmetry, Developmental Stability, and Evolution*. Oxford, UK: Oxford University Press.

Murray, J. D. (1989). *Mathematical Biology*. Biomathematics, Vol. **19**. Berlin: Springer-Verlag.

Ne'eman, Y. (1999). Symmetry as the leitmotif at the fundamental level in twentieth century physics. *Symmetry: Cult. Sci.*, **10**, 143–162.

Ne'eman, Y. (2002). Pythagoreanism in atomic, nuclear and particle physics. In: I. Hargittai and T. C. Laurent (Eds.), *Symmetry 2000*. Oxford, UK: Pergamon Press, pp. 265–278.

Ne'eman, Y., and Kirsh, Y. (1986). *The Particle Hunters*. Cambridge, UK: Cambridge University Press.

Negadi, T. (2001). Symmetry and proportion in the genetic code, and genetic information from the basic units of life. *Symmetry: Cult. Sci.*, **12**(3–4), 331–348.

Negadi, T. (2005). Symmetry and information in the genetic code. In: M. He, G. Narasimhan, and S. Petoukhov (Eds.), *Advances in Bioinformatics and Its Applications*. Series in Mathematical Biology and Medicine, Vol. **8**. Hackensack, NJ: World Scientific, pp. 502–511.

Negadi, T. (2006). The genetic code structure, from inside. *Symmetry: Cult. Sci.*, **17**(1–2), 317–340.

Nielsen, M. A., and Chuang, I. L. (2001). *Quantum Computation and Quantum Information*. Cambridge, UK: Cambridge University Press.

Oster, G. F., and Murray, J. D. (1989). Pattern formation models and developmental constraints. *J. Exp. Zool.*, **251**, 186–202.

Paun G., Rozenberg G., and Salomaa, A. (2006). *DNA Computing: New Computing Paradigms*. Upper Saddle River, NJ: Prentice Hall.

Penrose, R. (1989). *The Emperor's New Mind*. Oxford, UK: Oxford University Press.

Penrose, R. (2004). *The Road to Reality: A Complete Guide to the Laws of the Universe*. London: Jonathan Cape.

Peterson, W. W., and Weldon, E. J. (1972). *Error-Correcting Codes*. Cambridge, MA: MIT Press.

Petoukhov, S. V. (1981). *Biomechanics, Bionics and Symmetry*. Moscow: Nauka (in Russian).

Petoukhov, S. V. (1989). Non-Euclidean geometries and algorithms of living bodies. *Comput. Math. Appl.*, **17**(4–6), 505–534.

Petoukhov, S. V. (1990). Symmetric–algorithmic properties of regular biostructures. *Symmetry: Cult. Sci.*, **1**(3), 295–312.

Petoukhov, S. V. (1999a). *Biosolitons: The Basis of Solitonic Biology*. Moscow: GPKM (in Russian).

Petoukhov, S. V. (1999b). Genetic code and the ancient Chinese "Book of Changes." *Symmetry: Cult. Sci.*, **10**, 211–226.

Petoukhov, S. V. (2001a). *The Bi-periodic Table of Genetic Code and the Number of Protons*. Moscow: MKC (in Russian).

Petoukhov, S. V. (2001b). Genetic codes 1: binary sub-alphabets, bi-symmetric matrices and golden section; Genetic codes 2: numeric rules of degeneracy and the chrono-cyclic theory. *Symmetry: Cult. Sci.*, **12**(1), 255–306.

Petoukhov, S. V. (2003). The biperiodic table and attributive conception of genetic code: a problem of unification bases of biological languages. In: F. Valafar and H. Valafar (Eds.), *Proceedings of the 2003 International Conference on Mathematics and Engineering Techniques in Medicine and Biological Sciences*, session "Bioinformatics 2003." Las Vegas, NV: CSREA Press.

Petoukhov, S. V. (2003–2004). Attributive conception of genetic code, its bi-periodic tables and problem of unification bases of biological languages. *Symmetry: Cult. Sci.*, **14–15**(pt. 1), 281–307.

Petoukhov, S. V. (2005). The rules of degeneracy and segregations in genetic codes. The chronocyclic conception and parallels with Mendel's laws. In: M. He, G. Narasimhan, and S. Petoukhov (Eds.), *Advances in Bioinformatics and Its Applications*. Series in Mathematical Biology and Medicine, Vol. **8**. Hackensack, NJ: World Scientific, pp. 512–532.

Petoukhov, S. V. (2006). Bioinformatics: matrix genetics, algebras of the genetic code and biological harmony. *Symmetry: Cult. Sci.*, **17**(1–4), 251–290.

Petoukhov, S. V. (2008a). *Matrix Genetics, Algebras of the Genetic Code, and Noise Immunity*. Moscow: RCD (in Russian).

Petoukhov, S. V. (2008b). The degeneracy of the genetic code and Hadamard matrices. 1–8. Retrieved Feb. 2008, from http://arXiv:0802.3366.

Petoukhov, S. V., and He, M. (2009). *Symmetrical Analysis Techniques for Genetic Systems and Bioinformatics: Advanced Patterns and Applications*. Hershey, PA: IGI Global.

Ponnamperuma, C. (1972). *The Origins of Life*. Thames and Hudson, London: E.P. Dutton, New York.

Ratner, V. A. (2002). *Genetics, Molecular Cybernetics*. Novosibirsk, Russia: Nauka.

Roller, A. (1974). *Discovering the Basis of Life: An Introduction to Molecular Biology*. New York: McGraw-Hill.

Rosen, J. (1983). *Symmetry Primer for Scientists*. New York: Wiley.

Rosen, J. (1995). *Symmetry in Science: An Introduction to the General Theory*. New York: Springer-Verlag.

Schrödinger, E. (1955). *What Is Life? The Physical Aspect of the Living Cell*. Cambridge, UK: Cambridge University Press.

Schutskiy, Y. K. (1997). *The Chinese Classical "Book of Changes."* Moscow: Vostochnaya Literatura (in Russian).

Seeman, N. (2004). Nanotechnology and the double helix. *Sci. Am.*, **290**(6), 64–75.

Shapiro, E., and Benenson, Y. (2007). Bringing DNA computers to life. *Sci. Am.*, **17**(3), 40–47.

Shcherbak, V. I. (1988). The co-operative symmetry of the genetic code. *J. Theor. Biol.*, **132**, 121–124.

Shechtman, D., Blech, I., Gratias, D. and Cahn, J. (1984). Metallic phase with long-range orientational order and no translational symmetry. *Phys. Rev. Lett.*, **53**, 1951–1954.

Shervatov, V. G. (1954). *Hyperbolic Functions.* Moscow: GITTL (in Russian).

Shubnikov, A. V., and Koptsik, V. A. (1974). *Symmetry in Science and Art.* New York: Plenum Press.

Shults, G. E., and Schirmer, R. H. (1979). *Principles of Protein Structure.* Berlin: Springer-Verlag.

Sklar, B. (2001). *Digital Communication: Fundamentals and Applications.* Upper Saddle River, NJ: Prentice Hall.

Stambuk, N. (1999). Circular coding properties of gene and protein sequences. *Croat. Chem. Acta*, **72**(4), 999–1008.

Stambuk, N., Konyevoda, P., and Gotovac, N. (2005). Symbolic coding of amino acid and nucleotide properties. In: M. He, G. Narasimhan, and S. Petoukhov (Eds.), *Advances in Bioinformatics and Its Applications.* Series in Mathematical Biology and Medicine, Vol. **8**. Hackensack, NJ: World Scientific, pp. 512–532.

Stent, G. S. (1969). *The Coming of the Golden Age.* New York: Natural History Press.

Stent, G. S. (1971). *Molecular Genetics.* San Francisco: W.H. Freeman.

Stewart, I., and Golubitsky, M. (1992). *Fearful Symmetry: Is God a Geometer?* Oxford, UK: Blackwell.

Szabo, R., and He, M. (2006). Statistical analyses of patterns in tripetides. *Symmetry: Cult. Sci.*, **17**(1–2), 293–316.

Szabo, R., He, M., Burnham, E., and Jurani, J. (2005). Analyzing patterns of tripeptids using statistical approach and neural network paradigms. In: M. He, G. Narasimhan, and S. Petoukhov (Eds.), *Advances in Bioinformatics and Its Applications.* Series in Mathematical Biology and Medicine, Vol. **8**. Hackensack, NJ: World Scientific, pp. 544–553.

Thompson d'Arcy, W. (1942). *On Growth and Form.* Cambridge, UK: Cambridge University Press.

Trahtman, A. M. (1972). *Introduction to the Generalized Spectral Theory of Signals.* Moscow: Sovetskoie Radio (in Russian),

Trahtman, A. M., and Trahtman, V. A. (1975). *The Foundations of the Theory of Discrete Signals on Finite Intervals.* Moscow: Sovetskoie Radio (in Russian).

Turing, A. M. (1952). The chemical basis of morphogenesis. *Philos. Trans. R. Soc. Lond. B*, **237**, 37–72.

Vavilov, N. I. (1922). The law of homologous series in variation. *J. Genet.*, **12**(1), 47–89.

Vernadsky, V. I. (1965). *Chemical Structure of the Earth and Its Surrounding.* Moscow: Nauka.

Waterman, M. S. (Ed.) (1999). *Mathematical Methods for DNA Sequences*. Boca Raton, FL: CRC Press.

Watson, J. D. (1968). *The Double Helix; A Personal Account of the Discovery of the Structure of DNA*. New York: Atheneum.

Watson, J. D., and Crick, F. H. C. (1953). Molecular structure of nucleic acids: a structure of deoxyribose nucleic acid. *Nature*, **171**, 737–738.

Weyl, H. (1931). *The Theory of Groups and Quantum Mechanics*. New York: Dover.

Weyl, H. (1946). *The Classical Groups: Their Invariants and Representations*. Princeton, NJ: Princeton University Press.

Weyl, H. (1952). *Symmetry*. Princeton, NJ: Princeton University Press.

Wigner, E. P. (1965). Violations of symmetry in physics. *Sci. Am.*, **213**(6), 28–36.

Wigner, E. P. (1967). *Symmetries and Reflections: Scientific Essays of Eugene P. Wigner*. Bloomington, IN: Indiana University Press.

Wigner, E. W. (1970). *Symmetries and Reflections*. Bloomington, IN: Indiana University Press.

Wittmann, H. G. (1961). Ansatze zur Entschlusselung des genetishen Codes. *Naturwissenschaften*, **48**(24), 55.

Yang, C. M. (2001). Chemistry and the 28-gon polyhedral symmetry of the genetic code. *Symmetry: Cult. Sci.*, **12**(3–4), 320–333.

Yang, C. M. (2005). Molecular versus atomic information logic behind the genetic coding contents constrained by two evolutionary axes and the Fibonacci–Lucas sequence. In: M. He, G. Narasimhan, and S. Petoukhov (Eds.), *Advances in Bioinformatics and Its Applications*, Series in Mathematical Biology and Medicine, Vol. 8. Hackensack, NJ: World Scientific, pp. 554–564.

Yarlagadda, R., and Hershey, J. (1997). *Hadamard Matrix Analysis and Synthesis with Applications to Communications and Signal/Image Processing*. New York: Kluwer Academic.

Ycas, M. (1969). *The Biological Code*. Amsterdam: North-Holland.

3 Biological Sequences, Sequence Alignment, and Statistics

Biological sequences comprise primarily *DNA sequences* (also called *genetic sequences* or *nucleotide sequences*) and *amino acid sequences* (also called *peptide sequences* or *protein sequences*). DNA sequences direct the formation of amino acid sequences and determine the expression and regulation of genes. They determine the main aspects of the life process. Amino acid sequences determine the structures and functions of proteins. The abundant biological sequence data provide us with the most important information regarding life. Life is a manifestation of a combination of information, substance, and movement. Obtaining the sequence data is an initial step toward an understanding of these data. Biologists often produce biological sequence alignments in a manual manner using knowledge of DNA and protein structure and evolution. In bioinformatics, a sequence alignment is a way of arranging the primary sequences of DNA, RNA, or protein to identify regions of similarity that may be a consequence of a functional, structural, or evolutionary relationship between sequences. A true alignment of biological sequences is one that reflects the evolutionary relationship between two or more sequences that share a common ancestor.

In this chapter we define biological sequences, mathematical sequences, and binary sequences in theoretical computer science. We describe pairwise sequence alignment, multiple sequence alignment, and optimal sequence alignment. We discuss the scoring system used to rank alignments, the algorithms used to find optimal (or good) scoring alignments, and the statistical methods used to evaluate the significance of an alignment score.

3.1 INTRODUCTION

A *DNA* or *genetic sequence* is a succession of letters representing the primary structure of a real or hypothetical DNA molecule or strand, with the capacity to carry information. The possible letters are A, C, G, and T, representing the

Mathematics of Bioinformatics: Theory, Practice, and Applications, By Matthew He and Sergey Petoukhov
Copyright © 2011 John Wiley & Sons, Inc.

four nucleotide subunits of a DNA strand: adenine, cytosine, guanine, and thymine bases covalently linked to a phospho-backbone. In the typical case, the sequences are printed abutting one another without gaps, as in the sequence AAAGTCTGAC, going from 5′ to 3′ from left to right. A succession of any number of nucleotides greater than four is liable to be called a sequence. With regard to its biological function, which may depend on context, a sequence may be *sense* or *antisense*, and either coding or noncoding. DNA sequences may also contain "junk DNA."

In some special cases, letters other than A, T, C, and G are present in a sequence. These letters represent ambiguity. The rules of the International Union of Pure and Applied Chemistry (IUPAC) are as follows:

A = adenine	S = GC (strong bonds)
C = cytosine	W = AT (weak bonds)
G = guanine	B = GTC (all but A)
T = thymine	D = GAT (all but C)
R = GA (purine)	H = ACT (all but G)
Y = TC (pyrimidine)	V = GCA (all but T)
K = GT (keto)	N = AGCT (any)
M = AC (amino)	

A peptide or *amino acid sequence* is the order in which amino acid residues, connected by peptide bonds, lie in a chain in peptides and proteins. The sequence is generally reported from the N-terminal end, which contains a free amino group, to the C-terminal end, which contains a free carboxyl group. A peptide sequence is often called a *protein sequence* if it represents the primary structure of a protein. Amino acids are the basic structural building units of proteins. They form short polymer chains called *peptides* or longer chains called either *polypeptides* or *proteins*. The process of such formation from an mRNA template, known as *translation*, is part of protein biosynthesis. Twenty amino acids are encoded by the standard genetic code (Table 3.1). Proteins are defined by their unique sequence of amino acid residues; this sequence is the primary structure of the protein. Just as the letters of the alphabet can be combined to form an almost endless variety of words, amino acids can be linked in varying sequences to form a vast variety of proteins.

3.2 MATHEMATICAL SEQUENCES

In mathematics, a *sequence* is an ordered list of objects (or events). It contains *members* (also called *elements* or *terms*), and the number of members (possibly

TABLE 3.1   Standard Amino Acid Abbreviations[a]

Amino Acid	Three-Letter Abbreviation	One-Letter Abbreviation
Alanine	Ala	a
Arginine	Arg	r
Asparagine	Asn	n
Aspartic acid	Asp	d
Cysteine	Cys	c
Glutamic acid	Glu	e
Glutamine	Gln	q
Glycine	Gly	g
Histidine	His	h
Isoleucine	Ile	i
Leucine	Leu	l
Lysine	Lys	k
Methionine	Met	m
Phenylalanine	Phe	f
Proline	Pro	p
Serine	Ser	s
Threonine	Thr	t
Tryptophan	Trp	w
Tyrosine	Tyr	y
Valine	Val	v

[a]See Appendix A for more information on amino acids.

infinite) is called the *length* of the sequence. Unlike a set, order matters, and exactly the same elements can appear multiple times at different positions in the sequence.

In the language of manoids, a finite set, called an *alphabet* is denoted by Σ. For example, $\Sigma = \{0, 1\}$ is an alphabet of binary numbers, and $\Sigma = \{A, C, G, T\}$ is an alphabet of DNA basis. Let $I = \{1, 2, 3, \dots, n\}$ be a set of natural numbers. A sequence I (also called a *word* or *string*) of length n ($n \geq 0$) over the alphabet Σ is a mapping $a: I \rightarrow \Sigma$ denoted by $a = (a_1, a_2, \dots, a_n)$, where $a_i = a(i)$. If the sequence length is $n = 0$, we call this sequence the *empty sequence* and denote it by $\in$. The set of all sequences over the alphabet S sequence is denoted by S^*. For example, genetic or DNA sequences are sequences over the alphabet of nucleotides, and amino acid sequences are sequences over the alphabet of amino acids.

An *infinite sequence* over S is a mapping from $I^* = \{1, 2, \dots\}$ (the set of natural numbers without 0) to S.

A *subsequence* of a given sequence is a sequence formed from the sequence by deleting some of the elements without disturbing the relative positions of the remaining elements.

If the terms of the sequence are a subset of an ordered set, a *monotonically increasing sequence* is one for which each term is greater than or equal to the term before it; if each term is strictly greater than the one preceding it, the sequence is called *strictly monotonically increasing*. A *monotonically decreasing sequence* is defined similarly. Any sequence fulfilling the monotonicity property is called *monotonic* or *monotone*. This is a special case of the more general notion of monotonic function.

The terms *nondecreasing* and *nonincreasing* are used to avoid any possible confusion with *strictly increasing* and *strictly decreasing*, respectively. If the terms of a sequence are integers, the sequence is an *integer sequence*. If the terms of a sequence are polynomials, the sequence is a *polynomial sequence*.

If S is endowed with a topology, it becomes possible to consider convergence of an infinite sequence in S. Such considerations involve the concept of the limit of a sequence.

In theoretical computer science, infinite sequences of digits (or characters) drawn from a finite alphabet are of particular interest. They are often referred to simply as sequences (as opposed to finite strings). Infinite binary sequences, for instance, are infinite sequences of bits (characters drawn from the alphabet $\{0, 1\}$). The set $C = \{0, 1\}^{\infty}$ of all infinite binary sequences is sometimes called the *Cantor space*.

An infinite binary sequence can represent a formal language (a set of strings) by setting the nth bit of the sequence to 1 if and only if the nth string is in the language. Therefore, the study of complexity classes, which are sets of languages, may be regarded as the study of sets of infinite sequences.

An infinite sequence drawn from the alphabet $\{0, 1, \dots, b - 1\}$ may also represent a real number expressed in the base-b positional number system. This equivalence is often used to bring the techniques of real analysis to bear on complexity classes.

3.3 SEQUENCE ALIGNMENT

The foundation of sequence alignment and analysis is based on the fact that biological sequences develop from preexisting sequences instead of being invented by nature from the beginning. The sequence of a gene can be altered in a number of ways. Three types of changes can occur at any given position within a sequence. Gene mutations have varying effects on health, depending on where they occur and whether they alter the function of essential proteins. Structurally, mutations can be classified as follows:

- *Point mutations*, often caused by chemicals or the malfunction of DNA replication, involve the exchange of a single nucleotide for another. Most common is the transition that exchanges a purine for a purine (A $\leftrightarrow$ G) or a pyrimidine for a pyrimidine (C $\leftrightarrow$ T).
- *Insertions* add one or more extra nucleotides into the DNA. They are usually caused by transposable elements or errors during replication of

repeating elements (e.g., AT repeats). Insertions in the coding region of a gene may alter the splicing of the mRNA (splice site mutation) or cause a shift in the reading frame (frame shift), both of which can significantly alter the gene product. Insertions can be reverted by excision of the transposable element.

- *Deletions* remove one or more nucleotides from the DNA. Like insertions, these mutations can alter the reading frame of the gene. Note that a deletion is not the exact opposite of an insertion; the former is quite random, whereas the latter consists of a specific sequence inserting at locations that are not entirely random or even quite narrowly defined.

An alignment between two (or more) sequences is a pairwise (multiple) comparison between the characters of each sequence. The basic sequence analysis is to ask if two or more sequences are related. A true alignment of biological sequences is one that reflects the evolutionary relationship between two or more homologies, which are sequences that share a common ancestor. The key issues to sequence alignments are:

- What sorts of alignment should be considered
- The scoring system used to rank alignments
- The algorithm used to find optimal (or good) scoring alignments
- The statistical methods used to evaluate the significance of an alignment score

Here we first demonstrate the scope of alignments (the number of alignments) to show that alignment is a difficult problem. Later we describe major optimal methods of pairwise sequence alignment and multiple sequence alignment. The alignment algorithms are given at the end of the chapter.

Number of Alignments

Let $\mathbf{a} = a_1a_2 \cdots a_m$ and $\mathbf{b} = b_1b_2 \cdots b_n$ be two sequences over an alphabet Σ of length n and m. An alignment of the sequences $\mathbf{a}$ and $\mathbf{b}$ is a pair of sequences $\mathbf{a}^* = a_1^*a_2^* \cdots a_m^*$ and $\mathbf{b}^* = b_1^*b_2^* \cdots b_m^*$ of equal length 1, defined by inserting blanks in the sequences $\mathbf{a}$ and $\mathbf{b}$ over the extended alphabet $\Sigma^* = \Sigma \cup \{\cdot\}$. The alignment of a^* and b^* is represented in tabular form:

$$a_1^*a_2^* \cdots a_L^*$$

$$b_1^*b_2^* \cdots b_L^*$$

where $\max\{m, n\} \leq L \leq m + n$. When $L = m + n$, the alignment is given by

$$a_1^* a_2^* \cdots a_L^* \qquad - \; - \; \cdots \; -$$
$$- \; - \; \cdots \; - \qquad b_1^* b_2^* \cdots b_L^*$$

For example, two alignments of the sequences ACCGTT and AGCCCCT are

$$\text{A} - \text{C C G T T}$$
$$\text{A G C C C C T}$$

and

$$\text{A} - \text{C C} - \text{G T T}$$
$$\text{A G C C C C} - \text{T}$$

A column that contains two identical characters is called a *match*, a column that contains two different nonblank characters is called a *mismatch*, and a column that contains a blank is called an *indel* (insertion/deletion). A common question is to find how many alignments are possible between the two sequences **a** and **b**. To answer this question, we define $f(i, j)$ = number of all possible alignments of one sequence of i characters with another sequence of j characters. The idea is to focus on the end of alignment. Two sequences end in exactly one of three ways:

Case 1	Case 2	Case 3
$\cdots a_m^*$	$\cdots a_m^*$	$\cdots -$
$\cdots -$	$\cdots b_n^*$	$\cdots b_n^*$

The first end alignment corresponds to an indel of a_m^*. There exist $f(n - 1, m)$ alignments of the earlier part of the sequence. The second end alignment corresponds to a match or mismatch. There exist $f(m - 1, n - 1)$ alignments. The last end alignment corresponds to an indel of b_n^*. There exists $f(m, n - 1)$ alignments of the earlier part of the sequence. Therefore, the total number of alignments $f(m, n)$ satisfies the following recurrence relation:

$$f(m, n) = f(m-1, n) + f(m-1, n-1) + f(m, n-1)$$

This recurrence relation was derived by Waterman (1999) and it was demonstrated that this number increases rapidly. For example, two sequences of length 1000 have

$$f(1000, 1000) \approx 10^{767.4\cdots}$$

alignments.

Pairwise Sequence Alignment

Pairwise sequence alignment methods are used to find the best-matching piecewise (local) or global alignments of two query sequences. Pairwise alignments can only be used between two sequences at a time, but they are efficient to calculate and are often used for methods that do not require extreme precision (such as searching a database for sequences with high homology to a query). The three primary methods of producing pairwise alignments are global alignment, local alignment, and global–local alignment.

Global Alignment

Global alignments, which attempt to align every residue in every sequence, are most useful when the sequences in a query set are similar and of roughly equal size. It provides the common means to measure the degree of overall similarity between two sequences. FASTA (FAST ALL) developed by Pearson and Lipman (1988) is a heuristic algorithm for global sequence alignment. It is used widely to align a query sequence against all sequences of a database. We describe here a commonly used algorithm for optimal global alignment. We point out that the optimal alignments depend on the input sequences and the algorithm parameters. The algorithm parameters assigned to matches, mismatches, and indels are determined by experience.

Optimal sequence alignment is closely related to the problem of finding the optimal edit distance in binary code. This is an old problem in coding theory introduced by Levenshtein (1966). The theory of semigroups and manoids provides the mathematical background for the manipulation of words over a finite alphabet.

Let $\mathbf{a} = a_1a_2 \cdots a_m$ and $\mathbf{b} = b_1b_2 \cdots b_n$ be two sequences over the alphabet Σ^* of approximately the same length. We define the similarity scores $s(a, b)$ over the alphabet Σ^* as follows:

1. $s(a, a) > 0$ for all a
2. $s(a, b) < 0$ for some (a, b) pairs
3. $s(a, -) = s(-, a) = -g(a)$ [$-g(a)$ is the indel penalty associated with a]

The global pairwise similarity alignment problem is to find the maximum similarity between the two sequences:

$$S(\mathbf{a}, \mathbf{b}) = \max \sum_{i=1}^{L} s(a_i^*, b_i^*)$$

where the maximum is over all alignments. Here the individual score $s(x, y)$ may be defined as

$$s(x, y) = \log \frac{p_{x,y}}{q_x q_y}$$

where $p_{x,y}$ is the probability that the characters x and y occur as an aligned column pair in a pairwise alignment of the match model, defined as

$$P(a, b|M) = \prod p_{x,y}$$

and q_x is the relative frequency of the character x to occur in the sequences a and b in the random model R, defined as

$$P(a, b|R) = \prod q_x \prod q_y$$

For both match and random models, we used the conditional probability notation $P(A|B)$. The conditional probability is the probability of some event A, given the occurrence of some other event B, defined as follows:

$$P(A|B) = \frac{P(A \cap B)}{P(B)}$$

Multiplying through, this becomes

$$P(A|B)P(B) = P(A \cap B)$$

which can be generalized to

$$P(A \cap B \cap C) = P(A)P(B|A)P(C|A \cap B)$$

In addition to similarity measures, we also mention the commonly used distance measure that can be used as a score function for sequence alignment. The distance measure can be defined for the global pairwise distance alignment. Let $d(a, b)$ be the distance over the alphabet Σ^* as follows:

1. $d(a, a) = 0$ for all a
2. $d(a, b) = d(b, a)$, cost of a mutation of a into b
3. $d(a, -) = d(-, a) = g(a)$, positive cost of inserting or deleting of the character a

Define

$$D(\mathbf{a}, \mathbf{b}) = \min \sum_{i=1}^{L} d(a_i^*, b_i^*)$$

where the minimum is over all alignments of $\mathbf{a}$ with $\mathbf{b}$. The main results on global pairwise alignment are stated below.

Theorem 3.1 **(Optimal Global Similarity Alignment)** Let $\mathbf{a} = a_1a_2 \cdots a_m$ and $\mathbf{b} = b_1b_2 \cdots b_n$ be two sequences over the alphabet Σ, define

$$S(i, j) = S(a_1a_2 \cdots a_i, b_1b_2 \cdots b_j)$$

and set

$$S(0,0) = 0, \quad S(0, j) = \sum_{k=1}^{j} s(-, b_k), \quad S(i, 0) = \sum_{k=1}^{i} s(a_k, -)$$

Then

$$S(i, j) = \max\{S(i-1, j) + s(a_i, -), S(i-1, j-1) + s(a_i, b_j), S(i, j-1) + s(-, b_j)\}$$

In particular,

$$S(a, b) = S(m, n)$$

Similarly, we have

Theorem 3.2 **(Optimal Global Distance Alignment)** Let $\mathbf{a} = a_1a_2 \cdots a_m$ and $\mathbf{b} = b_1b_2 \cdots b_n$ be two sequences over the alphabet Σ, define

$$D(i, j) = D(a_1a_2 \cdots a_i, b_1b_2 \cdots b_j)$$

and set

$$D(0,0) = 0, \quad D(0, j) = \sum_{k=1}^{j} d(-, b_k), \quad D(i, 0) = \sum_{k=1}^{i} d(a_k, -)$$

Then

$$D(i, j) = \min\{D(i-1, j) + d(a_i, -), D(i-1, j-1) + d(a_i, b_j), D(i, j-1) + d(-, b_j)\}$$

In particular,

$$D(a, b) = D(m, n)$$

We illustrate the similarity alignment by the following examples.

Example 3.1 Consider two sequences, UAUAAU and AUAUAUAU, and score matches with a value of 2 and mismatches and indels with a value of −1. The matrix D is

D	j	0	1	2	3	4	5	6	7	8
i		—	A	U	A	U	A	U	A	U
0	—	0	-1	-2	-3	-4	-5	-6	-7	-8
1	U	-1	-1	1	0	-1	-2	-3	-4	-5
2	A	-2	1	0	3	2	1	0	-1	-2
3	U	-3	0	3	2	5	4	3	2	1
4	A	-4	-1	2	5	4	7	6	5	4
5	A	-5	-2	1	4	4	6	6	8	7
6	U	-6	-3	0	3	6	5	8	7	10

The optimal alignment score for these two sequences is $D(6, 8) = 10$.

Local Alignment

Biological sequences often contain similar subsequences that are preserved during the course of evolution. Local alignments are more useful for dissimilar sequences that are suspected to contain regions of similarity or similar sequence motifs within their larger sequence context. The problem of finding highly related subsequences of two sequences is accomplished by local alignment. The Smith–Waterman algorithm is a general local alignment method also based on dynamic programming. With sufficiently similar sequences, there is no difference between local and global alignments. The BLAST (Basic Local Alignment Sequence Tool) is a fast heuristic algorithm for local alignment developed by Altschul et al. (1990). BLAST finds regions of similarity. Here we consider only the subsequences of consecutive elements. Any subsequence of a sequence $a_1a_2 \cdots a_m$ has the form $a_ia_{i+1} \cdots a_{m+k}$ for some $1 \le i \le m$ and $k \le m - i$. We present the optimal local alignment developed in the Smith–Waterman algorithm (Smith and Waterman, 1981). Let $\mathbf{a} = a_1a_2 \cdots a_m$ and $\mathbf{b} = b_1b_2 \cdots b_n$ be two sequences over the alphabet Σ. Define

$$S(ij, kl) = S(a_i \cdots a_j, b_k \cdots b_l)$$

What is the maximum similarity between subsequences of $\mathbf{a}$ and $\mathbf{b}$? That is, find

$$L(a, b) = \max \left\{ S(ij, kl) = S(a_i \cdots a_j, b_k \cdots b_l) \mid 1 \le i \le j \le m, 1 \le k \le l \le n \right\}$$

Theorem 3.3   (Optimal Local Alignment)   Let $\mathbf{a} = a_1a_2 \cdots a_m$ and $\mathbf{b} = b_1b_2$ $\cdots b_n$ be two sequences over the alphabet Σ. Define

$$L(i, 0) = 0, \qquad 0 \le i \le m$$
$$L(0, j) = 0, \qquad 0 \le j \le n$$

and

$$L(i, j) = \max\{0, L(i-1, j-1)+s(a_i, b_j), L(i-1, j)+s(a_i, -),$$
$$L(i, j-1)+s(-, b_j)|1 \leq i \leq m, 1 \leq j \leq n\}$$

where $s(x, y) \geq 0$ if x and y match; $s(x, y) \leq 0$ if x and y do not match or one of them is a blank.

Then

$$L(j, l) = \max\{0, S(a_i \cdots a_j, b_k \cdots b_l)|1 \leq i \leq j \leq m, 1 \leq k \leq l \leq n\}$$

Each maximal entry $L(j^*, l^*)$ of the array L corresponds to an optimal local alignment of the sequences **a** and **b**.

Example 3.2 Consider the sequences GGTATGG and CCCTTTTCCC and score the matches with the value of 5, mismatches with the value of –4, and indels with the values of –7. The matrix L is then given as follows:

L	j	0	1	2	3	4	5	6	7	8	9
i		—	C	C	C	T	T	T	C	C	C
0	—	0	0	0	0	0	0	0	0	0	0
1	G	0	0	0	0	0	0	0	0	0	0
2	G	0	0	0	0	0	0	0	0	0	0
3	T	0	0	0	0	5	5	5	0	0	0
4	A	0	0	0	0	0	1	1	1	0	0
5	T	0	0	0	0	5	5	6	0	0	0
6	G	0	0	0	0	0	2	1	2	0	0
7	G	0	0	0	0	0	0	0	0	0	0

The optimal local alignment score for these two sequences is $L(5, 6) = 6$. This score leads to the optimal local alignment

$$T \quad A \quad T$$
$$T \quad T \quad T$$

Global–Local Alignment

Global–local alignment (hybrid alignment) compares a sequence with the subsequences of another sequence. This can be especially useful when the downstream part of one sequence overlaps with the upstream part of the other sequence. In this case, neither global nor local alignment is entirely appropriate: A global alignment would attempt to force the alignment to extend beyond the region of overlap, while a local alignment might not fully cover the region of overlap (Lipman et al., 1984). Here we present an optimal global–local alignment.

Let $\mathbf{a} = a_1a_2 \cdots a_m$ and $\mathbf{b} = b_1b_2 \cdots b_n$ be two sequences of different length over the alphabet Σ. Here we let $m \leq n$. The problem is to find the maximum matching of the shorter sequence with the longer one. That is, find

$$H(\mathbf{a}, \mathbf{b}) = \max\{S(\mathbf{a}, b_k \cdots b_l) | 1 \leq k \leq l \leq m\}$$

Theorem 3.4   (Optimal Global–Local Alignment)   Let $\mathbf{a} = a_1a_2 \cdots a_m$ and $\mathbf{b} = b_1b_2 \cdots b_n$ be two sequences over the alphabet Σ. Define

$$H(0, j) = 0, \qquad\qquad 0 \leq j \leq m$$
$$H(i, 0) = \sum_{k=1}^{i} s(a_k, -), \qquad 0 \leq i \leq n$$

and

$$H(i, j) = \max\{H(i-1, j-1) + s(a_i, b_j), H(i-1, j) + s(a_i, -),$$
$$H(i, j-1) + s(-, b_j) | 1 \leq i \leq m, 1 \leq j \leq n\}$$

where $s(x, y) \geq 0$ if x and y match; $s(x, y) \leq 0$ if x and y do not match or one of them is a blank.

Then

$$H(i, j) = \max\{S(a_i \cdots a_i, b_k \cdots b_j) | 1 \leq i \leq m, 1 \leq k \leq j \leq n\}$$

In particular,

$$H(\mathbf{a}, \mathbf{b}) = \max\{H(m, j) | 1 \leq j \leq n\}$$

Example 3.3   Consider the sequences AUUA and UAAUAAU and score the matches with a value of 5 and mismatches and indels with a value of –4. The matrix H is given as follows:

H	j	0	1	2	3	4	5	6	7
i		—	U	A	A	U	A	A	U
0	—	0	0	0	0	0	0	0	0
1	A	–4	–4	5	5	1	5	5	1
2	U	–8	1	1	1	10	6	2	10
3	U	–12	–3	–3	–3	6	6	2	7
4	A	–16	–7	2	2	2	11	11	7

The optimal alignment score for these two sequences is given by the maximum entries $H(4, 5) = H(4, 6) = 11$. This alignment leads to the respective optimal global–local alignments:

$$
\begin{array}{cccc}
\text{A} & \text{U} & \text{U} & \text{A} \\
\text{A} & \text{U} & \text{A} & \text{A}
\end{array}
$$

and

$$
\begin{array}{cccc}
\text{A} & \text{U} & \text{U} & \text{A} \\
\text{A} & \text{A} & \text{U} & \text{A}
\end{array}
$$

Multiple Sequence Alignment

Multiple sequence alignment is an extension of pairwise alignment used to incorporate more than two sequences at a time. Multiple sequence alignment invalues aligning a number of sequences simultaneously to determine common features among a collection of sequences. Multiple alignments are often used to identify conserved sequence regions across a group of sequences hypothesized to be related evolutionarily. Such conserved sequence motifs can be used in conjunction with structural and mechanistic information to locate the catalytic active sites of enzymes. To identify the common features, one needs to determine an optimal alignment for the entire collection of sequences. Multiple sequence alignments are computationally difficult to produce, and most formulations of the problem lead to NP-complete combinatorial optimization problems (Deken, 1983). Nevertheless, the utility of these alignments in bioinformatics has led to the development of a variety of methods suitable for aligning three or more sequences.

Let $\Omega = (\mathbf{a}_1 \mathbf{a}_2 \cdots \mathbf{a}_k)$ be a family of sequences over the alphabet Σ,

$$
a_1 = a_{11} \quad \cdots \quad a_{1n_1}
$$
$$
\vdots
$$
$$
a_k = a_{k1} \quad \cdots \quad a_{kn_k}
$$

and $\Sigma^* = (\mathbf{a}_1^* \mathbf{a}_2^* \cdots \mathbf{a}_k^*)$ be a corresponding family of sequences of equal length l over the extended alphabet $\Sigma^* = \Sigma \cup \{\cdot\}$,

$$
a_1^* = a_{11}^* \quad \cdots \quad a_{1l}^*
$$
$$
\vdots
$$
$$
a_k^* = a_{k1}^* \quad \cdots \quad a_{kl}^*
$$

by inserting blanks, where $\max\{n_1, n_2, \ldots, n_k\} \le l \le n_1 + n_2 + \cdots + n_k$.

For example, a multiple alignment of the three sequences AAGAA, ATAATG, and CTGGG is

$$
\begin{array}{ccccccc}
A & A & - & G & A & A & A \\
A & T & - & A & A & T & G \\
C & T & G & G & - & - & G
\end{array}
$$

The optimal global alignment is to find the maximum similarity between these sequences Ω in terms of a scoring function $s(\Omega^*)$, that is,

$$S(\Omega) = \max\{s(\Omega^*)|\Omega^* \text{ is a multiple alignment of } \Omega\}$$

where

$$s(\Omega^*) = \sum_{i=1}^{l} s(a_{1i}^*, \dots, a_{ki}^*)$$

is the sum of scores of the columns. Here it is assumed that the columns of the alignment are statistically independent. We are now in a position to state the optimal multiple sequence alignment result.

Theorem 3.5 (Optimal Global Multiple Sequence Alignment) Let $\Omega = (\mathbf{a_1 a_2} \cdots \mathbf{a_k})$ be a family of sequences over the alphabet Σ,

$$a_1 = a_{11} \quad \cdots \quad a_{1m_1}$$
$$\vdots$$
$$a_k = a_{k1} \quad \cdots \quad a_{kn_k}$$

and $B = (b_1, \dots, b_k)$ be a binary vector over $\{0, 1\}$ and define $b^*x = x$ if $b = 1$ and $b^*x = -x$ if $b = 0$. For all index vectors $(i_1, \dots, i_k)$, define

$$S(i_1, \dots, i_k) = \max\{S(i_1 - b_1, \dots, i_k - b_k) + s(b_1^* a_{1i_1}, \dots, b_k^* a_{ki_k})\}$$

where the maximum is taken over all nonzero binary vectors B. Also, we set

$$S(0, \dots, 0) = 0$$

Then

$$S(i_1, \dots, i_k) = S(a_{11}, \dots, a_{1i_1}, \dots, a_{k1}, \dots a_{ki_k})$$

In particular,

$$S(\Omega) = S(n_1, \dots, n_k)$$

Example 3.4 Figure 3.1 is a representation of a protein multiple sequence alignment produced using ClustalW (Chenna et al., 2003). The sequences are

FIGURE 3.1 First 90 positions of the alignment. The shadings represent the amino acid conservation according to the properties and distribution of amino acid frequencies in each column. Note the two completely conserved residues arginine (R) and lysine (K), marked with asterisks at the top of the alignment.

instances of the acidic ribosomal protein P0 homolog (L10E) encoded by the *Rplp0* gene from multiple organisms. The protein sequences were obtained through SwissProt searching using the gene name. This was generated by Miguel Andrade, February 2006 (UTC).

Profile and Sequence Alignment

Profile analysis has long been a useful tool in finding and aligning distantly related sequences and in identifying known sequence domains in new sequences. Basically, a *profile* is a description of the consensus of a multiple sequence alignment. It represents the common characteristics of a family of similar sequences where any single sequence is just one realization of a family's characteristics. It uses a position-specific scoring system to capture information about the degree of conservation at various positions in the multiple alignment. The profile method has several advantages over most sequence comparison methods. Since the profile represents the alignment of a number of known sequences, it contains information that defines where the family of sequences is conserved and where it is variable. Comparison of a new sequence to a profile search can emphasize similarity to conserved regions while tolerating diversity in variable regions. This makes it a much more sensitive and specific method for database searching than pairwise methods, such as those used by BLAST or FastA, that use position-independent scoring.

Example 3.5 Consider an optimal profile-sequence alignment that aligns a sequence against a profile. Let $\Omega = (\mathbf{a}_1\mathbf{a}_2 \cdots \mathbf{a}_k)$ be a family of sequences over the alphabet Σ and $\Omega^* = (\mathbf{a}_1^*\mathbf{a}_2^* \cdots \mathbf{a}_k^*)$ be a corresponding family of sequences of equal length l over the extended alphabet $\Sigma^* = \Sigma \cup \{\cdot\}$:

$$a_1^* = a_{11}^* \quad \cdots \quad a_{1l}^*$$
$$\vdots$$
$$a_k^* = a_{k1}^* \quad \cdots \quad a_{kl}^*$$

The profile of the alignment Ω^* is a sequence of l probability distributions $\mathbf{P}_j = (p_{j,x})$ on the alphabet Σ^* such that $p_{j,x}$ is the relative frequency of the character x to occur in the jth column of the alignment. We denote the profile of the alignment Ω^* by $P^*(\Omega^*) = (P_1^* \cdots P_L^*)$. An alignment of the profile $P(\Omega^*)$ and the sequence $\mathbf{a}^* = a_1^* \cdots a_L^*$ is a pair of sequences

$$P_1^* \cdots P_L^*$$
$$a_1^* \cdots a_L^*$$

A blank in the profile $P^*(\Omega^*)$ is the probability distribution denoted by $-_\mathrm{p}$:

$$
\begin{matrix}
1 \\
0 \\
\vdots \\
0
\end{matrix}
$$

which assigns probability 1 to the blank and probability 0 to all other characters. The optimal profile-sequence alignment is to find the maximum similarity between the profile $\mathbf{P}$ and the sequence $\mathbf{a}$, that is,

$$S(\mathbf{P}, \mathbf{a}) = \max\{s(\mathbf{P}^*, \mathbf{a}^*)|(\mathbf{P}^*, \mathbf{a}^*) \text{ is an alignment of } (\mathbf{P}, \mathbf{a})\}$$

where $s(\mathbf{P}^*, \mathbf{a}^*)$ is a score function that may be defined as

$$s(\mathbf{P}^*, \mathbf{a}^*) = \sum_{i=1}^{l} \sum_{x \in \Omega^*} s(a_i^*, x) p_x$$

with an individual similarity score $s(a, x)$ on the alphabet Σ^* and a score between the probability distribution $\mathbf{p} = (p_x)$ on the alphabet Ω^* and the character x in Σ^*.

Theorem 3.6   (Optimal Profile-Sequence Alignment)   Let $\mathbf{P} = \mathbf{p}_1\mathbf{p}_2 \cdots \mathbf{p}_n$ be the profile of a multiple sequence alignment and $\mathbf{a} = a_1 a_2 \cdots a_n$ be a sequence over the alphabet Σ^*. Define

$$S(i, j) = S(\mathbf{p}_1\mathbf{p}_2 \cdots \mathbf{p}_i, a_1 a_2 \cdots a_j), \qquad 1 \le i \le m, \quad 1 \le j \le n$$

and set

$$S(0, 0) = 0, \qquad S(i, 0) = \sum_{k=1}^{i} s(p_k, -), \qquad S(0, j) = \sum_{k=1}^{j} s(-_\mathrm{p}, a_k)$$

Then

$$S(i, j) = \max\{S(i-1, j) + s(\mathbf{p}_i, -), S(i-1, j-1) + s(\mathbf{p}_i, a_j), S(i, j-1) + s(-_\mathrm{p}, a_j)\}$$

In particular,

$$S(\mathbf{P}, \mathbf{a}) = S(m, n)$$

Example 3.6   Consider the sequences AGCA, AGAGA, ACCG, and CGGC over the DNA alphabet. The multiple alignment

$$
\begin{array}{ccccc}
A & G & - & C & A \\
A & G & A & G & A \\
A & C & - & C & G \\
C & G & - & G & C
\end{array}
$$

has the following profile P:

0	0	3/4	0	0
3/4	0	1/4	0	1/2
1/4	1/4	0	1/2	1/4
0	3/4	0	1/2	1/4
0	0	0	0	0

where the columns are labeled in turn by $-$, A, C, G, and T. The profile P can be viewed as a column stochastic matrix.

An alignment between this profile and the sequence AACCT is

$$
\begin{array}{cccccc}
p_1 & p_2 & p_3 & p_4 & p_5 & -_p \\
A & A & - & C & C & T
\end{array}
$$

A blank in the profile must be inserted into all sequences of the corresponding multiple alignment, so the resulting multiple alignment is

$$
\begin{array}{cccccc}
A & G & - & C & A & - \\
A & G & A & G & A & - \\
A & C & - & C & G & - \\
C & G & - & G & C & - \\
A & A & - & C & C & T
\end{array}
$$

Next we present an optimal profile-to-profile alignment in terms of the distance scoring function.

Theorem 3.7   (Optimal Profile-to-Profile Alignment)   Let $\mathbf{P} = \mathbf{p}_1\mathbf{p}_2 \cdots \mathbf{p}_m$ be the profile of a multiple sequence alignment and $\mathbf{Q} = \mathbf{q}_1\mathbf{q}_2 \cdots \mathbf{q}_n$ be the second profile of a multiple sequence alignment over the alphabet Σ^*. Then define

$$
D(\mathbf{P},\mathbf{Q}) = \min \left\{ d(\mathbf{P}^*,\mathbf{Q}^*) = \sum_{i=1}^{l} d(p_i^*,q_i^*) \,\middle|\, (\mathbf{P}^*,\mathbf{Q}^*) \text{ is an alignment of } (\mathbf{P},\mathbf{Q}) \right\}
$$

as the minimum distance between the profiles $\mathbf{P}$ and $\mathbf{Q}$. Let

$$D(i, j) = D(\mathbf{p}_1\mathbf{p}_2 \cdots \mathbf{p}_i, \mathbf{q}_1\mathbf{q}_2 \cdots \mathbf{q}_j), \qquad 1 \le i \le m, \quad 1 \le j \le n$$

and set

$$D(0,0) = 0, D(i,0) = \sum_{k=1}^{i} d(p_k, -_\text{p}), \qquad D(0, j) = \sum_{k=1}^{i} d(-_\text{p}, q_k)$$

Then

$$D(i, j) = \min\{D(i-1, j) + d(\mathbf{p}_i, -_\text{p}), D(i-1, j-1) + \\ s(\mathbf{p}_i, \mathbf{q}_j), S(i, j-1) + d(-_\text{p}, \mathbf{q}_j)\}$$

In particular,

$$D(\mathbf{P}, \mathbf{Q}) = D(m, n)$$

3.4 SEQUENCE ANALYSIS AND FURTHER DISCUSSION

Now we know how to find an optimal alignment. A major concern when inter-preting alignment results is whether similarity between sequences is biologi-cally significant. Good alignments can occur by chance alone. Many chance mechanisms are involved in the creation of these data. How do we know if it is a biologically meaningful alignment, especially when the similarity is only marginal? Here we present two approaches. One is the classical approach based on the traditional statistical approach of calculating the chance of a match score greater than the value observed. The other is the Bayesian approach, based on a comparison of models.

Under even the simplest random models and scoring systems, very little is known about the random distribution of optimal global alignment scores (Deken, 1983). Monte Carlo experiments can provide rough distributional results for some specific scoring systems and sequence compositions (Reich et al., 1984), but these cannot be generalized easily.

Therefore, one of the few methods available for assessing the statistical significance of a particular global alignment is to generate many random sequence pairs of the appropriate length and composition, and calculate the optimal alignment score for each (Altschul and Erickson, 1985; Fitch, 1983). Although it is then possible to express the score of interest in terms of standard deviations from the mean, it is a mistake to assume that the relevant distribu-tion is normal and convert this Z-value into a P-value; the tail behavior of global alignment scores is unknown. The most that one can say reliably is that if 100 random alignments have scores inferior to the alignment of interest, the P-value in question is probably less than 0.01. One further pitfall to avoid is exaggerating the significance of a result found among multiple tests. When many alignments have been generated (e.g., in a database search), the significance of the best must be discounted accordingly. An alignment with a *P*-value of 0.0001 in the context of a single trial may be assigned a *P*-value of 0.1 only if it was selected as the best among 1000 independent trials.

However, unlike those of global alignments, statistics for the scores of local alignments are well understood. This is particularly true for local alignments lacking gaps, which we consider first. Such alignments were precisely those sought by the original BLAST database search programs (Altschul et al., 1990) from each of the two sequences being compared. A modification of the Smith–Waterman (1981) or Sellers (1984) algorithms will find all segment pairs whose scores cannot be improved by extension or trimming. These are called *high-scoring segment pairs* (HSPs). To analyze how high a score is likely to rise by chance, a model of random sequences is needed. For proteins, the simplest model chooses the amino acid residues in a sequence independently, with specific background probabilities for the various residues. Additionally, the score expected for aligning a random pair of amino acid is required to be negative. Were this not the case, long alignments would tend to have high scores independent of whether the segments aligned were related, and the statistical theory would break down. Just as the sum of a large number of independent identically distributed (i.i.d.) random variables tends to a normal distribution, the maximum of a large number of i.i.d. random variables tends to an extreme value distribution (Gumbel, 1958). (We elide the many technical points required to make this statement rigorous.) In studying optimal local sequence alignments, we are essentially dealing with the latter case (Dembo et al., 1994; Karlin and Altschul, 1990). In the limit of sufficiently large sequence lengths m and n, the statistics of HSP scores are characterized by two parameters, K and λ (lambda). Most simply, the expected number of HSPs with a score of at least S is given by the formula $E = K_{mn}e^{-\lambda S}$. We call this the *E-value for the score S*.

This formula makes eminently intuitive sense. Doubling the length of either sequence should double the number of HSPs attaining a given score. Also, for an HSP to attain the score $2x$, it must attain the score x twice in a row, so one expects E to decrease exponentially with the score. The parameters K and λ can be thought of simply as natural scales for the search space size and the scoring system, respectively.

The other approach is based on a comparison of models.

1. *Hidden Markov model* (HMM). This is a statistical model in which the system being modeled is assumed to be a Markov process with unknown parameters, and the challenge is to determine the hidden parameters from the observable parameters. The extracted model parameters can then be used to perform further analysis: for example, for pattern recognition applications. In a regular Markov model, the state is directly visible to the observer, and therefore the state transition probabilities are the only parameters. In a *hidden* Markov model, the state is not directly visible, but variables influenced by the

state are visible. Each state has a probability distribution over the possible output tokens. Therefore, the sequence of tokens generated by an HMM gives some information about the sequence of states. Hidden Markov models are especially well known for their application in temporal pattern recognition, such as speech, handwriting, gesture recognition, musical score following, partial discharges, and bioinformatics.

2. *Profile hidden Markov models.* These have several advantages over standard profiles. Profile HMMs have a formal probabilistic basis and have a consistent theory behind gap and insertion scores, in contrast to standard profile methods, which use heuristic methods. HMMs apply a statistical method to estimate the true frequency of a residue at a given position in the alignment from its observed frequency, whereas standard profiles use the observed frequency itself to assign the score for that residue. This means that a profile HMM derived from only 10 to 20 aligned sequences can be equivalent in quality to a standard profile created from 40 to 50 aligned sequences. In general, producing good profile HMMs requires less skill and manual intervention than does producing good standard profiles.

3. *Pattern discovery.* Given a sequence of data such as a DNA or amino acid sequence, a motif or pattern is a repeating subsequence. Such repeated subsequences often have important biological significance, and hence discovering such motifs in various biological databases turns out to be a very important problem in computational biology. Of course, in biological applications the various occurrences of a pattern in the given sequence may not be exact, so it is important to be able to discover motifs even in the presence of small errors. Various tools are now available for carrying out automatic pattern discovery. This is usually the first step toward a more sophisticated task such as gene finding in DNA or secondary structure prediction in protein sequences at the system level.

4. *Scoring functions.* The choice of a scoring function that reflects biological or statistical observations about known sequences is important in producing good alignments. Protein sequences are frequently aligned using substitution matrices that reflect the probabilities of given character-to-character substitutions. A series of matrices called *PAM* (point accepted mutation) *matrices*, originally defined by Margaret Dayhoff and sometimes referred to as *Dayhoff matrices*) explicitly encode evolutionary approximations regarding the rates and probabilities of particular amino acid mutations. Another common series of scoring matrices, known as BLOSUM (blocks substitution matrix), encodes empirically derived substitution probabilities (Durbin et al., 1998). Variants of both types of matrices are used to detect sequences with differing levels of divergence, thus allowing users of BLAST or FASTA to restrict searches to more closely related matches or to expand to detect more divergent sequences (Durbin et al., 1998). Gap penalties account for the introduction of a gap—in the evolutionary model, an insertion or deletion mutation—in both nucleotide and protein sequences, and therefore the penalty values should be

proportional to the rate expected for such mutations. The quality of the alignments produced therefore depends on the quality of the scoring function. It can be very useful and instructive to try the same alignment several times with different choices for scoring matrix and/or gap penalty values, and to compare the results. Regions where the solution is weak or nonunique can often be identified by observing which regions of the alignment are robust to variations in alignment parameters.

5. *Structural alignments.* These are usually specific to protein and sometimes RNA sequences, and use information about the secondary and tertiary structure of the protein or RNA molecule to aid in aligning the sequences. These methods can be used for two or more sequences and typically produce local alignments; however, because they depend on the availability of structural information, they can only be used for sequences whose corresponding structures are known (usually through x-ray crystallography or NMR spectroscopy). Because both protein and RNA structure is more evolutionarily conserved than is sequence (Chothia and Lesk, 1986), structural alignments can be more reliable between sequences that are very distantly related and that have diverged so extensively that sequence comparison cannot reliably detect their similarity.

Structural alignments are used as the gold standard in evaluating alignments for homology-based protein structure prediction (Zhang and Skolnick, 2005) because they explicitly align regions of the protein sequence that are structurally similar rather than relying exclusively on sequence information. However, clearly, structural alignments cannot be used in structure prediction because at least one sequence in the query set is the target to be modeled, for which the structure is not known. It has been shown that given the structural alignment between a target and a template sequence, highly accurate models of the target protein sequence can be produced; a major stumbling block in homology-based structure prediction is the production of structurally accurate alignments given only sequence information.

We are witnessing the emergence of the "data-rich" era in biology. The myriad data available, ranging from sequence strings to complex phenotypic and disease-relevant data, pose a huge challenge to modern biology. The standard paradigm in biology that deals with "hypothesis to experimentation (low-throughput data) to models" is gradually being replaced by "data to hypothesis to models and experimentation to more data and models." And unlike data in physical sciences, those in the biological sciences are almost guaranteed to be highly heterogeneous and incomplete. To make significant advances in this data-rich era, it is essential that there be robust data repositories that allow interoperable navigation, query, and analysis across diverse data, a plug-and-play tools environment that will facilitate seamless interplay of tools and data, and versatile user interfaces that will allow biologists to visualize and present the results of analysis in the most intuitive and user-friendly manner. We address below several challenges posed by the enormous need for scientific data integration in biology, with specific examples and strategies. The issues that need to be addressed may include:

- Architecture of data and knowledge repositories
- Databases (flat, relational, and object-oriented; which is most appropriate?)
- The imminent need for ontologies in biology
- The middle layer (how to design it)
- Applications and integration of applications into the middle layer
- Reduction and analysis of data (the largest challenge!)
- How to integrate legacy knowledge with data
- User interfaces (Web browser and beyond)

The complex and diverse nature of biology mandates that there is no "one solution fits all" model for the issues listed above. Although there is a need to have similar solutions across multiple disciplines within biology, the dichotomy of having to deal with the context, which is everything in some cases, poses severe design challenges. For example, can a system that describes cellular signaling also describe developmental genetics? Can the ontologies that span different areas (e.g., anatomy, gene and protein data, cellular biology) be compatible and connective? Can the detailed biological knowledge accrued painstakingly over decades be integrated easily with high-throughput data? These are only few of the questions that arise in designing and building modern data and knowledge systems in biology.

3.5 CHALLENGES AND PERSPECTIVES

Although the human genome project has great potential, theoretical work is essential for sequencing and mapping all genomes, human and nonhuman, animal and plant. Mathematical and computational advances provide dramatic efforts in sequencing and mapping. Specific comparative analyses of the genomes of diverse organisms can increase our understanding of the natural world. For example, when a DNA sequence is determined, it is examined for a variety of sequence features known to be important: tRNAs, rRNAs, protein coding regions—introns and regulatory regions, promoters, and enhancers. It is often quite difficult to identify them, as these sequence features are not identical in all organisms. Even the widely studied bacterium *Escherichia coli* promoter sequences cannot be identified with certainty. As more and more DNA is sequenced, it becomes increasingly important to have accurate methods to identify these regions, without many false positives. Statistics and mathematics should make significant contributions in this area.

One of the most common comparative methods of biological sequences is pairwise alignment. However, multiple sequence alignments remain a serious problem, with a long computation time. Heuristic methods that align by building up pairwise alignments have been proposed, but they often fail to give good multiple alignments. Closely coupled with multiple alignment is the construction of evolutionary trees. Closely related sequences should be neighbors with few changes between them. DNA sequences are collected in the GenBank database, and protein sequences are collected in the Protein Identification Resource (PIR). When a new DNA sequence is determined, GenBank is searched for approximate similarities with the new sequence. Translations of the DNA sequence into the corresponding amino acid sequence are used to search the protein database. Sensitive search methods require time and space proportional to the product of the sequences being compared. Searching GenBank (now more than 40×10^6 bases) with a 5000-bp sequence requires time proportional to 2×10^{11} with traditional search techniques. Lipman and Pearson (1985) have developed techniques that greatly reduce the time needed. Using their techniques, one can screen the databases routinely with new sequences on IBM PCs, for example. These methods rapidly locate diagonals where possible similarities might lie and then perform more sensitive alignments. This family of programs (FASTA, FASTN, etc.) are the most widely used sequence analysis programs and have accounted for many important discoveries. An example of the impact of such analysis is the unexpected homology between an oncogene and a growth factor. This discovery became the basis of the molecular theory of carcinogenesis.

Many current and future challenges for statistics and probability that are motivated by questions in molecular biology, genetics, and molecular evolution will require new techniques and theories. One such set of challenges involves the use of DNA sequence data to reconstruct phylogenetic trees, analyze genetically complex traits, and study other problems. As more and more DNA sequence data are accumulated, patterns arise and exploratory data analysis techniques need to be developed to look through the wealth of data for patterns. The ordering and frequency of the four nucleotides are not random (even in noncoding regions). To compare two sequences of DNA or protein (or to compare a given sequence with a databank) and to look for matches or similarities requires the creation of new algorithms. Comparisons can answer both evolutionary and functional questions. Are sequences descended from a common ancestral sequence? Do they serve similar functions? One problem has been to calculate the probability of a long matching region between two DNA sequences, where some level of dependence occurs as a result of overlapping regions. Strong limit laws have been established that give rates for the longest matching sequences between different sequences (with a given proportion of mismatches) as the length of the sequences increases. Detailed distributional behavior has been obtained using the Chen–Stein method of approximation by a Poisson random variable. These new distributional results are now used as a basis for statistical tests. Arratia et al. (1990) contains a snapshot of current mathematical work on these questions.

More sensitive sequence analysis can be obtained by dynamic programming methods. In part they are used after the diagonals are located in the FASTN and FASTA programs. Here similar sequence elements are aligned with positive scores, and dissimilar elements are aligned with negative scores. Complicating the analysis are insertions and deletions, which also receive negative scores. The challenge of the problem is to arrange two sequences into the maximum number of scoring alignments. Additional difficulty arises from the fact that slightly similar regions of DNA or protein sequences might lie in otherwise unrelated sequences. Despite the complex nature of the problem, an efficient algorithm (Smith and Waterman, 1981) has been devised and is widely used.

The problem of sequence comparison creates a related statistical problem of estimating p-values (attained significance levels) for the alignment scores. The set of possible alignment scores from two sequences are dependent random variables, since they result from overlapping sequence segments. Another area of mathematical research that will be stimulated by biology is the probabilistic theory of discrete and dynamic structures. While the scattered beginnings of this field have extended over the past three decades, the major developments are yet to come. Illustrative developments in the field include random graphs and random directed graphs, interacting particle systems, stochastic cellular automata, products of random matrices, and nonlinear dynamical systems with random coefficients. For example, Erdös and Rényi (1960) created the field of random graphs to model apparently random connections in neural tissue. Erdös and Rényi discovered numerous examples of "phase transitions," and many more have been discovered since (see Bollobás, 1985).

REFERENCES

Altschul, S. F., and Erickson, B. W. (1985). Significance of nucleotide sequence alignments: a method for random sequence permutation that preserves dinucleotide and codon usage. *Mol. Biol. Evol.*, **2**, 526–538.

Altschul, S. F., Gish, W., Miller, W., Myers, E. W., and Lipman, D. J. (1990). Basic local alignment search tool. *J. Mol. Biol.*, **215**, 403–410.

Arratia, R., Goldstein, L., and Gordon, L. (1990). Poisson approximations and the Chen–Stein method. *Stat. Sci.*, **5**, 403–434.

Bollobás, B. (1985). *Random Graphs*. Orlando, FL: Academic Press.

Chenna, R., Sugawara, H., Koike, T., Lopez, R., Gibson, T. J., Higgins, D. G., and Thompson, J. D. (2003). Multiple sequence alignment with the Clustal series of programs. *Nucleic Acids Res.*, **31**(13), 3497–3500.

Chothia, C., and Lesk, A. M. (1986). The relation between the divergence of sequence and structure in proteins. *EMBO J.*, **5**(4), 823–826.

Deken, J. (1983). Probabilistic behavior of longest-common-subsequence length. In: D. Sankoff and J. B. Kruskal (Eds.), *Time Warps, String Edits and Macromolecules:*

The Theory and Practice of Sequence Comparison. Reading, MA: Addison-Wesley, pp. 55–91.

Dembo, A., Karlin, S., and Zeitouni, O. (1994). Limit distribution of maximal non-aligned two-sequence segmental score. *Ann. Probab.*, **22**, 2022–2039.

Durbin, R., Eddy, S., Krogh, A., and Mitchison, G. (1998). *Biological Sequence Analysis: Probabilistic Models of Proteins and Nucleic Acids*. Cambridge, UK: Cambridge University Press.

Erdös, P., and Rényi, A. (1960). On the evolution of random graphs. *Publ. Math. Inst. Hungar. Acad. Sci.*, **5**, 17–61.

Fitch, W. M. (1983). Random sequences. *J. Mol. Biol.*, **163**, 171–176.

Gumbel, E. J. (1958). *Statistics of Extremes*. New York: Columbia University Press.

Karlin, S., and Altschul, S. F. (1990). Methods for assessing the statistical significance of molecular sequence features by using general scoring schemes. *Proc. Natl. Acad. Sci. USA*, **87**, 2264–2268.

Levenshtein, V. I. (1966). Binary codes capable of correcting deletion, insertions, and reversals. *Sov. Phys. Dokl.*, **6**, 707–710.

Lipman, D. J., and Pearson, W. R. (1985). Rapid and sensitive protein similarity searches. *Science*, **227**, 1435–1441.

Lipman, D. J., Wilbur, W. J., Smith, T. F., and Waterman, M. S. (1984). On the statistical significance of nucleic acid similarities. *Nucleic Acids Res.*, **12**, 215–226.

Pearson, R. W., and Lipman, D. J. (1988). Improved tools for biological sequence comparison. *Proc. Natl. Acad. Sci. USA*, **85**, 2444–2448.

Reich, J. G., Drabsch, H., and Daumler, A. (1984). On the statistical assessment of similarities in DNA sequences, *Nucleic Acids Res.*, **12**, 5529–5543.

Sellers, P. H. (1984). Pattern recognition in genetic sequences by mismatch density. *Bull. Math. Biol.*, **46**, 501–514.

Smith, T. F., and Waterman, M. S. (1981). Identification of common molecular subsequences. *J. Mol. Biol.*, **147**, 195–197.

Waterman, M. S. (Ed.) (1999). *Mathematical Methods for DNA Sequences*. Boca Raton, FL: CRC Press.

Zhang, Y., and Skolnick, J. (2005). The protein structure prediction problem could be solved using the current PDB library. *Proc. Natl. Acad. Sci. USA*, **102**, 1029–1034.

4 Structures of DNA and Knot Theory

It is well known that DNA is the genetic material of all cells, containing coded information about cellular molecules and processes. DNA consists of two polynucleotide strands twisted around each other in a double helix. DNA packing can be visualized as two very long strands that have been intertwined millions of times, tied into knots, and subjected to successive coiling. DNA is involved in transcribing proteins that direct cell growth and activities. However, DNA is tightly packed into genes and chromosomes. For replication or transcription to take place, DNA must first unpack itself so that it can interact with enzymes. However, replication and transcription are much easier to accomplish if the DNA is neatly arranged rather than tangled up in knots. Enzymes are essential to unpacking DNA. Enzymes act to slice through individual knots and reconnect strands in a more orderly way. Enzymes maintain the proper geometry and topology during the transformation and also "cut" the DNA strands and recombine the loose ends.

Mathematics can be used to model these complicated processes. In this chapter we provide an introduction to the structures of DNA; key elements of knot theory, such as links, tangles, and knot polynomials; and applications of knot theory to the study of closed circular DNA. The physical and chemical properties of this type of DNA can be explained in terms of basic characteristics of the linking number, which is invariant under continuous deformation of the DNA structure and is the sum of two geometric quantities, twist and writhing. This chapter is in no way exhaustive of all the topological applications in DNA structures. For comprehensive coverage of the topology of DNA, readers should consult the excellent survey articles in the field (e.g., Sumners, 1987, 1990, 1992).

4.1 INTRODUCTION

DNA is a double-stranded molecule composed of two polarized strands (of deoxyribonucleotide polymers) which run in opposite directions (termed

Mathematics of Bioinformatics: Theory, Practice, and Applications, By Matthew He and Sergey Petoukhov
Copyright © 2011 John Wiley & Sons, Inc.

antiparallel) and wind around a central, common axis. One is entwined about the other such that an overall helical shape results (known as a *plectonemic helix*). Both are wound in a right-handed manner. This structure is to be contrasted with a *paranemic helix*, in which a pair of coils lie side by side without interwinding. The strands are occasionally distinguished as the Watson strand and the Crick strand.

In the case of the molecular structure of eukaryotic chromosomes in each human cell, two meztres of DNA is packaged into the cell nucleus. To access the information, the DNA must be unwound as a double helix and needs to be "spread out" in the nucleus. However, during cell division (mitosis), in order to move the strands around, they are packaged into dense bundles as follows :

- *Nucleosome formation* (beads on a string): 2.5 loops of DNA wrapped around core DNA
- *Solenoid formation* (beaded string is coiled): six nucleosomes per solenoid coil
- *Supercoiling* (coil of solenoids is itself coiled): the coiled coil is then folded, as in a mitotic chromosome (i.e., a 10,000-fold reduction in length)

Each nucleotide base of one strand is paired with a nucleotide base on the other strand to create a stable structure of the two polymers. The pairing of the four types of bases (A, T, C, G) by hydrogen bonds is not random: An A pairs with a T and a G pairs with a C. The bases on the outside of the helix are exposed to solvent within two grooves along the helix, the major groove and the minor groove. It is within these grooves that DNA interacts with other molecules. The three structural variations of these grooves (A, B and Z DNA), which differ in the relationship between the bases and the helical axis, offer one mechanism by which reactivity of DNA is modulated:

- *B-DNA*. This is fully hydrated DNA, the most common encountered in vivo. Owing to the location of the helical axis in the center of the base pairs, the edges of the base pairs are about equally deep in the interior.
- *A-DNA*. When B-DNA is dehydrated, there is a reversible structural change in A-DNA.
- *Z-DNA*. Unlike B-DNA and A-DNA, Z-DNA is a left-handed helix. The conformational change from B-DNA to Z-DNA is one mechanism for relief of the torsional strain found in B-DNA in vivo and may serve as a switch mechanism to regulate gene expression.

In circular double-helix DNA (closed circular ccDNA), the strands are joined covalently to form a circular duplex molecule. The geometry of such an assembly is such that its number of coils cannot be changed without first breaking one of its strands. This topological "dilemma" is resolved within the cell—

to ensure proper biological functioning—by specialized enzymes that unknot, untwist, and unwind the DNA to enable replication and then re-form the compact mode thereafter.

Forms of DNA

1. *Supercoiled (or knotted) DNA.* Double-stranded circular (or linear) DNA can have tertiary or higher-order structure. Superhelicity is therefore sometimes referred to as DNA's tertiary structure. Supercoils refer to the DNA structure in which the two strands of circular DNA twist around each other. This is termed *supercoiling, supertwisting,* or *superhelicity*—meaning the coiling of a coil, also understood in terms of knots. Only topologically closed domains (such as a covalently closed circle) can undergo supercoiling. A linear molecule can have topological domains as long as there is a region of the DNA bounded by constraints on the rotation of the DNA double helix. Eukaryotic DNAs in association with nuclear proteins acquire superhelical conformation in chromosomes. Adding a twist to the DNA (as catalyzed by an enzyme) imposes a strain. A DNA segment so strained that it is closed into a circle would then contort into a figure eight (or its topological equivalent)—the simplest supercoil. This is the shape that circular DNA assumes to accommodate one too many or one too few helical twists. For each additional helical twist that is accommodated, the lobes will show one more rotation about their axis. Such superhelicity results in more compact structures. In any other naturally found geometry, the DNA is either under- or overwound. Its helical axis does not lie in a plane or on the surface of a sphere because of writhing and twisting. This is the physical solution to the potential (torsional) energy minimization problem. Supercoiling can therefore be:

   a. *Negative (right-handed).* Supercoils formed by a deficit in link, called negative supercoils, result from underwinding, unwinding, or subtractive twisting of the DNA helix. The two lobes of the figure eight then appear rotated counterclockwise with respect to each other. All naturally occurring double-stranded DNAs are negatively supercoiled. Negative supercoiling facilitates DNA-strand separation during replication, recombination, and transcription. All the naturally occurring double-stranded DNAs are negatively supercoiled (including bacterial and viral circular duplex DNAs).

   b. *Positive (left-handed).* Supercoils formed by an increase in link, called positive supercoils, result from tighter winding or overwinding of the DNA helix, resulting in extrahelical twists. The two lobes of the figure eight then appear rotated clockwise with respect to each other. This would compact DNA as effectively as negative supercoiling but would make strand separation much more difficult.

In nondividing eukaryotic cells, chromosomal DNA is wrapped around a nucleosome core which consists of highly basic proteins called *histones*. The DNA is wrapped around the nucleosome in a left-handed solenoidal arrangement. This negative supercoiling is one of the forms taken up by under-wound DNA.

2. *Relaxed DNA.* Circular DNA without superhelical twist is known as a relaxed molecule. DNA in its relaxed (ideal) state usually assumes the B configuration. In a relaxed double-helical segment of DNA, the two strands twist around the helical axis once every 10.6 base pairs of sequence. Relaxed, closed circular DNA is defined as DNA that has no supercoils when constrained to lie flat in a plan. The following structures are consistent with the relaxed state: (a) linear DNA (either straight or curved); (b) closed circular DNA, provided that its axis lies in a plane or on the surface of a sphere.

Supercoiling is thus vital to two major functions. It helps pack large circular rings of DNA into a small space by making the rings highly compact. It also helps in the unwinding of DNA required for its replication and transcription. Supercoiled DNA is thus the biologically active form. The normal biological functioning of DNA occurs only if it is in the proper topological state.

4.2   KNOT THEORY PRELIMINARIES

Knots

A *knot* is a closed continuous curve in space that does not intersect itself anywhere. When a knot is deformed (i.e., stretched, compressed, bent, or twisted), but not cut or torn, all the deformed curves will be considered to be the same as the original closed knotted curve. The simplest knot of all is the unknotted circle, called an *unknot* or *trivial knot* and denoted C. The next simplest knot is called a *trefoil knot* (Figure 4.1).

In a projection of a knot into a plane, we call the places where the knot crosses itself in the graphs the *crossings* of the projection. The crossing number of a knot K, denoted c(K), is the smallest number of crossings that occur in any projection of the knot. If a knot is *nontrivial*, it has more than one crossing in a projection. A figure-eight knot (Figure 4.2) has four crossings.

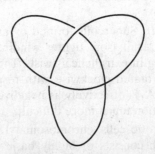

FIGURE 4.1   Trefoil knot.

FIGURE 4.2 Figure-eight knot.

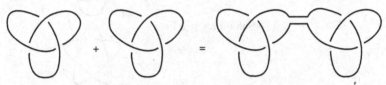

FIGURE 4.3 Composition (sum) of K_1 and K_2.

An orientation on a knot is defined by choosing a direction to travel around the knot. This direction is denoted by placing coherently directed arrows along the projection of the knot in the direction of our choice. We then say that the knot is *oriented*. Certain types of knots possess knot projections in which crossings alternate between under- and overpasses as one travels around the knot in a fixed direction. We call this type of knot an *alternating knot*. The trefoil knot and the figure-eight knot are alternating.

Given two projections of knots and assuming that the two projections do not overlap, one can compose a new knot by deleting a small arc from each knot projection and then connecting the four ending points by two new arcs, as in Figure 4.3. The resulting knot is called the *composition* (or knot sum) of the two knots, denoted $K_1 \# K_2$ (or $K_1 + K_2$).

A knot that can be expressed as the composition of two nontrivial knots is called a *composite knot*. The unknot is not a composite knot. The knots that make up a composite knot are called *factor knots*. The unknot or trivial knot may also be called an *identity knot*, as the composition of a knot K with an unknot is again K (i.e., $K + C = K$). A knot that is not the composition of any two nontrivial knots is called a *prime knot*. Both the trefoil and figure-eight knots are prime knots. It is often possible to combine two prime knots to create two different composite knots, depending on the orientation of the two. Schubert (1949) showed that every knot can be decomposed uniquely (up to the order in which the decomposition is performed) as a knot sum of prime knots. There is no known formula for giving the number of distinct prime knots as a function of the number of crossings. Rolfsen (1976) has provided a

TABLE 4.1 Prime Knots

Knot Symbol	Prime Knot	Knot Projection
0_1	Unknot	
3_1	Trefoil knot	
4_1	Figure-eight knot	
5_1	Solomon's seal knot	
6_1	Stevedore's knot	
6_2	Miller Institute knot	

pictorial enumeration of prime knots of up to 10 crossings. The kth knot having n crossings in this (arbitrary) ordering of knots is given the symbol n_k. Table 4.1 summarizes a number of named prime knots.

Suppose that we have two projections of the same knot. If we made a knot out of string that modeled the first of the two projections, we should be able to rearrange the string to resemble the second projection. We call this process of continuous deformation of the rearranging of the string through three-dimensional space without letting it pass through itself, *ambient isotopy*. Deformation of a knot projection is called *planar isotopy* if it deforms the projection plane.

Reidemeister was the first person to prove rigorously that knots exist which are distinct from an unknot. He did this in the 1930s by showing that all knot deformations can be reduced to a sequence of three types of moves (Figure 4.4):

1. *Twist move* (type I Reidemeister move): to put in, or take out, a twist in a knot
2. *Poke move* (type II Reidemeister move): to either add or remove two crossings

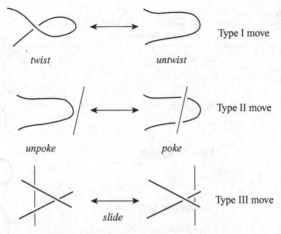

FIGURE 4.4   Reidemeister moves.

3. *Slide move* (type III Reidemeister move): to slide a strand of a knot from one side of a crossing to the other side

These moves are most commonly called *Reidemeister moves*, although the term *equivalence moves* is sometimes used. If two projections represent the same knot, there must be a sequence of Reidemeister moves to get from the one projection to the other.

Links

Next we consider a set of several knots. A *link* is the union of a finite number of disjoint knots in three-dimensional space. A knot will be considered a link of one component. Four common links—the trivial link (or unlink), the Hopf link, the Whitehead link, and the Borromean link—are shown in Table 4.2. The notation and ordering follow Rolfsen (1976), with c_k^r denoting the kth r-component link with crossing number c.

Two links are considered to be the same if we can deform the one link to the other link without ever having any one of the knots intersect itself or any of the other loops in the process. That is, two links are considered equal if they are isotopic. Many statements about knots also apply to links. This may be a good reason to extend the study to links. However, the most important rationale for including links is that certain operations that we will consider leave invariant the class of links, but not the class of knots.

Linking Number

Next, we define an important number known as the *linking number*. Let K_1 and K_2 be two components in a link L, and choose an orientation on each

TABLE 4.2   Links

Link Number	Link Name	Link Diagram
0_1^2	Trivial link	
2_1^2	Hopf link	
5_1^2	Whitehead link	
6_2^3	Borromean link (rings)	

Type I: +1   Type II -1

FIGURE 4.5   Computing the linking number.

component. Then at each crossing between the two components, we count a +1 for each crossing of the first type, and a −1 for each crossing of the second type (Figure 4.5). In other words, to each of these crossings is associated an index number of +1 or −1, according to the direction in which the tangent vector to the top curve must be rotated to coincide with the tangent vector to the bottom curve. If the rotation is clockwise, the index number is −1, and if it is counterclockwise, the index number is +1. Adding all the indices associated with all the crossings and dividing by 2 gives the link number of two knots denoted by $L(K_1, K_2)$. Formally, a linking number is defined as the sum of +1 crossings and −1 crossings over all crossings between the two links divided by 2 calculated by the formula

$$L(K_1, K_2) = \frac{1}{2} \sum_{p \in \alpha \cap \beta} \varepsilon(p)$$

where $\alpha \cap \beta$ is the set of crossings of α with β, and $\varepsilon(p)$ is the sign of the crossing. The linking number of a splittable two-component link is always 0. The linking number has four major properties:

1. The linking number $L(K_1, K_2)$ is a property of the curves in space and is independent of the planar projection.
2. The linking number $L(K_1, K_2)$ is unchanged if either of the curves is deformed continuously, provided that no breaks are made in either curve. Moreover, the Reidemeister moves do not affect the linking number.
3. The linking number $L(K_1, K_2)$ changes sign if the direction of one of the curves is reversed.
4. The linking number $L(K_1, K_2)$ changes sign if a pair of curves is reflected in a plane.

It is well known that the linking number is an invariant of the oriented links; that is, once the orientations are selected on the two components of the link, the linking number is unchanged by ambient isotopy. In special cases in which two oriented curves K_1 and K_2 bound a ribbonlike surface, the linking number $L(K_1, K_2)$ is the sum of two geometric quantities: twist $T(K_1, K_2)$, and writhe $W(K_1)$.

$$L(K_1, K_2) = T(K_1, K_2) + W(K_1) \qquad (4.1)$$

This important characteristic, together with the invariance of the linking number, have been applied to the study of circular DNA structure (Adams, 1994).

Basically, the twist $T(K_1, K_2)$ of one curve K_1 about another curve K_2 measures the magnitude of the spinning of K_1 around K_2. The twist of helices about a linear axis is the number of times the helix (K_1) resolves about the axis (K_2). This number, $T(K_1, K_2) > 0$ if the helix K_1 is right-handed and $T(K_1, K_2) < 0$ if the helix K_1 is left-handed, as illustrated in Figure 4.6.

For the more general cases in which K_2 is not linear, or planar, the definition of the twist is much more complex, for the concept is no longer geometrically obvious. To define the twist in the general case, we need the ribbonlike surface joining and bounded by the two curves called the *corresponding surface*. We assume this surface to be differentiable near the curve K_2 so that there is a tangent plane to the surface at every point of K_2. Let T be the unit tangent vector to the curve K_2 at a point x and V be a unit vector perpendicular to T at x and tangent to the surface at x pointing in the direction of K_1. Their cross-product $T \times V$ is a unit vector perpendicular to the surface at x. It varies along with point x along the curve K_2. The twist of K_1 around K_2 is defined to be the measure of the total change of V in the direction of $T \times V$ as x moves along

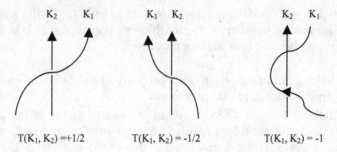

$T(K_1, K_2) = +1/2$ $T(K_1, K_2) = -1/2$ $T(K_1, K_2) = -1$

FIGURE 4.6   Twist of helices about a linear axis.

the entire curve K_2. This is given by the line integral (normalized in turns) over the curve K_2:

$$T(K_1, K_2) = \frac{1}{2\pi} \int_{K_2} (T \times V) dV \tag{4.2}$$

This integral is not necessarily an integer. It changes under deformations of either the curve K_2 or the corresponding surface. Since the cross-product operation is not commutative, the twist depends on the ordering of the curves. The twist of K_1 about K_2 is not necessarily the twist of K_2 about K_1.

The writhing number of a curve K_1, denoted by $W(K_1)$, is a knot property, defined as the sum of crossings p of a curve K_1,

$$W(K_1) = \sum_{p \in C(K_1)} \varepsilon(p) \tag{4.3}$$

where $\varepsilon(p)$ is defined to be ± 1 if the overpass slants from top left to bottom right or bottom left to top right, and $C(K_1)$ is the set of crossings of an oriented curve as illustrated in Figure 4.7.

The proof of this equation is beyond our scope in this chapter. The main characteristic of this fundamental equation should be noted. The linking number $L(K_1, K_2)$ is a topological invariant. However, the twist number $T(K_1, K_2)$ and writhing number $W(K_2)$ are not, and in fact, vary under deformation. Therefore, whereas the twist and a change in writhing could increase or increase linking, the linking number is invariant under deformation.

Tangle

A *tangle* in a knot or link projection is a region in the projection plane surrounded by a circle such that the knot or link crosses the circle exactly four times (Figure 4.8). We will always think of the four points where the knot or link crosses the circle as occurring in the four compass directions NW, NE, SW,

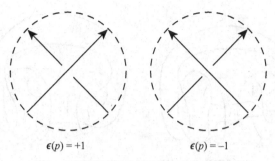

$\epsilon(p) = +1$ $\epsilon(p) = -1$

FIGURE 4.7 Writhe index.

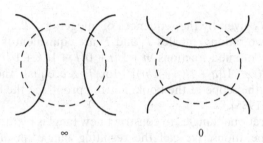

∞ 0

FIGURE 4.8 Tangles.

and SE. The tangles can be used to build blocks of knot and link projections. Understanding tangles will be very useful in understanding knots.

Two tangles are *equivalent* if a sequence of Reidemeister moves can be used to transform one into the other while keeping the four string endpoints fixed and not allowing strings to pass outside the circle. The simplest tangles are the ∞-tangle (trivial) and 0-tangle (trivial), shown in Figure 4.8. The family of tangles that can be converted to the trivial tangled by moving the endpoints of the strings is the family of *rational tangles*. Equivalently, a rational tangle is one in which the strings can continuously be deformed (fixing the endpoints) entirely into the boundary 2-sphere of the 3-ball, with no string passing through itself or through another string. An algebraic tangle is any tangle obtained by additions and multiplications of rational tangles. Rational tangles form a homologous family of two-string configurations in a 3-sphere and formed by a pattern of plectonemic supercoiling of pairs of strings.

The rational tangle may be represented by an even or an odd number of integers. If the rational tangle is represented by an even or odd number of integers, we start with two vertical or horizontal strings (i.e., the ∞ tangle/0 tangle) and alternately twist the two bottom/right-hand endpoints appropriately, followed by twisting the two right-hand/bottom endpoints appropriately. The equivalence between two rational tangles is well connected, with *continued fractions* corresponding to the integers. Suppose that we have two rational

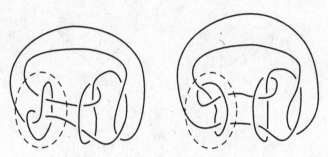

FIGURE 4.9   Kinoshita–Terasaka mutants.

tangles T_1 and T_2 given by the sequences of integers $i, j, k, \dots, l, m$ and $n, p,$ $q, \dots, r, s$. The two rational tangles T_1 and T_2 are equivalent if and only if the corresponding continued fractions $m + 1/[l + 1/(l \cdots 1/[k + 1/(j + 1/i)])]$ for T_1 and $s + 1/[r + 1/(r \cdots 1/[q + 1/(p + 1/n)])]$ for T_2 are equal. The proof of this result is beyond the scope of the book. For the proof, see the book by Burde and Zieschang (1985).

One can use rational tangles to construct new tangles by the multiplication and addition operations. We call the resulting tangle an *algebraic tangle*. Although many tangles are algebraic, there are tangles that are not algebraic. While discussing tangles, there is another way to obtain new knots, called *mutation*. Suppose that we have a knot K formed from two tangles. We cut the knot open along four points on each of the four strings coming out of T_2, flipping T_2 over, and gluing the four strings back together. We could also cut the four strings coming out of T_2, flip T_2 left to right, and then glue the strings back together. We can also do both operations in turn: It's as if we rotated the tangle 180° and then reglued it. Any of these three operations is called a mutation, and the three resulting knots together with the original knot are called *mutants* of one another. Figure 4.9 shows two famous mutants, called the *Kinoshita–Terasaka mutants*.

Although mutation can turn one knot into another, it cannot turn a non-trivial knot into a trivial knot. The mutants and tangles will be used to help us understand knotting in DNA. The mathematics of tangles has been applied to model protein–DNA binding. A tangle consists of strings properly embedded in a three-dimensional ball. The protein complex can be thought of as a three-dimensional ball, while the DNA segments bound by the protein complex can be thought of as strings embedded within the ball. This simple model can be used to determine the topology of protein-bound DNA.

In the 1980s, biochemists discovered knotting in DNA molecules. Concurrently, synthetic chemists realized that it is possible to create knotted molecules, where the type of knot determined the properties of the molecules. To perform various biological functions such as replication, transcription, and recombination, DNA has to be utilized. The knotting and tangling in the DNA molecules make the performance of these functional processes difficult, yet there must be a way of manipulating the tangled masses of DNA molecules. Applications of knot theory to DNA structures are discussed in the next section.

Knot Polynomials

Next, we introduce knot polynomials and compute the knot polynomial from a projection of the knot. We'll note that any two different projections of the same knot yield the same polynomials. So the polynomial is an invariant of the knot. A knot invariant in the form of a polynomial such as the Alexander polynomial and the Jones polynomial are discussed in detail.

A *polynomial* is a mathematical expression involving a sum of powers in one or more variables multiplied by coefficients. A polynomial in one variable (i.e., a univariate polynomial) with constant coefficients is given by

$$a_n x^n + \cdots + a_2 x^2 + a_1 x + a_0 \tag{4.4}$$

A *Laurent polynomial* with coefficients is an algebraic object that is typically expressed in the form

$$\cdots + a_{-n} t^{-n} + a_{-(n-1)} t^{-(n-1)} + \cdots + a_{-1} t^{-1} + a_0 + a_1 t + \cdots + a_n x^n + \cdots \tag{4.5}$$

A Laurent polynomial is an algebraic object in the sense that it is treated as a polynomial except that the indeterminant t can also have negative powers.

The *Alexander polynomial* is a knot invariant discovered in 1923 by J. W. Alexander (Alexander, 1928). The Alexander polynomial remained the *only* known knot polynomial until the Jones polynomial was discovered in 1984. Unlike the Alexander polynomial, the more powerful Jones polynomial *does*, in most cases, distinguish handedness.

The notation $[a + b + c + \cdots]$ is an abbreviation for the Alexander polynomial of a knot

$$a + b\left(x + x^{-1}\right) + c\left(x^2 + x^{-2}\right) + \cdots$$

The notation can be extended for links (Figure 4.10), in which case one or more matrices are used to generate the corresponding multivariate Alexander polynomial (Rolfsen, 1976, p. 389).

A second knot polynomial, the *Jones polynomial*, was discovered subsequently. Unlike the first-discovered Alexander polynomial, can sometimes distinguish handedness. Jones polynomials are Laurent polynomials in t assigned to an R^3 knot. The Jones polynomials are denoted $V_L(t)$ for links, $V_k(t)$ for knots, and normalized so that

$$V_{\text{unknot}}(t) = 1$$

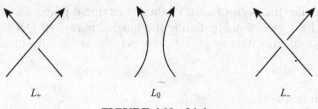

L_+ L_0 L_-

FIGURE 4.10 Links.

For example, the right- and left-hand trefoil knots have the polynomials

$$V_{\text{trefoil}}(t) = t + t^3 - t^4$$
$$V_{\text{trefoil}*}(t) = t^{-1} + t^{-3} - t^{-4}$$

respectively.

4.3 DNA KNOTS AND LINKS

Geneticists have discovered that DNA can form knots and links that can be described mathematically. By understanding knot theory more completely, scientists are becoming more able to comprehend the massive complexity involved in the life and reproduction of the cell. The particular fascination in this process for geneticists is the fact that chemical changes occur in the DNA strand as a result of this process. Changes in the DNA structure due to the actions of these enzymes have required geneticists to use very advanced mathematical topology (which includes knot theory) and geometry in their study of molecular biology.

Descriptive Properties Associated with Supercoiling

Supercoiling is an abstract mathematical property and represents the sum of twist and writhe. *Supercoil* is seldom used as a noun with reference to DNA topology. It is the combination of twists and writhes that imparts supercoiling, and these occur in response to a change in the linking number. A coiled structure is at a higher energy (less stable). When the linking number is reduced in closed circular DNA, the molecule supercoils by minimizing twisting and bending. To partially relieve the strain introduced by the change in linking number (a "deficit" in the link), the DNA must distort in other ways—compensating with a change in twist or writhe. These are, physically, the two ways that the DNA can do so. The relationship of twist, writhe, and supercoiling is expressed by the equation $S = T + W$ (known as *White's formula*). Twist and writhe are geometric quantities. Unusually, link as a topological property is equal to the sum of two geometric properties. Their values change if the ribbon is deformed in space. Link, twist, and writhe can be either positive or negative. Link is always an integer, whereas twist and writhe can take any real values.

1. *Writhing*. Global contortions of circular DNA are described as *writhe*. The writhing number describes the supertwisting or supercoiling of the helix in space. It is the number of turns that the duplex axis makes about the super-helix axis. Writhe describes the supercoiling, the coiling of the DNA coil. It is a measure of the DNA's superhelicity (supercoiling) and can be positive or negative. Writhe is a measure of the coiling, bending, or nonplanarity of the axis of the double helix. A right-handed coil is assigned a negative number (negative supercoiling) and a left-handed coil is assigned a positive number (positive supercoiling). When a molecule is relaxed and contains no supercoils, the linking number = the twist number since $W = 0$. The linking number of relaxed DNA is $L = N/10.5$, where N is the number of base pairs in the DNA fragment.

2. *Twisting*. Twist is the number of helical turns in the DNA: that is, the complete revolutions that one polynucleotide strand makes about the duplex axis in the particular conformation under consideration. Twist is normally the number of base pairs divided by 10.4: that is, the number of bases per turn of the helix. Twist is altered by deformation and is a local phenomenon. The total twist is the sum of all the local twists. Twist is a measure of deformation due to a twisting motion. Twist and writhe are interconvertible. In part because chromosomes may be very large, segments in the middle may act as if their ends are anchored. As a result, they may be unable to distribute excess twist to the rest of the chromosome or to absorb twist to recover from underwinding; the segments may become supercoiled, in other words. In response to supercoiling, they will assume an amount of writhe, just as if their ends were joined.

3. *Linking number*. This is a topological property that determines the degree of supercoiling. It defines the number of times a strand of DNA winds in the right-handed direction around the helix axis when the axis is constrained to lie in a plane. It is the number of times that one DNA strand crosses about the other when the DNA is made to lie flat on a plane. If both strands are covalently intact, the linking number cannot change. Link is thus a topological invariant, remaining unaltered even if the two curves are deformed in space— as long as neither is cut. Topology theory indicates that the sum of T and W equals the linking number: $L = T + W$. For example, in the circular DNA of 5400 base pairs, the linking number is $5400/10 = 540$. When a molecule is relaxed and contains no supercoils, the linking number = the twist number since $W = 0$. Thus, if there is no supercoiling, $W = 0$ and $T = L = 540$. If there is positive supercoiling, $W = +20$ and $T = L - W = 520$. In special cases in which the axis of the double helix remains in a plane or on the surface of a sphere, twist equals the linking number and there is no writhe, but all other

cases are considerably more complex. Supercoiling can even be caused by an increase in the linking number (although this does not occur in nature).

4. *Density*. The density of supercoiling is useful to define as a property that distinguishes DNAs varying significantly in size. Superhelical density is the number of supercoils per turn of helix. It is denoted by the Greek letter sigma and is defined as the number of turns that have been added or subtracted in the supercoiled DNA compared to the relaxed state, divided by the total number of turns in the DNA if it were relaxed (which would normally be bp/10.5). Typically, sigma is between −0.05 and −0.07 (5 to 7% underwinding) in isolated natural DNA.

5. *Link-altering enzymes*. The functionality of DNA is related to its topology, which is maintained by enzymes that are capable of altering it. Nature has come up with particular enzymes that control the knottedness (as well as other topological states such as twist-induced supercoiling) of DNA. The exact ability of these enzymes to locate a knot in a circular DNA is an unresolved question in molecular biology. Known as topoisomerases, these enzymes change the structure by altering the DNA link of a molecule. This is achieved by breaking one of the strands temporarily, passing the other strand through it and then resealing the bonds. This effectively changes the linking number in the DNA. The enzymes are of two types:

a. *Type 1*. These function by creating transient single-strand breaks in DNA, altering the link by one, cutting one strand, and passing the other strand through the break.

b. *Type 2*. These alter the link by two, by breaking both strands of the double helix at the same time and passing a segment of the double helix through the break.

Many topoisomerase enzymes sense supercoiling and either generate or dissipate it as they change DNA topology.

Energy Associated with Various Structures

The energy of a molecule changes if there is a change in pitch (i.e., the number of bases per full turn) or bending of the double-helix ring. Even a small change in the pitch of DNA results in a large increase in energy

1. *Minimum energy*. Linear DNA assumes the B-configuration because it is the configuration of minimum energy. Linear molecules of DNA assume a configuration known as the b-configuration. Deviation from this relaxed state increases the energy of the DNA molecule, although circular DNA of large diameter increases it least.

2. *Higher energy*. In the ring form, too, the DNA double helix tries to attain the state of minimum energy. The DNA ring approximates the b-configuration of the linear molecule while trying to attain the state of minimum energy. This packaging of DNA deforms it physically, thereby increasing its energy. Such

an increase in stored (potential) energy within the molecule is then available to drive reactions such as the unwinding events that occur during DNA replication and transcription. Too much stored energy is not necessarily a good thing, though. In nature, this problem is addressed by having DNA form supercoils, in which the helical axis of the DNA curves itself into a coil. Supercoiling or the formation of a superhelix structure minimizes the excess energy that builds up when DNA molecules are deformed during the packing process.

At this point, we should mention that supercoiling is not necessarily the only solution to the problem of normalizing the number of bases pairs per helix in an unwound piece of DNA. You could also separate the two strands by breaking the hydrogen bonds between complementary bases in contiguous base pairs until the remaining DNA has the correct number of bases per turn. In terms of energy needed, though, it requires a lot more energy to break the hydrogen bonds than to supercoil. Nevertheless, strand separation does occur during replication and transcription, and it turns out that it is the physics of the underwinding that facilitates strand separation. Cruciform structures also require some unpairing of the base pairs, and again, it is the underwinding that maintains the required strand separation.

4.4   CHALLENGES AND PERSPECTIVES

We can gain insight into the unknotting of DNA by using principles of topology. Topologists study the invariant properties of geometric objects, such as knots. Tightly packed DNA in the genes must quickly unknot itself in order for replication or transcription to occur. Principles of topology give cell biologists a quantitative, powerful, and invariant way to measure the properties of DNA. Principles of knot theory have helped elucidate the mechanisms by which enzymes unpack DNA. Additionally, topological methods have been influential in determining the left-handed winding of DNA around histones. Measuring changes in a crossing number have also been instrumental in understanding the termination of DNA replication and the role of enzymes in recombination. In the area of DNA structure, several subareas are particularly amenable to mathematical analysis:

- A complete analysis of the packaging of DNA in chromatin. Only first-order coiling into core nucleosomes is understood. By far the largest compaction of DNA comes from higher-order folding.
- Presentation of the topological invariants that describe the structure of DNA and its enzymatic transformations. The goal is to be able to predict the structure of interstate or products from enzymatic mechanisms and in turn to predict mechanisms from structure.
- An analysis of the reciprocal interaction between secondary and higher-order structures. This includes the phenomena of bending, looping, and phasing.

This work has implications for both biology and mathematics. Mathematics will be affected in both topology and geometry. Renewed interest in the study of embedding invariants for graphs has occurred because of the enumeration and classification topoisomers; the study of random knots has been used to study macromolecules in dilute solution, and tangle calculus and Dehn surgery theory have been used in the study of DNA enzyme mechanisms.

In the study of kinetoplast DNA, topology and the theory of interacting particles have been brought together in a unique way. Finally, in the study of DNA–protein interactions, theorems from differential geometry and differential topology have been recast in different frameworks to solve helical periodicity problems. Determination of the configuration of closed circular DNA brings together the fields of geometry and topology and nonlinear partial differential equations, or topology and Monte Carlo techniques. These will involve extensive use of computational techniques, including the creation of new codes to use nonlinear partial differential equations to solve elasticity problems for closed circular rods.

Differential geometry is the branch of mathematics that applies the methods of differential calculus to study the differential invariants of manifolds. Topology is the mathematical study of shape. It defines and quantizes properties of space that remain invariant under deformation. These two fields have been used extensively to characterize many of the basic physical and chemical properties of DNA. Specific examples of particular note follow.

The recent review of Dickerson (1989) summarizes how such geometric concepts as tilt, roll, shear, and propeller twist have been used to describe the secondary structure of DNA (i.e., the actual helical stacking of the bases, which forms a linear segment of DNA). In addition, these concepts can be used to describe the interaction of DNA with ligands such as intercalating drugs (Wang et al., 1983).

From the time that closed circular DNA was discovered, it has been clear that such DNA exhibits physical and chemical properties that differ in fundamental ways from those of related linear DNA. Using differential geometry and topology, both molecular biologists and mathematicians have been able to explain many of the properties of these molecules from two basic characteristics of the linking number: first, that it is invariant under deformations; and second, that it is the sum of the two geometric quantities, twist and writhe (White, 1969). Among the major applications are:

- An explanation for and extent of supercoiling in a variety of closed DNAs (Bauer, 1978)
- An analysis of the enzymes that change the topology of a DNA chain (Cozzarelli, 1980; Wasserman and Cozzarelli, 1986)
- An estimation of the extent of winding in nucleosomes (Travers and Klug, 1987)
- A determination of the free energy associated with supercoiling (Depew and Wang, 1975)

- Quantitative analysis of the binding of proteins and small ligands to DNA (Wang et al., 1983)
- A determination of the helical repeat of DNA in solution and DNA wrapped on protein surfaces (White et al., 1988)
- A determination of the average structure of supercoiled DNA in solution (Boles et al., 1990)

Topology and, in particular, knot and link theory of closed space curves have been used extensively to elucidate additional intertwining of closed DNA caused by catenation of two closed duplexes or knotting of a single duplex. In particular, recent developments in polynomial invariants for links and knots have been used to describe the structure of DNA and to characterize the action of recombinases (Wasserman and Cozzarelli, 1986; White et al., 1987).

Additional areas of mathematics recently have developed interactions with biology. Three-dimensional topology and low-dimensional differential geometry are two examples. Theorems about the global topological invariants of curves and ribbons in three-dimensional space have been instrumental in studying the structural conformation of closed circular DNA. These mathematical ideas apply to supercoiling in closed DNA, topoisomerases, nucleosome winding, the free energy associated with supercoiling, and binding between proteins and DNA. These applications were carried out by experimentalists, often in collaboration with mathematicians. As collaborative work continues and our knowledge of the role of conformational changes of biological macromolecules grows, the biological problems to be solved become more complicated and the mathematical questions deepen. For example, molecular biology has renewed interest in embedding invariants for graphs (used in studying topoisomers), the study of random knots (used to study solutions of macromolecules), and the tangle calculus (used in the study of the DNA enzyme mechanism).

Structural biology includes analysis of the topological and geometric structure of DNA and proteins. It also includes molecular dynamics simulation and drug design. Basic work must be done related to the structure and folding of crystalline and hydrated proteins. For many proteins, the structure is dictated by the sequence, so this area is closely related to genomics. Molecules are in continual motion in nature, but nuclear magnetic resonance spectroscopy (NMR) and x-ray crystallography necessarily involve snapshots. Mathematical and computational methods are essential to complement experimental structural biology by allowing the addition of motion to molecular structures.

Mathematics has made perhaps its most important contribution to cellular and molecular biology in the area of structural biology. This area is at the interface of three disciplines—biology, mathematics, and physics—because its success has involved the use of sophisticated physical methods to determine the structures of biologically important macromolecules, their assembly into specialized particles and organelles, and even at higher levels of organization more recently. A wide array of methods have been employed, but we focus on the two most powerful of these, x-ray crystallography and NMR, but with a mention of other methods.

Mathematics plays three roles. First, computational methods lie at the heart of these techniques because a large amount of information about local areas or short distances is encrypted in the raw data, and it is a major computational task to deduce a structure. Second, new mathematical methods of analysis are continually being developed to improve ways of determining the structure. Third, increasingly sophisticated computer graphics have been developed in response to the need to display and interpret such structure.

In crystallography the actual process of data collection has been enhanced by modern methods of detection (e.g., area detectors) and the use of intense synchrotron sources so that data collection per se is rarely rate limiting. Also, the use of modern techniques of recombinant DNA has greatly facilitated the isolation of material for crystallization.

Until the development of two-dimensional NMR in 1978 by Richard Ernst, the use of nuclear magnetic resonance for studying the structure of biological macromolecules was limited by the need to represent too much information in a limited space. With the pioneering development of the ability to represent NMR spectra in two frequency domains, it became possible to resolve the spectra of small proteins and oligonucleotides. A key benefit was that cross peaks, resulting from magnetic interactions of nuclei close to one another, could be measured. Since these cross peaks contained spatial information, there was an immediate movement to determine the structure of these molecules at atomic resolution. The technique has been remarkably effective. The structures of a number of proteins and oligonucleotides have been determined. The use of NMR to determine structures has proven to be an important complement to x-ray crystallography because the structures of many biologically important molecules [e.g., zinc fingers by Klevit (1991), Summers (1991), and Lee et al. (1991)] have resisted attempts at crystallization; these structures must be studied in solution. The success of this technique has been critically dependent on mathematics, beginning with the theoretical underpinnings by Ernst. The determination of structures is dependent on the mathematical technique of distance geometry that calculates all structures consistent with the distance constraints obtained from the NMR experiment. Other methods have included molecular dynamics and more recently the use by Altman and Jardetzky (1989) and Altman et al. (1991) of a Kalman filter to sample conformational space. There are significant limitations to two-dimensional NMR for structure determinations. First, the resolution obtained from NMR is less than that obtained from the best x-ray structures and is not sufficient to show in detail active sites of biologically important molecules. A major mathematical challenge is to obtain such detailed structural information from structures that are basically undetermined. One important approach is to use the structure to backcalculate the NMR data and, by iteration, improve resolution. Better computational techniques could extend the limit.

One cannot overestimate the importance of solving structures at atomic resolution. It has led directly to an understanding of the replication of DNA and its supercoiling in chromatin; the basis of protein and nucleic acid secondary, tertiary, and quaternary structures; how proteins act as enzymes and antibodies; and how electron transfer is achieved.

The area of molecular geometry and its interface with visualization has been underrepresented in research to date. This research, which would benefit from the involvement of geometers and would probably contribute to new mathematics, is a major limiting area in structural biology, especially in drug design and protein folding. As noted above, new methods will enhance the use of NMR for the determination of structures. Significant advances for solving the phase problem mathematically are being pursued. Important advances are being made in the field of computer-aided drug design.

Related to the structure of crystalline and hydrated proteins is the question of how proteins fold. For many proteins the folded structure and organelle formation (e.g., ribosomes) are dictated by the sequence. Reduction of the folding code has resisted intense efforts, but very recently important new approaches have been developed that have revealed significant new information. For example, two laboratories have shown that relatively short polypeptides can have significant secondary structure. This finding is important because it validates a piecemeal approach to protein folding, where secondary structure can be considered apart from tertiary structure. The second is the minimalist approach of DeGrado et al. (1989), in which model structures with predicted motifs are synthesized by chemical means. Experimental advances such as these, together with the explosive expansion of the available data and the development of more powerful decoding methods, means that members of families of protein folding codes will soon be readily identifiable. Once again this area requires mathematical innovation.

Three-dimensional structures as determined by x-ray crystallography and NMR are static since these techniques derive a single average structure. In nature, molecules are in continual motion; it is this motion that allows them to function (a static molecule is as functional as a static automobile). Mathematical and computational methods have been able to complement experimental structural biology by adding motion to the molecular structure. These techniques have been able to bring molecules to life in a most realistic manner, reproducing experimental data of a wide range of structural, energetic, and kinetic properties. Systems studied have extended from pure liquid water, through small solutes in water, to entire proteins and segments of DNA in solution.

The methods used for these calculations provide a glimpse of how simulation can be used generally in biology. Starting with a three-dimensional structure, a mathematical formulation for the forces between atoms gives the total force on each atom. These net forces are then used in Newton's second law of motion to give the accelerations, which are then integrated to give a numerical trajectory. The trajectory provides a complete description of the system, giving the position and velocity of every atom as a function of time. It is remarkable that simple forces and classical mechanics seem to give such a faithful picture of molecular motion.

In summary, many doubts and suspicions exist in understanding of the genetic language. How was life information accumulated and evolved in the DNA sequence? How can we understand the possible function of the large amount of nongenic DNA in the genome and extract life information from the DNA sequence under the background of strong noises? What principle governs the functional networks in a genome? How can we predict the molecular structure from its sequence information?

REFERENCES

Adams, C. (1994). *The Knot Book: An Elementary Introduction to Mathematical Theory of Knots*. New York: W.H. Freeman.

Alexander, J. W. (1928). Topological invariants of knots and links. *Trans. Amer. Math. Soc.*, **30**(2), 275–306.

Altman, R. B., and Jardetzky, O. (1989). The heuristic refinement method for the determination of the solution structure of proteins from NMR data. In: N. J. Oppenheimer and T. L. James (Eds.), *Nuclear Magnetic Resonance*, Part B: *Structure and Mechanisms*. Methods in Enzymology, Vol. **177**. New York: Academic Press, pp. 218–246.

Altman, R. B., Arrowsmith, C., Pachter, R., and Jardetzky, O. (1991). Determination of large protein structures from NMR data: definition of the solution structure of the trp repressor. In: J. C. Hoch, F. M. Poulsen, and C. Redfield (Eds.), *Computational Aspects of the Study of Biological Macromolecules by NMR Spectroscopy*. New York: Plenum, Press, pp. 363–374.

Bauer, W. R. (1978). Structure and reactions of closed duplex data. *Annu. Rev. Biophys. Bioeng.*, **7**, 287–313.

Boles, T. C., White, J. H., and Cozzarelli, N. R. (1990). Structure of plectonemically supercoiled DNA. *J. Mol. Biol.*, **213**, 931–951.

Burde, G., and Zieschang, H. (1985). *Knots*. New York: deGruyter.

Cozzarelli, N. R. (1980). DNA gyrase and the supercoiling of DNA. *Science*, **207**, 953–960.

DeGrado, W. F., Wasserman, Z. R., and Lear, J. D. (1989). Protein design, a minimalist approach. *Science*, **243**, 622–628.

Depew, R. E., and Wang, J. C. (1975). Conformational fluctuations of DNA helix. *Proc. Natl. Acad. Sci. USA*, **72**, 4275–4279.

Dickerson, R. E. (1989). Definitions and nomenclature of nucleic acid structure components. *Nucleic Acids Res.*, **17**(5), 1797–1803.

Klevit, R. E. (1991). Recognition of DNA by Cys2, His2 zinc fingers. *Science*, **253**(5026), 1367, 1393.

Lee, M. S., Gottesfeld, J. M., and Wright, P. E. (1991). Zinc is required for folding and binding of a single zinc finger to DNA. *FEBS Lett.*, **279**(2), 289–294.

Rolfsen, D. (1976). *Knots and Links*, Berkeley, CA: Publish or Perish.

Schubert, H. (1949). Sitzungsber. *Heidelb. Akad. Wiss. Math.-Naturwiss. Klasse*, **3**.

Summers, M. F. (1991). Zinc finger motif for single-stranded nucleic acids? Investigations by nuclear magnetic resonance. *J. Cell. Biochem.*, **45**(1), 41–48.

Sumners, D. W. (1987). The role of knot theory in DNA research. In: C. McCrory and T. Shifrin (Eds.), *Geometry and Topology*. New York: Marcel Dekker, pp. 297–318.

Sumners, D. W. (1990). Untangling DNA. *Math. Intelligencer*, **12**, 71–80.

Sumners, D. W. (Ed.) (1992). *Knot Theory and DNA: New Scientific Applications of Geometry and Topology* (Proc. Symp. Appl. Math., Vol. 45). Providence RI: American Mathematical Society.

Travers, A. A., and Klug, A. (1987). The bending of DNA in nucleosomes and its wider implications. *Philos. Trans. R. Soc. Lond. B*, **317**, 537–561.

Wang, J. C., Peck, L. F., and Becherer, K. (1983). DNA supercoiling and its effects on DNA structure and function. *Quant. Biol.*, **47**, 85–91.

Wasserman, S. A., and Cozzarelli, N. R. (1986). Biochemical topology: applications to DNA recombination and replication. *Science*, **232**, 951–960.

White, J. H. (1969). Self-linking and the Gauss integral in higher dimensions. *Am. J. Math.*, **91**, 693–728.

White, J. H., Millett, K. C., and Cozzarelli, N. R. (1987). Description of the topological entanglement of DNA catenanes and knots by a powerful method involving strand passage and recombination. *J. Mol. Biol.*, **197**, 585–603.

White, J. H., Cozzarelli, N. R., and Bauer, W. R. (1988). Helical repeat and linking number of surface-wrapped DNA. *Science*, **241**, 323–327.

5 Protein Structures, Geometry, and Topology

Proteins play crucial roles in almost every biological process. They are responsible in one form or another for a variety of physiological functions. They function as catalysts, they transport and store other molecules (e.g., oxygen), they provide mechanical support and immune protection, they generate movement, they transmit nerve impulses, and they control growth and differentiation. Proteins are linear polymers built of monomer units called *amino acids*. The construction of a vast array of macromolecules from a limited number of monomer building blocks is a recurring theme in biochemistry. Does protein function depend on the linear sequence of amino acids? The function of a protein is directly dependent on its three-dimensional structure. Remarkably, proteins fold up spontaneously into three-dimensional structures that are determined by the sequence of amino acids in the protein polymer. Thus, proteins are the embodiment of the transition from the one-dimensional world of sequences to the three-dimensional world of molecules capable of diverse activities.

In this chapter we introduce protein primary structures, secondary structures, tertiary structure, and quaternary structure by geometric means. We also discuss the classification of proteins, physical forces in proteins, protein motion (folding and unfolding), and basic methods for secondary structure and tertiary structure prediction.

5.1 INTRODUCTION

A protein comprises a sequence of amino acids, which are the building blocks of proteins. There are 20 amino acids that commonly appear in proteins. Recently, a twenty-first naturally occurring amino acid was found (Atkins and Gesteland, 2002). Each amino acid is represented by one or more sequences of three RNA nucleotides, known as a *codon* or *triplet*. The combination of four possible nucleotides in groups of three yields 64 codons. Amino acids are coded by more than one codon. An *organelle* performs the translation of

Mathematics of Bioinformatics: Theory, Practice, and Applications, By Matthew He and Sergey Petoukhov
Copyright © 2011 John Wiley & Sons, Inc.

mRNA into proteins. The process of translation is coordinated by start and stop codons. *Start codons* signal the location on the RNA molecule where translation should begin, while *stop codons* signal the location where the translation should terminate. Once the chain of amino acids that made up a particular protein is assembled, the protein disassociates from the organelle and folds into a specific three-dimensional structure. The chain of several amino acids is referred to as a *peptide*. Longer chains are often called *polypeptides* or *proteins*. Proteins are synthesized as linear polymers (chains). The order of the amino acids in a protein's primary sequence plays an important role in determining its secondary structure and, ultimately, its tertiary structure. The sequence of amino acids that comprises a protein completely determines its three–dimensional shape, its physical and chemical properties, and ultimately, its biological function. Proteins perform a variety of functions in the cell, covering all aspects of cellular functions, from metabolism to growth to division. Most proteins are fully biologically active when folded into their native globular structure, and understanding the forces behind this process is one of the most important questions in biology.

In this chapter we present the basic concepts of geometry and topology, followed by protein primary structures, secondary structures, tertiary structure, and quaternary structure by geometric means. We also discuss the classification of proteins, physical forces in proteins, protein motion (folding and unfolding), and basic methods (optimization and statistical methods) for secondary structure and tertiary structure prediction.

5.2 COMPUTATIONAL GEOMETRY AND TOPOLOGY PRELIMINARIES

Computational Geometry

Computational geometry is the study of efficient algorithms to solve geometric problems, such as: Given N points in a plane, what is the fastest way to find the nearest neighbor of a point? Given N straight lines, find the lines that intersect. Computational geometry emerged from the field of algorithm design and analysis in the late 1970s. It has grown into a recognized discipline. The success of the field as a research discipline can, on the one hand, be explained by the beauty of the problems studied and the solutions obtained, and, on the other hand, by the many application domains—computer graphics, geographic information systems, robotics, proteins, and others—in which geometric algorithms play a fundamental role.

The connections and interactions between molecular modeling and computational geometry have been growing recently. Many questions in molecular modeling can be understood geometrically in terms of arrangements of spheres in three dimensions. Problems include computing properties of such arrangements, such as their volume and topology, testing intersections and collisions between molecules, finding offset surfaces, data structures for computing interatomic forces and performing molecular dynamics simulations, and computer graphic algorithms for rendering molecular models accurately and efficiently. Computational geometry can also be used as a tool for studying topology and architecture of macromolecules and macromolecular complexes. Here we introduce briefly the common terms and algorithmic problems in computational geometry. Detailed descriptions may be found in Skiena (2008).

Polygon   A *polygon* is a collection of line segments that form a cycle and do not cross each other. A polygon can be represented as a sequence of points. For example, the points

$$(0,0), \quad (0,1), \quad (1,1), \quad (1,0)$$

form a square. The line segments of the polygon connect adjacent points in the list, together with one additional segment connecting the first and last points. A *simple polygon* is one in which no two segments cross. A *convex polygon* is one in which any two points inside the polygon can be connected by a line segment that does not cross the polygons. The smallest convex polygon containing a collection of points is known as a *convex hull*.

Convex Hull   The *convex hull* of a set of points S in n dimensions is the intersection of all convex sets containing S. Finding the convex hull of a set of points is *the* most elementarily interesting problem in computational geometry, just as the minimum spanning tree is the most elementarily interesting problem in graph algorithms. It arises because the hull quickly captures a rough idea of the shape or extent of a data set. Convex hull also serves as a first preprocessing step to many, if not most, geometric algorithms. For example, consider the problem of finding the diameter of a set of points, which is the pair of points a maximum distance apart. The diameter will always be the distance between two points on the convex hull. The convex hull representation has recently been used for supervised classification of protein structures (Wang et al., 2006a,b, 2008). Specifically, the novel patterns based on convex hull representation are first extracted from a protein structure, then the classification system is constructed and machine learning methods such as neural networks and hidden Markov models are employed (Wang et al., 2008).

Triangulation   *Triangulation* is the division of a surface or plane polygon into a set of triangles, usually with the restriction that each triangle side is shared entirely by two adjacent triangles. Triangulation is a fundamental problem in computational geometry, because the first step in working with complicated geometric objects is to break them into simple geometric objects. The simplest geometric objects are triangles in two dimensions, and tetrahedra in three. Classical applications of triangulation include finite-element analysis and computer graphics. Recently, triangulation has been applied to computation of a molecular surface (Ryu et al., 2007a,b, 2009). A molecular surface is used for both the visualization of a molecule and the computation of various molecular properties, such as the area and volume of a protein, which are important for studying problems such as protein docking and folding.

Voronoi Diagram   *Voronoi diagrams* represent the region of influence around each of a given set of sites. Given a set S of points $p_1, \ldots, p_n$, Voronoi diagrams decompose the space into regions around each point, such that all the points in the region around p_i are closer to p_i than to any other point in S. It involves partitioning a plane with points into convex polygons such that each polygon contains exactly one generating point, and every point in a given polygon is closer to its generating point than to any other. A Voronoi diagram is sometimes known as a *Dirichlet tessellation*. The cells are called *Dirichlet regions*, *Thiessen polytopes*, or *Voronoi polygons*. Voronoi diagrams have been used to compute molecular surfaces on proteins (Ryu et al., 2007a,b).

Nearest-Neighbor Search   *Nearest-neighbor search* (or *similarity search*) is a search to quickly find the nearest neighbor of a query point; that is, given a set S of n points in d dimensions and a query point q, which point in S is closest to q? Nearest-neighbor search is important in classification. Such nearest-neighbor classifiers are widely used, often in high-dimensional spaces. The vector-quantization method of image compression partitions an image into 8×8 pixel regions. This method uses a predetermined library of several thousand 8×8 pixel tiles and replaces each image region by the most similar library tile. The most similar tile is the point in 64-dimensional space that is closest to the image region in question. Compression is achieved by reporting the identifier of the closest library tile instead of the 64 pixels, at some loss of image fidelity. The nearest-neighbor search has been used to approximate the protein structure (Lotan and Schwarzer, 2004).

Polygon Partitioning   *Polygon partitioning* is an important preprocessing step for many geometric algorithms, because most geometric problems are simpler and faster on convex objects than on nonconvex objects. Given a polygon or polyhedron P, how can P be partitioned into a small number of simple (typically, convex) pieces? It is easier to work with the pieces independently than with the original object.

Shape Similarity   *Shape similarity* is a problem that underlies much of pattern recognition. Given two polygonal shapes, P_1 and P_2, how similar are P_1 and P_2? Definition of similarity is application dependent. There is no single algorithmic approach that can solve all shape-matching problems. Consider a system for optical character recognition (OCR). We have a known library of shape models representing letters and the unknown shapes we obtain by scanning a page. We seek to identify an unknown shape by matching it to the most similar shape model. The shape similarity measures are widely used in protein structure comparison and prediction (Lotan and Schwarzer, 2004; Sael et al., 2008).

Topology

Topology is a branch of mathematics that can be defined as the study of qualitative properties of certain objects (called *topological spaces*) that are invariant under certain types of transformations (called *continuous maps*), especially those properties that are invariant under a certain type of equivalence (called *homeomorphism*). The mathematical definition of topology is described briefly here.

Let **X** be any set and let *T* be a family of subsets of **X**. Then *T* is a topology on **X** if:

- Both the empty set and **X** are elements of *T*.
- Any union of arbitrarily many elements of *T* is an element of *T*.
- Any intersection of finitely many elements of *T* is an element of *T*.

If *T* is a topology on **X**, then **X** together with *T* is called a *topological space*.

All sets in *T* are called *open*; note that in general not all subsets of **X** need be in *T*. A subset of **X** is said to be *closed* if its complement is in *T* (i.e., it is open). A subset of **X** may be open, closed, both, or neither.

A function or map from one topological space to another is called *continuous* if the inverse image of any open set is open. If the function maps the real numbers to the real numbers (both spaces with the standard topology), this definition of continuous is equivalent to the definition of continuous in calculus. If a continuous function is one-to-one and onto and if the inverse of the function is also continuous, the function is called a *homeomorphism* and the domain of the function is said to be *homeomorphic* to the range. Another way of saying this is that the function has a natural extension to the topology. If two spaces are homeomorphic, they have identical topological properties and are considered to be topologically the same. A cube and a sphere are homeomorphic, as are a coffee cup and a doughnut. But the circle is not homeomorphic to the doughnut. DNA topology and protein topology are active research areas.

Mathematical Space   *Mathematical space* is an informal term for any of many different types of sets with added structure. Mathematical spaces often form a hierarchy (i.e., one space may inherit all the characteristics of a parent space). For example, all inner product spaces are also normed vector spaces, all normed vector spaces are also metric spaces, and all metric spaces are topological spaces, because the inner product induces a norm on the inner product space such that

$$\|x\| = \sqrt{<x, x>}$$

and so on.

Mathematical Optimization   In mathematics programming, an *optimization problem* is a problem of finding the *best* solution from all feasible solutions. More formally, an optimization problem has the general form

$$\min_{x \in S} f(x) \quad \text{or} \quad \max_{x \in S} f(x) \tag{5.1}$$

where:

- $f(x)$ is a real-valued function defined on the space R^n, called an *objective function*.
- S is a subset of the space R^n, called a *feasible set*.
- The points x^* in S are called *feasible*.

A point x^* in S is said to be a local minimum of the $f(x)$ if

$$f(x^*) \le f(x), \forall x \in S \cap \{x, \|x - x^*\| < \delta, \delta > 0\} \tag{5.2}$$

A point x^* in S is said to be a global minimum of the function $f(x)$ if

$$f(x^*) \le f(x) \quad \forall x \in S \tag{5.3}$$

Local and global maximum points can be defined similarly. Maximization and minimization are related by the relation

$$\max\{f(x), \forall x \in S\} = -\min\{-f(x), \forall x \in S\} \tag{5.4}$$

Therefore, any maximization problem can be converted into an equivalent minimization problem, and vice versa.

5.3 PROTEIN STRUCTURES AND PREDICTION

In this section we begin with a discussion on amino acids and present their three-dimensional geometric shapes. We introduce protein primary, secondary, tertiary, and quaternary structure by geometric means.

Chemical Structure of Amino Acids

We first present the chemical structure of 20 amino acids. Each amino acid contains an amino group NH_2 and the carboxyl group $COOH$. The NH_2 group is a proton acceptor with the following equilibrium at pH 7:

$$RNH_2 + H_2O \leftrightarrow RNH_3^- + OH^- \tag{5.5}$$

The COOH group is a proton donator with the following equilibrium at pH 7:

$$RCO_2H + H_2O \leftrightarrow RNH_3^- + OH^- \tag{5.6}$$

Protein Shape Representation

A protein can be viewed as a set of its individual atoms. Each atom type can be modeled as a sphere of a given radius. The radii are restricted to a relatively small interval, and the minimal distances between the centers of these atomic spheres are also restricted. This volumetric representation is important in studying the protein-to-protein interaction. The computational geometry plays important roles in dealing with intersection and location queries (Halperin and Overmars, 1998).

A protein can also be viewed as a folded three-dimensional curve of amino acids (polypeptide chain) (Lesk, 2001). A molecule made up of amino acids is needed for the body to function properly. Proteins are an important class of biological macromolecules present in all biological organisms, made up of such elements as carbon, hydrogen, nitrogen, phosphorus, oxygen, and sulfur. All proteins are polymers of amino acids. Proteins are the basis of body structures such as skin and hair and of substances such as enzymes and antibodies. Proteins fold in three dimensions. Protein structure is organized hierarchically from primary structure to quaternary structure. Higher-level structures are *motifs* and *domains*. Protein structures are commonly grouped into four levels of structure:

1. *Primary structure.* The amino acid sequence of the peptide chains (Figure 5.1). The primary structure is held together by covalent or peptide bonds, which are made during the process of protein biosynthesis or translation. These peptide bonds provide rigidity to a protein. The two ends of the amino acid chain are referred to as the *C-terminal end* or *carboxyl terminus* (C-terminus) and the *N-terminal end* or *amino terminus* (N-terminus) based on the nature of the free group on each extremity.

2. *Secondary structure.* Highly regular substructures (α-*helix* and *strands of* β-*sheet*; Figure 5.2), which are locally defined, meaning that there can be many different secondary motifs present in a single protein molecule.

3. *Tertiary structure.* Three-dimensional structure of a single protein molecule; a spatial arrangement of the secondary structures (Figure 5.3). It also describes the completely folded and compacted polypeptide chain.

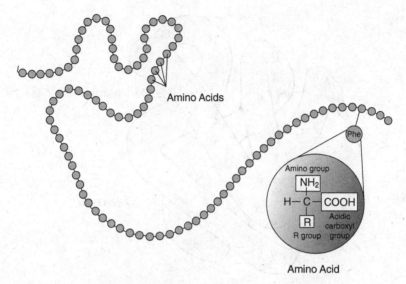

FIGURE 5.1   Primary structure of a protein.

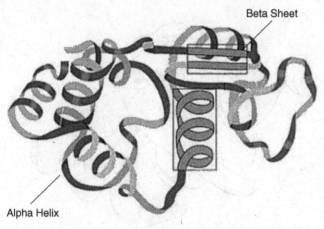

FIGURE 5.2   Secondary structure of protein.

4. *Quaternary structure.* Complex of several protein molecules or polypeptide chains (Figure 5.4), usually called *protein subunits* in this context, which function as part of the larger assembly or protein complex.

In addition to these levels of structure, a protein may shift between several similar structures in performing its biological function. This process is also reversible. In the context of these functional rearrangements, tertiary or quaternary structures are usually referred to as *chemical conformation*, and transitions between them are called *conformational changes.*

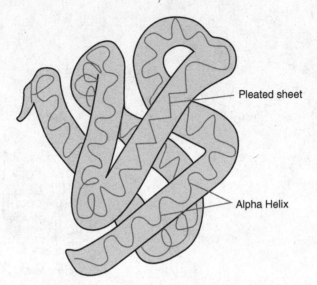

FIGURE 5.3   Tertiary structure of protein.

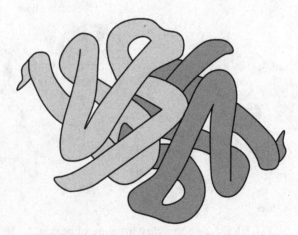

FIGURE 5.4   Quaternary structure of protein.

Protein Motion (Folding and Unfolding)

Folding and unfolding is an exciting area of geometry. It is attractive in the way that problems and even results can easily be understood, with little knowledge of mathematics or computer science, yet the solutions are difficult and involve many sophisticated techniques. The general sort of problem considered is how a particular object (e.g., linkage, piece of paper, polyhedron, protein) can be reconfigured or *folded* according to a few constraints, which depend on the object being folded and the problem of interest. In particular,

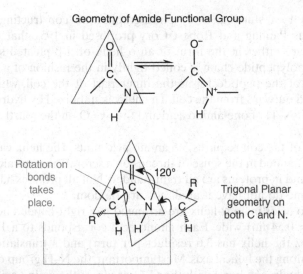

Geometry of Amide Functional Group

Rotation on bonds takes place.

120°

Trigonal Planar geometry on both C and N.

FIGURE 5.5   Planar triangle geometry of the carbonyl unit (C=O).

we are interested in efficient algorithms for characterizing fold ability and finding efficient folding processes, or in proving that such algorithms are impossible. Most folding and unfolding problems are attractive from a pure mathematical standpoint, from the beauty of the problems themselves. Nonetheless, most of the problems have close connections to important industrial applications. Linkage folding has applications in robotics and hydraulic tube bending, and has connections to protein folding.

Secondary Structure Prediction

The purpose of secondary protein structure prediction is to locate all α-helices and β-strands within a protein. The secondary structures of a protein are formed by short- and long-ranging interactions during the protein's folding process. This can be viewed as the specific geometric shape caused by intra-molecular and intermolecular hydrogen bonding of amide groups. The geometry assumed by the protein chain is directly related to molecular geometry concepts of hybridization theory. Experimental evidence shows that the amide unit is a rigid planar structure. This is derived from the planar triangle geometry of the carbonyl unit (C=O) (Figure 5.5).

The geometry around the nitrogen is derived from an unusual situation with planar triangle geometry. Apparently, the double bond on oxygen can alternate to make a double bond between carbon and nitrogen. Rotation around bonds C–C and N–C does take place. The C=O and NH are always in a rigid plane. Notice that the carbonyl group and the hydrogen on nitrogen are almost always *trans* to each other. The result is that chains of amino acids as peptides with amide bonds reflect this geometry.

As a result of studying x-ray photographs and constructing molecular models, Linus Pauling and Robert Cory proposed in 1951 that the protein structures were either in the form of an α-helix or a β-pleated sheet. In an *α-helix*, the polypeptide chain is coiled tightly in the fashion of a spring. The "backbone" of the peptide forms the inner part of the coil, while the side chains extend outward from the coil. The helix is stabilized by hydrogen bonds between the >N–H of one amino acid and the >C=O on the fourth amino acid away from it.

One turn of the coil requires 3.6 amino acid units. The helix can be either right- or left-handed in the sense of threads on a screw. The naturally occurring α-helixes found in proteins are all right-handed. Not all proteins have a helical structure; some do not have it at all and are random.

The amino acids in an α-helix are arranged in a right-handed helical structure, 5.4 Å (= 0.54 nm) wide. Each amino acid corresponds to a 100° turn in the helix (i.e., the helix has 3.6 residues per turn) and a translation of 1.5 Å (= 0.15 nm) along the helical axis. Most important, the N–H group of an amino acid forms a hydrogen bond with the C=O group of the amino acid *four* residues earlier; this repeated hydrogen bonding defines an α-helix. Similar structures include the 3_{10} helix (hydrogen bonding) and the π-helix (hydrogen bonding). These alternative helices are relatively rare, although the 3_{10} helix is often found at the ends of α-helices, "closing" them off. Transient helices (sometimes called δ-helices) have also been reported as intermediates in molecular dynamics simulations of α-helical folding.

Residues in α-helices typically adopt backbone (φ, ψ) dihedral angles around (−60°, −45°). More generally, they adopt dihedral angles such that the ψ dihedral angle of one residue and the φ dihedral angle of the *next* residue sum to roughly −105°. Consequently, α-helical dihedral angles generally fall on a diagonal stripe on the Ramachandran plot (of slope −1), ranging from (−90°, −15°) to (−35°, −70°). For comparison, the sum of the dihedral angles for a 3_{10} helix is roughly −75°, whereas that for the π-helix is roughly −130°. The general formula for the rotation angle Ω per residue of any polypeptide helix with *trans* isomers is given by the equation

$$3\cos\Omega = 1 - \cos^2 \frac{\phi + \psi}{2} \qquad (5.7)$$

The α-helix is tightly packed; there is almost no free space within the helix.

The β-*sheet* (also β-*pleated sheet*) is the second form of regular secondary structure in proteins, consisting of β-strands connected laterally by three or more hydrogen bonds, forming a generally twisted, pleated sheet (the most common form of regular secondary structure in proteins is the α-helix). A β-*strand* is a stretch of amino acids, typically 5 to 10 amino acids long, whose peptide backbones are almost fully extended.

The majority of β-strands are arranged adjacent to other strands and form an extensive hydrogen bond network with their neighbors in which the N–H groups in the backbone of one strand establish hydrogen bonds with the C=O groups in the backbone of the adjacent strands. In the fully extended β-strand, successive side chains point straight up, then straight down, then straight up, and so on. Adjacent β-strands in a β-sheet are aligned so that their C^α atoms are adjacent and their side chains point in the same direction.

However, β-strands are rarely perfectly extended; rather, they exhibit a slight twist due to the chirality of their component amino acids. The energetically preferred dihedral angles $(\varphi, \psi) = (-135°, 135°)$ diverge somewhat from the fully extended conformation $(\varphi, \psi) = (-180°, 180°)$ (Voet and Voet, 2004). The twist is often associated with alternating fluctuations in the dihedral angles to prevent the individual β-strands in a larger sheet from splaying apart. A good example of such a twisted β-hairpin can be seen in the protein BPTI. The side chains point outward from the folds of the pleats, roughly perpendicularly to the plane of the sheet; successive residues point outward on alternating faces of the sheet.

Information-Theoretic Method of Protein Secondary Structure Prediction

The prediction of protein secondary structure from its amino acid sequence can be considered as the problem of finding the correlation between the two objects. It can be studied in the framework of information theory. The amino acid sequence can be regarded as an information source. The corresponding secondary structure can be considered as an information receiver. For an amino acid sequence of length N, one can construct a secondary structure sequence of the same length written by three letters α, β, and c following the one-to-one correspondence between residue and secondary structure.

Let $p(a_i)$ be the probability of structure a_i in the secondary structure sequence $(a_i = \alpha, \beta, c)$ and let $p(s_i)$ be the probability of amino acid s_i in the protein $(j = 1, 2, \ldots, 20)$. Define average mutual information

$$I(X;Y) = H(X) - H(X|Y) = -\sum_i p(a_i)\log p(a_i) + \sum_i \sum_j p(s_i)p(a_i|s_i)\log p(a_i|s_i)$$

$$(5.8)$$

Similarly, we can also define

$$I(Y;X) = H(Y) - H(Y|X) = -\sum_j p(s_j)\log p(s_i) + \sum_i \sum_j p(a_i)p(s_i|a_i)\log p(s_i|a_i)$$

It is easy to prove that

$$I(X;Y) = I(Y;X)$$

The maximum of $H(X|Y)$ is $H(X)$, which corresponds to no correlation between X and Y. So the correlation between secondary structure (X) and amino acid (Y) is defined by

$$r_1 = \frac{I(X;Y)}{H(X)} \qquad (a_i = \alpha, \beta, c; s_j = A, C, \ldots, W, Y) \qquad (5.9)$$

where r_1 takes values between 0 and 1:

- $r_1 = 0$ indicates no correlation.
- $r_1 = 1$ the full determination of secondary structure by amino acid, which occurs in the case of $p(a_i|s_j) = 0$ or 1 for all a_i and s_j.

The single peptide-structure correspondence can easily be extended to dipeptide (tripeptide)-structure correspondence through residue numeration by shifting a window of width 2 (3). The equations above can be generalized in these cases. For the case of dipeptide-structure correspondence, a_i takes nine confirmations:

$$\alpha\alpha, \alpha\beta, \alpha c, \beta\alpha, \beta\beta, \beta c, c\alpha, c\beta, cc$$

s_j takes 400 dipeptides in the equations above; that is,

$$AA, AC, \ldots, WY, YY$$

The correlation between secondary structure and neighboring dipeptide can be defined by

$$r_2 = \frac{I(X;Y)}{H(X)} \qquad (5.10)$$

The correlation between secondary structure and tripeptide can be defined by

$$r_3 = \frac{I(X;Y)}{H(X)} \qquad (a_i = \alpha\alpha\alpha, \alpha\alpha\beta, \ldots, ccc; \quad s_j = AAA, AAC, \ldots, WYY, YYYY)$$

$$(5.11)$$

It can be demonstrated that the correlation of protein secondary structure with dipeptide frequency is much stronger than that with a single peptide and the correlation with tripeptide frequency is much stronger than that with a dipeptide. Therefore, the prediction of protein secondary structure from dipeptide and tripeptide distribution is a better approach than single-peptide prediction. Thus, the information-theoretic approach provides a method to estimate the efficiency of a structural prediction. The averaged mutual information $I(X;Y)$ is a useful quantity for the estimate.

Tertiary Structure Prediction

According to a protein's tertiary structure, proteins can be divided into globular and fibrous proteins. *Globular proteins* are nearly spherical. All enzymes are globular. Proteins are predominantly globular. *Fibrous proteins* contain a variety of structure proteins and normally exhibit regularities in their primary structures. These regularities are generally so strong that the native conformations of structural proteins are much easier to characterize than those of globular proteins. The conformational search of the global minimum energy conformation of a protein *ab initio* from the amino acid sequence is one of the greatest challenges in computational biology.

A challenge in the area of computational biology has been to develop a method to theoretically predict the correct three-dimensional structure of a protein *ab initio* from the primary structure. The two most common approaches to the problem of predicting protein structure from sequence would be either to search the native structure of the protein among the entire conformational space available to the polypeptide, or to simulate the folding process in detail.

The former appears to be beyond our reach. Even the structures of small organic molecules cannot be generated using algorithmic implementations of the laws of physics for atomic interactions. Full atom protein folding simulations are completely beyond current computational resources. Short simulations from the folded state, known as *molecular dynamics simulations*, are possible but do not accurately recreate the behavior of folded proteins in solution.

Exhaustive conformational search is also out of reach; the number of possible conformations is immense and would take too long to explore either computationally or in vivo during folding (Levinthal, 1968). In an attempt to reduce the search space, a common approach is to use a simplified polypeptide representation and restrain atom or residue positions to a lattice (Dill et al., 1995). Folding or conformational search experiments are rarely successful, even for small proteins.

Potential Energy Surface Defined by Force Fields

Let's consider a molecule with N atoms. The position of the ith atom is denoted by the vector x_i. We describe the potential energy surface of a protein by molecular mechanics. Molecular mechanics states that the potential energy of a protein can be approximated by the potential energy of the nuclei. Therefore, the energy contribution of the electrons is neglected. This approximation allows one to write the potential energy of a protein as a function of the nuclear coordinates. A typical molecular modeling force field contains five types of potentials. These potentials correspond to deformation of covalent bond length and bond angles, torsional motion associated with rotation about bonds, electrostatic interaction, and van der Waals interaction.

$$V(x) = V_{\text{length}} + V_{\text{angle}} + V_{\text{torsion}} + V_{\text{electrostatic}} + V_{\text{weak}} \tag{5.12}$$

The potential energy $V = V(x)$ is a function of the atomic coordinate x of the molecule. The distance is measured in angstroms (Å), energy in kilocalories per mole (kcal/mol), and mass in the atomic mass unit, the dalton (Da). The bond length potential is given by

$$V_{\text{length}} = \sum_{i,j \text{ bonds}} k_0 (r_{ij} - r_0)^2 \tag{5.13}$$

where $r_{ij} = \|x_i - x_j\|$ is the bond length, r_0 the reference bond length, and k_0 a force constant. Reference bond lengths and force constants depend on the bond type. The bond potential corresponds to covalent bond deformation. The bond length deformations are sufficiently small at ordinary temperatures and in the absence of chemical reactions. The bond deformation energy between the ith and jth atoms is given by a harmonic potential,

$$k_0 (r_{ij} - r_0)^2$$

The bond angle potential is given by

$$V_{\text{angle}} = \sum_{\theta \text{ angle}} k_0 (\theta - \theta_0)^2 \tag{5.14}$$

where θ_0 is the reference bond angle and k_0 is a force constant, both of which depend on the type of atom involved. The angle θ between the bonds $p = x_j - x_i$ and $r = x_k - x_j$ is given by

$$\cos \theta = \frac{p \cdot r}{\|p\|\|r\|}, \qquad \theta \in [0, \pi] \tag{5.15}$$

The bond angle potential corresponds to angle deformation. Bond angle deformations are sufficiently small at ordinary temperatures and in the absence of chemical reactions.

The potentials for bond length and bond angle deformation are considered as the hard degrees of freedom in a molecular system in the sense that considerable energy is necessary to cause significant deformation from their reference values. The most variation in structure and relative energy comes from the remaining potential energy terms.

The torsion potential corresponds to the barriers of bond rotation, which involves the dihedral angles of the rotatable bonds. The barriers of torsion can be expressed as a series of cosine functions. The mathematical expression for the torsion potential is given by

$$V_{\text{torsion}} = \sum_{\theta::\text{dihedral}} |k_0| - k_0 \cos (n_0 \theta)^2 \tag{5.16}$$

where n_0 is the multiplicity of the angle and k_0 is a force constant, both of which depend on the type of atoms involved. The dihedral angle θ can be obtained from

$$\cos\theta = \frac{|(p \times r) \cdot (r \times q)|}{\|p \times r\| \|r \times q\|}, \qquad \theta \in [-\pi, \pi] \tag{5.17}$$

where

$$p = x_j - x_i, \qquad r = x_k - x_j, \qquad q = x_l - x_k$$

and the sign of the angle θ is given by the sign of the inner product $(p \times q) \cdot r$. The complementary angle $\pi - \theta$ is the torsion angle of the bond, $x_j - x_k$.

The electrostatic potential corresponds to the nonbounded interaction between the charged atoms in a molecule. The interaction is attractive when the charges have opposite sign and repulsive when the charges have the same sign. The electrostatic potential of a molecule is given by

$$V_{\text{electrostatic}} = \sum_{\substack{i<j \\ \text{atoms}}} \frac{q_i q_j}{4\pi\delta_0 r_{ij}} \tag{5.18}$$

where q_i is the point charge of the ith atom, δ_0 is the dielectric constant of vacuum, and r_{ij} is the distance between the ith and jth atoms.

The van der Waals potential corresponds to the interaction between non-bounded atoms in a molecule. This interaction comes from attractive and repulsive forces. The van der Waals potential is given by

$$V_{\text{weak}} = \sum_{\substack{i<j \\ \text{atoms}}} \left(\frac{A_{ij}}{r_{ij}^{12}} - \frac{B_{ij}}{r_{ij}^{6}} \right) \tag{5.19}$$

where A_{ij} and B_{ij} are given by

$$A_{ij} = \frac{1}{2} B_{ij} (R_i + R_j)^6$$

$$B_{ij} = \frac{3}{2} \frac{1}{\sqrt{4\pi\delta_0}} \frac{1}{\sqrt{m_e}} \frac{e\hbar\alpha_i\alpha_j}{\sqrt{\alpha_i/N_i} + \sqrt{\alpha_j/N_j}}$$

where e is the electron charge, $\hbar$ the reduced Planck constant, m_e the electron mass, α_i the polarizability of the ith atom, N_i the effective number of outer shell electrons in the ith atom, and R_i the van der Waals radius of the ith atom.

Conformational Search Methods

The conformational search of the global minimum energy surface of a protein from the amino acid sequence is one of the challenging problems in bioinformatics. In recent years, several optimization approaches to solve this problem have appeared in the literature. The most common approach is to model the protein surface by using a force field. Among the most commonly used force fields are CHARMM, developed by Brooks et al. (1983). Conformational search based on force fields can be approached by the global optimization techniques of Horst and Pardalos (1994). These methods are currently better suited for lower-dimensional problems. For higher-dimensional problems, one of the most successful optimization techniques for conformational search is conformational space annealing (CSA), introduced by Lee et al. (1997). CSA has been designed to search a large portion of the potential energy surface. It is an iterative algorithm maintaining local minimum energy conformations in each iteration of a population. It has been applied successfully to proteins with 100 to 150 residues (Scheraga, 1996). It is currently one of the leading conformational search algorithms. The protein conformation generation can be found at http://www.bbmb.iastate.edu/jerniganresearch.shtml.

The *smoothing method*, also known as the *diffusion equation method*, invented by Kostrowicki et al. (1991) [see also Kostrowicki and Scheraga (1992)] is another useful technique for conformational search. This method can be used to approximate the potential energy surface such that the number of local minima largely decreases while the deepest local minimum is retained. When a force field is smoothed such that the potentials for bond lengths and bond angles are smoothed as well, the entire molecular structure will become a single point. Comprehensive coverage of smoothing various potentials is available in a book by Zimmermann (2003). The general scheme is to define a smooth operator that is linear where each term of the potential can be smoothed separately. For example, the exponential operator is given by

$$\Psi_t = \exp\left(t \frac{d^2}{dx^2} \right) \tag{5.20}$$

This smooth operator is linear and transforms polynomial functions into polynomial functions of the same degree. For example,

$$\Psi_t x^4 = x^4 + 12x^2 t + 12t^2 \tag{5.21}$$

Here we describe the process of smoothing the torsion potential of a protein. Let's recall that the torsion potential of a protein is expressed as a linear combination of cosine terms of dihedral angles (5.3). To smooth this potential, we express the dihedral angles by distances. We assume that bond lengths and bond angles are fixed to their reference values. Then the cosine of a dihedral angle θ can be expressed by the distance $r = \|x_l - x_i\|$ of the first and last of the atoms involved:

$$\cos\theta = \alpha + \beta r^2$$

where α and β are constants depending on the reference bond lengths and reference bond angles. In general, $\cos n\theta$ of a multiple dihedral angle can be represented as a Chebyshev polynomial in $\cos\theta$, which is a polynomial in r^2.

Let $x = \cos\theta$; then the Chebyshev polynomials can be written as

$$T_n(x) = \cos n\theta = \cos(n \arccos x) \tag{5.22}$$

Furthermore, we have

$$T_n(x) = \cos n\theta = T_n(\alpha + \beta r^2) \tag{5.23}$$

Consequentially, the torsion potential can be expressed as a linear combination of Chebyshev polynomials:

$$V_{\text{torsion}} = \sum_{\theta::\text{dihedral}} |k_0| - k_0 T_n(\alpha + \beta r^2) \tag{5.24}$$

Each term is a polynomial in r^2, so the torsion potential $V_{\text{torsion}}(x)$ can be smoothed by the linear operator Ψ_t,

$$\tilde{V}_{\text{torsion}}(x, t) = \Psi_t V_{\text{torsion}}(x) \tag{5.25}$$

The potential energy surface of a protein and the smoothed potential energy surface of a protein are illustrated in (Figures 5.6 and 5.7).

FIGURE 5.6 Potential energy surface of protein.

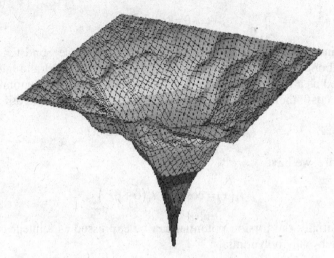

FIGURE 5.7 Smoothed potential energy surface of protein.

5.4 STATISTICAL APPROACH AND DISCUSSION

The objective of conformational search is to find all preferred conformations of a molecule. An alternative to conformational search is fold recognition. Proteins may have similar tertiary structures even if their primary structures are not sufficiently similar or different. This observation has led to the hypothesis that there are only a limited number of significantly distinct tertiary structures. The main goal of fold recognition is to predict the tertiary structure of a protein from its amino acid sequence by finding the best match between the amino acid sequence and some tertiary structure in a protein database (Figure 5.8).

A basic approach to fold recognition is comparative modeling. Let A be the amino acid sequence of a protein with unknown tertiary structure, and align the sequence A to the primary structures of all proteins in the database of tertiary protein structures. Suppose that the sequence A best aligns to the primary structure of B. This sequence alignment can be used to inter the structural alignment. For example, if the residue a_i of A aligns with the residue b_j of B, the position of the residue a_i in the unknown tertiary structure is defined as the position of the residue b_j in the tertiary structure in the database. Subsequences of the sequence of A aligned with a series of blanks of the sequence of B are modeled as a coil region.

A more sophisticated approach to fold recognition makes use of the method of three-dimensional profile-sequence alignment. For this, we make use of both a sequence and a protein database. Let A be a sequence of amino acids and P be the three-dimensional profile of a protein. We align A to P. Let

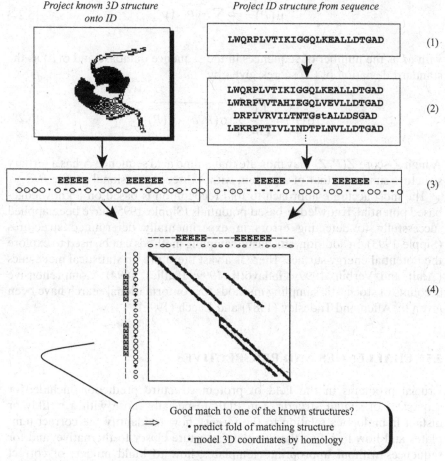

FIGURE 5.8 Threading predicted one-dimensional structure profiles into known three-dimensional structures: (1) input a sequence; (2) generate sequence alignment; (3) predict the one-dimensional structure; (4) align the predicted and known structure(s).

$\sigma(P, A)$ be the corresponding alignment score. To estimate the significance of these alignment scores, we align the protein with three-dimensional profile P against all amino acid sequences of a sequence database. The Z-score for aligning the amino acid sequence **A** to the protein with three-dimensional profile P is given by

$$Z(P, A) = \frac{\sigma(P, A) - \mu(P)}{\sigma(P)} \qquad (5.26)$$

where $\mu(P)$ is the mean score of alignment scores given by

$$\mu(P) = \frac{1}{M} \sum_A \sigma(P, A) \tag{5.27}$$

with M as the number of sequences in the sequence database and $\sigma(P)$ as the standard deviation of the scores, given by

$$\sigma(P) = \sqrt{\frac{1}{M} \sum_A [\sigma(P, a) - \mu(P)]^2} \tag{5.28}$$

A high Z-score $Z(P, Z)$ may indicate that amino acid sequence **A** has a tertiary structure similar to that of a protein with a three-dimensional profile P.

The most accurate approach to fold recognition is based on a knowledge-based potential. Knowledge-based potentials (Sipple, 1995) have been applied successfully to detecting errors in experimentally determined structures (Sipple, 1993). In addition, stochastic sampling methods can be used to explore the potential energy surface. There is a vast literature on statistical mechanics (Amit and Verbin, 1999; Gallavotti, 1999; Phillies, 1994). Comprehensive accounts of stochastic sampling methods for conformational search have been given by Allen and Tildesley (1987) and Leach (1996).

5.5 CHALLENGES AND PERSPECTIVES

Crucial problems in the field of protein structure prediction include, for sequences of similar structures in PDB (especially those with a weakly or distant homologous relation to the target), how to identify the correct templates and how to refine the template structure closer to the native; and for sequences without appropriate templates, how to build models of correct topology from scratch. Since a detailed physicochemical description of protein folding principles does not yet exist, the protein structure prediction problem is defined largely by the evolutionary or structural distance between the target and the solved proteins in the PDB library. For proteins with close templates, full-length models can be constructed by copying the template framework.

In recent years, despite many debates, structure genomics has probably become one of the most noteworthy efforts in protein structure determination, which aims to obtain three-dimensional models of all proteins by an optimized combination of experimental structure solution and computer-based structure prediction (Burley et al., 1999; Chandonia and Brenner, 2006). Two factors will dictate the success of structure genomics: experimental structure determination of optimally selected proteins and efficient computer modeling algorithms. Depending on whether similar structures are found in the PDB library, the protein-structure prediction can be categorized into template-based modeling and free modeling. Although threading is an efficient tool for detecting structural analogs, advancements in methodology development have arrived at a steady state. Encouraging progress is observed in structure refinement, which aims at drawing template structures closer to the native. This has been driven primarily by the use of multiple structure templates and the development of hybrid knowledge- and physics-based force fields. For free modeling, exciting examples have been witnessed in folding small proteins to atomic resolutions. However, predicting structures for proteins larger than 150 residues remains a challenge, with bottlenecks from both force field and conformational search.

Based on about 40,000 structures in the PDB library (many are redundant) (Berman et al., 2000), 4 million models/fold assignments can be obtained by a simple combination of the PSI-BLAST search and the comparative modeling technique (Pieper et al., 2006). Development of more sophisticated and automated computer modeling approaches will dramatically enlarge the scope of modelable proteins in structure genomics.

REFERENCES

Allen, M. P., and Tildesley, D. J. (1987). *Computer Simulation of Liquids*. Oxford, UK: Clarendon Press.

Amit, D. J., and Verbin, Y. (1999). *Statistical Physics: An Introductory Course*. Singapore: World Scientific.

Atkins, J. F., and Gesteland, R. (2002). The 22nd amino acid. *Science*, **296**(5572), 1409–1410.

Berman, H. M., Westbrook, J., Feng, Z., Gilliland, G., Bhat, T. N., Weissig, H., Shindyalov, I. N., and Bourne, P. E. (2000). The Protein Data Bank. *Nucleic Acids Res.*, **28**, 235–242.

Brooks, B., Bruccoleri, R., Olafson, B., States, D., Swaminathan, S., and Karplus, M. (1983). CHARMM: a program for macromolecular energy minimization and dynamics calculations. *J. Comp. Chem.*, **4**, 187–217.

Burley, S. K., Almo, S. C., Bonanno, J. B., Capel, M., Chance, M. R., Gaasterland, T., Lin, D., Sali, A., Studier, F. W., and Swaminathan, S. (1999). Structural genomics: beyond the human genome project. *Nat Genet.*, **23**, 151–157.

Chandonia, J. M., and Brenner, S. E. (2006). The impact of structural genomics: expectations and outcomes. *Science*, **311**, 347–351.

Dill, K. A., Bromberg, S., Yue, K. Z., Fiebig, K. M., Yee, D. P., Thomas, P. D., and Chan, H. S. (1995). Principles of protein-folding: a perspective from simple exact models. *Protein Sci.*, **4**, 561–602.

Gallavotti, G. (1999). *Statistical Mechanics*. New York: Springer-Verlag.

Halperin, D., and Overmars, M. H. (1998). Spheres, molecules and hidden surface removal. *Comput. Geom. Theory Appl.*, **11**(2), 83–102.

Horst, R., and Pardalos, P. M. (1994). *Handbook of Global Optimization*. Dordrecht, The Netherlands: Kluwer.

Kostrowicki, J., and Scheraga, H. A. (1992). Application of the diffusion equation method for global optimization of oligopepetides. *J. Phys. Chem.*, **96**, 7442–7449.

Kostrowicki, J., Piela, L., Cherayil, J., and Scheraga, H. A. (1991). Performance of the diffusion equation method in searches for optimum structures of clusters of Lennard-Jones atoms. *J. Phys. Chem.*, **95**, 4113–4119.

Leach, A. R. (1996). *Molecular Modeling: Principles and Applications*. Reading, MA: Addison-Wesley.

Lee, J., Scheraga, H. A., and Rackovsky, S. (1997). New optimization method for conformational energy calculations on polypeptides: conformational space annealing. *J. Comp. Chem.*, **18**, 1222–1232.

Lesk, A. M. (2001). *Introduction to Protein Architecture: The Structural Biology of Proteins*. New York: Oxford University Press.

Levinthal, C. (1968). Are there pathways for protein folding? *J. Chem. Phys.*, **65**, 44–45.

Lotan, I., and Schwarzer, F. (2004). Approximation of protein structure for fast similarity measures. *J. Comp. Biol.*, **11**(2–3), 299–317.

Phillies, G. D. J. (1994). *Elementary Lectures in Statistical Mechanics*. New York: Springer-Verleg.

Pieper, U., Eswar, N., Davis, F. P., Braberg, H., Madhusudhan, M. S., Rossi, A., Marti-Renom, M., Karchin, R., Webb, B. M., Eramian, D., et al. (2006). MODBASE: a database of annotated comparative protein structure models and associated resources. *Nucleic Acids Res.*, **34**, D291–D295.

Ryu, J., Park, R., Cho, Y., Seo, J., and Kim, D.-S. (2007a). Beta-shape-based computation of blending surfaces on a molecule. *Proceedings of the 4th International Symposium on Voronoi Diagrams in Science and Engineering*, July 9–11, pp. 189–198.

Ryu, J., Cho, Y., and Kim, D.-S. (2007b). Molecular surfaces on proteins via beta shapes. *Comput. Aid. Des.*, **39**(12), 1042–1057.

Ryu, J., Cho, Y., and Kim, D.-S. (2009). Triangulation of molecular surfaces. *Comput. Aid. Des.*, **41**(6), 463–478.

Sael, L., Li, B., La, D., Fang, Y., Ramani, K., Rustamov, R, and Kihara, D. (2008). Fast protein tertiary structure retrieval based on global surface shape similarity: 1. *Proteins*, **72**(4), 1259–1273.

Scheraga, H. A. (1996). Recent developments in the theory of protein folding: searching for the global energy minimum. *Biophys. Chem.*, **59**, 329–339.

Sipple, M. J. (1993). Recognition of errors in three-dimensional structures of proteins. *Proteins Struct. Funct. Genet.*, **12**, 355–362.

Sipple, M. J. (1995). Knowledge-based potentials for proteins. *Curr. Biol.*, **5**, 229–235.

Skiena, S. (2008). *The Algorithm Design Manual*, 2nd ed. New York: Springer-Verlag.

Voet, D., and Voet, J. G. (2004). *Biochemistry*, Vol. **1**, 3rd ed. Hoboken, NJ: Wiley. See especially pp. 227–231.

Wang, Y., Wu, L.-Y., Zhang, X.-S., and Chen, L. (2006a). Automatic classification of protein structures based on convex hull representation by integrated neural network. In: J.-Y. Cai, S. B. Cooper, and A. Li (Eds.), *Theory and Applications of Models of Computation*, Vol. **3959**. New York: Springer-Verlag.

Wang, Y., Wu, L.-Y., Zhang, X.-S., and Chen, L. (2006b). Exploring the classification of protein structures on geometric patterns by neural networks. *Int. J. Comput. Intell. Res.*, **2**(1), 100–104.

Wang, Y., Wu, L.-Y., Zhang, X.-S., and Chen, L. (2008). Supervised classification of protein structures based on convex hull representation. *Int. J. Bioinf. Res. Appl.*, **3**(2), 123–144.

Zimmermann, K. H. (2003). *An Introduction to Protein Informatics*. Dardrecht, The Netherlands: Kluwer Academic.

6 Biological Networks and Graph Theory

Biological systems ranging from food webs in ecology to biochemical interactions in molecular biology can be modeled and analyzed as networks. Biological networks are abstract representations of biological systems which capture many of their essential characteristics. A mathematical graph is an abstract representation of a set of objects where some pairs of the objects are connected by links. With the availability of complete genome sequences and high-throughput technologies and postgenomics experimental data, we have seen a growing interest in the study of networks of biomolecular interactions in recent years. Graph theory plays an important role in a wide variety of disciplines, ranging from communications to molecular and population biology. Network approaches offer the tools to analyze and understand a host of biological systems. In particular, within the cell the variety of interactions among genes, proteins, and metabolites are captured by network representations. In this chapter we focus our discussions on biological applications of the theory of graphs and networks.

6.1 INTRODUCTION

Recent advances in molecular biology and high-throughput technologies for biological measurement have led to a high volume of data sets on systems at different levels, ranging from molecules to populations. Typically, these data sets consist of a list of biological objects and their interactions. Naturally, their interactions could be captured by network representations at various levels. Broadly speaking, biological networks may be grouped at the molecular, cellular, and population levels. At the population level, ecological networks, food-web networks, and epidemiological networks are the most common. At the cellular level, neuronal networks and immunological networks have attracted attention recently. At the molecular level,

Mathematics of Bioinformatics: Theory, Practice, and Applications, By Matthew He and Sergey Petoukhov
Copyright © 2011 John Wiley & Sons, Inc.

gene regulatory networks, protein interaction networks, and metabolic networks have attracted the most attention to date. A large number of data sets on these networks are now available. It is possible to investigate the structural properties of networks and identify their key properties in living cells.

One of the ultimate goals of biological networks is to improve our understanding of the processes and events that lead to pathologies and diseases. The analysis of biological pathways can provide a more efficient way of browsing through biologically relevant information and offer a quick overview of underlying biological processes. Protein interactions help put biological processes in context, allowing researchers to characterize specific pathway biology. Hence, the analysis of biological networks is crucial to an understanding of complex biological systems and diseases.

The mathematical theory that underpins the study of complex networks is graph theory (Diestel, 2000). In mathematics, graph theory is the study of graphs. A *graph* is an abstract representation of a set of objects where some pairs of the objects are connected by links. The interconnected objects are represented by mathematical abstractions called *vertices*, and the links that connect some pairs of vertices are called *edges*. Typically, a graph is depicted in diagrammatic form as a set of dots for the vertices, joined by lines or curves for the edges. Table 6.1 provides a partial list of graph models on various complex networks.

Motivated by the considerations outlined above, a substantial literature and databases on the analysis of biological networks have emerged in recent years. These include studies on identifying and interpreting the structures of biological networks. Our primary goal in the present chapter is to describe, as broadly as possible, the major advances made in this field in relation to graph theory. In this chapter we focus on the three biomolecular networks:

1. Transcriptional regulatory networks (or genetic regulatory networks), which describe the regulatory interactions between different genes
2. Protein interaction networks of the physical interactions between an organism's proteins
3. Metabolic networks of biochemical reactions between metabolic substrates

6.2   GRAPH THEORY PRELIMINARIES AND NETWORK TOPOLOGY

In this section we introduce the principal notations of graph theory and recall some basic definitions and facts from graph theory. While the material of this section is mathematical in nature, we shall see in the remainder of the chapter that all the concepts recalled here arise in real biological networks.

TABLE 6.1   Examples of Networks

Graph	Nodes (Vertices)	Links (Edges)	Networks	References
Undirected graphs	Routers	Wires	Internet	Faloutsos et al., 1999
Directed graphs	Web pages	URL	World Wide Web networks	Barabási et al., 2002
Directed graphs/ undirected graphs	Genes	Expressions of genes A and B are correlated/ regulatory influences	Gene regulatory networks	Lee et al., 2001
Directed graphs	Genes and proteins	Transcription factor regulates a gene	Transcriptional regulatory networks	Guelzim et al., 2002
Directed bipartite graphs	Metabolites/ reactions	Production/ consumption	Metabolic networks	Savageau, 1991
Directed graphs	Proteins	Interaction	Protein interaction networks	Uetz et al., 2000
Directed graphs	People	Friendship	Societal networks	Milgram, 1967
		Collaborations		Wasserman and Faust, 1994
		Sexual contacts		Liljeros et al., 2001
		Coauthorship of scientific papers		Barabási et al., 2002

Graph Theory Preliminaries

A graph is an ordered pair $G := (V, E)$ comprising a set V of vertices or nodes together with a set E of edges or lines. The vertices belonging to an edge are called the *ends*, *endpoints*, or *end vertices* of the edge. A vertex may exist in a graph and not belong to an edge. V and E are usually taken to be finite. The order of a graph is the number of vertices. A graph's size is the number of edges. The *degree* of a vertex is the number of edges that connect to it, where an edge that connects to the vertex at both ends (a loop) is counted twice.

Graphs or networks can be divided into two broad classes: undirected and directed. A graph may be *undirected* if there is no distinction between the two vertices associated with each edge, or its edges may be directed from one vertex to another. Formally, *a directed graph* or *digraph* is an ordered pair $D := (V, A)$ with

- V a set whose elements are called *vertices* or *nodes*
- A a set of ordered pairs of vertices, called *arcs*, *directed edges*, or *arrows*

An arc $a = (x, y)$ is considered to be directed from x to y; y is called the *head* and x is called the *tail* of the arc; y is said to be a direct *successor* of x, and x is said to be a direct *predecessor* of y. If a path leads from x to y, then y is said to be a successor of x and reachable from x, and x is said to be a predecessor of y. The arc (y, x) is called the arc (x, y) inverted. A directed graph D is called *symmetric* if for every arc in D, the corresponding inverted arc also belongs to D. A symmetric loopless directed graph $D = (V, A)$ is equivalent to a simple undirected graph $G = (V, E)$, where the pairs of inverse arcs in A correspond one-to-one with the edges in E; thus, the edges in G number $|E| = |A|/2$, or half the number of arcs in D.

A *mixed graph G* is a graph in which some edges may be directed and some may be undirected. It is written as an ordered triple $G := (V, E, A)$ with V, E, and A defined as above. Directed and undirected graphs are special cases.

A *loop* is an edge (directed or undirected) which starts and ends on the same vertex; these may be permitted or not permitted according to the application. In this context, an edge with two different ends is called a *link*.

A *simple graph* has three vertices and three edges. Each vertex has degree 2, so this is also a regular graph. As opposed to a multigraph, a simple graph is an undirected graph that has no loops and no more than one edge between any two different vertices. In a simple graph the edges of the graph form a set (rather than a multiset), and each edge is a pair of distinct vertices. In a simple graph with n vertices, every vertex has a degree that is less than n (the inverse, however, is not true—there exist nonsimple graphs with n vertices in which every vertex has a degree smaller than n).

A graph is a *weighted graph* if a number (weight) is assigned to each edge. Such weights might represent, for example, costs, lengths, or capacities, depending on the problem. The *weight* of the graph is the sum of the weights given to all edges.

A *regular graph* is a graph where each vertex has the same number of neighbors (i.e., every vertex has the degree). A regular graph with vertices of degree k is called a *k-regular graph* or a *regular graph of degree k*.

Complete graphs have the feature that each pair of vertices has an edge connecting them. In an undirected graph G, two vertices u and v are called *connected* if G contains a path from u to v. Otherwise, they are called *disconnected*. A graph is called connected if every pair of distinct vertices in the graph is connected, and is disconnected otherwise.

A graph is called *k-vertex-connected* or *k-edge-connected* if removal of k or more vertices (respectively, edges) makes the graph disconnected. A k-vertex-connected graph is often simply called k-*connected*.

A directed graph is called *weakly connected* if replacing all of its directed edges with undirected edges produces a connected (undirected) graph. It is *strongly connected* or *strong* if it contains a directed path from u to v and a directed path from v to u for every pair of vertices u and v.

Two edges of a graph are called *adjacent* (sometimes *coincident*) if they share a common vertex. Two arrows of a directed graph are called *consecutive* if the head of the first arrow is at the nock (notch end) of the second. Similarly, two vertices are called adjacent if they share a common edge (consecutive if they are at the notch and at the head of an arrow), in which case the common edge is said to join the two vertices. An edge and a vertex on that edge are called *incident*.

The graph with only one vertex and no edges is called a *trivial graph*. A graph with only vertices and no edges is known as an *edgeless graph*. The graph with no vertices and no edges is sometimes called a *null graph* or *empty graph*, but not all mathematicians allow this object.

In a weighted graph or digraph, each edge is associated with some value, variously called its *cost*, *weight*, *length*, or other term depending on the application; such graphs arise in many contexts: for example, in optimal routing problems such as the traveling salesman problem. Normally, the vertices of a graph, by their nature as elements of a set, are distinguishable. This type of graph may be called *vertex-labeled*. However, for many questions it is better to treat vertices as indistinguishable; then the graph may be called *unlabeled*. (Of course, the vertices may still be distinguishable by the properties of the graph itself, e.g., by the numbers of incident edges.) The same remarks apply to edges, so that graphs that have labeled edges are called *edge-labeled graphs*. Graphs with labels attached to edges or vertices are more generally designated as labeled. Consequently, graphs in which vertices are indistinguishable and edges are indistinguishable are called unlabeled. (Note that in the literature the term *labeled* may apply to other types of labeling besides that which serves only to distinguish different vertices or edges.)

A binary relation R on a set X is a directed graph. Two edges x and y of X are connected by an arrow if $x \mathrm{R} y$. Basic examples are:

- In a complete graph each pair of vertices is joined by an edge; that is, the graph contains all possible edges.
- In a bipartite graph, the vertices can be divided into two sets, W and X, so that every edge has one vertex in each of the two sets.
- In a complete bipartite graph, the vertex set is the union of two disjoint subsets, W and X, so that every vertex in W is adjacent to every vertex in X but there are no edges within W or X.
- In a path of length n, the vertices can be listed in order, $v_0, v_1, \ldots, v_n$, so that the edges are $v_{i-1}v_i$ for each $i = 1, 2, \ldots, n$.
- A cycle or circuit of length n is a closed path without self-intersections; equivalently, it is a connected graph with degree 2 at every vertex. Its

vertices can be named $v_1, \ldots, v_n$, so that the edges are $v_{i-1}v_i$ for each $i = 2, \ldots, n$ and v_nv_1.

- A planar graph can be drawn in a plane with no crossing edges (i.e., embedded in a plane).
- A forest is a graph with no cycles.
- A tree is a connected graph with no cycles.

Power Law and Power Law Distribution

Power laws are abundant in nature. The power-law distribution has become the signature of biological networks. A *power law* is any polynomial relationship that exhibits the property of scale invariance. The most common power laws relate two variables and have the form

$$P(x) = ax^k + o(x^k) \tag{6.1}$$

where a and k are constants and $o(x^k)$ is an asymptotically small function of x. Here, k is typically called the *scaling exponent*, the word *scaling* denoting the fact that a power-law function satisfies $P(cx) \propto P(x)$, where c is a constant. That is, a rescaling of the function's argument changes the constant of proportionality but preserves the shape of the function itself. This point becomes clearer if we take the logarithm of both sides:

$$\log P(x) = k \log x + \log a \tag{6.2}$$

Notice that this expression has the form of a linear relationship with slope k. Rescaling the argument produces a linear shift of the function up or down but leaves both the basic form and the slope k unchanged.

Power-law relations characterize a staggering number of naturally occurring phenomena. For instance, inverse-square laws, such as gravitation and the Coulomb force are power laws, as are many common mathematical formulas, such as the quadratic law of area of the circle. However, it is mainly in the study of probability distributions that power laws have attracted recent interest. A wide variety of observed probability distributions appear, at least approximately, to have tails asymptotically following power-law forms, an observation connected closely with the study of the theory of large deviations, which considers the frequency of extremely rare events such as stock market crashes and large natural disasters. It is primarily in the study of statistical distributions that the name *power law* is used; in other areas the power-law functional form is more often referred to simply as a polynomial form or polynomial function. A few notable examples of power laws are the Gutenberg–Richter law for earthquake sizes, Pareto's law of income distribution, structural self-similarity of fractals, and scaling laws in biological systems.

A power-law distribution is any that in the most general sense has the form

$$P(x) \propto L(x)x^{-\alpha} \tag{6.3}$$

where $\alpha > 1$, and $L(x)$ is a slowly varying function, which is any function that satisfies $L(tx)/L(x) \to 1$ as $x \to \infty$ with t constant. This property of $L(x)$ follows directly from the requirement that $p(x)$ be asymptotically scale invariant; thus, the form of $L(x)$ controls only the shape and finite extent of the lower tail.

Network Topology and Network Models

There are many tools and measures available now to study the structure and dynamics of complex networks. Statistical graph properties include the distribution of vertex degrees, the distribution of the clustering coefficients and other notions of density, the distribution of vertex–vertex distances, and the distribution of network motif occurrences. In the following we discuss four of the most fundamental quantities:

1. Degree distribution
2. Clustering coefficient
3. Subgraphs and motifs
4. Centrality (degree, closeness, betweenness, and eigenvector) and essentiality

Degree Distribution   In the study of various networks, the *degree* (or connectivity) of a node in a network is the number of connections (edges) it has to other nodes. If a network is directed, nodes have two different degrees: the *in-degree*, which is the number of incoming edges, and the *out-degree*, which is the number of outgoing edges. The degree distribution is the probability distribution of these degrees over the entire network. Formally, the degree distribution $P(k)$ of a network is then defined to be the fraction of nodes in the network with degree k. Thus, if there are n nodes in total in a network and n_k of them have degree k, we have

$$P(k) = \frac{n_k}{n} \tag{6.4}$$

The degree distribution is very important in studying biological networks and other complex networks. The simplest network model, for example, the (Bernoulli) random network, in which each of n nodes is connected (or not) with independent probability p (or $1 - p$), has a binomial distribution of degrees

$$P(k) = \binom{n-1}{k} p^k (1-p)^{n-1-k} \tag{6.5}$$

or a Poisson distribution in the limit of large n,

$$P(k) = \frac{\lambda^k e^{-\lambda}}{k!} \tag{6.6}$$

where λ is a constant.

Most networks in the real world, however, have degree distributions very different from this. Most are highly right-skewed, meaning that a large majority of nodes are of low degree, but a small number, known as *hubs*, are of high degree. Some networks, notably the Internet, the World Wide Web, and some social networks are found to have degree distributions that approximately follow a power law:

$$P(k) \approx k^{-\lambda} \tag{6.7}$$

where λ is a constant. Such networks, called *scale-free networks*, have attracted particular attention for their structural and dynamical properties.

Clustering Coefficient   The *clustering coefficient* is a measure that gives insight into the local structure of a network. Mathematically, we define the clustering coefficient as follows. Let $G = (V, E)$ be a graph with a set of vertices, V, and a set of edges, E. An edge e_{ij} connects vertex i with vertex j. The neighborhood N of vertex v_i is defined as its immediately connected neighbors, as follows:

$$N_i = \{v_i : e_{ij} \in E \lor e_{ji} \in E\} \tag{6.8}$$

Let k_i be the degree (number of vertices) in its neighborhood N_i. The clustering coefficient C_i for a vertex v_i is defined as

$$C_i = \frac{|\{e_{jk}\}|}{k_i(k_i - 1)} : v_j, v_k \in N_i; e_{jk} \in E \tag{6.9}$$

representing the proportion of links between the vertices within its neighborhood divided by the number of links that could possibly exist between them.

For a directed graph, e_{ij} is distinct from e_{ji}, and therefore for each neighborhood N_i there are $k_i(k_i - 1)$ links that could exist among the vertices within the neighborhood (k_i is the total (in + out) degree of the vertex). An undirected graph has the property that e_{ij} and e_{ji} are considered identical. Therefore, if a vertex v_i has k_i neighbours, edges could exist among the vertices within the neighborhood. Thus, the clustering coefficient for undirected graphs can be defined as

$$C_i = \frac{2|\{e_{jk}\}|}{k_i(k_i - 1)} : v_j, v_k \in N_i; e_{jk} \in E \tag{6.10}$$

For a vertex that is a part of a fully interconnected graph, $C_i = 1$; for a vertex where none of its neighbors are interconnected, $C_i = 0$. The clustering coefficient for the entire system is given by Watts and Strogatz (1998) as the average of the clustering coefficient for each vertex:

$$\langle C \rangle = \frac{\sum C_i}{N} \tag{6.11}$$

A graph is considered small-world if its average clustering coefficient is significantly higher than a random graph constructed on the same vertex set. For all metabolic networks available, the average clustering coefficient assembles a power-law form as

$$C_k = k^{-\lambda} \tag{6.12}$$

This suggests the existence of a hierarchy of vertices with different degrees of modularity.

Subgraphs and Motifs   In graph theory, a *subgraph* of a graph G is a graph whose vertex set is a subset of that of G, and whose adjacency relation is a subset of that of G restricted to this subset. A subgraph H is a *spanning subgraph*, or *factor*, of a graph G if it has the same vertex set as G. We say that *H spans G*.

In genetics, a *sequence motif* is a nucleotide or aminoacid sequence pattern that is widespread and has, or is conjectured to have, biological significance. For proteins, a sequence motif is distinguished from a *structural motif*, a motif formed by the three-dimensional arrangement of amino acids, which may not be adjacent.

A number of complex biological networks were recently found to contain *network motifs*. In proteins, structure motifs usually consist of just a few elements; for example, a helix–turn–helix has just three. Note that while the spatial sequence of elements is the same in all instances of a motif, they may be encoded in any order within the underlying gene. Protein structural motifs often include loops of variable length and unspecified structure, which in effect create the "slack" necessary to bring together in space two elements that are not encoded by immediately adjacent DNA sequences in a gene. Note also that even when two genes encode secondary structural elements of a motif in the same order, they may specify somewhat different sequences of amino acids.

Centrality and Essentiality   Within graph theory and network analysis, there are various measures of the centrality of a vertex within a graph that determine the relative importance of a vertex within the graph. There are four measures of centrality that are widely used in network analysis: degree centrality, closeness, betweenness, and eigenvector centrality.

Degree centrality is the most basic of the centrality measures. It is defined as the number of links incident upon a node (i.e., the number of ties that a node has). Degree is often interpreted in terms of the immediate risk of a node for catching whatever is flowing through the network (such as a virus, or some information). If the network is directed, we usually define two separate measures of degree centrality, in-degree and out-degree. *In-degree* is a count of the number of ties directed to the node, and *out-degree* is the number of ties that the node directs to others. For a graph $G := (V, E)$ with n vertices, the degree centrality $C_D(v)$ for vertex v is

$$C_D(v) = \frac{\deg(v)}{n-1} \qquad (6.13)$$

Closeness is a centrality measure of a vertex within a graph. Vertices that are "shallow" to other vertices (i.e., those that tend to have short geodesic distances to other vertices within the graph) have higher closeness. Closeness is preferred in network analysis to mean shortest path length, as it gives higher values to more central vertices, and so is usually positively associated with other measures, such as degree. It is defined as the mean geodesic distance (i.e., the shortest path) between a vertex v and all other vertices reachable from it:

$$\frac{\sum_{t \in V \setminus v} d_G(v, t)}{n-1} \qquad (6.14)$$

where $n > 1$ is the size of the network's connectivity component V reachable from v. Closeness can be regarded as a measure of how long it will take information to spread from a given vertex to other reachable vertices in the network.

Betweenness is a centrality measure of a vertex within a graph. Vertices that occur on many shortest paths between other vertices have higher betweenness than those that do not. For a graph $G := (V, E)$ with n vertices, the betweenness $C_B(v)$ for vertex v is

$$C_B(v) = \sum_{s \neq v \neq t} \frac{\sigma_{st}(v)}{\sigma_{st}} \qquad (6.15)$$

where σ_{st} is the number of shortest geodesic paths from s to t, and $\sigma_{st}(v)$ is the number of shortest geodesic paths from s to t that pass through a vertex v. This may be normalized by dividing through the number of pairs of vertices not including v, which is $(n-1)(n-2)$. Calculating the betweenness and closeness centralities of all the vertices in a graph involves calculating the shortest paths between all pairs of vertices on a graph.

Eigenvector centrality is a measure of the importance of a node in a network. It assigns relative scores to all nodes in the network based on the principle that connections to high-scoring nodes contribute more to the score of the node in question than do equal connections to low-scoring nodes.

Let x_i denote the score of the ith node. Let $A_{i,j}$ be the adjacency matrix of the network. Hence, $A_{ij} = 1$ if the ith node is adjacent to the jth node, and $A_{i,j} = 0$ otherwise. More generally, the entries in A can be real numbers representing connection strengths. For the ith node, let the centrality score be proportional to the sum of the scores of all nodes that are connected to it. Hence,

$$x_i = \frac{1}{\lambda} \sum_{j \in M(i)} x_j = \frac{1}{\lambda} \sum_{j=1}^{N} A_{i,j} x_j \qquad (6.16)$$

where $M(i)$ is the set of nodes that are connected to the ith node, N is the total number of nodes, and λ is a constant. In vector notation this can be rewritten

$$X = \frac{1}{\lambda} AX, \quad AX = \lambda X \qquad (6.17)$$

In general, there will be many different eigenvalues λ for which an eigenvector solution exists. However, the additional requirement that all the entries in the eigenvector be positive implies (by the Perron–Frobenius theorem) that only the greatest eigenvalue results in the desired centrality measure. The ith component of the related eigenvector then gives the centrality score of the ith node in the network. Power iteration is one of many eigenvalue algorithms that may be used to find this dominant eigenvector.

The network model is a database model conceived as a flexible way of representing objects and their relationships. Where the hierarchical model structures data as a tree of records, with each record having one parent record and many children, the network model allows each record to have multiple parent and child records, forming a lattice structure. Next, we describe three models that can be seen as network paradigms.

Random Network   Graph theory focused initially on regular graphs. Since the 1950s, large networks with no apparent design principles were described by random graphs as the simplest model of a complex network (Bollobas, 1985). A *random network* is obtained by starting with a set of n vertices and adding edges between them at random. Different random graph models produce different probability distributions on graphs. Most commonly studied is the Erdös–Rényi model (Erdös and Rényi, 1960), denoted $G(n, p)$, in which every possible edge occurs independently with probability p. This process generates a graph with approximately $pN(N - 1)/2$ randomly distributed edges. A closely related model, denoted $G(n, M)$, assigns equal probability to all graphs with exactly M edges. The latter model can be viewed as a snapshot at a particular time of the random graph process, which is a stochastic process that starts with n vertices and no edges and at each step adds one new edge chosen uniformly from the set of missing edges. The theory of random graphs studies typical properties of random graphs, those that hold with high probability for graphs drawn from a particular distribution. For example, we might ask, for a given value of n and p, what the probability is that $G(n, p)$ is connected. In studying such questions, researchers often concentrate on the asymptotic behavior of random graphs—the values that various probabilities converge to as n grows very large.

Scale-Free Network   A *scale-free network* is a network whose degree distribution follows a power law, at least asymptotically. That is, the fraction $P(k)$ of nodes in the network having k connections to other nodes goes for large values of k as $P(k) \sim k^{-\gamma}$, where γ is a constant whose value is typically in the range $2 < \gamma < 3$, although occasionally it may lie outside these bounds. Scale-free networks are noteworthy because many empirically observed networks appear to be scale-free, including the World Wide Web, protein networks, citation networks, and some social networks.

The power-law distribution strongly influences the network topology. It turns out that the major hubs are closely followed by smaller ones. These, in turn, are followed by other nodes with an even smaller degree, and so on. This hierarchy allows for a fault-tolerant behavior. Since failures occur at random and the vast majority of nodes are those with small degree, the likelihood that a hub would be affected is almost negligible. Even if such an event occurs, the network will not lose its connectedness, which is guaranteed by the remaining hubs. On the other hand, if we choose a few major hubs and take them out of the network, it simply falls apart and is turned into a set of rather isolated graphs. Thus, hubs are scale-free networks. Another important characteristic of scale-free networks is the clustering coefficient distribution, which decreases as the node degree increases. This distribution also follows a power law. That means that the low-degree nodes belong to very dense subgraphs and those subgraphs are connected to each other through hubs.

Hierarchical Network   A *Hierarchical network* is a network topology in which a central "root" node (the top level of the hierarchy) is connected to one or more other nodes that are one level lower in the hierarchy (i.e., the second level) with a point-to-point link between each of the second-level nodes and the top-level central root node. At the same time, each of the second-level nodes that are connected to the top-level central root node will also have one or more other nodes that are one level lower in the hierarchy (i.e., the third level) connected to it, also with a point-to-point link, the top-level central root node being the only node that has no other node above it in the hierarchy. (The hierarchy of the tree is symmetrical.)

6.3 MODELS OF BIOLOGICAL NETWORKS

A network model can be used to present a synthetic view of the current state of biological knowledge on a given network and can be used to simulate the process it represents. A biological network model allows a variety of analyses, ranging from statistical properties of its topology to predictions of features of its dynamic behavior, or even prediction of cellular phenotypes. If these predictions can be compared with experimental results, they should allow either confirmation of the model's accuracy or, better yet, correction of the model. Several mathematical framework structures, such as a system of differential equations and Boolean networks for biological networks are discussed in this section.

Gene Regulatory Networks

A *gene regulatory network* (GRN) or *genetic regulatory network* is a collection of DNA segments in a cell which interact with each other and with other substances in the cell, thereby governing the rates at which genes in the network are transcribed into mRNA. As we see here, a GRN involves interactions among DNA, RNA, proteins, and other molecules. In general, each mRNA molecule goes on to make a specific protein (or set of proteins). These mRNA molecules and proteins interact with each other with various degrees of specificity. Some diffuse around the cell. Others are bound to cell membranes, interacting with molecules in the environment. These molecules and their interactions comprise a gene regulatory network.

A gene regulatory network can be viewed as a directed graph: a pair (V, E), where V is a set of vertices (genes) and E a set of directed edges (regulatory influences), and a pair (A, B) of vertices, where A is the source vertex and B the target vertex. A gene A directly regulates a gene B if the protein that is encoded by A is a transcription factor for gene B. This simple model can be improved by adding an additional attribute on vertices or edges: for example, "+" or "−" labels on edges may indicate positive or negative regulatory influence.

Genes can be viewed as nodes in the network, with input being proteins such as transcription factors, and outputs being the level of gene expression. The node itself can also be viewed as a function that can be obtained by combining basic functions upon the inputs (in the Boolean network described below these are Boolean functions, typically AND, OR, and NOT). These functions have been interpreted as performing a type of information processing within the cell, which determines cellular behavior. The basic drivers within cells are concentrations of some proteins, which determine both spatial (location within the cell or tissue) and temporal (cell cycle or developmental stage) coordinates of the cell, as a kind of "cellular memory."

Mathematical models of GRNs have been developed to capture the behavior of the system being modeled, and in some cases generate predictions corresponding to experimental observations. In other cases, models have proven to make accurate novel predictions, which can be tested experimentally, thus suggesting new approaches to explore in an experiment that sometimes wouldn't be considered in the design of the protocol of an experimental laboratory. The most common modeling technique involves the use of coupled ordinary differential equations. Several other promising modeling techniques have been used, including Boolean networks, Petri nets, Bayesian networks, and graphical Gaussian models.

Typically, a gene regulatory network is modeled as a system of rate equations describing the reaction kinetics of the constituent parts and governing the evolution of mRNA and protein concentrations. Suppose that our regulatory network has N nodes, and let $S_1(t)$, $S_2(t)$, ... , $S_N(t)$ represent the concentrations of the N corresponding substances at time t. Then the temporal evolution of the system can be described approximately by

$$\frac{dS_j}{dt} = f_j\left(S_1(t), S_2(2), \ldots, S_N(t)\right) \tag{6.18}$$

where the functions f_j express the dependence of S_j on the concentrations of other substances present in the cell. The functions f_j are ultimately derived from basic principles of chemical kinetics or simple expressions derived from these (e.g., Michaelis–Menten enzymatic kinetics). Hence, the functional forms of the f_j are usually chosen as low-order polynomials that serve as an ansatz for the real molecular dynamics. Such models are then studied using the mathematics of nonlinear dynamics.

By solving for the fixed point of the system,

$$\frac{dS_j}{dt} = 0 \tag{6.19}$$

for all j, one obtains (possibly several) concentration profiles of proteins and mRNAs that are theoretically sustainable (although not necessarily stable). Steady states of kinetic equations thus correspond to potential cell types, and oscillatory solutions to equation (6.19) correspond to naturally cyclic cell types. Mathematical stability of these attractors can usually be characterized by the sign of higher derivatives at critical points and then correspond to the biochemical stability of the concentration profile. Critical points and bifurcations in the equations correspond to critical cell states in which small state or parameter perturbations could switch the system between one of several stable differentiation fates. Trajectories correspond to the unfolding of biological pathways and transients of the equations to short-term biological events. For a more mathematical discussion, see the reference section for articles on nonlinearity, dynamical systems, bifurcation theory, and chaos theory.

The following example illustrates how a Boolean network can model a GRN together with its gene products (the outputs) and the substances from the environment that affect it (the inputs). Stuart Kauffman was among the first biologists to use the metaphor of Boolean networks to model genetic regulatory networks (Kauffman, 1993).

- Each gene, each input, and each output is represented by a node in a directed graph in which there is an arrow from one node to another if and only if there is a causal link between the two nodes.
- Each node in the graph can be in one of two states: on or off.
- For a gene, "on" corresponds to the gene being expressed; for inputs and outputs, "on" corresponds to the substance being present.
- Time is viewed as proceeding in discrete steps. At each step, the new state of a node is a Boolean function of the prior states of the nodes with arrows pointing toward it.

The validity of the model can be tested by comparing simulation results with time-series observations. Continuous network models of GRNs are an extension of the Boolean networks described above. Nodes still represent genes and connections between them, regulatory influences on gene expression. Genes in biological systems display a continuous range of activity levels, and it has been argued that using a continuous representation captures several properties of gene regulatory networks not present in the Boolean model (Vohradsky, 2001).

Recent experimental results (Blake et al., 2003; Elowitz et al., 2002) have demonstrated that gene expression is a stochastic process. Thus, many authors are now using stochastic formalism, after the work of Arkin and McAdams (1998). Works on single gene expression (Raser and O'Shea, 2005) and small synthetic genetic networks (Elowitz and Leibler, 2000; Gardner et al., 2000), such as the genetic toggle switch of Tim Gardner and Jim Collins, provided additional experimental data on the phenotypic variability and the stochastic nature of gene expression. The first versions of stochastic models of gene expression involved only instantaneous reactions and were driven by the Gillespie algorithm (Gillespie, 1976).

Since some processes, such as gene transcription, involve many reactions and could not be modeled correctly as an instantaneous reaction in a single step, it was proposed to model these reactions as single-step multiple delayed reactions, to account for the time it takes for the entire process to be completed (Roussel and Zhu, 2006).

From here a set of reactions was proposed (Ribeiro et al., 2006) that allow generating GRNs. These are then simulated using a modified version of the Gillespie algorithm. It can simulate multiple time-delayed reactions.

For example, basic transcription of a gene can be represented by the following single-step reaction (RNAP is the RNA polymerase, RBS is the RNA ribosome binding site, and Pro_i is the promoter region of gene i):

$$\text{RNAP} + \text{Pro}_i \xrightarrow{K_{i,base}} \text{Pro}_i(\tau_i^1) + \text{RBS}_i(\tau_i^1) + \text{RNAP}(\tau_i^2) \qquad (6.20)$$

A recent work proposed a simulator (SGNSim, Stochastic Gene Networks Simulator) (Ribeiro and Lloyd-Price, 2007) that can model GRNs where transcription and translation are modeled as multiple time-delayed events, and its dynamics is driven by a stochastic simulation algorithm able to deal with multiple time-delayed events. The time delays can be drawn from several distributions and the reaction rates from complex functions or from physical parameters. SGNSim can generate ensembles of GRNs within a set of user-defined parameters, such as topology. It can also be used to model specific GRNs and systems of chemical reactions. Genetic perturbations such as gene deletions, gene overexpression, insertions, and frame shift mutations can be modeled as well.

The GRN is created from a graph with the desired topology, imposing in-degree and out-degree distributions. Gene promoter activities are affected by other gene expression products that act as inputs, in the form of monomers or combined into multimers and set as direct or indirect. Next, each direct input is assigned to an operator site and different transcription factors can be allowed, or not, to compete for the same operator site, while indirect inputs are given a target. Finally, a function is assigned to each gene, defining the gene's response to a combination of transcription factors (promoter state). The transfer functions (i.e., how genes respond to a combination of inputs) can be assigned to each combination of promoter states as desired.

In other recent work, multiscale models of gene regulatory networks have been developed that focus on synthetic biology applications. Simulations have been used that model all biomolecular interactions in transcription, translation, regulation, and induction of gene regulatory networks, guiding the design of synthetic systems (Kaznessis, 2007).

Protein Interaction Networks

A key feature of the biological organization in all organisms is the tendency of proteins with a common function to associate physically via stable protein-to-protein interactions (PPIs) to form larger macromolecular assemblies. These protein complexes are often linked together by extended networks of weaker, transient PPIs, to form interaction networks that integrate pathways mediating the major cellular processes. Consequently, the cell is viewed increasingly as an assembly of interconnected functional modules that integrate and coordinate the cell's major biochemical activities and responses to external and intrinsic signals. Given their broad significance, systematic analyses of PPI networks have become a major experimental focus.

One of the ultimate goals of biological networks is to improve our understanding of the processes and events that lead to pathologies and diseases. The analysis of biological pathways can provide a more efficient way of browsing through biologically relevant information and offer a quick overview of underlying biological processes.

Protein interactions help put biological processes in context, allowing researchers to characterize specific pathway biology. Hence, an analysis of biological networks is crucial for an understanding of complex biological systems and diseases. The analysis of protein interaction networks is an important and very active research area in bioinformatics and computational biology (Dyke, 1988).

Metabolic Networks

Metabolic networks comprise the chemical reactions of metabolism as well as the regulatory interactions that guide these reactions. With the sequencing of complete genomes, it is now possible to reconstruct the network of biochemical reactions in many organisms, from bacteria to human beings. Several of these networks are available online: Kyoto Encyclopedia of Genes and Genomes, (a database resource for linking genome to life and the environment developed by the Kanehisa Laboratories in the Kyoto University Bioinformatics Center and the Human Genome Center of the University of Tokyo as part of their research activities); EcoCyc, a scientific database for the bacterium *Escherichia coli* K-12 MG1655 comprising literature-based descriptions of the entire genome and of transcriptional regulation, transporters, and metabolic pathways; and BioCyc, a collection of 376 Pathway/Genome Databases, each of which describes the genome and metabolic pathways of a single organism.

In the final analysis, the biological function of life is determined by the organizational form of atoms and molecules, determined especially by the confirmation changes and movements of proteins and nucleic acid molecules. The self-organization phenomena are observed from the molecular to the cellular to the ecological level. Biological networks are dynamic and dependent on the cell environment. Based on networks, we are able to understand how individual components are integrated together into a complete system to perform some biological functions. As a fundamental element of the network, the protein–protein interaction should be deduced by using the sequential, structural, and evolutionary information on individual proteins.

6.4 CHALLENGES AND PERSPECTIVES

In network models, the relevant components in a system are identified as vertices or nodes. The interactions between vertices are represented as edges or links. A major challenge consists of identifying with reasonable accuracy the complex molecular interactions that take place at different levels, from genes to metabolites through proteins. Although an understanding of the interactions of proteins continues to be important, an understanding of a system's structure and dynamics is the latest trend. The approach advocated in systems biology requires a shift in our notion of what to look for in biology. Because a system is not just an assembly of genes and proteins, its properties cannot be fully understood merely by drawing diagrams of their interconnections. Although such a diagram represents an important first step, it is analogous to a static road map, whereas what we really seek to know are the traffic patterns, why such traffic patterns emerge, and how we can control them. Identifying all the genes and proteins in an organism is like listing all the parts of an airplane. Although such a list provides a catalog of the individual components, by itself it is not sufficient for an understanding of the complexity underlying the engineered object. We need to know how these parts are assembled to form the structure of the airplane. This is analogous to drawing an exhaustive diagram of gene-regulatory networks and their biochemical interactions. Such diagrams provide limited knowledge of how changes to one part of a system may affect other parts, but to understand how a particular system functions, we must first examine how the individual components interact dynamically during operation. We must seek answers to such questions as: What is the voltage on each signal line? How are the signals encoded? How can we stabilize the voltage against noise and external fluctuations? How do the circuits react when a malfunction occurs in the system? What are the design principles and possible circuit patterns, and how can we modify them to improve system performance and applications (Kitano, 2001)?

A fundamental activity over the next two decades will involve analysis of the integrated structure and behavior of the complex genetic regulatory systems underlying development in higher organisms, a massive task since the human genome encodes perhaps 100,000 genes. Its accomplishment will require uniting work in molecular and developmental genetics with new mathematical and computational tools.

In more detail, recent progress in molecular genetics in eukaryotes is revealing the detailed composition of structural genes as well as *cis*-acting regulatory loci, such as promoters, homeoboxes, and tissue- and stage-specific enhancer sequences, as well as *trans*-acting components. These genetic elements, together with their RNA and protein products, comprise a genomic regulatory network that coordinates patterns of gene expression in cell types, cell differentiation, and ontogeny from the zygote. Understanding the structure, logic, integrated dynamic behavior, and evolution of such networks is central to molecular, developmental, and evolutionary biology.

The Human Genome Initiative will provide massive sequence data from which we can eventually identify the diverse locations in the genome of each regulatory sequence, as well as the locations of many or most structural genes. These data are fundamental to understanding the "wiring diagram" of the genomic regulatory networks in eukaryotes. Analysis will require development of appropriate computer databases and development of new theory and algorithms in the mathematical theory of directed graphs. Understanding the evolution of such genomic networks under the influence of point and chromosomal mutations that literally scramble the genomic wiring diagram will require new uses of random directed graph theory, stochastic processes, and population genetic models.

In addition to understanding the structure and evolution of genomic regulatory networks, we must understand the coordinated behavior of such systems that integrate the behavior of 100,000 molecular variables. It is here, in an effort to relate the information that we can achieve about small parts of the genomic system to the overall behavior of the integrated system, that a new marriage of mathematics and biology must be found. We have no hope of understanding the integrated behavior of such complex systems, linking the "microlevel" of structure and logic with the macrolevel of behavior, without mathematical theories. Although no approach is yet clearly adequate, new avenues are available.

A first approach is via ensembles. Statistical mechanics is the paradigmatic example of a theory that links microscopic and macroscopic levels. There it is possible to explain macroscopic behaviors without knowing all the details of the microscopic dynamics. Similarly, it may be possible to build up statistical understanding of the integrated behavior of extremely complex genomic regulatory systems without knowing all the details of the microscopic structure.

Molecular genetic techniques reveal small-scale features of genomic systems, such as the sequences that regulate a gene and biases in the "rules" governing the activity of genes as a function of their molecular inputs. Using these local features, one can construct mathematically the ensemble of all genomic systems consistent with those local constraints. This ensemble constitutes the proper null hypothesis about the structure and logic of genomic systems that are random members of such an ensemble. Thus, the typical or generic behavior of ensemble members involves predictions about the large-scale features of random members of the ensemble. This is a new kind of statistical mechanics, averaging over ensembles of systems (Derrida, 1981; Kauffman, 1969, 1974). If the distributions of properties parallel those seen in genomic regulatory systems, those properties may be explained as consequences of membership in the ensemble. Indeed, past work based on this approach (Kauffman, 1969, 1974) has shown that many features of model genomic systems are parallel and hence may explain a number of features of cell differentiation, such as the numbers of cell types in an organism, the similarity of gene expression patterns in different cell types in an organism, and other statistical features. Improved ensemble models, coupled with population genetic models, offer the hope of understanding how evolution can mold the structure, logic, and behavior of integrated genomic systems.

A second approach may be the development of new mathematical and experimental tools to "parse" the genomic system into structurally or functionally isolated subcircuits. Thus, clusters of genes may be regulated in overlapping hierarchical batteries, or some genes may fall to fixed steady states of activities that are common to many or all cell types, while other subsets of genes oscillate or exhibit complex patterns of temporal activity unique to different subsets of cell types. Analysis of such temporal patterns by time-series techniques, and based on a temporal series of two-dimensional protein gel data, where each gel shows the synthesis patterns of up to 2000 genes at a time, may help resolve the genome into behavioral "chunks." If so, this will help block out the overall behavioral organization of the genomic system. Thereafter, analysis of detailed midsized subcircuits, with perhaps several to 100 or so genes, will require use of promoter constructs allowing activation or inhibition of arbitrary genes in arbitrary cell types at arbitrary moments, with analysis of the cascading consequences. Union with dynamic systems theory for modestly small systems, where the inverse problem of guessing plausible circuitry to yield observed synthesis patterns is practical, can then be carried out.

In summary, to understand biology at the system level, we must examine the structure and dynamics of cellular function, in addition to the characteristics of isolated parts of a cell or organism. Properties of systems, such as robustness, emerge as central issues, and understanding these properties may have an impact on the future of medicine. However, many breakthroughs in experimental devices, advanced software, and analytical methods are required before the achievements of systems biology can live up to their much-touted potential.

REFERENCES

Arkin, A., and McAdams, H. H. (1998). Stochastic kinetic analysis of developmental pathway bifurcation in phage lambda-infected *Escherichia coli* cells. *Genetics*, **149**, 1633–1648.

Barabási, A. L., Jeong, H., Ravasz, R., Zeda, E., Vicsek, T., and Schubert, A. (2002). On the topology of the scientific collaboration networks. *Physica A*, **311**, 590.

Blake, W. J., Kaern, M., Cantor, C. R., and Collins, J. J. (2003). Noise in eukaryotic gene expression. *Nature*, **422**, 633–637.

Bollobas, B. (1985). *Random Graphs*. London: Academic Press.

Derrida, B. (1981). Random energy model: an exactly solvable model of disordered systems. *Phys. Rev. B*, **24**, 2613.

Diestel, R. (2000). *Graph Theory*. New York: Springer-Verlag.

Dyke, C. (1988). *The Evolutionary Dynamics of Complex Systems: A Study in Biosocial Complexity*. New York: Oxford University Press.

Elowitz, M. B., and Leibler, S. (2000). A synthetic oscillatory network of transcriptional regulators. *Nature*, **403**, 335–338.

Elowitz, M. B., Levine, A. J., Siggia, E. D., and Swain, P. S. (2002). Stochastic gene expression in a single cell. *Science*, **297**, 1183–1186.

Erdös, P., and Rényi, A. (1960). On the evolution of random graphs. *Publ. Math. Inst. Hung. Acad. Sci.*, **5**, 17–61.

Faloutsos, M., Faloutsos, P., and Faloutsos, C. (1999). On power-law relationships of the Internet topology. *Comput. Commun. Rev.*, **29**, 251–262.

Gardner, T. S., Cantor, C. R., and Collins, J. J. (2000). Construction of a genetic toggle switch in *Escherichia coli*. *Nature*, **403**, 339–342.

Gillespie, D. T. (1976). A general method for numerically simulating the stochastic time evolution of coupled chemical reactions. *J. Comput. Phys.*, **22**, 403–434.

Guelzim, N., Bottani, S., Bourgine, P., and Kepes, F. (2002). Topological and causal structure of the yeast transcriptional regulatory network. *Nat. Genet.*, **31**(1), 60–63.

Kauffman, S. (1993). *The Origins of Order.* New York: Oxford University Press.

Kauffman, S. A. (1969). Metabolic stability and epigenesis in randomly constructed genetic nets. *J. Theor. Biol.*, **22**, 437–467.

Kauffman, S. A. (1974). The large scale structure and dynamics of gene control circuits: an ensemble approach. *J. Theor. Biol.*, **44**, 167–190.

Kaznessis, Y. N. (2007). Models for synthetic biology. *BMC Syst. Biol.*, **1**, 47.

Kitano, H. (2001). *Foundations of Systems Biology.* Cambridge, MA: MIT Press.

Lee, T. I., Rinaldi, N. J., Robert, F., Odom, D. T., Bar-Joseph, Z., Gerber, G. K., Hannett, N. M., Harbison, C. T., Thompson, C. M., Simon, I., et al., (2001). The web of human sexual contacts. *Nature*, **411**, 907–908.

Liljeros, F., Edling, C. R., Amaral, L. A. N., Stanley, H. E., and Aberg, Y. (2001). The web of human sexual contacts. *Nature*, **411**, 907–908.

Milgram, S. (1967). The small-world problem. *Psychol. Today*, **2**, 60–67.

Raser, J. M., and O'Shea, E. K. (2005). Noise in gene expression: origins, consequences, and control. *Science*, **309**, 2010–2013.

Ribeiro, A. S., and Lloyd-Price, J. (2007). SGN Sim, a stochastic genetic networks simulator. *Bioinformatics*, **23**(6), 777–779.

Ribeiro, A. S., Zhu, R., and Kauffman, S. A. (2006). A general modeling strategy for gene regulatory networks with stochastic dynamics. *J. Comp. Biol.*, **13**(9), 1630–1639.

Roussel, M. R., and Zhu, R. (2006). Validation of an algorithm for delay stochastic simulation of transcription and translation in prokaryotic gene expression. *Phys. Biol.*, **3**, 274–284.

Savageau, M. A. (1991). Biochemical systems theory: operational differences among variant representations and their significance. *J. Theor. Biol.*, **151**(4): 509–530.

Uetz P., et al. (2000). A comprehensive analysis of protein–protein interactions in *Saccharomyces cerevisiae. Nature*, **403**, 623–627.

Vohradsky, J. (2001). Neural model of the genetic network. *J. Biol. Chem.*, **276**, 36168–36173.

Wasserman, S., and Faust, K. (1994). *Social Network Analysis: Methods and Application.* Cambridge, UK: Cambridge University Press.

Watts, D. J., and Strogatz, S. (1998). Collective dynamics of "small-world" networks. *Nature*, **393**, 440–442.

7 Biological Systems, Fractals, and Systems Biology

Modern science connects many basic secrets of living matter with the genetic codes. Biological organisms belong to a category of very complex natural systems, which correspond to a huge number of biological species with inherited properties. But surprisingly, molecular genetics has discovered that all organisms are identical to each other by their basic molecular-genetic structures. Due to this revolutionary discovery, a great unification of all biological organisms has resulted in science. The information-genetic line of investigations has become one of the most prospective lines not only in biology, but also in science as a whole.

To understand complex biological systems at the various levels of molecules, cells, tissues, and organs, we must examine their structures, dynamics, and functions. It requires the integration of experimental, computational, and theoretical explorations. Many breakthroughs in experimental devices, high-throughput technologies, and mathematical framework are required before any achievements in understanding biological systems. While computational biology, through pragmatic modeling and theoretical exploration, provides a powerful foundation from which to address critical scientific questions head-on, in this chapter we focus on analytical methods of fractal geometry in biological systems. We explain how the presence of fractal geometry can be used in an analytical way to study genetic code systems and predict outcomes in systems, to generate hypotheses, and to help design experiments. At the end of the chapter we discuss the emerging field of systems biology, as well as challenges and perspectives in biological systems.

7.1 INTRODUCTION

The discovery of DNA structure in 1953 was the turning point in the history of science, culture, and society. The underlying principle of this discovery is that it has a digital nature: It contains specific, clear information; it is a code. This information allows scientists to approach the study of all biological

Mathematics of Bioinformatics: Theory, Practice, and Applications, By Matthew He and Sergey Petoukhov
Copyright © 2011 John Wiley & Sons, Inc.

systems (they all share the same code) within a defined, fully delineated framework. The challenge is therefore to decode this information. Biological systems contain two main types of digital information: genes, which encode the proteins through the intermediary of RNA, and biological networks, which specify interactions in time and space at different levels of molecules, cells, tissues, organs, and systems.

The study of biological systems cannot be limited simply to listing its parts (i.e., proteins, genes, cells, etc.). A deeper understanding of biological systems can demonstrate how these parts are assembled and how they interact with each other and with the surrounding environment. The systems approach brings with it a sense of wholeness. In the words of Ludwig von Bertalanffy, the author of general system theory, contemporary science should recognize the importance of *wholeness*, defined as "problems of organization, phenomena not resolvable into local events, dynamic interactions manifest in the difference of behavior of parts when isolated or in higher configuration, etc.; in short, 'systems' of various orders not understandable by investigation of their respective parts in isolation" (Ge et al., 2003).

It was only recently that system-level analysis can be grounded in discoveries at the molecular level. With the progress of the genome sequence project and a range of other molecular biology projects that accumulate in-depth knowledge of the molecular nature of biological systems, we are now at the stage of looking into the possibility of a system-level understanding that is solidly grounded in molecular-level understanding. Although systems are composed of matter, the essence of these systems lies in dynamics and it cannot be described merely by enumerating components of the system. Both the structure of the system and its components play an indispensable role in forming a symbiotic state of the system as a whole. This may include an understanding of the structure of the system, such as gene regulatory and biochemical networks, and an understanding of the dynamics of the system: both quantitative and qualitative analysis. There are numbers of exciting and profound issues that are actively investigated, such as the robustness of biological systems, network structures and dynamics, and applications to drug discovery. Systems biology and network biology are in their infancy, but these are the areas that have to be explored and the areas that demonstrate the mainstream in biological sciences in this century (Kitano, 2002a,b).

Biologists have traditionally modeled nature using Euclidean representations of natural objects or series. They represented heartbeats as sine waves, conifer trees as cones, animal habitats as simple areas, and cell membranes as curves or simple surfaces. However, scientists have come to recognize that many natural constructs are better characterized using fractal geometry. Biological systems and processes are typically characterized by many levels of substructure, with the same general pattern repeated in an ever-decreasing cascade.

Scientists discovered that the basic architecture of a chromosome is treelike; every chromosome consists of many "minichromosomes" and therefore can be treated as fractal. For a human chromosome, for example, a fractal dimension D equals 2.34 (between the plane and the space dimension). Self-similarity has also been found in DNA sequences. In the opinion of some biologists, fractal properties of DNA can be used to resolve evolutionary relationships in animals. Perhaps in the future, biologists will use the fractal geometry to create comprehensive models of the patterns and processes observed in nature.

7.2 FRACTAL GEOMETRY PRELIMINARIES

Fractals as Mathematical and Biological Objects

Fractal geometry provides a new perspective from which to view the world. For centuries we've used the line as a basic building block to understand the objects around us. Fractal geometry is a new language used to describe, model, and analyze complex forms found in nature. A *fractal* is a geometric shape that has two most important properties:

1. The object is self-similar.
2. The object has fractional dimensions.

What is *self-similarity*? If you look carefully at a fern leaf, you will notice that every little leaf—part of the bigger one—has the same shape as that of the whole fern leaf. You can say that the fern leaf is self-similar. The same goes for fractals: You can magnify them many times, and after every step you will see the same shape, which is characteristic of that particular fractal.

The noninteger dimension is more difficult to explain. Classical geometry deals with objects of integer dimensions: zero-dimensional points, one-dimensional lines and curves, two-dimensional plane figures such as squares and circles, and three-dimensional solids such as cubes and spheres. However, many natural phenomena are better described using a dimension between two whole numbers. So while a straight line has a dimension of 1, a fractal curve will have a dimension between 1 and 2, depending on how much space it takes up as it twists and curves. The more the flat fractal fills a plane, the closer it approaches two dimensions. Similarly, a "hilly fractal scene" will reach somewhere between two and three dimensions. So a fractal landscape made up of a large hill covered with tiny mounds would be close to the second dimension, while a rough surface composed of many medium-sized hills would be close to the third dimension.

There are a lot of different types of fractals. In this section we present two of the most popular types: complex number fractals and iterated function system (IFS) fractals. The two most famous complex number fractals are the Mandelbrot set and Julia fractals. A *Mandelbrot set* is a set of points on a complex plain. To build a Mandelbrot set, we have to use an algorithm based on the recursive formula

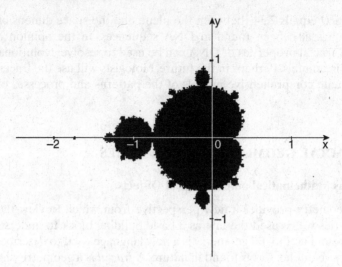

FIGURE 7.1   Mandelbrot set.

$$Z_n = Z_{n-1} + c \tag{7.1}$$

separating the points of the complex plane into two categories: (1) points inside the Mandelbrot set, and (2) points outside the Mandelbrot set. Figure 7.1 shows a portion of the complex plane. The points of the Mandelbrot set are shown in black.

Julia fractals are strictly connected with Mandelbrot fractals. The iterative function that is used to produce them is the same as for the Mandelbrot set. The only difference is the way in which this formula is used. The value of c determines the shape of the Julia set; in other words, each point of the complex plane is associated with a particular Julia set.

Iterated function system (IFS) *fractals* are created on the basis of simple plane transformations: scaling, dislocation, and the plane axes rotation. Creating an IFS fractal consists of the following steps:

1. Defining a set of plane transformations.
2. Drawing an initial pattern on the plane (any pattern).
3. Transforming the initial pattern using the transformations defined in step 1.
4. Transforming the new picture (combination of initial and transformed patterns) using the same set of transformations.
5. Repeating step 4 as many times as possible (in theory, this procedure can be repeated an infinite number of times).

The most famous ISF fractals are the *Sierpinski triangles*, the fractals we can get by taking the midpoints of each side of an equilateral triangle and

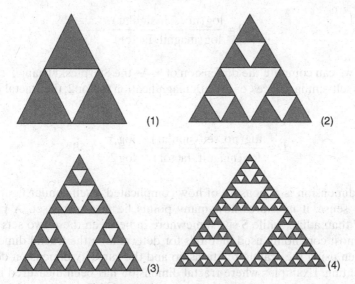

FIGURE 7.2   Sierpinski triangles.

connecting them. The iterations should be repeated an infinite number of times. Figure 7.2 presents the four initial steps of the construction of Sierpinski triangles. Using this fractal as an example, we can prove that the fractal dimension is not an integer.

First, we have to find out how the "size" of an object behaves when its linear dimension increases. In one dimension we can consider a line segment. If the linear dimension of the line segment is doubled, the length (characteristic size) of the line has also doubled. In two dimensions, if the linear dimensions of a square are doubled, for example, the characteristic size, the area, increases by a factor of 4. In three dimensions, if the linear dimension of a box is doubled, the volume increases by a factor of 8.

So what is the dimension of a Sierpinski triangle? How do we find the exponent in this case? For this, we need logarithms. Note that for the square, we have N^2 self-similar pieces, each with magnification factor **N**. So we can write

$$D = \frac{\log(\text{no. self-similar})}{\log(\text{magnif. factor})} = \frac{\log N^2}{\log N} = 2 \qquad (7.2)$$

Similarly, the dimension of a cube is

$$D = \frac{\log(\text{no. self-similar})}{\log(\text{magnif. factor})} = \frac{\log N^3}{\log N} = 3$$

Thus, we take as the definition of the fractal dimension of a self-similar object,

$$D = \frac{\log(\text{no. self-similar})}{\log(\text{magnif. factor})}$$

Now we can compute the dimension of **S**. As the Sierpinski triangle consists of three self-similar pieces, each with magnification factor 2, the fractal dimension is

$$D = \frac{\log(\text{no. self-similar})}{\log(\text{magnif. factor})} = \frac{\log 3}{\log 2} \approx 1.58$$

Fractal dimension is a measure of how complicated a self-similar figure is. In a rough sense, it measures how many points lie in a given set. A plane is "larger" than a line, while **S** sits somewhere in between these two sets.

The most commonly used methods for determining the fractal dimensions have been using the scaling relationship and the capacity dimension done by box counting. Examples where fractal dimension has been measured include the surfaces of proteins, cell membranes, cells of the cornea, and bacterial colonies.

7.3   FRACTAL GEOMETRY IN BIOLOGICAL SYSTEMS

Fractal geometry reveals the regularity behind matter with apparently irregular forms. A fractal implies a complex pattern with self-similarity and self-affinity, that is, a fractal has a shape made of parts similar to the whole in some way. DNA sequences and the structures of protein have such a complex form. Scaling behavior can be seen in fundamental biological structures. DNA structure demonstrates fractal properties in the distribution of sequence information. Fractal geometry can be used for approximate analyses of these biological objects. Fractal research into proteins and enzymes is currently an active field of bioinformatics (Iannaccone et al., 1996). In this section we first summarize several examples of fractal applications in DNA sequences, cell, protein, and chromosome structures, and enzyme and ion channel kinetics. We discuss DNA walks, fractal and symmetrical properties in genetic code systems, and fractal properties of proteins and polymers.

Fractals in DNA Sequences   Self-similarity has recently been found in DNA sequences (Nonnenmacher et al., 1994; Stanley, 1992). The multifractal spectrum approach has been used to reconstruct the evolutionary history of organisms from mDNA sequences (Glazier et al., 1995). The multifractal spectra for invertebrates and vertebrates were quite different, allowing for the recognition of broad groups of organisms. They concluded that DNA sequences display fractal properties and that these can be used to resolve evolutionary relationships in animals. Furthermore, Xiao et al. (1995) found that nucleotide sequences in animals, plants, and humans display fractal properties. They also showed that exon and intron sequences differ in their fractal properties.

Fractals in Cell, Protein, and Chromosome Structures   Takahashi (1989) hypothesized that the basic architecture of a chromosome is treelike, consisting of a concatenation of "minichromosomes." A fractal dimension of $D = 2.34$ was determined from an analysis of first- and second-order branching patterns in a human metaphase chromosome. Xu et al. (1994) hypothesized that the twistings of DNA binding proteins have fractal properties.

Lewis and Rees (1985) determined the fractal dimension of protein surfaces ($2 \Leftarrow D \Leftarrow 3$) using microprobes. A mean surface dimension of $D = 2.4$ was determined using microprobe radii ranging from 1 to 3.5 Å. More highly irregular surfaces ($D > 2.4$) were found to be sites of interprotein interaction. Wagner et al. (1985) estimated the fractal dimension of heme and iron–sulfur proteins using crystallographic coordinates of the carbon backbone. They found that the structural fractal dimension correlated positively with the temperature dependence of protein relaxation rates. Smith et al. (1989) used fractal dimension as a measure of contour complexity in two-dimensional images of neural cells. They recommend D as a quantitative morphological measure of cellular complexity.

Fractals in Enzyme and Ion Channel Kinetics   The kinetics of protein ion channels in the phospholipid bilayer were examined by Liebovitch et al. (1987). The timing of openings and closings of ion channels had fractal properties, implying that processes operating at different time scales are related, not independent (Liebovitch and Koniarek 1992). López-Quintela and Casado (1989) developed a fractal model of enzyme kinetics, based on the observation that kinetics is a function of substrate concentration. They found that some enzyme systems displayed classical Michaelis–Menten kinetics ($D = 1$), whereas others showed fractal kinetics ($D < 1$).

Fractals and DNA Walk   A DNA walk of a genome represents how the frequency of each nucleotide of a pairing nucleotide couple changes locally. This analysis implies measurement of the local distribution of G's in the content of GC and of T's in the content of TA. Lobry was the first to propose this analysis (1996).

As you probably already know, DNA is a long sequence of nucleotides that code all the genetic information about us. The nucleotides can be either adenine, guanine, cytosine, or thymine (abbreviated A, G, C, and T). One of the fractal patterns that were studied was in the sequence of nucleotides in what is called the *DNA walk*, a graphical representation of the DNA sequence in which you move up if you hit C or T and down if you hit A or G. For example, Figure 7.3 represents the sequence CATG. Fractal patterns were found in many DNA walks. These patterns are remarkably similar to *Brownian motion*. Figure 7.4 is a model of a fractal DNA walk.

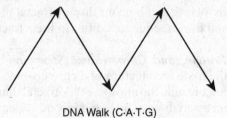

DNA Walk (C·A·T·G)

FIGURE 7.3   DNA walk.

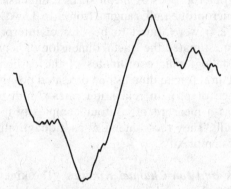

FIGURE 7.4   Fractal model of a DNA walk.

As we have shown above, the DNA walk is a geometrical representation of the nucleotide sequence. This DNA walk scheme could be applied to demonstrate the symmetric and fractal structure of the genetic codon system. Next we present a simple approach to constructing the biperiodic table of the genetic code (Petoukhov, 2001) by using a triple of RNA tetrahedrons. We then use various methods to classify the codon table and demonstrate the symmetric and fractal structure of the genetic codon system.

RNA Tetrahedron   A regular tetrahedron has four equal faces, four vertices, and six edges (the minimal number of faces required to form a three-dimensional polyhedron, similar to the fact that a triangle is the first polygon in two-dimensional space). RNA bases consists of four bases: A, C, G, and U. We label each letter to each face of a regular tetrahedron. We color each tetrahedron red, green, and blue, respectively (Figure 7.5).

To construct a biperiodic table of the genetic code, we roll three tetrahedrons and record three letters covered at the bottom of each toss. Assume that each event is equally likely. It's easy to see that there are a total of $4 \times 4 \times 4 = 4^3 = 64$ possible outcomes. We list all these 64 elements in the table $G(i, j), i, j = 1, 2, 3, 4, 5, 6, 7, 8$.

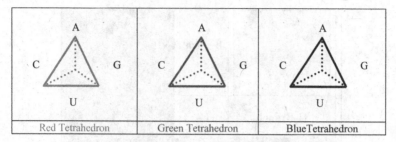

FIGURE 7.5   RNA tetrahedron.

AAA	ACA	AGA	AUA	CAA	CCA	CGA	CUA
AAC	ACC	AGC	AUC	CAC	CCC	CGC	CUC
AAG	ACG	AGG	AUG	CAG	CCG	CGG	CUG
AAU	ACU	AGU	AUU	CAU	CCU	CGU	CUU
GAA	GCA	GGA	GUA	UAA	UCA	UGA	UUA
GAC	GCC	GGC	GUC	UAC	UCC	UGC	UUC
GAG	GCG	GGG	GUG	UAG	UCG	UGG	UUG
GAU	GCU	GGU	GUU	UAU	UCU	UGU	UUU

FIGURE 7.6   Genetic code from a full 4-ary tree.

Theoretically, for each cell of the table, there are 64 possible ways to arrange a codon. The total number of codons in the table is 64!. One way to list all 64 codons is to use a full 4-ary tree structure. One may label A, C, G, and U to each edge of the tree, respectively, from left to right. Allow the tree to grow up to three levels (the height of the tree is 3). The total number of the nodes of this full 4-ary tree with level 3 is $4^3 = 64$. A complete list of the codons is given in Figure 7.6. This table may be visualized by the three levels of the 4 × 4 table shown in Figure 7.7.

An important variation of Figure 7.6 is the *biperiodical table of genetic code* (Petoukhov, 2001; Figure 7.8). This table demonstrates a great fractal structure and has led to many discoveries. The distribution of the RNA codons may provide some patterns and relations for the genetic code. Next we introduce three different methods to classify the codes in Figure 7.8. The first method is based on the equivalence properties of A, C, G, and U (attribute-based method). The second method connects the RAN codon with a six-digit binary table (binary code method). The third method uses the Fibonacci numbers and six-digit binary code to classify the genetic code (Fibonacci method). The

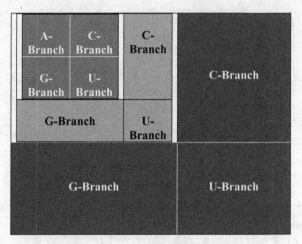

FIGURE 7.7   Genetic code from a full 4-ary tree.

CCC	CCA	CAC	CAA	ACC	ACA	AAC	AAA
CCU	CCG	CAU	CAG	ACU	ACG	AAU	AAG
CUC	CUA	CGC	CGA	AUC	AUA	AGC	AGA
UCC	UCA	UAC	UAA	GCC	GCA	GAC	GAA
CUU	CUG	CGU	CGG	AUU	AUG	AGU	AGG
UCU	UCG	UAU	UAG	GCU	GCG	GAU	GAG
UUC	UUA	UGC	UGA	GUC	GUA	GGC	GGA
UUU	UUG	UGU	UGG	GUU	GUG	GGU	GGG

FIGURE 7.8   Biperiodical table of genetic code.

distributions of the genetic code based on these three methods demonstrate the great symmetries of the codons.

Attribute-Based Method   Recently, Petoukhov (2001) pointed out that regular matrices of the genetic code arise if one takes into consideration the existence of the three subalphabets of the genetic alphabet, in accordance with the three types of attributes of nitrogenous bases A, C, G, and U. Table 2.2 shows that each letter of the code alphabet has three "faces" or meanings in three binary subalphabets in connection with the three types of attributes. We'll use these attributes to assign A, C, G, and U values of 1, 2, and 3 to each equivalence pair. The following are all possible combinations of these assignments:

27	18	18	12	18	12	12	8
18	27	12	18	12	18	8	12
18	12	27	18	12	8	18	12
18	12	12	8	27	18	18	12
12	18	18	27	8	12	12	18
12	18	8	12	18	27	12	18
12	8	18	12	18	12	27	18
8	12	12	18	12	18	18	27

FIGURE 7.9 $C = G = 3$, $A = U = 2$. P_1, product of hydrogen bonds.

- $C = G = 3$, $A = U = 2$, hydrogen bond–based (2,3)-combination
- $C = U = 1$, $A = G = 2$, pyrimidine/purine ring–based (1,2)-combination
- $G = U = 1$, $A = C = 3$, amino group–based (1,3)-combination

For each case, we apply two basic operations, addition and multiplication, to generate numerical tables. These tables are used to construct corresponding frequency tables of the distributions of the genetic code. For example, with $C = G = 3$, $A = U = 2$, if we apply the multiplication to Figure 7.6, we have the results shown in Figure 7.9. We have the distribution of codons with equal numbers shown in Table 7.1. A symmetrical histogram is illustrated in Figure 7.10.

Binary Code Method   Next we consider a 3-bit binary code: 111, 110, 101, 100, 011, 010, 001, and 000. Using these codes, we construct the 8×8 table $B(i, j)$, $i, j = 1, 2, 3, 4, 5, 6, 7, 8$, shown in Figure 7.11, where the asterisk implies the append operation between three-digit binary code. Various distributions of $G(i, j)$ may be constructed by using these correspondences. Let X be the number of 1's in table $B(i, j)$. Then the possible values of X are 0, 1, 2, 3, 4, 5, and 6. Seven classes of the codons are divided. The frequency table of the genetic code is given in Table 7.2. It is easy to see that the table demonstrates a normal distribution of the random variable X (Figure 7.12).

Fibonacci Method   This method was used initially in the article by A. Stakhov (2008) and in his book (Stakhov, 2009). The Fibonacci code could have an X-digit code. X is the first few numbers in the Fibonacci sequence. If there is a six-digit code, the first few numbers would be 1, 1, 2, 3, 5, and 8. Let's consider

TABLE 7.1   C = G = 3, A = U = 2

Product of Hydrogen Bonds	Codons	Frequency of Codons
8	AAA, AAU, AUA, UAA, AUU, UAU, UUA, UUU	8
12	CAA, ACA, AAC, CAU, ACU, AAG, CUA, AUC, AGA, UCA, UAC, GAA, CUU, AUG, AGU, UCU, UAG, GAU, UUC, UGA, GUA, UUG, UGU, GUU	24
18	CCA, CAC, ACC, CCU, CAG, ACG, CUC, CGA, AGC, UCC, GCA, GAC, CUG, CGU, AGG, UCG, GCU, GAG, UGC, GUC, GGA, UGG, GUG, GGU	24
27	CCC, CCG, CGC, GCC, CGG, GCG, GGC, GGG	8

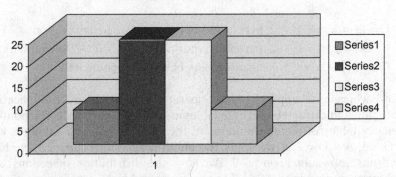

FIGURE 7.10   Attribute-based distribution of genetic code.

*	111	110	101	100	011	010	001	000
111	111111	111110	111101	111100	111011	111010	111001	111000
110	110111	110110	110101	110110	110011	110010	110001	110000
101	101111	101110	101101	101100	101011	101010	101001	101000
100	100111	100110	100101	100100	100011	100010	100001	100000
011	011111	011110	011101	011100	011011	011010	011001	011000
010	010111	010110	010101	010100	010011	010010	010001	010000
001	001111	001110	001101	001100	001011	001010	001001	001000
000	000111	000110	000101	000100	000011	000010	000001	000000

FIGURE 7.11   Six-digit binary code B(i, j).

TABLE 7.2   Frequency Table of the Genetic Code

X	Elements	No. of Elements
0	GGG	1
1	GGU, GGA, UGG. GAA, GUG, GAG	6
2	AAG, GGC, UUG, GUU, AGG, UAA, UGU, GCG, AGA, GUA, UGA, GAU, GCU, UAG, GAC, GCA	15
3	UUU, AAA, AAU, UUA, CGG, GCC, AUA, GUC, UAU, UCG, UGC, GCU, AGU, AUG, UAC, UCA, AGC, CGA, ACG, CAG	20
4	AAC, CCG, UUC, AUU, UCC, CAA, ACA, UCU, UCU, CGU, CUG, AUC, CUA, ACU, CAU	15
5	CCA, CCU, ACC, CUU, CUC, CAC	6
6	CCC	1

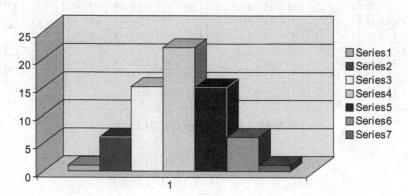

FIGURE 7.12   Binary code–based distribution of genetic code.

the six-digit Fibonacci code using Fibonacci numbers $1, 1, 2, 3, 5$, and 8 as digit weights. We first label each cell of the 8×8 table by C0 to C63, as shown in Figure 7.13. Applying the formula

$$N = a_6 \times 8 + a_5 \times 5 + a_4 \times 3 + a_3 \times 2 + a_2 \times 1 + a_1 \times 1$$

to both tables $B(i, j)$ and $C(i, j)$, we obtain another table $F(i, j)$ of the Fibonacci code (Figure 7.14). For example,

$$C63 = 1 \times 8 + 1 \times 5 + 1 \times 3 + 1 \times 2 + 1 \times 1 + 1 \times 1 = 20$$
$$C0 = 0 \times 8 + 0 \times 5 + 0 \times 3 + 0 \times 2 + 0 \times 1 + 0 \times 1 = 0$$
$$C1 = 1 \times 8 + 0 \times 5 + 0 \times 3 + 0 \times 2 + 0 \times 1 + 0 \times 1 = 8$$

Since all four tables have the same 8×8 dimensions, we assume the following one-to-one correspondence for each $i, j = 1, 2, 3, 4, 5, 6, 7, 8$:

C63	C62	C61	C60	C59	C58	C57	C56
C55	C54	C53	C52	C51	C50	C49	C48
C47	C46	C45	C44	C43	C42	C41	C40
C39	C38	C37	C36	C35	C34	C33	C32
C31	C30	C29	C28	C27	C26	C25	C24
C23	C22	C21	C20	C19	C18	C17	C16
C15	C14	C13	C12	C11	C10	C9	C8
C7	C6	C5	C4	C3	C2	C1	C0

FIGURE 7.13   Fibonacci code $C(i, j)$.

C63 = 20	C62 = 12	C61 = 15	C60 = 7	C59 = 17	C58 = 9	C57 = 12	C56 = 4
C55 = 18	C54 = 10	C53 = 13	C52 = 5	C51 = 15	C50 = 7	C49 = 10	C48 = 2
C47 = 19	C46 = 11	C45 = 14	C44 = 6	C43 = 16	C42 = 8	C41 = 11	C40 = 3
C39 = 17	C38 = 9	C37 = 12	C36 = 4	C35 = 14	C34 = 6	C33 = 9	C32 = 1
C31 = 19	C30 = 11	C29 = 14	C28 = 6	C27 = 16	C26 = 8	C25 = 11	C24 = 3
C23 = 17	C22 = 9	C21 = 12	C20 = 4	C19 = 14	C18 = 6	C17 = 9	C16 = 1
C15 = 18	C14 = 10	C13 = 13	C12 = 5	C11 = 15	C10 = 7	C9 = 10	C8 = 2
C7 = 16	C6 = 8	C5 = 11	C4 = 3	C3 = 13	C2 = 5	C1 = 8	C0 = 0

FIGURE 7.14   Fibonacci code $F(i, j)$.

$$G(i, j) \leftrightarrow B(i, j) \leftrightarrow C(i, j) \leftrightarrow F(i, j)$$

Next we use tables $F(i, j)$ and $G(i, j)$ to construct a frequency table (Table 7.3). We have a total number of 21 groups according to this method. The frequency distribution of Table 7.3 can be illustrated by a histogram, as shown in Figure 7.15.

Scale-Invariant Features of Coding and Noncoding DNA Sequences

The role of genomic DNA sequences in coding for protein structure is well known. The coding region of a gene is the portion of DNA or RNA that is transcribed into another RNA, such as a messenger RNA or a noncoding RNA (e.g., a transfer RNA or a ribosomal RNA). A transcript can then be translated into proteins. A noncoding DNA describes DNA which does not contain instructions for making proteins (or other cell products, such as noncoding RNAs). In eukaryotes, a large percentage of many organisms' total genome size comprises noncoding DNA (a puzzle known as the *C-value enigma*). Some noncoding DNA is involved in regulating the activity of coding regions. However, much of this DNA has no known function and is sometimes referred to as *junk DNA*. An open question in computational molecular biology is

TABLE 7.3   Fibonacci Code–Based Frequency Table of Genetic Code

Fibonacci Code	Genetic Codons				
0	GGG				
1	GAA	GAG			
2	GGA	AAG			
3	UGG	AGG	AGA		
4	UAG	UAA	AAA		
5	GUG	UGA	CAG		
6	GCG	CGG	GCA	CGA	
7	GUA	ACG	CAA		
8	GGU	UUG	AUG	AUA	
9	GAU	UCG	GAU	UCA	ACA
10	GGC	UUA	AAU	CCG	
11	UGU	AGU	CUG	AGC	CUA
12	UAU	UAC	AAC	CCA	
13	GUU	UGC	CAU		
14	GCU	CGU	GCC	CGC	
15	GUC	ACU	CAC		
16	UUU	AUU	AUC		
17	UCU	UCC	ACC		
18	UUC	CCU			
19	CUU	CUC			
20	CCC				

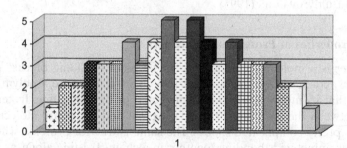

FIGURE 7.15   Fibonacci code–based distribution of genetic code.

whether long-range correlation is present in both coding and noncoding DNA or only in the latter.

To answer this question, systematic analyses of biological databases have been performed by Buldyrev et al. (1995). The authors considered all thirty-three 301 coding and all twenty-nine 453 noncoding eukaryotic sequences, each of length greater than 512 base pairs (bp) in the present release of the GenBank, to determine whether there is any statistically significant distinction in their long-range correlation properties. Standard fast Fourier transform (FFT) analysis indicates that coding sequences have practically no correlations in the range 10 to 100 bp (spectral exponent $\beta = 0.00 \pm 0.04$, where the uncertainty is two standard deviations). In contrast, for noncoding sequences, the average value of the spectral exponent β is positive (0.16 ± 0.05), which unambiguously shows the presence of long-range correlations. Buldyrev et al. also separately analyzed the 874 coding and the 1157 noncoding sequences that have more than 4096 bp and found a larger region of power-law behavior. Buldyrev et al. calculated the probability that these two data sets (coding and noncoding) were drawn from the same distribution and found that it is less than 10^{-10}. They also obtained independent confirmation of these findings using the method of detrended fluctuation analysis (DFA), which is designed to treat sequences with statistical heterogeneity, such as DNA's known mosaic structure ("patchiness") arising from the nonstationarity of nucleotide concentration. The nearly perfect agreement between the two independent analysis methods, FFT and DFA, increases the confidence in the reliability of the conclusion regarding long-range correlation properties of coding and noncoding sequences. Recently, long-range correlation in DNA sequences was analyzed by Bacry et al. (1995) using wavelet analysis. The wavelet transform modulus maxima method was used to analyze the fractal scaling properties of DNA sequences. This method, based on the definition of partition functions, which use the values of the wavelet transform at its modulus maxima, allows one to determine accurately the singularity spectrum of a given singular signal. It was found that there exist long-range correlations in noncoding regions and no long-range correlations in coding regions, in excellent agreement with the results of Buldyrev et al. (1995).

Fractal Properties of Proteins and Polymers

A *polymer* is a molecule composed of a series of "building blocks" (called *monomers*) connected to one another in a chain. If you take a polymer, you will find that its monomers are not connected in a straight line. Instead, the angles between the monomers can be different and the entire molecule can twist into pretty complicated shapes. The same is true for proteins, which are formed by amino acids bonding together in a chain. Twisting alone, as well as folding and breaking, often implies that the shape is fractal. Proteins and many other polymers are, indeed, fractal, and various methods exist for finding their fractal dimension. The results for some interesting proteins are shown in Table 7.4. Note that the dimensions are much higher than 1, which you would expect from a linear chain. This is another proof that proteins are fractal.

The numerical value of the fractal dimension D gives us a quantitative measure of self-similarity. It tells us how many small pieces $N(r)$ are revealed when an object is viewed at finer resolution r. The quantitative relationship between $N(r)$ and the fractal dimension is that $N(r)$ is proportional to r^{-D}. The larger the fractal dimension, the larger the number of small pieces that are

TABLE 7.4   Fractal Dimensions of Some Proteins

Protein	Fractal Dimension
Lysozyme (egg white)	1.614
Hemoglobin (oxygen carrier in the blood)	1.583
Myoglobin (muscle protein)	1.728

Source: Ideker et al. (2001).

revealed as the object is viewed at finer resolution. The fractal dimension measures the correlations between the small and large pieces and the correlations between the small pieces themselves. In addition, the fractal dimension can be used to classify different objects. For example, the fractal dimension of the blood vessels in a normal retina is different from the fractal dimension in a retina changed by diseases. The fractal dimension may serve as a method to diagnose different diseases and as an index to quantify the severity of these diseases. Fractal dimension may also provide hints about biological mechanisms. Different mechanisms produce fractals with different dimensions. Hence, measuring the fractal dimension of an object may give us clues as to how to determine the mechanism that produced it. For example, the process of diffusion-limited aggregation produces fractals with a fractal dimension of about 1.7. The blood vessels in the retina have a fractal dimension of about 1.7. Thus, it is worthwhile to speculate if the growth of these blood vessels was produced by diffusion-limited aggregation. This would mean that the growth of the blood vessels was proportional to the gradient of a diffusible substance, such as oxygen or a growth factor.

Fractal surfaces can be used to characterize the roughness or irregularity of protein surfaces (Lewis and Rees, 1985). The degree of irregularity of a surface may be described by the fractal dimension D. For protein surfaces defined by probes in the range 1.0 to 3.5 Å in radius, D is approximately 2.4, or intermediate between the value for a completely smooth surface ($D = 2$) and that for a completely space-filling surface ($D = 3$). Individual regions of proteins show considerable variation in D. These variations may be related to structural features such as active sites and subunit interfaces, suggesting that surface texture may be a factor influencing molecular interactions.

In summary, fractal theory is a unifying concept integrating scale dependence and complexity, both of which are central to our understanding of biological patterns and processes (Lam and Quattrochi, 1992; West and Goldberger 1987; Wiens 1989). Given that fractal and chaos theory are comparatively new fields, it is perhaps not surprising that biologists are still grappling with these concepts. Recognition of the fractal geometry of nature has important implications in biology, as evidenced by the numerous examples presented here. Zeide and Gresham (1991) describe as self-evident the fractal nature of biological structures and systems. We feel that one of the great challenges facing biologists lies in translating these self-evident concepts into comprehensive models of the patterns and processes observed in nature.

7.4 SYSTEMS BIOLOGY

The emerging field of systems biology involves the application of experimental, theoretical, and modeling techniques to the study of biological organisms at all levels, from the molecular, through the cellular, to the behavioral. Its aim is to understand biological processes as entire systems instead of as isolated parts. Developments in the field have been made possible by advances in molecular biology—in particular, new technologies for determining DNA sequence, gene expression profiles, protein–protein interactions, and so on.

The systems biology approach starts with the definition of the structure of the system under study. To determine its functional properties, the attention shifts to the system dynamics. The structure and dynamics provide a baseline that can be used to analyze an essential property of biological systems: robustness.

Robustness of biological systems manifests itself in various ways. First, biological systems constantly adapt to internal or external changes. Second, they show certain insensitivity, which enables them to deal with the noise generated by the stochastic signals to which they are exposed. Finally, they also exhibit what could be called a graceful degradation, which is a slow and gradual end as opposed to the catastrophic failure that occurs when functions are damaged (Hood and Galas, 2003).

The overall systems biology methodology includes the formulation of a model once the components of the system have been defined, followed by the systematical perturbation (either genetically or environmentally) and monitoring of the system. The experimentally observed responses are then reconciled with those predicted by the model. Finally, new perturbation experiments are designed and performed to distinguish between multiple or competing model hypotheses (Ideker et al., 2001).

In summary, to understand biology at the system level, we must examine the structure and dynamics of cellular function rather than the characteristics of isolated parts of a cell or organism. Properties of systems, such as robustness, emerge as central issues, and understanding these properties may have an effect on the future of medicine. However, many breakthroughs in experimental devices, advanced software, and analytical methods are required before the achievements of systems biology can live up to their much-touted potential (Kitano, 2002a,b).

7.5 CHALLENGES AND PERSPECTIVES

At every level of organization, biological systems are complex hierarchies in which ensembles of lower-level units become the units in higher-order ensembles. The analysis of complex hierarchical systems therefore represents one of the most important open areas in biology. At both the molecular and cellular levels, the components of biological systems are being revealed by modern experimental methodology. The organization and integration of these details into a functional biological system will require the techniques of the mathematician as well as the data of the biologist. Problems of this sort are at the core of genetics, neurobiology, developmental biology, and immunology. Similar problems exist in understanding how individuals are organized into populations, and populations into communities.

The analysis of complex hierarchical systems is one of the most important open areas in modern biology. This holds true at all levels of organization. The essence of the matter is this: On several levels, the components of biological systems are being revealed by modern experimental biology. The techniques of molecular biology are most important here; other experimental advances are also of major utility. The central theoretical question is how the molecular details are integrated into a functional unity, a question central to at least three major fields: neurobiology, developmental biology, and immunology.

The immune system contains 10^{12} cells, comprising at least 10^7 specificities. These cells move within the body and communicate both by cell–cell contact and via tens, maybe hundreds, of regulatory molecules. The system is capable of pattern recognition, learning and memory expression, and thus has many features in common with the nervous system.

Theoretical ideas have played a major role in the development of the field. Controversies such as instructive vs. selective theories of antibody formation, germ-line vs. somatic mutation models for the generation of antibody diversity, and regulatory circuits vs. idiotypic networks have dominated the intellectual development of the field and determined the direction of much experimental effort. Mathematical theories have not been nearly as important, but this appears to be changing as the field addresses more quantitative issues, such as the role of somatic mutation in the generation of antibody diversity, the role of receptor clusters in cell stimulation and desensitization signals, the effects of different concentrations of cytokines, receptor affinities, and receptor number on cell stimulation, cell proliferation, cell differentiation, and the engagement of effector functions.

Modeling the immune system requires the same type of hierarchical approach as does neurobiological modeling. At the lowest level, one must develop quantitative models of the action of single lymphocytes as they interact with antigens and cytokines. A large amount of effort involving the study of infinite systems of ordinary differential equations and branching processes has gone into the mathematical modeling of receptor cross-linking by multivalent ligands (cf. Perelson, 1984). Cell response in terms of proliferation or differentiation has been examined from an optimal control perspective (Perelson et al., 1976). The effects of the T-cell growth factor IL-2 have also been incorporated into cellular models (Kevrekidis et al., 1988). At the next-higher levels, small idiotypic networks containing two complementary cell populations have been modeled, as well as networks containing hundreds to thousands of B-cell clones (Perelson, 1989; Segel and Perelson, 1989; Weisbuch et al. 1990). In the immune system, not only is the number of components large, but in distinction to the nervous system, the components turn over rapidly. The average life span of a B cell is on the order of four days, that of serum antibody, one to two weeks. Thus, on a rather rapid time scale, many immune system components may be replaced, although the system as a whole remains intact.

New ideas and mathematical representations are required to handle systems with large numbers of constantly changing components. Some promising approaches involve the formulation of models in terms of a potentially infinite-dimensional *shape space*, where emphasis is placed on determining interactions among molecules based on their shapes. In computer models binary strings have been used to represent molecular shape, with the obvious advantage of fast algorithms to determine complementarities and the ability to represent 4×10^9 different molecular shapes with 32 bits (Farmer et al., 1986). To handle the perpetual novelty that the elimination of old components and the generation of new components introduces into the immune system, models can be formulated using "metadynamical" rules, wherein an algorithm is used to update the dynamical equations of the model, depending on the components present in the system at the time of update (Bagley et al., 1989). One needs to understand in a mathematical sense the dynamics of a system in which the variables of the model are in constant flux. What does it mean to have an attractor if the variables describing the attractor are eliminated from the system before a trajectory approaches the attractor? Formulation of models appropriate to unravel the observed complexity in the immune system is the first major step. Next, a massive effort is required to unravel the behavioral modes of these complex models and compare them with experiment. Here, theoretical immunology merges into the mainstream of theoretical biology.

There are other areas in which we see the future growth of theoretical ideas in immunology. For example, vaccine design depends on the ability to predict T-cell epitopes. DeLisi and Berzofsky (1985) suggested that T-cell epitopes tend to be amphipathic structures. Alternative algorithms have been suggested (e.g., Rothbard and Taylor, 1988), and databases have been used to identify sequence patterns characteristic of T-cell epitopes (Claverie et al., 1988). This area is clearly one in which we will see future growth and which will rely heavily on theoretical and computational analyses.

Understanding the dynamics of HIV infection (AIDS) and its effects on the immune system is another important area for future research. Quantitative questions include: How can the $CD4^+$ T-cell population be depleted if only one in 100 cells is infected? Why is there such a long incubation period from time of infection to the clinical symptoms of AIDS? Why is this incubation period different in children than in adults? In a seropositive patient, what does the level of serum antibody predict about the course of the disease? Can one define quantitative measures of a person's chance of infecting a sex partner based on antibody or antigen levels measured in the blood? Models will also help in determining the pathogenesis of the disease and in isolating primary effects of HIV from the secondary effects of immune dysfunction. Mathematics can also play a role in the development of optimal treatment schedules and in the design of clinical trials of multiple drug therapies for AIDS. Development of epidemiological models is currently an active area of mathematical endeavor and one that will continue at a high level as we attempt to track the course of this epidemic and develop vaccine strategies aimed at its eventual eradication.

The theory of dynamical systems has been stimulated by biological questions. For example, iterations of a single nonlinear function, described via a population model of a simple kind, capture the dynamics of an isolated population with discrete generations, subject to influences that regulate the population numbers exclusively through the population size. More explicitly, the population size at generation $n + 1$ is assumed to be a given nonlinear function of the population size at generation n. Models of this type were introduced in population studies a long time ago. Isolated studies of the iteration of functions were conducted near the beginning of the twentieth century. Some of this work, notably that by Julia (1918) and Fatou (1919) and then by Myrberg (1963) and Sarkovskii (1964), pointed to a rich mathematical structure. However, it was only in the 1970's that a widespread appreciation of the depth and beauty of the mathematical phenomena involved in these mathematical problems emerged. Population biologists, especially May, played a role in stimulating this appreciation. One can only speculate as to whether the theory of these iterations would have taken off as it did without this influence from population biology, but clearly, the motivation from population biology was an important part of the chain of historical events that led to very significant scientific and mathematical discoveries.

The study of simple population models provides a classic example of mutual stimulation of mathematics and biology, with resulting benefits to both. The interlocking efforts of mathematicians, biologists, and physicists formed a network of positive feedbacks that moved the subject to new levels of sophistication. Their investigations showed clearly the existence of universal sequences of bifurcations in iterations of one-dimensional maps. Libchaber provided striking confirmation of Feigenbaum's discoveries about period-doubling bifurcations in fluid convection experiments.

Computation has played an important role in dynamical systems theory, especially in its application to specific problems. Applications in biology require the development of effective computational methods for the analysis of dynamical systems and their bifurcations. New mathematics is emerging from work in this direction.

REFERENCES

Bacry, E., Arneodo, A., Muzy, J. F., and Graves, P.-V. (1995).Wavelet analysis of DNA sequences. In: F. L. Andrew, A. U. Michael, and V. W. Mladen (Eds.), *Proceedings of Wavelet Applications in Signal and Image Processing III. Proc. SPIE*, **2569**, 489–498.

Bagley, R. J., Farmer, J. D., Kauffman, S. A., Packard, N. H., Perelson, A. S., and Stadnyk, I. M. (1989). Modeling adaptive biological systems. *Biosystems*, **23**, 113–137.

Buldyrev, S. V., Goldberger, A. L., Havlin, S., Mantegna, R. N., Matsa, M. E., Peng, C.-K., Simons, M., and Stanley, H. E. (1995). Long-range correlation properties of coding and noncoding DNA sequences. *Phys. Rev. E*, **51**, 5084–5091.

Claverie, J.-M., Kourilsky, P., Langlade-Demoyen, P., Chalfour-Prohnicka, A., Dadaglio, G., Tekais, F., Plata, F., and Bougueleret, L. (1988). T-immunogenic peptides are constituted of rare sequence patterns: use in the identification of T epitopes in the human immunodeficiency virus gag protein. *Eur. J. Immunol.*, **18**, 1547–1553.

DeLisi, C., and Berzofsky, J. A. (1985). T-cell antigenic sites tend to be amphipathic structures. *Proc. Natl. Acad. Sci. USA*, **82**, 7048–7052.

Farmer, J. D., Packard, N. H., and Perelson, A. S. (1986). The immune system, adaptation, and machine learning. *Physica D*, **22**, 187–204.

Fatou, M. P. (1919). Sur les équations fonctionelles. *Bull. Soc. Math. France*, **47**, 161–271; and (1920), *Ibid.*, **48**, 33–94, 208–314.

Ge, H., et al. (2003). Integrating "omic" information: a bridge between genomics and systems biology. *Trends Genet.*, **19**(10), 551–560.

Glazier, J. A., Raghavachari, S., Berthlesen, C. L., and Skolnick, M. H. (1995). Reconstructing phylogeny from the multifractal spectrum of mitochondrial DNA. *Phys. Rev. E*, **51**, 2665–2668.

Hood, L., and Galas, D. (2003). The digital code of DNA. *Nature*, **421**, 444–448.

Iannaccone, P. M., and Khokha, M. (Eds.) (1996). *Fractal Geometry in Biological Systems: An Analytical Approach*. Boca Raton, FL: CRC Press.

Ideker, T. et al. (2001). A new approach to decoding life: systems biology. *Annu. Rev. Genom. Hum. Genet.*, **2**, 343–372.

Julia, C. (1918). Mémoire sur l'itération des fonctions rationelles. *J. Math. Pures Appl.*, **4**, 47–245.

Kevrekidis, I. G., Zecha, A. D., and Perelson, A. S. (1988). Modeling dynamical aspects of the immune response: I. T cell proliferation and the effect of IL-2. In: A. S. Perelson (Ed.), *Theoretical Immunology*, Part 1, SFI Studies in the Sciences of Complexity. Readings MA: Addison-Wesley, pp. 167–197.

Kitano, H. (2002a). Computational systems biology. *Nature*, **420**, 206–210.

Kitano, H. (2002b). Systems biology: a brief overview. *Science*, **295**, 1662–1664.

Lam, N. S., and Quattrochi, D. A. (1992). On the issues of scale, resolution, and fractal analysis in the mapping sciences. *Prof. Geogr.*, **44**, 88–98.

Lewis, M., and Rees, D. C. (1985). Fractal surfaces of proteins. *Science*, **230**, 1163–1165.

Liebovitch, L. S., and Koniarek, J. P. (1992). Ion channel kinetics: protein switching between conformational states is fractal in time. *IEEE Eng. Med. Biol.*, **11**, 53–56.

Liebovitch, L. S., Fischbargand, J., and Koniarek, J. P. (1987). Ion channel kinetics: a model based on fractal scaling rather than multistate Markov processes. *Math. Biosci.*, **84**, 37–68.

Lobry, J. R. (1996). A simple vectorial representation of DNA sequences for the detection of replication origins in bacteria. *Biochimie*, **78**, 323–326.

López-Quintela, M. A., and Casado, J. (1989). Revision of the methodology in enzyme kinetics: a fractal approach. *J. Theor. Biol.*, **139**, 129–139.

Myrberg, P. J. (1963). Iteration der reellen Polynome zweiten Grades III. *Ann. Acad. Sci. Fenn.*, **336**(3), 1–18.

Nonnenmacher, T. F., Losa, G. A., and Weibel, E. R. (1994). *Fractals in Biology and Medicine.* Boston: Birkhäuser.

Perelson, A. S. (1984). Some mathematical models of receptor clustering by multivalent ligands. In: A. S. Perelson, C. DeLisi, and F. W. Wiegel (Eds.), *Cell Surface Dynamics: Concepts and Models.* New York: Marcel Dekker, pp. 223–276.

Perelson, A. S. (1989). Immune network theory. *Immunol. Rev.*, **5**, 36.

Perelson, A. S., Mirmirani, M., and Oster, G. F. (1976). Optimal strategies in immunology: I. B-cell differentiation and proliferation. *J. Math. Biol.*, **3**, 325–367.

Petoukhov, S. V. (2001). *The Bi-periodic Table of Genetic Code and Number of Protons.* Moscow: MKC (in Russian).

Rothbard, J. B., and Taylor, W. R. (1988). A sequence pattern common to T cell epitopes. *EMBO J.*, **7**, 93–100.

Sarkovskii, A. N. (1964). Coexistence of cycles of a continuous map of a line into itself. *Ukr. Mat. Zh.*, **16**, 61–71.

Segel, L. A., and Perelson, A. S. (1989). Shape space: an approach to the evaluation of cross-reactivity effects, stability and controlability in the immune system. *Immunol. Lett.*, **22**, 91–99.

Smith, T. G., Marks, W. B., Lange, G. D., Sheriff, W. H., and Neale, E. A. (1989). A fractal analysis of cell images. *J. Neurosci. Methods*, **27**, 173–180.

Stakhov, A. P. (2008). Fibonacci numbers and genetic code. In: Museum of Harmony and Golden Section, http://www.goldenmuseum.com/index_engl.html.

Stakhov, A. P. (2009). *The Mathematics of Harmony. From Euclid to Contemporary Mathematics and Computer Science.* New Jersey, London, Singapore, Beijing, Shanghai, Hong Kong, Taipei, Chennai: World Scientific.

Stanley, H. E. (1992). Fractal landscapes in physics and biology. *Physica A*, **186**, 1–32.

Takahashi, M. (1989). A fractal model of chromosomes and chromosomal DNA replication. *J. Theor. Biol.*, **141**, 117–136.

Wagner, G. C., Colvin, J. T., Allen, J. P., and Stapleton, H. J. (1985). Fractal models of protein structure, dynamics and magnetic relaxation. *J. Am. Chem. Soc.*, **107**, 5589–5594.

Weisbuch, G., De Boer, R. J., and Perelson, A. S. (1990). Localized memories in idiotypic networks. *J. Theor. Biol.*, **146**, 483–499.

West, B. J., and Goldberger, A. L. (1987). Physiology in fractal dimensions. *Am. Sci.*, **75**, 354–365.

Wiens, J. A. (1989). Spatial scaling in ecology. *Funct. Ecol.*, **3**, 385–397.

Xiao, Y., Chen, R., Shen, R., Sun, J., and Xu, J. (1995). Fractal dimension of exon and intron sequences. *J. Theor. Biol.*, **175**, 23–26.

Xu, J., Chao, Y., and Chen, R. (1994). Fractal geometry study of DNA binding proteins. *J. Theor. Biol.*, **171**, 239–249.

Zeide, B., and Gresham, C. A. (1991). Fractal dimensions of tree crowns in three loblolly pine plantations of coastal South Carolina. *Can. J. For. Res.*, **21**, 1208–1212.

8 Matrix Genetics, Hadamard Matrices, and Algebraic Biology

In this chapter we continue the discussion introduced in Chapter 2 about genetic matrices, their symmetries, and their algebraic properties. The algebraic theory of coding is one of the modern fields of applications of algebra. This theory uses matrix algebra intensively. This chapter is devoted to matrix forms of presentations of the genetic code for algebraic analysis of a basic scheme of degeneracy of the genetic code. Similar matrix forms are utilized in the theory of signal processing and encoding. The Kronecker family of genetic matrices is investigated, which is based on the genetic matrix [C A; U G], where C, A, U, and G are the letters of the genetic alphabet. This matrix in the third Kronecker power is the 8×8 matrix, which contains all 64 genetic triplets in a strict order, with a natural binary numeration of the triplets by the numbers 0 to 63. Peculiarities of the basic scheme of the genetic code degeneracy are reflected in the symmetrical black-and-white mosaic of this genetic 8×8 matrix. Unexpectedly, this mosaic matrix is connected algorithmically with Hadamard matrices, which are well known in the theory of signal processing and encoding, spectral analysis, quantum mechanics, and quantum computers. Furthermore, many types of cyclic permutations of genetic elements lead to reconstruction of initial Hadamard matrices into new Hadamard matrices unexpectedly. This demonstrates that matrix algebra is one of the promising instruments and an adequate language in bioinformatics and algebraic biology.

8.1 INTRODUCTION

Algebraic biology uses matrix algebra as a promising instrument for its investigation. Many biological structured phenomena have an inherited character and are connected with genetic code systems which provide their transmission along a chain of generations. One may suggest that algebraic features of the genetic code are reflected in structural features of inherited physiological systems and define many structural peculiarities of vital functions. Achievements

Mathematics of Bioinformatics: Theory, Practice, and Applications, By Matthew He and Sergey Petoukhov
Copyright © 2011 John Wiley & Sons, Inc.

in molecular genetics, which have uncovered the fact that all biological organisms are identical in their molecular-genetic bases, have led to a new viewpoint about the nature of life: "Life is a partnership between genes and mathematics" (Stewart, 1999).

Genetic information is transferred by means of discrete elements: four letters of the genetic alphabet, 64 triplets, 20 amino acids, and so on. The general theory of signal processing utilizes the encoding of discrete signals by means of special mathematical matrices and spectral representations of signals to increase reliability and efficiency of information transfer (see, e.g., Ahmed and Rao, 1975; Sklar, 2001). The authors develop a special branch of mathematical biology called *matrix genetics* which is based on using matrix algebra and matrix methods of the algebraic theory of coding to study the genetic code (He, 2001, 2003a,b; He and Petoukhov, 2007; He et al., 2004; Petoukhov, 2001a,b, 2005a,b, 2008a–d). One can mention here that an investigation of structural analogies between computer informatics and genetic informatics is one of the important tasks of modern science in connection with the creation of DNA computers and with the development of bioinformatics. We describe some new results in this field which are related to the discovery of an unexpected connection of Rademacher functions, Walsh functions (Ahmed and Rao, 1975), and Hadamard matrices with a structural phenomenology of the genetic code. Hadamard matrices are used in many scientific and technological fields, due to their advantageous properties: for example, in error-correcting codes such as the Reed–Muller code, in spectral analysis and multichannel spectrometers with Hadamard transformations, in quantum mechanics in their normalized forms as unitary operators, and in quantum computers with Hadamard gates.

8.2   GENETIC MATRICES AND THE DEGENERACY OF THE GENETIC CODE

The genetic code is named the *degeneracy code* because its 64 triplets encode 20 amino acids, and different amino acids are encoded by different quantities of triplets. Hypotheses about a connection between this degeneracy and the noise immunity of genetic information have existed since the time of the discovery of the genetic code. The specifics of the degeneracy of the genetic code provoke many questions. One of them is the following: Was the code degeneracy an accidental choice of nature, or not? Deep investigations of symmetries using a matrix map of the code degeneracy can give many useful results for such questions.

Modern science recognizes many variants (or dialects) of the genetic code, data about which are shown on NCBI's Web site, http://www.ncbi.nlm.nih.gov/Taxonomy/Utils/wprintgc.cgi. Seventeen variants (or dialects) of the genetic code exist, which differ one from another by some details of correspondences between triplets and objects encoded by them. Most of these dialects (including the Standard Code and the Vertebrate Mitochondrial Code) have the

THE STANDARD CODE	
8 subfamilies of the "two-position NN-triplets" ("black triplets") and the amino acids, which are encoded by them	8 subfamilies of the "three-position NN-triplets" („white triplets") and the amino acids, which are encoded by them
CCC, CCU, CCA, CCG ➔ Pro	CAC, CAU, CAA, CAG ➔ His, His, Gln, Gln
CUC, CUU, CUA, CUG ➔ Leu	AAC, AAU, AAA, AAG ➔ Asn, Asn, Lys, Lys
CGC, CGU, CGA, CGG ➔ Arg	AUC, AUU, AUA, AUG ➔ Ile, Ile, Ile, Met
ACC, ACU, ACA, ACG ➔ Thr	AGC, AGU, AGA, AGG ➔ Ser, Ser, Arg, Arg
UCC, UCU, UCA, UCG ➔ Ser	UAC, UAU, UAA, UAG ➔ Tyr, Tyr, Stop, Stop
GCC, GCU, GCA, GCG ➔ Ala	UUC, UUU, UUA, UUG ➔ Phe, Phe, Leu, Leu
GUC, GUU, GUA, GUG ➔ Val	UGC, UGU, UGA, UGG ➔ Cys, Cys, Stop, Trp
GGC, GGU, GGA, GGG ➔ Gly	GAC, GAU, GAA, GAG ➔ Asp, Asp, Glu, Glu

THE VERTEBRATE MITOCHONDRIAL CODE	
8 subfamilies of the "two-position NN-triplets" ("black triplets") and the amino acids, which are encoded by them	8 subfamilies of the "three-position NN-triplets" („white triplets") and the amino acids, which are encoded by them
CCC, CCU, CCA, CCG ➔ Pro	CAC, CAU, CAA, CAG ➔ His, His, Gln, Gln
CUC, CUU, CUA, CUG ➔ Leu	AAC, AAU, AAA, AAG ➔ Asn, Asn, Lys, Lys
CGC, CGU, CGA, CGG ➔ Arg	AUC, AUU, AUA, AUG ➔ Ile, Ile, Met, Met
ACC, ACU, ACA, ACG ➔ Thr	AGC, AGU, AGA, AGG ➔ Ser, Ser, Stop, Stop
UCC, UCU, UCA, UCG ➔ Ser	UAC, UAU, UAA, UAG ➔ Tyr, Tyr, Stop, Stop
GCC, GCU, GCA, GCG ➔ Ala	UUC, UUU, UUA, UUG ➔ Phe, Phe, Leu, Leu
GUC, GUU, GUA, GUG ➔ Val	UGC, UGU, UGA, UGG ➔ Cys, Cys, Trp, Trp
GGC, GGU, GGA, GGG ➔ Gly	GAC, GAU, GAA, GAG ➔ Asp, Asp, Glu, Glu

FIGURE 8.1   Two examples of the basic scheme of the genetic code degeneracy with 32 black triplets and 32 white triplets. (Initial data from http://www.ncbi.nlm.nih.gov/Taxonomy/Utils/wprintgc.cgi.)

following general scheme of their degeneracy, where 32 "black" triplets with "strong roots" and 32 "white" triplets with "weak roots" exist.

In this general or basic scheme, the set of 64 triplets contains 16 subfamilies of triplets, every of which contains four triplets with the same two letters in the first positions of each triplet (an example of such subsets is the case of the four triplets CAC, CAA, CAU, and CAG with the same two letters on their first positions). We shall name such subfamilies the subfamilies of *NN*-triplets. In the basic scheme of degeneracy described, the set of these 16 subfamilies of *NN*-triplets is divided into two equal subsets from the viewpoint of degeneration properties of the code (Figure 8.1). The first subset contains eight subfamilies of two-position *NN*-triplets, a coding value of which is independent of a letter in their third position. An example of such a subfamily is that of the four triplets CGC, CGA, CGU, and CGC (Figure 8.1), all of which encode the same amino acid, Arg, although they have different letters in their third position. All members of such subfamilies of *NN*-triplets are shown in black in Figures 8.1 and 8.2.

CCC	CCA	CAC	CAA	ACC	ACA	AAC	AAA
Pro	Pro	His	Gln	Thr	Thr	Asn	Lys
CCU	CCG	CAU	CAG	ACU	ACG	AAU	AAG
Pro	Pro	His	Gln	Thr	Thr	Asn	Lys
CUC	CUA	CGC	CGA	AUC	AUA	AGC	AGA
Leu	Leu	Arg	Arg	Ile	Met	Ser	Stop
CUU	CUG	CGU	CGG	AUU	AUG	AGU	AGG
Leu	Leu	Arg	Arg	Ile	Met	Ser	Stop
UCC	UCA	UAC	UAA	GCC	GCA	GAC	GAA
Ser	Ser	Tyr	Stop	Ala	Ala	Asp	Glu
UCU	UCG	UAU	UAG	GCU	GCG	GAU	GAG
Ser	Ser	Tyr	Stop	Ala	Ala	Asp	Glu
UUC	UUA	UGC	UGA	GUC	GUA	GGC	GGA
Phe	Leu	Cys	Trp	Val	Val	Gly	Gly
UUU	UUG	UGU	UGG	GUU	GUG	GGU	GGG
Phe	Leu	Cys	Trp	Val	Val	Gly	Gly

FIGURE 8.2   Genomatrix $P^{(3)} = P_{123}^{CAUG} = [C \ A; \ U \ G]^{(3)}$ (Figure 2.2) for the Vertebrate Mitochondrial Code. The matrix contains 64 triplets and 20 amino acids with their traditional abbreviations. Stop codons are marked "Stop." Numeration of columns and rows in decimal notation is shown. Black cells of the genomatrix contain the black triplets and white cells contain the white triplets. Rademacher functions for rows are shown on the right side.

The second subset contains eight subfamilies of three-position NN-triplets, the coding value of which depends on a letter in their third position. An example of such a subfamily in Figure 8.1 is that of the four triplets CAC, CAA, CAU, and CAC, two of which (CAC, CAU) encode the amino acid His and the other two of which (CAA, CAG) encode the amino acid Gln. All members of such subfamilies of NN-triplets are indicated white in the genomatrix $P^{(3)} = [C \ A; \ U \ G]^{(3)}$ in Figure 8.2. So the genomatrix $[C \ A; \ U \ G]^{(3)}$ has 32 black triplets and 32 white triplets. Each subfamily of four NN-triplets is disposed in an appropriate 2×2 subquadrant of the genomatrix $[C \ A; \ U \ G]^{(3)}$, due to the Kronecker algorithm of construction of the genomatrix $[C \ A; \ U \ G]^{(3)}$ of triplets from the alphabet genomatrix P (Figure 2.2).

Here one should recall the work of Rumer (1968), in which a combination of letters in the first two positions of each triplet was termed a *root* of this triplet. A set of 64 triplets contains 16 possible variants of such roots. Taking into account properties of triplets, Rumer has divided the set of 16 possible roots into two subsets with eight roots in each. The roots CC, CU, CG, AC, UC, GC, GU, and GG form the first of such octets were termed *strong roots* by Rumer. The other eight roots, CA, AA, AU, AG, UA, UU, UG, and GA, form the second octet and were termed *weak roots*. When Rumer published his works, the Vertebrate Mitochondrial Code and some of the other code dialects were unknown. But one can easily check that the set of 32 black (white) triplets, which we show in Figure 8.1 for the Standard Code and the Vertebrate Mitochondrial Code, is identical to the set of 32 triplets with strong (weak) roots described by Rumer. So, using notions proposed by Rumer, the black triplets can be called *triplets with strong roots* and the white triplets can be called *triplets with weak roots*. Rumer believed that this symmetrical division into two binary-oppositional categories of roots is very important for understanding the nature of genetic code systems.

One can check easily on the basis of data from NCBI's Web site (http://www.ncbi.nlm.nih.gov/Taxonomy/Utils/wprintgc.cgi) that the following 11 dialects of the genetic code have the same basic scheme of degeneracy, with 32 black triplets and with 32 white triplets: (1) the Standard Code; (2) the Vertebrate Mitochondrial Code; (3) the Yeast Mitochondrial Code; (4) the Mold, Protozoan, and Coelenterate Mitochondrial Code and the Mycoplasma/Spiroplasma Code; (5) the Ciliate, Dasycladacean and Hexamita Nuclear Code; (6) the Euplotid Nuclear Code; (7) the Bacterial and Plant Plastid Code; (8) the Ascidian Mitochondrial Code; (9) the Blepharisma Nuclear Code; (10) the Thraustochytrium Mitochondrial Code; and (11) the Chlorophycean Mitochondrial Code. In this chapter we consider this basic scheme of the degeneracy that is presented by means of a black-and-white mosaic of the genetic matrix $P^{(3)} = [\text{C A; U G}]^{(3)}$ in Figure 8.2.

It should be mentioned that the other six dialects of the genetic code—the Invertebrate Mitochondrial Code, the Echinoderm and Flatworm Mitochondrial Code, the Alternative Yeast Nuclear Code, the Alternative Flatworm Mitochondrial Code, the Trematode Mitochondrial Code, and the Scenedesmus Obliquus Mitochondrial Code—have only small differences from the basic scheme of degeneracy described.

According to general traditions, the theory of symmetry studies initially those natural objects that possess the most symmetrical character, and then it constructs a theory for cases of violations of this symmetry in other kindred objects. For this reason, we pay special attention here to the Vertebrate Mitochondrial Code, which is the most symmetrical code among dialects of the genetic code and which corresponds to the basic scheme of the degeneracy. Additionally, we should mention that some authors consider this dialect not only the most "perfect" but also the most ancient (Frank-Kamenetskiy, 1988); but this last statement is debatable. Figure 8.1 shows the correspondence between the set of 64 triplets and the set of 20 amino acids with stop signals of protein synthesis in the Standard Code and the Vertebrate Mitochondrial Code.

Figure 8.2 demonstrates the unexpected phenomenological fact of the symmetrical character of dispositions for the 32 white triplets and the 32 black triplets (from Figure 8.1) in the genomatrix $[\text{C A; U G}]^{(3)}$ described in Chapter 2. All triplets are shown together with amino acids and a stop codon, which are encoded by triplets in the Vertebrate Mitochondrial Code. Black cells of the genomatrix contain black triplets and white cells contain white triplets.

So the black-and-white mosaic of the genomatrix $[\text{C A; U G}]^{(3)}$ in Figure 8.2 reflects the specificity of the basic scheme of the degeneracy with 32 black triplets and 32 white triplets, but the disposition of amino acids and of stop codons corresponds to the particular case of the Vertebrate Mitochondrial Code. Unexpectedly, it has a few interesting symmetrical peculiarities, as follows:

- The left and right halves of the matrix mosaic are mirror-antisymmetric to each other in color; any pair of cells, disposed in mirror-symmetrical manner in these halves, possesses opposite colors.
- Mosaics of all rows have a meander-line character, which is connected with Rademacher functions from the theory of discrete signal processing. Each row presents one of the Rademacher functions if each black (white) cell is interpreted such that it contains the number +1 (−1).
- The black-and-white matrix mosaic has the symmetric figure of a diagonal cross; diagonal quadrants of the matrix are equivalent to each other from the viewpoint of their mosaic.
- The genomatrix [C A; U G]$^{(3)}$ consists of the four pairs of neighbor rows with even and odd numeration numbers in each pair: 0–1, 2–3, 4–5, 6–7. For the case of the basic scheme of code degeneracy, the rows of each pair are equivalent to each other from the viewpoint of their mosaic (for the particular case of the Vertebrate Mitochondrial Code, the rows of each pair are equivalent to each other additionally from the viewpoint of the disposition of the same amino acids in their appropriate cells).
- The turning of the genomatrix [C A; U G]$^{(3)}$ into a cylinder with an agglutination of its upper and lower borders reveals an ornamental pattern of a cyclic shift. This pattern has the character of cyclic shifts, which permits one to think about a possible genetic meaning of cyclic codes, which play a significant role in the theory of digital signal processing. This pattern is demonstrated more clearly by a tessellation of a plane with this mosaic genomatrix (Figure 8.3, left). The plane with this tessellation possesses the ornamental pattern with two pattern units that are identical in their forms but contrary in their colors (black and white) and orientations (left and right).

It should be noted that a huge quantity 64! ≈ 10^{89} of variants exists for dispositions of 64 triplets in an 8 × 8 matrix. Modern physics estimates the time of existence of the universe in 10^{17} s. That means the following: If for consideration of each of these variants we spend only 1 s, then during all the time of existence of the universe we shall have time to consider only an insignificant part of these 10^{89} variants. It is obvious that in such a situation an accidental disposition of the 20 amino acids and the corresponding triplets in a 8 × 8 matrix will almost never give any symmetry in their disposition in matrix halves, quadrants, and rows.

This symmetrical character of the degeneracy of the genetic code, which is presented by the matrix mosaic (Figure 8.2), is the key to many secrets of the

FIGURE 8.3   *Left:* tessellation of a plane with the mosaic of genomatrix $[C\ A;\ U\ G]^{(3)}$ from Figure 8.2. *Right:* tessellation of a plane with the mosaic of genomatrix P_{231}^{CAUG} from Figure 8.4.

genetic code. It verifies that the degeneracy is not an accidental thing but is a consequence of some hidden regular laws. In our opinion, one of the most important features of the mosaic genomatrix in Figure 8.2 is that each of its rows fits one of the famous Rademacher functions, which are known in the theory of digital communication and are described in Chapter 1. The fact that the left and right halves of the matrix mosaic are mirror-antisymmetric to each another can be interpreted as a consequence of this connection between the matrix rows and Rademacher functions.

It seems essential that this connection between the matrix rows (or columns in some cases) and Rademacher functions is a conserved stability in a great number of new genomatrices which are produced by means of positional and alphabetic permutations of genetic elements inside triplets in the initial genomatrix $P_{123}^{CAUG} = [C\ A;\ U\ G]^{(3)}$ (Petoukhov, 2006, 2008a–d). A positional permutation inside triplets is a permutation of positions inside each triplet simultaneously, which replaces an initial order 1–2–3 of its letters into some new order: for example, into the order 2–3–1; in this case the triplet CAG is replaced by the triplet AGC in its matrix cell, and so on, and a new genomatrix P_{231}^{CAUG} appears as a result (Figure 8.4).

It is unexpected that this "cyclic-generated" genomatrix P_{231}^{CAUG} with new matrix dispositions of triplets and amino acids possesses similar symmetric characteristics (Petoukhov, 2006, 2008a,c):

- All rows of the 8×8 genomatrix and its 4×4 quadrants have a meander-line character again, which is connected by Rademacher functions.
- All its 4×4 quadrants are identical to each other by the mosaics.
- The upper and the lower halves of P_{231}^{CAUG} are identical to each other from the viewpoint of dispositions of all amino acids and stop signals.

	0 (000)	2 (010)	4 (100)	6 (110)	1 (001)	3 (011)	5 (101)	7 (111)	
0	CCC Pro	CAC His	ACC Thr	AAC Asn	CCA Pro	CAA Gln	ACA Thr	AAA Lys	⊓⊔⊓⊔
2	CUC Leu	CGC Arg	AUC Ile	AGC Ser	CUA Leu	CGA Arg	AUA Met	AGA Stop	⊓⊔
4	UCC Ser	UAC Tyr	GCC Ala	GAC Asp	UCA Ser	UAA Stop	GCA Ala	GAA Glu	⊓⊔⊓⊔
6	UUC Phe	UGC Cys	GUC Val	GGC Gly	UUA Leu	UGA Trp	GUA Val	GGA Gly	⊔⊓
1	CCU Pro	CAU His	ACU Thr	AAU Asn	CCG Pro	CAG Gln	ACG Thr	AAG Lys	⊓⊔⊓⊔
3	CUU Leu	CGU Arg	AUU Ile	AGU Ser	CUG Leu	CGG Arg	AUG Met	AGG Stop	⊓⊔
5	UCU Ser	UAU Tyr	GCU Ala	GAU Asp	UCG Ser	UAG Stop	GCG Ala	GAG Glu	⊓⊔⊓⊔
7	UUU Phe	UGU Cys	GUU Val	GGU Gly	UUG Leu	UGG Trp	GUG Val	GGG Gly	⊔⊓

FIGURE 8.4 Genomatrix P_{231}^{CAUG}, which is produced from the genomatrix P_{123}^{CAUG} (Figure 8.2) by the cyclic shift of positions in triplets (1–2–3 → 2–3–1). Rademacher functions for rows are shown on the right side.

- The genomatrix P_{231}^{CAUG} possesses four pairs of identical rows as well: 0–1, 2–3, 4–5, 6–7 (but the rows with these numbers are disposed in new matrix positions in Figure 8.2 and they differ from the rows with the same numbers in Figure 8.2).

To work with a set of positional and alphabetic permutations, we use the following denotations. We change the symbol of the genomatrix $P^{(3)} = [\text{C A; U G}]^{(3)}$ by the symbol P_{123}^{CAUG}, which is more comfortable for the comparative analysis of this 8×8 genomatrix with other 8×8 genomatrices given below. Here the bottom index "123" shows the appropriate queue of positions 1–2–3 in triplets; the upper index shows the type of kernel [C A; U G] of the Kronecker family of genomatrices. The exponent (3) is not written because the bottom index is enough to indicate that this symbol means the 8×8 genomatrix of triplets. This change of symbol is useful because we shall consider the genomatrices not only with permutations of positions in triplets (2–3–1, 3–1–2, etc.) but with alphabetic permutations of the genetic letters that lead to other kernels of Kronecker families of genomatrices ([G C; A U], [C A; G U], etc.). In the last cases of alphabetic permutations, matrices P_{123}^{GCAU}, P_{123}^{CAGU}, and so on, arise.

Note that the mosaic of the initial 8×8 genomatrix P_{123}^{CAUG} is reproduced in 4×4 quadrants of this P_{231}^{CAUG} in a fractal manner: the coefficient of fractal ranging of areas is equal to 4. The tessellations of a plane by the mosaics of P_{123}^{CAUG} and of P_{231}^{CAUG} demonstrate their fractal correspondence very clearly (Figure 8.3). Such a scale transformation of areas in the mosaics of the code degeneracy can be called a *tetra-reproduction transformation*. Due to this tetra-reproduction, the cyclic-generated genomatrix P_{231}^{CAUG} has a quantity of pattern units four times greater than that of the initial genomatrix P_{123}^{CAUG} (Figures 8.2 to 8.4).

This fact is interesting because an analogical tetra-reproduction (or a tetra-division) exists in living nature in the course of the division of gametal cells, which are transmitters of genetic information. In this mysterious act of meiosis, one gamete is divided into four new gametes. This fact was mentioned notably in a famous book by Schrödinger (1955, Sec. 13). The tetra-reproduction of the mosaics of the genomatrices that was described can be utilized, in particular, in formal models of meiosis.

Permutations of elements play an important role in the theory of signals processing (Ahmed and Rao, 1975; Trahtman and Trahtman, 1975). Only six variants of permutations of positions in triplets are possible: 1–2–3, 2–3–1, 3–1–2, 1–3–2, 2–1–3, and 3–2–1. The genomatrices P_{123}^{CAUG} and P_{231}^{CAUG} for the first two of these permutations were considered above (see Figures 8.2 and 8.4). Let us consider the other four variants that lead to genomatrices: P_{312}^{CAUG}, P_{132}^{CAUG}, P_{213}^{CAUG}, and P_{321}^{CAUG}, presented in Figure 8.5. It is an unexpected phenomenological fact that each row of all these genomatrices is connected with a relevant Rademacher function again, and that these new genomatrices have symmetrical peculiarities which are similar to the symmetrical peculiarities of P_{123}^{CAUG} and P_{231}^{CAUG}. It means that the basic scheme considered for the degeneracy of the genetic code is in close agreement with these types of permutations and with the Rademacher functions.

The revelation of the permutation group of the six symmetric genomatrices $P_{123}^{CAUG(3)}$, $P_{231}^{CAUG(3)}$, $P_{213}^{CAUG(3)}$, $P_{321}^{CAUG(3)}$, $P_{312}^{CAUG(3)}$, $P_{132}^{CAUG(3)}$ seems to be the essential fact because of heuristic associations with the mathematical theory of digital signal processing, where similar permutations have long been utilized as a useful tool. For example, the book (Ahmed and Rao, 1975, Sec. 4.6) gives an example of the important role of the method of data permutations and of the binary inversion for one of variants of the algorithm of a fast Fourier transformation. In this example the numeric sequence $0, 1, 2, 3, 4, 5, 6, 7$ is re-formed into the sequence $0, 4, 2, 6, 1, 5, 3, 7$. But the same change of numeration of the columns and the rows takes place in our case (Figure 8.5), where the genomatrix P_{123}^{CAUG} is re-formed into the genomatrix P_{321}^{CAUG} as a result of the inversion of binary numbering of the columns and the rows (or of the inversion of the positions in the triplets). These and other facts permit one to think that the genetic system has a connection with a fast Fourier transformation (or with a fast Hadamard transformation) (Petoukhov, 2006, 2008a–c).

Until now we have considered the Kronecker family of genomatrices with the kernel [C A; U G] and have revealed some interesting properties of the mosaic genomatrices [C A; U G]$^{(3)}$. But one can consider other variants of kernels for genetic matrices: $P_{123}^{CAGU} = [C\ A;\ G\ U]^{(3)}$, $P_{123}^{GCAU} = [G\ C;\ A\ U]^{(3)}$, and so on. These new variants of kernels of the Kronecker families of genomatrices are produced by alphabetic permutations of the four letters C,

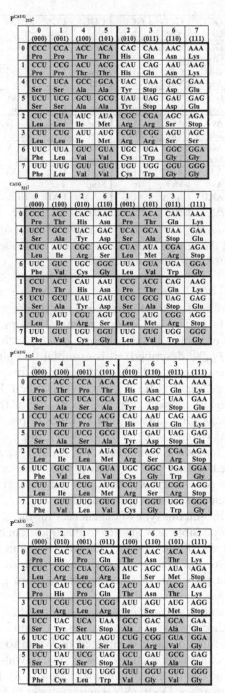

P^{CAUG}_{213}:

	0 (000)	1 (001)	4 (100)	5 (101)	2 (010)	3 (011)	6 (110)	7 (111)
0	CCC Pro	CCA Pro	ACC Thr	ACA Thr	CAC His	CAA Gln	AAC Asn	AAA Lys
1	CCU Pro	CCG Pro	ACU Thr	ACG Thr	CAU His	CAG Gln	AAU Asn	AAG Lys
4	UCC Ser	UCA Ser	GCC Ala	GCA Ala	UAC Tyr	UAA Stop	GAC Asp	GAA Glu
5	UCU Ser	UCG Ser	GCU Ala	GCG Ala	UAU Tyr	UAG Stop	GAU Asp	GAG Glu
2	CUC Leu	CUA Leu	AUC Ile	AUA Met	CGC Arg	CGA Arg	AGC Ser	AGA Stop
3	CUU Leu	CUG Leu	AUU Ile	AUG Met	CGU Arg	CGG Arg	AGU Ser	AGC Ser
6	UUC Phe	UUA Leu	GUC Val	GUA Val	UGC Cys	UGA Trp	GGC Gly	GGA Gly
7	UUU Phe	UUG Leu	GUU Val	GUG Val	UGU Cys	UGG Trp	GGU Gly	GGG Gly

$^{CAUG}_{321}$:

	0 (000)	4 (100)	2 (010)	6 (110)	1 (001)	5 (101)	3 (011)	7 (111)
0	CCC Pro	ACC Thr	CAC His	AAC Asn	CCA Pro	ACA Thr	CAA Gln	AAA Lys
4	UCC Ser	GCC Ala	UAC Tyr	GAC Asp	UCA Ser	GCA Ala	UAA Stop	GAA Glu
2	CUC Leu	AUC Ile	CGC Arg	AGC Ser	CUA Leu	AUA Met	CGA Arg	AGA Stop
6	UUC Phe	GUC Val	UGC Cys	GGC Gly	UUA Leu	GUA Val	UGA Trp	GGA Gly
1	CCU Pro	ACU Thr	CAU His	AAU Asn	CCG Pro	ACG Thr	CAG Gln	AAG Lys
5	UCU Ser	GCU Ala	UAU Tyr	GAU Asp	UCG Ser	GCG Ala	UAG Stop	GAG Glu
3	CUU Leu	AUU Ile	CGU Arg	AGU Ser	CUG Leu	AUG Met	CGG Arg	AGG Stop
7	UUU Phe	GUU Val	UGU Cys	GGU Gly	UUG Leu	GUG Val	UGG Trp	GGG Gly

P^{CAUG}_{312}:

	0 (000)	4 (100)	1 (001)	5 (101)	2 (010)	6 (110)	3 (011)	7 (111)
0	CCC Pro	ACC Thr	CCA Pro	ACA Thr	CAC His	AAC Asn	CAA Gln	AAA Lys
4	UCC Ser	GCC Ala	UCA Ser	GCA Ala	UAC Tyr	GAC Asp	UAA Stop	GAA Glu
1	CCU Pro	ACU Thr	CCG Pro	ACG Thr	CAU His	AAU Asn	CAG Gln	AAG Lys
5	UCU Ser	GCU Ala	UCG Ser	GCG Ala	UAU Tyr	GAU Asp	UAG Stop	GAG Glu
2	CUC Leu	AUC Ile	CUA Leu	AUA Met	CGC Arg	AGC Ser	CGA Arg	AGA Stop
6	UUC Phe	GUC Val	UUA Leu	GUA Val	UGC Cys	GGC Gly	UGA Trp	GGA Gly
3	CUU Leu	AUU Ile	CUG Leu	AUG Met	CGU Arg	AGU Ser	CGG Arg	AGG Stop
7	UUU Phe	GUU Val	UUG Leu	GUG Val	UGU Cys	GGU Gly	UGG Trp	GGG Gly

P^{CAUG}_{132}:

	0 (000)	2 (001)	1 (001)	3 (011)	4 (100)	6 (110)	5 (101)	7 (111)
0	CCC Pro	CAC His	CCA Pro	CAA Gln	ACC Thr	AAC Asn	ACA Thr	AAA Lys
2	CUC Leu	CGC Arg	CUA Leu	CGA Arg	AUC Ile	AGC Ser	AUA Met	AGA Stop
1	CCU Pro	CAU His	CCG Pro	CAG Gln	ACU Thr	AAU Asn	ACG Thr	AAG Lys
3	CUU Leu	CGU Arg	CUG Leu	CGG Arg	AUU Ile	AGU Ser	AUG Met	AGG Stop
4	UCC Ser	UAC Tyr	UCA Ser	UAA Stop	GCC Ala	GAC Asp	GCA Ala	GAA Glu
6	UUC Phe	UGC Cys	UUA Ile	UGA Ser	CUG Leu	CGG Arg	GUA Val	GGA Gly
5	UCU Ser	UAU Tyr	UCG Ser	UAG Stop	GCU Ala	GAU Asp	GCG Ala	GAG Glu
7	UUU Phe	UGU Cys	UUG Leu	UGG Trp	GUU Val	GGU Gly	GUG Val	GGG Gly

FIGURE 8.5 Genomatrices P^{CAUG}_{213}, P^{CAUG}_{321}, P^{CAUG}_{312}, and P^{CAUG}_{132}. Each matrix cell has a triplet and an amino acid (or a stop signal) coded by this triplet. The black-and-white mosaic reflects the specificity of the basic scheme of the degeneracy of the genetic code.

GGG	GGC	GCG	GCC	CGG	CGC	CCG	CCC
Gly	Gly	Ala	Ala	Arg	Arg	Pro	Pro
GGA	GGU	GCA	GCU	CGA	CGU	CCA	CCU
Gly	Gly	Ala	Ala	Arg	Arg	Pro	Pro
GAG	GAC	GUG	GUC	CAG	CAC	CUG	CUC
Glu	Asp	Val	Val	Gln	His	Leu	Leu
GAA	GAU	GUA	GUU	CAA	CAU	CUA	CUU
Glu	Asp	Val	Val	Gln	His	Leu	Leu
AGG	AGC	ACG	ACC	UGG	UGC	UCG	UCC
Stop	Ser	Thr	Thr	Trp	Cys	Ser	Ser
AGA	AGU	ACA	ACU	UGA	UGU	UCA	UCU
Stop	Ser	Thr	Thr	Trp	Cys	Ser	Ser
AAG	AAC	AUG	AUC	UAG	UAC	UUG	UUC
Lys	Asn	Met	Ile	Stop	Tyr	Leu	Phe
AAA	AAU	AUA	AUU	UAA	UAU	UUA	UUU
Lys	Asn	Met	Ile	Stop	Tyr	Leu	Phe

FIGURE 8.6   Genomatrix $P_{123}^{GCAU} = [G\ C;\ A\ U]^{(3)}$ and the mosaic of the basic scheme of the degeneracy of the genetic code (dispositions of amino acids and stop codons correspond to the Vertebrate Mitochondrial Code).

A, U, and G on positions in the kernel 2×2 matrix: for example, by mutual interchanges $C \leftrightarrow G$ and $A \leftrightarrow U$ (such permutations produce a change of letter compositions of triplets in the cells of a genetic 8×8 matrix, in contract to the genomatrix P_{123}^{CAUG} described). It is essential that all these new mosaic genomatrices possess analogical phenomenological properties, in contrast to the case of the genomatrix $[C\ A;\ U\ G]^{(3)}$ described. First, all these new genomatrices are again connected in their rows (or in their columns) with Rademacher functions. One can add that all kinds of possible positional permutations in triplets (from 1–2–3 to 2–3–1, 3–1–2, etc.), which generate new genomatrices (e.g., mosaic genomatrices P_{231}^{GCAU}, P_{312}^{GCAU}, P_{321}^{GCAU}, P_{213}^{GCAU}, and P_{132}^{GCAU} are produced from P_{123}^{GCAU} in such a way), conserve the same close connections of new genomatrices with Rademacher functions. Figures 8.6 to 8.17 show some examples of such genomatrices.

Why has nature chosen this type of degeneracy for the genetic code? Matrix genetics proposes a possible new answer to this question: because this degeneracy connects systems of the genetic code with Rademacher functions (and with Walsh functions and Hadamard matrices, which are described below), which allow for the provision of some technologies of genetic information processing.

Rademacher functions are an incomplete set of orthogonal functions which are well known in discrete signal processing (see Chapter 1). The incomplete set of Rademacher functions was completed by Walsh to form the complete orthogonal set of rectangular functions, now known as Walsh functions. Taking into account the close connection of genomatrices with Rademacher functions described, a question arises: Do the 8×8 genomatrices of 64 triplets described possess a hidden connection with Walsh functions by means of some natural genetic algorithm? This question has a positive answer. A special simple

GGG Gly	GCG Ala	CGG Arg	CCG Pro	GGC Gly	GCC Ala	CGC Arg	CCC Pro
GAG Glu	GUG Val	CAG Gln	CUG Leu	GAC Asp	GUC Val	CAC His	CUC Leu
AGG Stop	ACG Thr	UGG Trp	UCG Ser	AGC Ser	ACC Thr	UGC Cys	UCC Ser
AAG Lys	AUG Met	UAG Stop	UUG Leu	AUC Ile	AUC Ile	UAC Tyr	UUC Phe
GGA Gly	GCA Ala	CGA Arg	GCA Ala	GGU Gly	GCU Ala	CGU Arg	CCU Pro
GAA Glu	GUA Val	CAA Gln	CUA Leu	GAU Asp	GUU Val	CAU His	CUU Leu
AGA Stop	ACA Thr	UGA Trp	UCA Ser	AGU Ser	ACU Thr	UGU Cys	UCU Ser
AAA Lys	AUA Met	UAA Stop	UUA Leu	AAU Asn	AUU Ile	UAU Tyr	UUU Phe

FIGURE 8.7   Genomatrix P_{231}^{GCAU}.

GGG Gly	CGG Arg	GGC Gly	CGC Arg	GCG Ala	CCG Pro	GCC Ala	CCC Pro
AGG Stop	UGG Trp	AGC Ser	UGC Cys	ACG Thr	UCG Ser	ACC Thr	UCC Ser
GGA Gly	CGA Arg	GGU Gly	CGU Arg	GCA Ala	CCA Pro	GCU Ala	CCU Pro
AGA Stop	UGA Trp	AGU Ser	UGU Cys	ACA Thr	UCA Ser	ACU Thr	UCU Ser
GAG Glu	CAG Gln	GAC Asp	CAC His	GUG Val	CUG Leu	GUC Val	CUC Leu
AAG Lys	UAG Stop	AAC Asn	UAC Tyr	AUG Met	UUG Leu	AUC Ile	UUC Phe
GAA Glu	CAA Gln	GAU Asp	CAU His	GUA Val	CUA Leu	GUU Val	CUU Leu
AAA Lys	UAA Stop	AAU Asn	UAU Tyr	AUA Met	UUA Leu	AUU Ile	UUU Phe

FIGURE 8.8   Genomatrix P_{312}^{GCAU}.

GGG Gly	GCG Ala	GGC Gly	GCC Ala	CGG Arg	CCG Pro	CGC Arg	CCC Pro
GAG Glu	GUG Val	GAC Asp	GUC Val	CAG Gln	CUG Leu	CAC His	CUC Leu
GGA Gly	GCA Ala	GGU Gly	GCU Ala	CGA Arg	CCA Pro	CGU Arg	CCU Pro
GAA Glu	GUA Val	GAU Asp	GUU Val	CAA Gln	CUA Leu	CAU His	CUU Leu
AGG Stop	ACG Thr	AGC Ser	ACC Thr	UGG Trp	UCG Ser	UGC Cys	UCC Ser
AAG Lys	AUG Met	AAC Asn	AUC Ile	UAG Stop	UUG Leu	UAC Tyr	UUC Phe
AGA Stop	ACA Thr	AGU Ser	ACU Thr	UGA Trp	UCA Ser	UGU Cys	UCU Ser
AAA Lys	AUA Met	AAU Asn	AUU Ile	UAA Stop	UUA Leu	UAU Tyr	UUU Phe

FIGURE 8.9   Genomatrix P_{132}^{GCAU}.

GGG	GGC	CGG	CGC	GCG	GCC	CCG	CCC
Gly	Gly	Arg	Arg	Ala	Ala	Pro	Pro
GGA	GGU	CGA	CGU	GCA	GCU	CCA	CCU
Gly	Gly	Arg	Arg	Ala	Ala	Pro	Pro
AGG	AGC	UGG	UGC	ACG	ACC	UCG	UCC
Stop	Ser	Trp	Cys	Thr	Thr	Ser	Ser
AGA	AGU	UGA	UGU	ACA	ACU	UCA	UCU
Stop	Ser	Trp	Cys	Thr	Thr	Ser	Ser
GAG	GAC	CAG	CAC	GUG	GUC	CUG	CUC
Glu	Asp	Gln	His	Val	Val	Leu	Leu
GAA	GAU	CAA	CAU	GUA	GUU	CUA	CUU
Glu	Asp	Gln	His	Val	Val	Leu	Leu
AAG	AAC	UAG	UAC	AUG	AUC	UUG	UUC
Lys	Asn	Stop	Tyr	Met	Ile	Leu	Phe
AAA	AAU	UAA	UAU	AUA	AUU	UUA	UUU
Lys	Asn	Stop	Tyr	Met	Ile	Leu	Phe

FIGURE 8.10   Genomatrix P_{213}^{GCAU}.

GGG	CGG	GCG	CCG	GGC	CGC	GCC	CCC
Gly	Arg	Ala	Pro	Gly	Arg	Ala	Pro
AGG	UGG	ACG	UCG	AGC	UGC	ACC	UCC
Stop	Trp	Thr	Ser	Ser	Cys	Thr	Ser
GAG	CAG	GUG	CUG	GAC	CAC	GUC	CUC
Glu	Gln	Val	Leu	Asp	His	Val	Leu
AAG	UAG	AUG	UUG	AAC	UAC	AUC	UUC
Lys	Stop	Met	Leu	Asn	Tyr	Ile	Phe
GGA	CGA	GCA	CCA	GGU	CGU	GCU	CCU
Gly	Arg	Ala	Pro	Gly	Arg	Ala	Pro
AGA	UGA	ACA	UCA	AGU	UGU	ACU	UCU
Stop	Trp	Thr	Ser	Ser	Cys	Thr	Ser
GAA	CAA	GUA	CUA	GAU	CAU	GUU	CUU
Glu	Gln	Val	Leu	Asp	His	Val	Leu
AAA	UAA	AUA	UUA	AAU	UAU	AUU	UUU
Lys	Stop	Met	Leu	Asn	Tyr	Ile	Phe

FIGURE 8.11   Genomatrix P_{321}^{GCAU}.

CCC	CCA	CAC	CAA	ACC	ACA	AAC	AAA
Pro	Pro	His	Gln	Thr	Thr	Asn	Lys
CCG	CCU	CAG	CAU	ACG	ACU	AAG	AAU
Pro	Pro	Gln	His	Thr	Thr	Lys	Asn
CGC	CGA	CUC	CUA	AGC	AGA	AUC	AUA
Arg	Arg	Leu	Leu	Ser	Stop	Ile	Met
CGG	CGU	CUG	CUU	AGG	AGU	AUG	AUU
Arg	Arg	Leu	Leu	Stop	Ser	Met	Ile
GCC	GCA	GAC	GAA	UCC	UCA	UAC	UAA
Ala	Ala	Asp	Glu	Ser	Ser	Tyr	Stop
GCG	GCU	GAG	GAU	UCG	UCU	UAG	UAU
Ala	Ala	Glu	Asp	Ser	Ser	Stop	Tyr
GGC	GGA	GUC	GUA	UGC	UGA	UUC	UUA
Gly	Gly	Val	Val	Cys	Trp	Phe	Leu
GGG	GGU	GUG	GUU	UGG	UGU	UUG	UUU
Gly	Gly	Val	Val	Trp	Cys	Leu	Phe

FIGURE 8.12   Genomatrix $P_{123}^{\mathrm{CAGU}} = [\mathrm{C\ A;\ G\ U}]^{(3)}$ and the mosaic of the basic scheme of the degeneracy of the genetic code (dispositions of amino acids and stop codons correspond to the Vertebrate Mitochondrial Code).

CCC	CAC	ACC	AAC	CCA	CAA	ACA	AAA
CGC	CUC	AGC	AUC	CGA	CUA	AGA	AUA
GCC	GAC	UCC	UAC	GCA	GAA	UCA	UAA
GGC	GUC	UGC	UUC	GGA	GUA	UGA	UUA
CCG	CAG	ACG	AAG	CCU	CAU	ACU	AAU
CGG	CUG	AGG	AUG	CGU	CUU	AGU	AUU
GCG	GAG	UCG	UAG	GCU	GAU	UCU	UAU
GGG	GUG	UGG	UUG	GGU	GUU	UGU	UUU

FIGURE 8.13   Genomatrix P_{231}^{CAGU}.

CCC	ACC	CCA	ACA	CAC	AAC	CAA	AAA
GCC	UCC	GCA	UCA	GAC	UAC	GAA	UAA
CCG	ACG	CCU	ACU	CAG	AAG	CAU	AAU
GCG	UCG	GCU	UCU	GAG	UAG	GAU	UAU
CGC	AGC	CGA	AGA	CUC	AUC	CUA	AUA
GGC	UGC	GGA	UGA	GUC	UUC	GUA	UUA
CGG	AGG	CGU	AGU	CUG	AUG	CUU	AUU
GGG	UGG	GGU	UGU	GUG	UUG	GUU	UUU

FIGURE 8.14   Genomatrix P_{312}^{CAGU}.

CCC	CAC	CCA	CAA	ACC	AAC	ACA	AAA
CGC	CUC	CGA	CUA	AGC	AUC	AGA	AUA
CCG	CAG	CCU	CAU	ACG	AAG	ACU	AAU
CGG	CUG	CGU	CUU	AGG	AUG	AGU	AUU
GCC	GAC	GCA	GAA	UCC	UAC	UCA	UAA
GGC	GUC	GGA	GUA	UGC	UUC	UGA	UUA
GCG	GAG	GCU	GAU	UCG	UAG	UCU	UAU
GGG	GUG	GGU	GUU	UGG	UUG	UGU	UUU

FIGURE 8.15   Genomatrix P_{132}^{CAGU}.

CCC	CCA	ACC	ACA	CAC	CAA	AAC	AAA
CCG	CCU	ACG	ACU	CAG	CAU	AAG	AAU
GCC	GCA	UCC	UCA	GAC	GAA	UAC	UAA
GCG	GCU	UCG	UCU	GAG	GAU	UAG	UAU
CGC	CGA	AGC	AGA	CUC	CUA	AUC	AUA
CGG	CGU	AGG	AGU	CUG	CUU	AUG	AUU
GGC	GGA	UGC	UGA	GUC	GUA	UUC	UUA
GGG	GGU	UGG	UGU	GUG	GUU	UUG	UUU

FIGURE 8.16   Genomatrix P_{213}^{CAGU}.

CCC	ACC	CAC	AAC	CCA	ACA	CAA	AAA
GCC	UCC	GAC	UAC	GCA	UCA	GAA	UAA
CGC	AGC	CUC	AUC	CGA	AGA	CUA	AUA
GGC	UGC	GUC	UUC	GGA	UGA	GUA	UUA
CCG	ACG	CAG	AAG	CCU	ACU	CAU	AAU
GCG	UCG	GAG	UAG	GCU	UCU	GAU	UAU
CGG	AGG	CUG	AUG	CGU	AGU	CUU	AUU
GGG	UGG	GUG	UUG	GGU	UGU	GUU	UUU

FIGURE 8.17   Genomatrix P_{321}^{CAGU}.

algorithm was discovered (Petoukhov, 2005b) which inverts the color of some cells in these matrices and leads to the generation of a new set of mosaic genomatrices (Figures 8.20 and 8.21) related to the Walsh functions and to Hadamard matrices. If the black (white) color of each cell of these new matrices is interpreted such that this cell contains the element +1 (–1), these numerical matrices demonstrate the following:

- Each row (or each column in some cases) of these new genomatrices coincides with one of the Walsh functions.
- A set of all rows (or columns in some cases) of each genomatrix is a complete set of eight different Walsh functions, and each genomatrix is one of the Hadamard 8 × 8 matrices.

Later we describe this genetic algorithm, called the *U-algorithm* because it is constructed on the basis of the special molecular status of uracil U (or thymine T). But next we review Hadamard matrices.

8.3 THE GENETIC CODE AND HADAMARD MATRICES

By definition, a Hadamard matrix of dimension n is the $n \times n$ matrix $H(n)$ with elements +1 and –1. It satisfies the condition

$$H(n)H(n)^{T} = nI_{n} \tag{8.1}$$

where $H(n)^{T}$ is the transposed matrix and $H(n)$ is the $n \times n$ identity matrix. Some Hadamard matrices of dimension 2^{k} are formed, for example, by the recursive formula $H(2^{k}) = H(2)^{(k)} = H(2) \otimes H(2^{k-1})$ for $2 \leq k \in N$, where $\otimes$ denotes the Kronecker (or tensor) product and (k) the Kronecker exponentiation, k and N are integers, and $H(2)$ is as shown in Figure 8.18. In this chapter we will indicate by black (white) all cells in the Hadamard matrices that contain the element +1 (the element –1, correspondingly).

Rows of a Hadamard matrix are mutually orthogonal; that is, every two different rows in a Hadamard matrix represent two perpendicular vectors, a

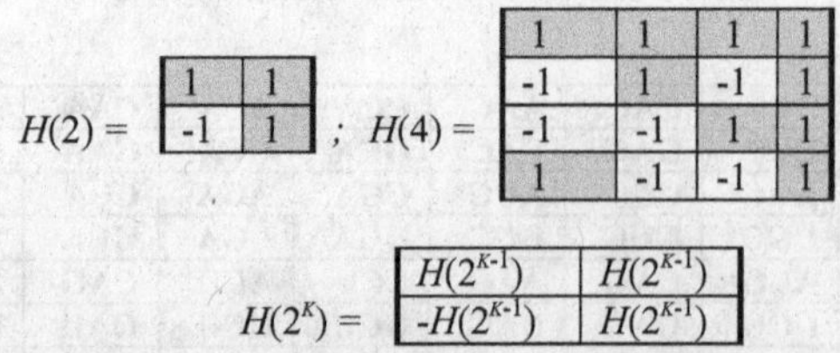

$$H(2) = \begin{array}{|c|c|} \hline 1 & 1 \\ \hline -1 & 1 \\ \hline \end{array} \; ; \; H(4) = \begin{array}{|c|c|c|c|} \hline 1 & 1 & 1 & 1 \\ \hline -1 & 1 & -1 & 1 \\ \hline -1 & -1 & 1 & 1 \\ \hline 1 & -1 & -1 & 1 \\ \hline \end{array}$$

$$H(2^{k}) = \begin{array}{|c|c|} \hline H(2^{k-1}) & H(2^{k-1}) \\ \hline -H(2^{k-1}) & H(2^{k-1}) \\ \hline \end{array}$$

FIGURE 8.18 Family of Hadamard matrices $H(2^{k})$ based on the Kronecker product. Matrix cells with elements +1 are shown in black.

scalar product of which is equal to 0. The element −1 can be disposed in any of four positions in a Hadamard matrix $H(2)$.

A Kronecker product of two Hadamard matrices is a Hadamard matrix as well. A permutation of any columns or rows of a Hadamard matrix leads to a new Hadamard matrix. Hadamard matrices and their Kronecker powers are used widely in spectral methods of analysis and processing of discrete signals and in quantum computers. A transform of a vector ā by means of a Hadamard matrix H gives the vector ū = Hā, generally called the *Hadamard spectrum of the vector* ā. A greater analogy exists between Hadamard transforms and Fourier transforms (Ahmed and Rao, 1975). In particular, the fast Hadamard transform exists in parallel with the fast Fourier transform. An entire class of multichannel *spectrometers with Hadamard transforms* is known (Tolmachev, 1976), where the principle of tape masks (or chain masks) is used, reminiscent of the principles of a chain construction of genetic texts in DNA. Hadamard matrices are used widely in the theory of coding. For example, they are connected with Reed–Muller error-correcting codes and with Hadamard codes (Peterson and Weldon, 1972), with the theory of compression of signals and images, with a realization of Boolean functions by means of spectral methods, with the theory of planning of multiple-factor experiments, and in many other branches of mathematics.

Rows of Hadamard matrices called Walsh functions (see Chapter 1) are used for a spectral presentation and for a transfer of discrete signals (Ahmed and Rao, 1975; Geramita, 1979; Yarlagadda and Hershey, 1997). Walsh functions can be represented in terms of products of Rademacher functions $r_n(t) = \text{sign}(\sin 2^n \pi t), n = 1, 2, 3, \dots$, which accept the two values +1 and −1 only (here "sign" is the function that gives the sign of the argument). When united in square matrices, sets of numerated Walsh functions form systems that depend on features of the union. Figure 8.19 shows two examples of systems

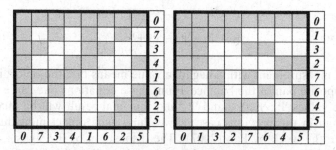

FIGURE 8.19   Examples of two systems of Walsh functions which are used frequently in the theory of digital signal processing. *Left:* the Walsh–Hadamard system. *Right:* the Walsh–Paley system. Each black (white) cell contains the number +1 (−1). Quantities of changes of the signs + and − are shown for each row and each column. (From Trahtman and Trahtman, 1975.)

of such functions, which are used widely in the theory of digital signal processing.

Hadamard matrices are connected with Walsh–Hadamard transforms, which are the most famous among nonsinusoidal orthogonal transforms and which can be calculated by means of mathematical operations of addition and subtraction only [for more details, see the literature (Ahmed and Rao, 1975; Trahtman and Trahtman, 1975; Yarlagadda and Hershey, 1997)]. Hereafter we use the simplified designations of matrix elements in illustrations of Hadamard matrices: the symbol "+" or a black matrix cell represents the element +1; the symbol − or a white matrix cell represents the element −1. The theory of discrete signals pays special attention to quantities of changes of the signs + and − along each row and each column in Hadamard matrices. These quantities are connected through the important notion of *sequency* as a generalization of the notion of *frequency* (Ahmed and Rao, 1975, p. 85).

Biological organisms are sets of biochemical molecules. A wide use of Hadamard matrices in analytical chemistry can be found, for example, in the work of Pan (2007), which draws special attention to applications of Hadamard matrices to enhance signal-to-noise ratio. This is explained in a simple example of weighing. The basic idea is connected with weighing of objects in groups, but not separately, for a more accurate determination of their individual weights. In the example of four objects, we can weigh them in two different ways. First, we can weigh each of them individually by means of a single pan spring balance well calibrated to give us correct values Ψ_1, Ψ_2, Ψ_3, and Ψ_4 for objects 1, 2, 3, and 4 with a small random error e. Second, we can weigh all four objects in groups by means of a two-pan balance to arrive at their general weights η_1, η_2, η_3, and η_4 in the next four weighings, with appropriate random errors e_1, e_2, e_3, and e_4:

$$\eta_1 = \Psi_1 + \Psi_2 + \Psi_3 + \Psi_4 + e_1$$

$$\eta_2 = \Psi_1 - \Psi_2 + \Psi_3 - \Psi_4 + e_2$$

$$\eta_3 = \Psi_1 + \Psi_2 - \Psi_3 - \Psi_4 + e_3$$

$$\eta_4 = \Psi_1 - \Psi_2 - \Psi_3 + \Psi_4 + e_4$$

Here a measurement with a negative value means that the object is placed on the opposite pan of the balance. From these equations one can easily calculate the values Ψ_1, Ψ_2, Ψ_3, and Ψ_4, and this final result will be much more precise than in the previous case of weighing each object individually [for details, see the work by Pan (2007)]. The disposition of the signs + and − in this system of four equations is identical to their disposition in the relevant Hadamard 4×4 matrix. In this way, applications of Hadamard transforms enhance the signal-to-noise ratio.

Some of the normalized Hadamard matrices are unitary operators (e.g., $2^{-0.5}[1\ 1;\ 1\ -1]$). They serve as one of the important instruments in creating quantum computers, which utilize Hadamard gates (as the evolution of the closed quantum system is unitary) (Nielsen and Chuang, 2001). Next we demonstrate connections of Hadamard matrices with the Kronecker families of genetic matrices described above.

Algebraic biology already includes examples of applications of Walsh functions (alongside other systems of basic functions) to the spectral analysis of various aspects of genetic algorithms and sequences (Forrest and Mitchell, 1991; Geadah and Corinthios 1977; Goldberg, 1989; Lee and Kaveh, 1986; Shiozaki, 1980; Vose and Wright, 1998; Waterman, 1999). The book by Zalmanzon (1989, p. 416) contains a review of investigations made by various authors about Walsh orthogonal functions in physiological systems of supracellular levels as well. We investigate whether structures of the genetic code have such direct relations with Hadamard matrices, which can justify systematic applications of Walsh–Hadamard functions to spectral and other analyses of many inherited biological structures at various levels. In this section we put forth evidence regarding connections of Hadamard matrices with the genetic code in its Kronecker matrix forms of presentation.

The genetic alphabet with its four letters A (adenine), C (cytosine), G (guanine), and U/T (uracil in RNA and thymine in DNA) is characterized by a phenomenological disturbance of symmetry related with the special status of the letter U/T:

- The three nitrogenous bases A, C, and G have one amide (amino group), NH_2, but the fourth basis, U/T, does not have this amide (Figure 2.1).
- The letter U is replaced by the letter T in genetic sequences only at transitions from RNA to DNA, and vice versa, for unknown reasons (in contrast to the three letters A, C, and G, which are not replaced).
- This special status of U/T leads to a special U-algorithm, which transforms a wide set of genetic 8×8 matrices of 64 triplets into appropriate Hadamard 8×8 matrices.

Here we should mention the importance of amino group NH_2. The amino group of amino acids bears a base function that provides recognition of an amino acid by an enzyme (Chapeville and Haenni, 1974). The importance of nitrogen compounds in molecular genetics is reflected in such names as "amino acids" (organic acids containing amino groups), "nitrogenous bases"; the "N-end" of a nucleotide circuit, with which protein synthesis always begins; and so on. All proteins are polyamides. A lack of proteins in food leads to a number of heavy infringements in the nitrogenous exchange. Beginning with works by Gierer and Mundry (1958) and Schuster and Schramm (1958), it has been known that action of nitrous acid, NHO_2, on RNA leads to the amino-mutation of RNA. More precisely, this action deletes the amino group NH_2 at the nitrogenous bases A and C and leads finally to a replacement of the nitrogenous bases A and C by the bases G and U, respectively: A $\rightarrow$ G and C $\rightarrow$ U. These amino-mutations are utilized traditionally to demonstrate molecular mechanisms as the origin of genetic mutations. Nitrogenous acid exists only in diluted water solutions, which are similar to solutions in biological organisms.

The phenomenological division of the four-letter genetic alphabet in the ratio 3:1 reminds one of the division of four components of the simplest Hadamard matrix $H(2) = [+1\ +1;\ -1\ +1]$ in the same ratio with three components +1 and a single component −1 (Figure 8.18). Taking it into account that the genetic alphabet can be represented in the form of a 2×2 matrix $P = [C\ A;\ U\ G]$ by analogy with the Hadamard matrix $H(2)$ (Figure 8.18).

Let us return now to the U-algorithm, which transforms the genomatrices of 64 triplets (Figures 8.2 and 8.4 to 8.17) into relevant Hadamard 8×8 matrices. A definition of the *U-algorithm* is the following:

- Each triplet in the black-and-white genomatrices (Figures 8.2 and 8.4 to 8.17) should change its own color into the opposite color each time the letter U stands in an odd position (in the first or third position) inside the triplet.
- Each triplet, which is disposed in a black (white) cell of such a changed genomatrix is interpreted as the number +1 (−1).

For example, according to the U-algorithm, the cells with the triplets UCA and GAU change their sign once, while the cell with the triplet UAU changes its sign twice, which means that the sign of this cell is unchanged. As a result of such U-algorithmic sign changes, a new mosaic in each of the same genomatrices appears. Such a mosaic is identical to the corresponding mosaic of a Hadamard matrix. Actually, if each black triplet (white triplet) in these genomatrices is replaced by the number +1 (−1), numeric matrices are formed (Figures 8.20 and 8.21). One can easily check that these new numeric matrices satisfy definition (8.1) of Hadamard 8×8 matrices: $H(8)H(8)^{\mathrm{T}} = 8I_n$. One can suppose that this U-algorithm (of inverting the signs every time the letter U or T appears in an odd position of triplets) is connected with the biological mechanism of mutual replacement of the letters U and T at transition from RNA to DNA, and vice versa.

One should note a special feature of the genetic Hadamard matrices in Figure 8.20: A quantity of changes of the signs + and − is equal to 14 for each of the halves of these matrices (we say upper, lower, left, and right halves). Such a "symmetrical" feature is typical of many other genetic Hadamard matrices (see some additional examples in Figure 8.21). One can call Hadamard matrices with such a feature *balanced Hadamard matrices*. One can check that each of the 4×4 quadrants of these Hadamard 8×8 matrices is a balanced Hadamard matrix as well. This feature distinguishes the genetic Hadamard matrices described from the Hadamard matrices in Figure 8.19, which are widely used in technical applications. For some reason nature has chosen the genetic code, which is connected with balanced Hadamard matrices. One can

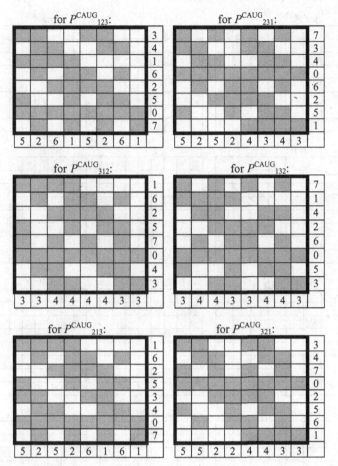

FIGURE 8.20 Some examples of balanced Hadamard matrices, which are produced from the six genomatrices indicated by means of the U-algorithm. The black cells correspond to the elements +1 and the white cells correspond to the elements −1. Numbers of changes of the signs + and − (or changes of colors) are shown for each row and each column.

find additional details on this theme in the literature (He and Petoukhov, 2009; Kappraff and Petoukhov, 2009; Petoukhov, 2008a–d; Petoukhov and He, 2009).

All such Hadamard matrices represent various basic systems of orthogonal functions, which are coordinated with the structural peculiarities of molecular systems of the genetic code. They can be utilized in genetic systems for spectral methods of genetic information processing with the use of noise-immunity coding, of compression of signals, and of other useful possibilities that Hadamard matrices and Walsh functions possess.

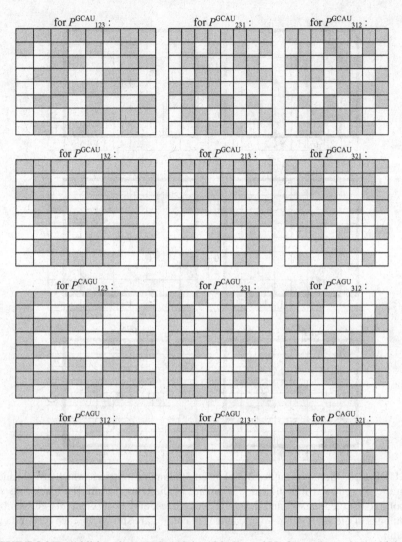

FIGURE 8.21 Additional examples of the 12 balanced Hadamard matrices which are produced from the 12 genomatrices of triplets by means of the U-algorithm. Black cells correspond to elements +1, and white cells correspond to elements −1.

More can be added about cyclic relations inside the set of described genomatrices. For example, the set of genomatrices P_{123}^{CAUG}, P_{231}^{CAUG}, P_{312}^{CAUG}, P_{321}^{CAUG}, P_{213}^{CAUG}, P_{132}^{CAUG} (see Figures 8.2, 8.4, and 8.5) was produced on the basis of two subsets of cyclic shifts of positions in triplets: 1–2–3 → 2–3–1 → 3–1–2 → 1–2–3 and 3–2–1 → 2–1–3 → 1–3–2 → 3–2–1. These cyclic relations are presented graphically in Figure 8.22.

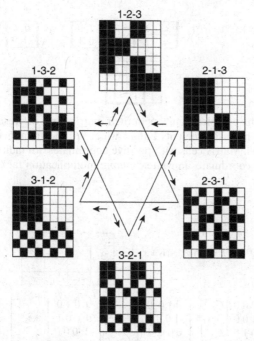

FIGURE   8.22 Two   cyclic   sequences   of   the   mosaic   genomatrices $P_{123}^{CAUG} \rightarrow P_{231}^{CAUG} \rightarrow P_{312}^{CAUG} \rightarrow P_{123}^{CAUG}$ and $P_{321}^{CAUG} \rightarrow P_{213}^{CAUG} \rightarrow P_{132}^{CAUG} \rightarrow P_{321}^{CAUG}$, which arise as a result of relevant cyclic permutations of positions in triplets: 1–2–3 → 2–3–1 → 3–1–2 and 3–2–1 → 2–1–3 → 1–3–2. The number over each matrix shows a relevant type of permutation of positions in all triplets. (From Petoukhov, 2008e.)

It is obvious that an analogous scheme can be demonstrated for appropriate subsets of Hadamard genomatrices as well. Such cyclic relations among different genomatrices can be used in mathematical models of inherited cyclic processes in living organisms.

8.4   GENETIC MATRICES AND MATRIX ALGEBRAS OF HYPERCOMPLEX NUMBERS

Complex and hypercomplex numbers, which are utilized in physics and mathematics, possess matrix forms for their representation. The notion of number is the main notion of mathematics and mathematical natural sciences. In view of this, an investigation of a possible connection of the genetic code to multi-dimensional numbers in their matrix presentations should be undertaken.

Algebras of complex numbers $z = x_0^* \mathbf{1} + x_1^* \mathbf{i}$ and hypercomplex numbers $x_0^* \mathbf{1} + x_1^* \mathbf{i}_1 + \cdots + x_k^* \mathbf{i}_k$ are well known. It is also known that complex and hypercomplex numbers have presentation as well as matrix forms of linear and

$$z = x_0*\mathbf{1} + x_1*\mathbf{i} = \begin{array}{|c|c|} \hline x_0 & x_1 \\ \hline -x_1 & x_0 \\ \hline \end{array} = x_0* \begin{array}{|cc|} \hline 1 & 0 \\ 0 & 1 \\ \hline \end{array} + x_1* \begin{array}{|cc|} \hline 0 & 1 \\ -1 & 0 \\ \hline \end{array}$$

	1	i
1	1	i
i	i	-1

FIGURE 8.23   *Top:* complex numbers in their matrix form of presentation and their decomposition on the basic elements **1** and **i**, which are shown in their matrix forms of presentation as well. Matrix cells with positive coordinates are indicated in black and cells with negative coordinates in white. *Bottom:* multiplication table of the basic elements **1** and **i**.

$$Q = x_0*\mathbf{1} + x_1*\mathbf{i_1} + x_2*\mathbf{i_2} + x_3*\mathbf{i_3} = \begin{array}{|c|c|c|c|} \hline x_0 & x_1 & x_2 & x_3 \\ \hline -x_1 & x_0 & -x_3 & x_2 \\ \hline -x_2 & x_3 & x_0 & -x_1 \\ \hline -x_3 & -x_2 & x_1 & x_0 \\ \hline \end{array} =$$

$$= x_0* \begin{vmatrix} 1&0&0&0 \\ 0&1&0&0 \\ 0&0&1&0 \\ 0&0&0&1 \end{vmatrix} + x_1* \begin{vmatrix} 0&1&0&0 \\ -1&0&0&0 \\ 0&0&0&-1 \\ 0&0&1&0 \end{vmatrix} + x_2* \begin{vmatrix} 0&0&1&0 \\ 0&0&0&1 \\ -1&0&0&0 \\ 0&-1&0&0 \end{vmatrix} + x_3* \begin{vmatrix} 0&0&0&1 \\ 0&0&-1&0 \\ 0&1&0&0 \\ -1&0&0&0 \end{vmatrix}$$

	1	i_1	i_2	i_3
1	1	i_1	i_2	i_3
i_1	i_1	-1	i_3	$-i_2$
i_2	i_2	$-i_3$	-1	i_1
i_3	i_3	i_2	$-i_1$	-1

FIGURE 8.24   *Top:* quaternions by Hamilton in the matrix form of presentation; cells with positive coordinates are shown in black and cells with negative coordinates are shown in white. *Middle:* the decomposition of quaternions in their matrix form in the basic elements **1**, i_1, i_2, and i_3, which are shown in the matrix form of presentation. *Bottom:* multiplication table of these basic elements.

vector forms. For example complex numbers $z = x*\mathbf{1} + y*\mathbf{i}$ (where **1** is the real unit and *i* is the imaginary unit: $\mathbf{i}^2 = -1$) possess the matrix form of presentation shown in Figure 8.23. By the way, complex numbers are utilized in computers in this matrix form.

The quaternions by Hamilton $Q = x_0^*\mathbf{1} + x_1^*\mathbf{i_1} + x_2^*\mathbf{i_2} + x_3^*\mathbf{i_3}$ (where $\mathbf{i_1^2} = \mathbf{i_2^2} = \mathbf{i_3^2} = -1$, $\mathbf{i_1^*i_2} = -\mathbf{i_2^*i_1} = \mathbf{i_3}$, $\mathbf{i_1^*i_3} = -\mathbf{i_3^*i_1} = -\mathbf{i_2}$, $\mathbf{i_2^*i_3} = -\mathbf{i_3^*i_2} = \mathbf{i_1}$), which are utilized widely in both physics and mathematics, have a matrix form of presentation as well. Figure 8.24 shows this form and its decomposition in the basic elements **1**, i_1, i_2, and i_3 in their matrix forms of presentation. In addition, the multiplication table of the basic elements **1**, i_1, i_2, and i_3 is demonstrated.

	000 (0)	001 (1)	010 (2)	011 (3)	100 (4)	101 (5)	110 (6)	111 (7)
000 (0)	x_0	x_1	$-x_2$	$-x_3$	x_4	x_5	$-x_6$	$-x_7$
001 (1)	x_0	x_1	$-x_2$	$-x_3$	x_4	x_5	$-x_6$	$-x_7$
010 (2)	x_2	x_3	x_0	x_1	$-x_6$	$-x_7$	$-x_4$	$-x_5$
011 (3)	x_2	x_3	x_0	x_1	$-x_6$	$-x_7$	$-x_4$	$-x_5$
100 (4)	x_4	x_5	$-x_6$	$-x_7$	x_0	x_1	$-x_2$	$-x_3$
101 (5)	x_4	x_5	$-x_6$	$-x_7$	x_0	x_1	$-x_2$	$-x_3$
110 (6)	$-x_6$	$-x_7$	$-x_4$	$-x_5$	x_2	x_3	x_0	x_1
111 (7)	$-x_6$	$-x_7$	$-x_4$	$-x_5$	x_2	x_3	x_0	x_1

$YY_8 =$ (label to the left of the matrix rows)

FIGURE 8.25   Matrix YY_8, the black cells of which contain coordinates with the sign + and the white cells of which contain coordinates with the sign −. The numeration of the columns and rows is identical to the numeration of the columns and rows of the matrix $[C\ A;\ U\ G]^{(3)}$ in Figure 2.2.

Is the mosaic genomatrix $P^{(3)} = [C\ A;\ U\ G]^{(3)}$ (Figure 8.2) connected with a matrix form of presentation of algebra of a multidimensional numeric system? In this section we answer this question positively.

Taking into account the molecular characteristics of the nitrogenous bases A, C, G, and U/T of the genetic alphabet, one can re-form this genomatrix $[C\ A;\ U\ G]^{(3)}$ into the new matrix YY_8 algorithmically (Figure 8.25).

The cells of the matrix YY_8, which are occupied by components with the sign +, are indicated in black. The cells of the matrix YY_8, which are occupied by components with the sign −, are marked in white. Such a black-and-white mosaic of the matrix YY_8 is identical to the black-and-white mosaic of the genomatrix $[C\ A;\ U\ G]^{(3)}$ (Figure 8.2). The matrix YY_8 has the eight independent parameters $x_0, x_1, x_2, x_3, x_4, x_5, x_6$, and x_7, which are interpreted here as real numbers. It has been discovered that the matrix YY_8 is the matrix form of presentation of a special eight-dimensional algebra (or the eight-dimensional algebra over the field of real numbers) and of the appropriate eight-dimensional numerical system. Below we list other structural analogies of the genomatrix $[C\ A;\ U\ G]^{(3)}$ with the matrix YY_8, the set of which allows one to consider that the matrix YY_8 and its algebra play a meaningful role in the model of the genetic code. But, initially, we draw attention to the "alphabetical" algorithm of *bipolar digitization* of 64 triplets (or *yin–yang digitization* as it was called initially), which produces the matrix YY_8 from the genomatrix $[C\ A;\ U\ G]^{(3)}$. This algorithm has received such an unusual name because of the special properties of the matrix YY_8 and its algebra (Petoukhov, 2008a,d,e; Petoukhov and He, 2009).

Alphabetic Algorithm of the Bipolar Digitization of 64 Triplets

This algorithm is based on utilizing the following two binary-oppositional attributes of the genetic letters A, C, G, and U/T: "purine or pyrimidine" and "two or three" hydrogen bonds. It also uses the famous thesis of molecular genetics that different positions inside triplets have different code meanings. For example, Konopelchenko and Rumer (1975) have reported that the first two positions of each triplet form the root of the codon and that they differ drastically from the third position by their essence and by their special role. In view of this alphabetical algorithm, the transformation of the genomatrix $[C\ A;\ U\ G]^{(3)}$ into the matrix YY_8 is not an abstract and arbitrary action at all, but such a transformation can be utilized by biocomputer systems of organisms materially.

The alphabetical algorithm of bipolar digitization defines the special scheme of reading each triplet: the first two positions of the triplet are read by genetic systems from the viewpoint of one attribute and the third position of the triplet is read from the viewpoint of another attribute. By this alphabetical algorithm, which allows one to recode the symbolic matrix $[C\ A;\ U\ G]^{(3)}$ into the numerical bipolar matrix YY_8 (Figure 8.25), each triplet is read in the following way:

- Two first positions of each triplet are filled out by the symbol α instead of the complementary letters C and G on these positions and by the symbol β instead of the complementary letters A and U, respectively.
- The third position of each triplet is filled out by the symbol γ instead of the pyrimidine (C or U) in this position, and by the symbol δ instead of the purine (A or G).
- The triplets, which have the letter C or G in their first position, receive the sign − only when their second position is occupied by the letter A. The triplets, which have the letters A or U in their first position, receive the sign + only when their second position is occupied by the letter C.

For example, the triplet CAG receives the symbol $-\alpha\beta\delta$, because its first letter C is symbolized by α, its second letter A is symbolized by β, and its third letter G is symbolized by δ. This triplet possesses the sign − because its first position has the letter C and its second position has the letter A. One can see that this algorithm recodes all triplets from the traditional alphabet C, A, U, G into the new alphabet α, β, γ, δ. As a result, each triplet receives one of the following eight expressions: $\alpha\alpha\gamma = x_0$, $\alpha\alpha\delta = x_1$, $\alpha\beta\gamma = x_2$, $\alpha\beta\delta = x_3$, $\beta\alpha\gamma = x_4$, $\beta\alpha\delta = x_5$, $\beta\beta\gamma = x_6$, and $\beta\beta\delta = x_7$. We will suppose that the symbols α, β, γ, and δ are real numbers. This algorithm transforms the initial symbolic matrix $[C\ A;\ U\ G]^{(3)}$ into the numeric matrix YY_8 with the eight coordinates x_0, x_1, x_2, x_3, x_4, x_5, x_6, and x_7. We shall name these matrix components x_0, x_1, ... , x_7, which are real numbers, *bipolar coordinates* or *YY-coordinates*.

Let us now switch our attention to algebraic properties of the matrix YY_8. By analogy with decompositions of the matrices of complex numbers and of quaternions by Hamilton (Figures 8.23 and 8.24), one can represent the eight-parametric matrix YY_8 (Figures 8.25 and 8.26) as the sum of the eight basic matrices, each of which is connected with one of the coordinates x_0, x_1, x_2, x_3,

	000 (0)	001 (1)	010 (2)	011 (3)	100 (4)	101 (5)	110 (6)	111 (7)
000 (0)	CCC ααγ x_0	CCA ααδ x_1	CAC -αβγ $-x_2$	CAA -αβδ $-x_3$	ACC βαγ x_4	ACA βαδ x_5	AAC -ββγ $-x_6$	AAA -ββδ $-x_7$
001 (1)	CCU ααγ x_0	CCG ααδ x_1	CAU -αβγ $-x_2$	CAG -αβδ $-x_3$	ACU βαγ x_4	ACG βαδ x_5	AAU -ββγ $-x_6$	AAG -ββδ $-x_7$
010 (2)	CUC αβγ x_2	CUA αβδ x_3	CGC ααγ x_0	CGA ααδ x_1	AUC -ββγ $-x_6$	AUA -ββδ $-x_7$	AGC -βαγ $-x_4$	AGA -βαδ $-x_5$
011 (3)	CUU αβγ x_2	CUG αβδ x_3	CGU ααγ x_0	CGG ααδ x_1	AUU -ββγ $-x_6$	AUG -ββδ $-x_7$	AGU -βαγ $-x_4$	AGG -βαδ $-x_5$
100 (4)	UCC βαγ x_4	UCA βαδ x_5	UAC -ββγ $-x_6$	UAA -ββδ $-x_7$	GCC ααγ x_0	GCA ααδ x_1	GAC -αβγ $-x_2$	GAA -αβδ $-x_3$
101 (5)	UCU βαγ x_4	UCG βαδ x_5	UAU -ββγ $-x_6$	UAG -ββδ $-x_7$	GCU ααγ x_0	GCG ααδ x_1	GAU -αβγ $-x_2$	GAG -αβδ $-x_3$
110 (6)	UUC -ββγ $-x_6$	UUA -ββδ $-x_7$	UGC -βαγ $-x_4$	UGA -βαδ $-x_5$	GUC αβγ x_2	GUA αβδ x_3	GGC ααγ x_0	GGA ααδ x_1
111 (7)	UUU -ββγ $-x_6$	UUG -ββδ $-x_7$	UGU -βαγ $-x_4$	UGG -βαδ $-x_5$	GUU αβγ x_2	GUG αβδ x_3	GGU ααγ x_0	GGG ααδ x_1

FIGURE 8.26 Result of the algorithmic transformation of 64 triplets into the numerical coordinates $x_0, x_1, \ldots, x_7$, which are based on the four symbols α, β, γ, and δ.

x_4, x_5, x_6, and x_7 (Figure 8.27). Let us symbolize any basic matrix related to any of the YY coordinates with even indexes (i.e., x_0, x_2, x_4, and x_6) by the symbol $\mathbf{f}_k$ (where "f" is the first letter of the word "female" and $k = 0, 2, 4, 6$). And let us symbolize any matrix that is related to any of YY coordinates with odd indexes (i.e., x_1, x_3, x_5, x_7 by the symbol $\mathbf{m}_s$ (where "m" is the first letter of the word "male" and $s = 1, 3, 5, 7$). In this case one can present the matrix YY_8 by the expression

$$YY_8 = x_0^* \mathbf{f}_0 + x_1^* \mathbf{m}_1 + x_2^* \mathbf{f}_2 + x_3^* \mathbf{m}_3 + x_4^* \mathbf{f}_4 + x_5^* \mathbf{m}_5 + x_6^* \mathbf{f}_6 + x_7^* \mathbf{m}_7 \qquad (8.2)$$

whose the matrix form is shown in Figure 8.27.

The important and unexpected fact is that the set of these eight basic matrices $\mathbf{f}_0, \mathbf{m}_1, \mathbf{f}_2, \mathbf{m}_3, \mathbf{f}_4, \mathbf{m}_5, \mathbf{f}_6$, and $\mathbf{m}_7$ forms a closed set relative to multiplications: A multiplication between any two matrices from this set generates a matrix from this set again. Figure 8.28 presents the results of multiplications among these eight matrices. The result of multiplying any two basic elements, which are taken from the left column and the upper row, is shown in the cell on the intersection of its row and column (e.g., in accordance with this multiplication table, $\mathbf{f}_2^* \mathbf{m}_5 = -\mathbf{m}_7$).

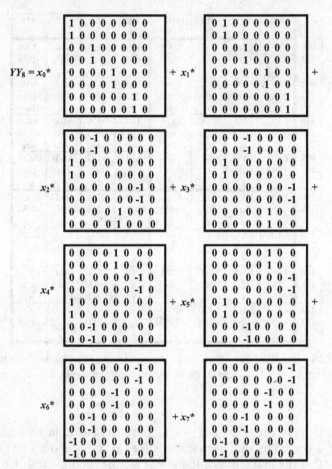

FIGURE 8.27 Matrix YY_8 as the sum of the eight basic matrices. The left column shows the basic matrices that are related to the coordinates with even indexes: x_0, x_2, x_4, and x_6. The right column shows the basic matrices that are related to the coordinates with odd indexes: x_1, x_3, x_5, and x_7.

	f_0	m_1	f_2	m_3	f_4	m_5	f_6	m_7
f_0	f_0	m_1	f_2	m_3	f_4	m_5	f_6	m_7
m_1	f_0	m_1	f_2	m_3	f_4	m_5	f_6	m_7
f_2	f_2	m_3	$-f_0$	$-m_1$	$-f_6$	$-m_7$	f_4	m_5
m_3	f_2	m_3	$-f_0$	$-m_1$	$-f_6$	$-m_7$	f_4	m_5
f_4	f_4	m_5	f_6	m_7	f_0	m_1	f_2	m_3
m_5	f_4	m_5	f_6	m_7	f_0	m_1	f_2	m_3
f_6	f_6	m_7	$-f_4$	$-m_5$	$-f_2$	$-m_3$	f_0	m_1
m_7	f_6	m_7	$-f_4$	$-m_5$	$-f_2$	$-m_3$	f_0	m_1

FIGURE 8.28 Multiplication table of the basic matrices f_0, m_1, f_2, m_3, f_4, m_5, f_6, and m_7 of the matrix YY_8 from Figures 8.25 and 8.27.

We noted above that such multiplication tables define appropriate algebras over a field. Correspondingly, the multiplication table in Figure 8.28 defines the genetic eight-dimensional algebra YY_8. Multiplication of any two members of the octet algebra YY_8 generates a new member of the same algebra. Multiplication of such numbers in their matrix forms of presentation implies that both factors have the identical matrix disposition of their eight parameters $x_0, x_1, \ldots, x_7$ (in the first factor) and $y_0, y_1, \ldots, y_7$ (in the second factor), and the final matrix has the same matrix disposition of its eight relevant parameters $z_0, z_1, \ldots, z_7$. This situation is similar to the situation of real numbers (or of complex numbers, or of hypercomplex numbers) when multiplication of any two members of the numerical system generates a new member of the same numerical system. In other words, the expression $YY_8 = x_0^* f_0 + x_1^* m_1 + x_2^* f_2 + x_3^* m_3 + x_4^* f_4 + x_5^* m_5 + x_6^* f_6 + x_7^* m_7$ is some kind of eight-dimensional number (*octet genonumber*) (Petoukhov, 2008a,d,e). We assign the symbol YY_8 conditionally to both this algebra and these octet genonumbers.

Let us give a numerical example of multiplication of two octet genonumbers: $V = 3^* f_0 + 2^* m_1 - 4^* f_2 + 1^* m_3 - 5^* f_4 + 6^* m_5 + 8^* f_6 - 7^* m_7$ and $W = 2^* f_0 - 4^* m_1 + 5^* f_2 + 3^* m_3 - 6^* f_4 - 8^* m_5 - 1^* f_6 + 5^* m_7$. The result of multiplication depends on the order of factors because of the nonsymmetrical character of the multiplication table relative to its main diagonal, which means that the algebra YY_8 is noncommutative:

$$V^*W = 18^* f_0 - 14^* m_1 + 24^* f_2 + 40^* m_3 - 30^* f_4 - 62^* m_5 - 16^* f_6 + 0^* m_7$$
$$W^*V = 128^* f_0 - 124^* m_1 - 60^* f_2 + 88^* m_3 + 48^* f_4 - 100^* m_5 + 92^* f_6 + 40^* m_7$$

These results can be arrived at by multiplication of appropriate matrix forms of presentation of the octet genonumbers V and W or by multiplication of linear forms of their presentation using the multiplication table in Figure 8.28. One should pay special attention to the cells on the main diagonal of the multiplication table. These cells contain squares of the basic elements. In cases of hypercomplex numbers, these diagonal cells contain elements ± 1 typically (e.g., see the multiplication tables of complex numbers and of quaternions by Hamilton in Figures 8.23 and 8.24). In our case these diagonal cells contain no real units at all, but all diagonal cells are occupied by the elements $\pm f_0$ and $\pm m_1$. Thereby the set of the eight basic matrices $f_0, m_1, f_2, m_3, f_4, m_5, f_6,$ and m_7 is divided into two equal subsets by the criterion of their squares. The first subset consists of elements with the even indexes: $f_0, f_2, f_4,$ and f_6. The squares of members of this f_0 subset are always equal to $\pm f_0$. The second subset consists of elements with the odd indexes: $m_1, m_3, m_5,$ and m_7. The squares of members of this m_1-subset are always equal to $\pm m_1$.

The basic element f_0 possesses all the properties of the real unit in relation to the members of the f_0 subset: $f_0^2 = f_0$, $f_0^* f_2 = f_2^* f_0 = f_2$, $f_0^* f_4 = f_4^* f_0 = f_4$, and $f_0^* f_6 = f_6^* f_0 = f_6$. But the element f_0 does not possess the commutative property of the real unit in relation to the members of the $\mathbf{m}_1$ subset: $\mathbf{f}_0^*\mathbf{m}_p \neq \mathbf{m}_p^*\mathbf{f}_0$, where $p = 1, 3, 5, 7$. For this reason, $\mathbf{f}_0$ is called the *quasi-real unit from the* $\mathbf{f}_0$ *subset*.

The basic element $\mathbf{m}_1$ possesses all the properties of the real unit in relation to the members of the $\mathbf{m}_1$ subset: $\mathbf{m}_1^2 = \mathbf{m}_1$, $\mathbf{m}_1^*\mathbf{m}_3 = \mathbf{m}_3^*\mathbf{m}_1 = \mathbf{m}_3$, $\mathbf{m}_1^*\mathbf{m}_5 = \mathbf{m}_5^*\mathbf{m}_1 = \mathbf{m}_5$, and $\mathbf{m}_1^*\mathbf{m}_7 = \mathbf{m}_7^*\mathbf{m}_1 = \mathbf{m}_7$. But the element $\mathbf{m}_1$ does not possess the commutative property of the real unit in relation to the members of the $\mathbf{f}_0$ subset: $\mathbf{m}_1^*\mathbf{f}_k \neq \mathbf{f}_k^*\mathbf{m}_1$, where $k = 0, 2, 4, 6$. For this reason, $\mathbf{m}_1$ is called the *quasi-real unit from the* $\mathbf{m}_1$ *subset*.

The even–odd principle exists in this YY_8 algebra. Really all members of the $\mathbf{f}_0$ subset and their coordinates x_0, x_2, x_4, and x_6 have even indexes, and they are disposed in columns with the even numbers 0, 2, 4, and 6 in the matrix YY_8 (Figure 8.25) and in its multiplication table (Figure 8.28). These coordinates x_0, x_2, x_4, and x_6 correspond to triplets with the pyrimidine suffixes C and U (Figure 8.26). For this reason the $\mathbf{f}_0$ subset can be called the *pyrimidine subset*.

All members of the $\mathbf{m}_1$ subset and their coordinates x_1, x_3, x_5, and x_7 have odd indexes and they are disposed in columns with the odd numbers 1, 3, 5, and 7 in the matrix YY_8 (Figures 8.25 and 8.26) and in its multiplication table (Figure 8.28). These coordinates x_1, x_3, x_5, and x_7 correspond to triplets with the purine suffixes A and G (Figure 8.26). For this reason the $\mathbf{m}_1$ subset can be called the *purine subset*.

In accordance with Pythagorean and ancient Chinese traditions, all even numbers are called *female* or *yin numbers*, and all odd numbers are called *male* or *yang numbers*. From the viewpoint of this tradition, the elements $\mathbf{f}_0, \mathbf{f}_2, \mathbf{f}_4, \mathbf{f}_6$, x_0, x_2, x_4, x_6 with the even indexes play the role of female or yin elements, and the elements $\mathbf{m}_1, \mathbf{m}_3, \mathbf{m}_5, \mathbf{m}_7, x_1, x_3, x_5, x_7$ with the odd indexes play the role of male or yang elements. Correspondingly the eight-dimensional algebra YY_8 can be termed *octet bipolar algebra* (or even–odd algebra, or yin-yang algebra, or bisexual algebra, or pyrimidine–purine algebra for triplets with pyrimidine and purine suffixes). Such an algebra, which possesses two quasi-real units and no real unit, gives new effective possibilities for modeling binary opposites in biological objects at different levels, including sets of triplets, amino acids, male and female gametal cells, male and female chromosomes, and so on. It should be pointed out that this genetic bipolar algebra is constructed in close connection with the special ordered set of Rademacher functions.

The octet bipolar numbers YY_8 (octet genonumbers) differ essentially from classical hypercomplex numbers, which have the real unit in the set of their basic elements. By traditional definition, hypercomplex numbers are the elements of algebras with real units. Complex and hypercomplex numbers were constructed historically as generalizations of real numbers with the obligatory inclusion of the real unit in the set of their basic elements. The octet bipolar numbers YY_8 do not have the real unit in the set of their basic elements at all, but they have two quasi-real units, $\mathbf{f}_0$ and $\mathbf{m}_1$. In comparison with hypercomplex numbers, bipolar numbers are, in principle, a new category of numbers in the mathematical natural sciences. In our opinion, knowledge of this category of numbers is necessary for a deep understanding of biological phenomena and

	f_0	f_2	f_4	f_6			m_1	m_3	m_5	m_7
f_0	f_0	f_2	f_4	f_6		m_1	m_1	m_3	m_5	m_7
f_2	f_2	$-f_0$	$-f_6$	f_4		m_3	m_3	$-m_0$	$-m_6$	m_4
f_4	f_4	f_6	f_0	f_2		m_5	m_5	m_6	m_0	m_2
f_6	f_6	$-f_4$	$-f_2$	f_0		m_7	m_7	$-m_4$	$-m_2$	m_0

FIGURE 8.29 Multiplication tables of the yin genoquaternion G_f (*left*) and yang genoquaternions G_m (*right*).

will perhaps be useful for the mathematical natural sciences as a whole. The mathematical theory of YY numbers represents a new formal and conceptual apparatus for modeling phenomena of reproduction and self-organization in living nature.

It can easily be demonstrated that bipolar algebras are a special generalization of the algebras of hypercomplex numbers in the form of *double-hypercomplex numbers*. Bipolar numbers (YY numbers) become the appropriate hypercomplex numbers in those cases when all their female (or male) coordinates are equal to zero. Traditional hypercomplex numbers can be represented as the "*monopolar*" *half* (a yin half or a yang half) of appropriate YY numbers. We denote yin-yang numbers by double letters (e.g., YY) to distinguish them from traditional (complex and hypercomplex) numbers. More details on this theme are available in the literature (Petoukhov, 2008a–e; Petoukhov and He, 2009).

If all male coordinates are equal to 0 ($x_1 = x_3 = x_5 = x_7 = 0$), the numbers YY_8 become the yin genoquaternions $G_f = x_0^* f_0 + x_2^* f_2 + x_4^* f_4 + x_6^* f_6$, the multiplication table for which is shown in Figure 8.29. These *yin quaternions* can also be called *pyrimidine quaternions* conditionally because their coordinates x_0, x_2, x_4, x_6 correspond to triplets with the pyrimidine suffixes C or U (Figure 8.26).

If all female coordinates are equal to 0 ($x_0 = x_2 = x_4 = x_6 = 0$), the numbers YY_8 become the yang genoquaternions $G_m = x_1^* m_1 + x_3^* m_3 + x_5^* m_5 + x_7^* m_7$, the multiplication table for which is shown in Figure 8.29. These *Yang quaternions* can be called also *purine quaternions* conditionally because their coordinates x_1, x_3, x_5, x_7 correspond to triplets with the purine suffixes A or G (Figure 8.26).

These genetic quaternions G_f and G_m have identical multiplication tables, which differ from the multiplication table of Hamilton quaternions (see Figure 8.24). Taking these facts into account, the octet genonumbers YY_8 can be termed *double genetic quaternions*. This leads to heuristic associations with a double helix of DNA, which is the bearer of genetic information. Just as the structure of three-dimensional physical space corresponds to the algebra of quaternions by Hamilton, so the structure of the genetic code corresponds to the algebra of the double genoquaternions.

The set of basic elements of the YY_8 algebra forms a semigroup. Two squares are marked out by bold lines in the left upper corner of the multiplication table in Figure 8.28. The first two basic elements, $\mathbf{f}_0$ and $\mathbf{m}_1$, are disposed in the smaller 2×2 square of this table only. The greater 4×4 square contains the four first basic elements $\mathbf{f}_0$, $\mathbf{m}_1$, $\mathbf{f}_2$, and $\mathbf{m}_3$. These aspects say that subalgebras YY_2 and YY_4 exist inside the algebra YY_8.

Each genetic triplet, which is disposed in the genomatrix $[C\ A;\ G\ U]^{(3)}$ in Figure 8.26 together with one of the female YY-coordinates x_0, x_2, x_4, and x_6 in a mutual matrix cell, is called a *female triplet* or *yin triplet*. The third position of all female triplets is occupied by the letter γ, which corresponds to the pyrimidine C or U/T. The female triplets can therefore be named *pyrimidine triplets* as well. Each triplet which is disposed in the genomatrix $[C\ A;\ G\ U]^{(3)}$ in Figure 7.4 together with one of the male YY coordinates x_1, x_3, x_5, x_7 in a mutual matrix cell is called a male triplet or yang triplet. The third position of all male triplets is occupied by the letter δ, which corresponds to the purine A or G. The male triplets can therefore be named *purine triplets*. In such an algebraic way the entire set of 64 triplets is divided into two subsets of pyrimidine triplets (or female triplets) and purine triplets (or male triplets). This algebraic division of the set of triplets defines a relevant internal structure in the set of 20 amino acids coded by them, which reveals some new approach to investigating structures of amino acid sequences in proteins (Petoukhov, 2008a–c; Petoukhov and He, 2009).

Now let us consider the close connection of structures of the genetic code with the octet bipolar matrices in many aspects.

Structural Analogies Between the Genomatrix $[C\ A;\ G\ U]^{(3)}$ and the Bipolar Matrix YY_8

The main interest of bioinformatics in octet bipolar algebra is connected with the possibility of its use as an adequate model of the structure of the genetic code. This possibility depends on structural coincidences between the bipolar matrix YY_8 and the genetic matrix $[C\ A;\ G\ U]^{(3)}$. A list of such nontrivial coincidences includes the following:

1. *First coincidence.* The black-and-white mosaics of the bipolar matrix YY_8 and the genetic matrix $[C\ A;\ G\ U]^{(3)}$ are identical. (For an unknown reason, nature has divided the set of the 64 genetic triplets into two subsets of 32 black triplets and 32 white triplets, which are disposed in the cells of 32 positive coordinates and 32 negative coordinates of the bipolar matrix YY_8.)

2. *Second coincidence.* In the bipolar matrix YY_8, the pairs of adjacent rows 0–1, 2–3, 4–5, and 6–7 are identical to each other by the assortment and the disposition of numerical coordinates x_0, x_1, x_2, x_3, x_4, x_5, x_6, and x_7.

In the genetic matrix $[C\ A;\ G\ U]^{(3)}$, the same pairs of adjacent rows 0–1, 2–3, 4–5, and 6–7 are identical to each other by the assortment and disposition of amino acids and stop codons.

3. *Third coincidence.* In the bipolar matrix YY_8, the female coordinates x_0, x_2, x_4, and x_6 occupy the columns with even numbers 0, 2, 4, and 6, and the male

coordinates x_1, x_3, x_5, and x_7 occupy the columns with odd numbers 1, 3, 5, and 7.

In the genetic matrix $[C\ A;\ G\ U]^{(3)}$, triplets with pyrimidine C or U in their third positions occupy the columns with even numbers 0, 2, 4, and 6; and triplets with purine A or G in their third positions occupy the columns with the odd numbers 1, 3, 5, and 7.

4. *Fourth coincidence.* In the bipolar matrix YY_8, one half of the numerical coordinates (x_0, x_1, x_2, x_3) exist in the two quadrants along the main diagonal only; the second half of the numerical coordinates (x_4, x_5, x_6, x_7) exist in the two quadrants along the second diagonal only.

In the genetic matrix $[C\ A;\ G\ U]^{(3)}$, one half of the amino acids exist in the two quadrants along the main diagonal only (Ala, Arg, Asp, Gln, Glu, Gly, His, Leu, Pro, Val); the second half of the amino acids exist in the two quadrants along the second diagonal only (Asn, Cys, Ile, Lys, Met, Phe, Ser, Thr, Trp, Tyr).

5. *Fifth coincidence.* In the bipolar matrix YY_8, the six different types of numerical matrices are generated by means of some kind of permutation of columns and rows of the matrix, each of which possesses its own type of the eight-dimensional bipolar algebra.

In the genetic matrix $[C\ A;\ G\ U]^{(3)}$, the same six types of permutations of columns and rows fit the six possible types of permutations of positions inside the 64 triplets (1–2–3, 2–3–1, 3–1–2, 3–2–1, 2–1–3, 1–3–2), which lead to the new genomatrices with symmetric and interrelated mosaics (see Figures 8.2, 8.4, and 8.5).

The fifth coincidence will be explained further. One should note that the black cells of the genomatrix $[C\ A;\ U\ G]^{(3)}_{123}$ contain the black NN-triplets, which encode the eight high-degeneracy amino acids, the coding meaning of which does not depend on the letter in the third position. Each of the amino acids in the set of eight high-degeneracy amino acids is encoded by four triplets or more: Ala, Arg, Gly, Leu, Pro, Ser, Thr, Val. The white cells of the genomatrix $[C\ A;\ U\ G]^{(3)}_{123}$ contain the white NN-triplets, the coding meaning of which depends on the letter in their third position; these triplets encode the 12 low-degeneracy amino acids together with stop signals: Asn, Asp, Cys, Gln, Glu, His, Ile, Lys, Met, Phe, Trp, Tyr.

The structural coincidences described for the two matrices YY_8 and $[C\ A;\ U\ G]^{(3)}_{123}$ allow us to consider the octet algebra YY_8 as a meaningful model of the structure of the genetic code. One can postulate such an algebraic model and then deduce some peculiarities of the genetic code from this model. These results of the comparison analysis give the following answer to the question of mysterious principles in the degeneracy of the Vertebrate Mitochondrial Code from the viewpoint of the algebraic model proposed. The matrix disposition of the 20 amino acids and the stop signals is determined by algebraic principles of the matrix disposition of the YY coordinates. Moreover, the disposition of the 32 black triplets and the high-degeneracy amino acids in this basic dialect of the genetic code is determined by the disposition of the YY coordinates with the sign +; and the disposition of the 32 white triplets, low-degeneracy amino acids, and stop signals is determined by the disposition of the YY coordinates with the sign −. One recalls here that the division of the set of 20 amino acids into the two subsets of eight high-degeneracy amino acids and the 12 low-degeneracy amino acids is practically the invariant rule of all the dialects of the genetic code (see below). The structural coincidences between both matrices do not exhaust the interconnections between the genetic code systems and the bipolar matrices. One can find additional information about applications of these genetic bipolar algebras for investigations in bioinformatics in the literature [Petoukhov, 2008a–e; Petoukhov and He, 2009].

The Six Kinds of Genetic Octet Bipolar Algebras Connected with Permutations of Positions in Triplets

Now we continue to study beautiful and unexpected mathematical properties of octet bipolar algebras.

In this chapter we have described the six mosaic genetic matrices $[C\ A;\ U\ G]_{123}^{(3)}, [C\ A;\ U\ G]_{231}^{(3)}, [C\ A;\ U\ G]_{312}^{(3)}, [C\ A;\ U\ G]_{321}^{(3)}, [C\ A;\ U\ G]_{213}^{(3)}$, and $[C\ A;\ U\ G]_{132}^{(3)}$, which have corresponded to the six possible types of permutation of positions in triplets. Each of these genetic matrices can be obtained from the initial matrix $[C\ A;\ U\ G]_{123}^{(3)}$ by an appropriate permutation of its columns and rows. One can make the same permutations of columns and rows in the bipolar matrix YY_8, which is denoted $(YY_8)_{123}$ in this section. In this way the appropriate matrices $(YY_8)_{123}$, $(YY_8)_{231}$, $(YY_8)_{312}$, $(YY_8)_{321}$, $(YY_8)_{213}$, and $(YY_8)_{132}$ arise. It is quite unexpected that not only the initial matrix $(YY_8)_{123}$ (Figure 8.25) but each of the other five matrices $(YY_8)_{231}$, $(YY_8)_{312}$, $(YY_8)_{321}$, $(YY_8)_{213}$, and $(YY_8)_{132}$ is the matrix form of presentation of its own eight-dimensional bipolar algebra. For example, Figure 8.30 shows the bipolar matrix $(YY_8)_{231}$, which corresponds to the genomatrix $[C\ A;\ U\ G]_{231}^{(3)}$, together with its multiplication table of the basic elements. Figure 8.31 demonstrates the multiplication tables for the other four bipolar matrices: $(YY_8)_{312}$, $(YY_8)_{132}$, $(YY_8)_{213}$, and $(YY_8)_{321}$. The degeneracy of the genetic code is thereby connected with the bunch of six genetic bipolar algebras (Petoukhov, 2008a,d; Petoukhov and He, 2009).

All these bipolar matrices have secret connections with Hadamard matrices: When all their coordinates are equal to the real unit 1 ($x_0 = x_1 = \cdots = x_7 = 1$) and when the signs of the components of the matrices are changed by means of the U-algorithm described above, all these octet bipolar matrices become Hadamard matrices. In necessary cases the biological computers of organisms can transform these bipolar matrices into Hadamard matrices to operate with systems of orthogonal vectors.

Two facts can be mentioned here as well. The complementary triplets (codon and anticodon) play an essential role in the genetic code systems. One

CCC x_0	CAC $-x_2$	ACC x_4	AAC $-x_6$	CCA x_1	CAA $-x_3$	ACA x_5	AAA $-x_7$
CUC x_2	CGC x_0	AUC $-x_6$	AGC $-x_4$	CUA x_3	CGA x_1	AUA $-x_7$	AGA $-x_5$
UCC x_4	UAC $-x_6$	GCC x_0	GAC $-x_2$	UCA x_5	UAA $-x_7$	GCA x_1	GAA $-x_3$
UUC $-x_6$	UGC $-x_4$	GUC x_2	GGC x_0	UUA $-x_7$	UGA $-x_5$	GUA x_3	GGA x_1
CCU x_0	CAU $-x_2$	ACU x_4	AAU $-x_6$	CCG x_1	CAG $-x_3$	ACG x_5	AAG $-x_7$
CUU x_2	CGU x_0	AUU $-x_6$	AGU $-x_4$	CUG x_3	CGG x_1	AUG $-x_7$	AGG $-x_5$
UCU x_4	UAU $-x_6$	GCU x_0	GAU $-x_2$	UCG x_5	UAG $-x_7$	GCG x_1	GAG $-x_3$
UUU $-x_6$	UGU $-x_4$	GUU x_2	GGU x_0	UUG $-x_7$	UGG $-x_5$	GUG x_3	GGG x_1

	f_0	f_1	f_2	f_3	m_4	m_5	m_6	m_7
f_0	f_0	f_1	f_2	f_3	m_4	m_5	m_6	m_7
f_1	f_1	$-f_0$	$-f_3$	f_2	m_5	$-m_4$	$-m_7$	m_6
f_2	f_2	f_3	f_0	f_1	m_6	m_7	m_4	m_5
f_3	f_3	$-f_2$	$-f_1$	f_0	m_7	$-m_6$	$-m_5$	m_4
m_4	f_0	f_1	f_2	f_3	m_4	m_5	m_6	m_7
m_5	f_1	$-f_0$	$-f_3$	f_2	m_5	$-m_4$	$-m_7$	m_6
m_6	f_2	f_3	f_0	f_1	m_6	m_7	m_4	m_5
m_7	f_3	$-f_2$	$-f_1$	f_0	m_7	$-m_6$	$-m_5$	m_4

FIGURE 8.30   *Top:* the bipolar matrix $(YY_8)_{231}$, which corresponds to the genomatrix $[C \ A; \ U \ G]_{231}^{(3)}$. *Bottom:* its multiplication table of the eight basic elements.

can replace each codon by its anticodon in the genomatrices $[C \ A; \ U \ G]_{123}^{(3)}$, $[C \ A; \ U \ G]_{231}^{(3)}, [C \ A; \ U \ G]_{312}^{(3)}, [C \ A; \ U \ G]_{132}^{(3)}, [C \ A; \ U \ G]_{213}^{(3)}, [C \ A; \ U \ G]_{321}^{(3)}$. Six new genomatrices appear in this case. Have they any connection with bipolar algebras? This question has a positive answer. The multiplication tables for the basic elements of bipolar matrices, connected with these new genomatrices, are identical to the multiplication tables for the initial genomatrices. In other words, the complementary transformations of the genomatrices $[C \ A; \ U \ G]_{123}^{(3)}, [C \ A; \ U \ G]_{231}^{(3)}, [C \ A; \ U \ G]_{312}^{(3)}, [C \ A; \ U \ G]_{132}^{(3)}, [C \ A; \ U \ G]_{213}^{(3)}$, and $[C \ A; \ U \ G]_{321}^{(3)}$ change the matrix forms of presentation of the initial YY_8 numbers only and do not change the bipolar algebras of the genomatrices. But if we consider the transposed matrices which are generated from the matrices $(YY_8)_{123}^{CAUG}$, $(YY_8)_{231}^{CAUG}$, and so on, they correspond to new octet bipolar algebras.

Matrix genetics has already proved its usefulness in bioinformatics, but in our opinion, we are in the very beginning stages of exporing its rich

	f_0	f_1	m_2	m_3	f_4	f_5	m_6	m_7
f_0	f_0	f_1	m_2	m_3	f_4	f_5	m_6	m_7
f_1	f_1	f_0	m_3	m_2	f_5	f_4	m_7	m_6
m_2	f_0	f_1	m_2	m_3	f_4	f_5	m_6	m_7
m_3	f_1	f_0	m_3	m_2	f_5	f_4	m_7	m_6
f_4	f_4	$-f_5$	m_6	$-m_7$	$-f_0$	f_1	$-m_2$	m_3
f_5	f_5	$-f_4$	m_7	$-m_6$	$-f_1$	f_0	$-m_3$	m_2
m_6	f_4	$-f_5$	m_6	$-m_7$	$-f_0$	f_1	$-m_2$	m_3
m_7	f_5	$-f_4$	m_7	$-m_6$	$-f_1$	f_0	$-m_3$	m_2

	f_0	f_1	m_2	m_3	f_4	f_5	m_6	m_7
f_0	f_0	f_1	m_2	m_3	f_4	f_5	m_6	m_7
f_1	f_1	$-f_0$	m_3	$-m_2$	$-f_5$	f_4	$-m_7$	m_6
m_2	f_0	f_1	m_2	m_3	f_4	f_5	$m6$	m_7
m_3	f_1	$-f_0$	m_3	$-m_2$	$-f_5$	f_4	$-m_7$	m_6
f_4	f_4	f_5	m_6	m_7	f_0	f_1	m_2	m_3
f_5	f_5	$-f_4$	m_7	$-m_6$	$-f_1$	f_0	$-m_3$	m_2
m_6	f_4	f_5	m_6	m_7	f_0	f_1	m_2	m_3
m_7	f_5	$-f_4$	m_7	$-m_6$	$-f_1$	f_0	$-m_3$	m_2

FIGURE 8.31 Multiplication tables of the basic elements of the octet bipolar algebras $(YY_8)_{312}$, $(YY_8)_{132}$.

opportunities. Below we give an example of one of the results that has already been arrived at in the field of matrix genetics.

8.5 SOME RULES OF EVOLUTION OF VARIANTS OF THE GENETIC CODE

Modern science knows many variants (or dialects) of the genetic code, data about which are shown on NCBI's Web site, http://www.ncbi.nlm.nih.gov/Taxonomy/Utils/wprintgc.cgi. Seventeen variants (or dialects) of the genetic

	f_0	m_1	f_2	m_3	f_4	m_5	f_6	m_7
f_0	f_0	m_1	f_2	m_3	f_4	m_5	f_6	m_7
m_1	f_0	m_1	f_2	m_3	f_4	m_5	f_6	m_7
f_2	f_2	m_3	f_0	m_1	f_6	m_7	f_4	m_5
m_3	f_2	m_3	f_0	m_1	f_6	m_7	f_4	m_5
m_5	f_4	m_5	$-f_6$	$-m_7$	$-f_0$	$-m_1$	f_2	m_3
m_5	f_4	m_5	$-f_6$	$-m_7$	$-f_0$	$-m_1$	f_2	m_3
f_6	f_6	m_7	$-f_4$	$-m_5$	$-f_2$	$-m_3$	f_0	m_1
m_7	f_6	m_7	$-f_4$	$-m_5$	$-f_2$	$-m_3$	f_0	m_1

	f_0	f_1	f_2	f_3	m_4	m_5	m_6	m_7
f_0	f_0	f_1	f_2	f_3	m_4	m_5	m_6	m_7
f_1	f_1	f_0	f_3	f_2	m_5	m_4	m_7	m_6
f_2	f_2	$-f_3$	$-f_0$	f_1	m_6	$-m_7$	$-m_4$	m_5
f_3	f_3	$-f_2$	$-f_1$	f_0	m_7	$-m_6$	$-m_5$	m_4
m_4	f_0	f_1	f_2	f_3	m_4	m_5	m_6	m_7
m_5	f_1	f_0	f_3	f_2	m_5	m_4	m_7	m_6
m_6	f_2	$-f_3$	$-f_0$	f_1	m_6	$-m_7$	$-m_4$	m_5
m_7	f_3	$-f_2$	$-f_1$	f_0	m_7	$-m_6$	$-m_5$	m_4

FIGURE 8.31   *Continued.* $(YY_8)_{213}$, and $(YY_8)_{321}$.

code exist, which differ one from another by their *numbers of degeneracy* (NDs; see Figure 8.32). By definition, the numbers of degeneracy of an amino acid are equal to the number of triplets that encode this amino acid in the dialect considered. Numbers of degeneracy, which are observed in the dialects, are equal to numbers from 1 to 8. For example, the first dialect of the genetic code (the Vertebrate Mitochondrial Code) in Figure 8.32 possesses 12 amino acids, for which the number of degeneracy is 2 (Asn, Asp, Cys, Gln, Glu, His, Ile, Lys, Met, Phe, Trp, Tyr); six amino acids, for which the number of degeneracy is 4 (Ala, Arg, Gly, Pro, Thr, Val), and two amino acids, for which the number of degeneracy is 6 (Leu, Ser).

One can see from the genomatrix in Figure 8.2 that in the Vertebrate Mitochondrial Code, the set of 20 amino acids is divided into two subsets: the

Dialects	Distribution of numbers of degeneracy from 1 to 8 among 20 AA								ΣAA with ND from **1 to 3**	ΣAA with ND from **4 to 8**
	1	2	3	4	5	6	7	8		
1		12		6		2			12	8
2	2	9	1	5		3			12	8
3	1	10	1	5		3			12	8
4		12		6		1		1	12	8
5	2	8	2	6		1		1	12	8
6	2	8	2	5		3			12	8
7	2	9	1	5		3			12	8
8		12		5		3			12	8
9	2	7	3	6		1		1	12	8
10	2	8	2	5		3			12	8
11	2	9	1	5		2	1		12	8
12	1	10	1	6		1		1	12	8
13	2	9	1	5	1	1	1		12	8
14	2	9	1	5	1	2			12	8
15	2	9	1	5	1	1	1		12	8
16		13		5		1		1	13	7
17	2	8	1	6		3			11	9

FIGURE 8.32   The 17 dialects of the genetic code and distributions of their numbers of degeneracy (ND) among 20 amino acids (AA). The two columns on the right show quantities of low and high-degenerate acids (ΣAA). Bold frames mark two categories of numbers of the degeneracy: from 1 to 3 and from 4 to 8 (Petoukhov, 2001a,b). (Data from http://www.ncbi.nlm.nih.gov/Taxonomy/Utils/wprintgc.cgi.)

subset of the eight high-degeneracy amino acids, which are coded by four or more triplets (Ala, Arg, Gly, Leu, Pro, Ser, Thr, Val), and the subset of 12 low-degeneracy amino acids, which are coded by three or fewer triplets (Asn, Asp, Cys, Gln, Glu, His, Ile, Lys, Met, Phe, Trp, Tyr). This division corresponds to the division of the set of cells of the bipolar matrix YY_8 into two subsets: the subset of cells with the sign + and the subset of cells with the sign − (Figures 8.25 and 8.26).

We consider this dialect, which is shown in Figure 8.32 as number 1 in the first column, as the basic dialect with which to compare other dialects. Let us analyze the 17 dialects of the genetic code to reveal the possible phenomenological rules and numerical invariants of evolution of the genetic code.

At first it seems that in Figure 8.32 the distribution of numbers of degeneracy in a set of the 17 dialects of the genetic codes is chaotic on the whole. But this impression disappears if one divides the set of 20 amino acids into the two subsets that were mentioned above in accordance with the genomatrix in Figure 8.2: the subset of low-degeneracy amino acids, each of which is encoded by three or fewer triplets in the Vertebrate Mitochondrial Code, and the subset of high-degeneracy amino acids, each of which is encoded by four or more triplets in the same basic dialect. Such a division reveals hidden regularities. Other types of division of the set of 20 amino acids into two subsets does not reveal hidden regularities.

The numbers of the dialects of the genetic code in Figure 8.32 correspond to the following dialects: (1) the Vertebrate Mitochondrial Code; (2) the Standard Code; (3) the Mold, Protozoan, and Coelenterate Mitochondrial Code and the Mycoplasma/Spiroplasma Code; (4) the Invertebrate Mitochondrial Code; (5) the Echinoderm and Flatworm Mitochondrial Code; (6) the Euplotid Nuclear Code; (7) the Bacterial and Plant Plastid Code; (8) the Ascidian Mitochondrial Code; (9) the Alternative Flatworm Mitochondrial Code; (10) the Blepharisma Nuclear Code; (11) the Chlorophycean Mitochondrial Code; (12) the Trematode Mitochondrial Code; (13) the Scenedesmus Obliquus Mitochondrial Code; (14) the Thraustochytrium Mitochondrial Code; (15) the Alternative Yeast Nuclear Code; (16) the Yeast Mitochondrial Code; and (17) the Ciliate, Dasycladacean and Hexamita Nuclear Code.

The data in Figure 8.32 permit us to formulate the following phenomenological rules (Petoukhov, 2001a,b).

Phenomenological Rule 1   In the dialects of the genetic code, the set of 20 amino acids contains two opposite subsets: the first consisting of 12 low-degeneracy amino acids (with their numbers of degeneracy from 1 to 3), and the second consisting of eight high-degeneracy amino acids (with their numbers of degeneracy from 4 to 8).

As the authors conclude, this rule about the canonical ratio 12:8 for two categories of amino acids holds true in nature without exception for dialects of the genetic code of autotrophic organisms. These types of organisms play the main role in biogeochemical cycles. But this rule has small exceptions in two cases of heterotrophic organisms in a form of minimal numeric shifting from the regular ratio 12:8 to the nearest integer ratios: The Yeast Mitochondrial Code possesses the ratio 13:7 for these two categories of amino acids, and the Ciliate, Dasycladacean and Hexamita Nuclear Code possesses the ratio 11:9. These nonstandard ratios encircle the canonical ratio 12:8 from opposing sides of the numerical axis. These nonstandard ratios demonstrate additionally the main role of the canonical ratio 12:8 as that center, around which minimal numeric fluctuations exist.

The data about evolution of the genetic code also demonstrate the existence of the following rule about canonical subsets of low- and high-degeneracy amino acids.

Phenomenological Rule 2   If a triplet encodes different amino acids in different genetic codes, these amino acids belong to the same canonical subset of amino acids. In other words, it is practically forbidden for those triplets that encode amino acids from one canonical subset of degeneracy to pass into the group of triplets during biological evolution, which encode amino acids from another canonical subset.

A single exception to this rule exists: The triplet UAG can encode amino acids Leu or Gln in the different canonical subsets. The rule says nothing about stop codons, so it does not consider those evolutionary cases when triplets that encode stop codons (or amino acids) in one genetic code begin to encode amino acids (or stop codons, respectively) in another code.

The phenomenological rules described above testify that two independent branches of evolution of the genetic code exist in billions of biological species: one branch for canonical subsets of high-degeneracy amino acids, and another branch for canonical subsets of low-degeneracy amino acids. These evolutionary branches within the consolidated code system can be compared with a parallel evolution of male and female organisms within a frame of one biological species. It reveals simultaneously that nature realizes an association of two very different subsets of 8 and 12 amino acids in the set of 20 amino acids. The matrix genetics thereby reveals the existence of such an internal structure in the set of 20 amino acids, which possesses the invariant properties in the evolution of the genetic code. One can find additional details about such phenomenological rules of the dialects in the literature (Petoukhov, 2001a,b, 2008a; Petoukhov and He, 2009).

During evolution of the genetic code, only some triplets change their code—meaning in the different dialects in comparison with the basic case of the Vertebrate Mitochondria Code in the sense that they begin to encode other amino acids or stop signals. What are the limitations utilized by nature in its choice of such changeable (or evolutional) triplets? Has the matrix disposition of these variable triplets any relation to the YY-coordinates $x_0, x_1, \ldots, x_7$ of the matrix YY_8 (Figures 8.25 and 8.26) and to their disposition in the genomatrix? Or do the bipolar coordinates have no relation to evolution of the genetic code and to systemic disposition of the variable triplets in the genomatrix $[C\ A;\ U\ G]^{(3)}$?

If such a relation is discovered, it gives additional evidence that the genetic octet bipolar algebra can be utilized as the adequate model of the genetic code or as the algebraic basis of the genetic code (the algebraic precode). It can be useful in tasks of sorting, putting in order, and in a deeper understanding of the genetic language. It can help to create new effective methods of information processing for many applied tasks as well. The appropriate algebraic model of the genetic code should give opportunities to deduce some evolutional peculiarities of the genetic code from such a fundamental mathematical system.

The results of a corresponding comparison analysis have shown the expressed connection between the disposition of the variable triplets in the genomatrix $[C\ A;\ U\ G]^{(3)}$ and disposition of the YY-coordinates $x_0, x_1, \ldots, x_7$

together with their signs, + and –, in the matrix YY_8. The results obtained lead to a few phenomenological rules of evolution of the dialects of the genetic code on the basis of the genetic octet bipolar algebra. In other words, the scheme, which is defined by this matrix algebra, holds true in the evolution of the genetic code in some significant aspects. These results give additional evidence of the appropriateness of such in each iteration of a population of an algebraic approach in bioinformatics.

The matrix form of presentation of members of the genetic octet bipolar algebra (Figures 8.25 and 8.26) contains 32 components with the sign + and 32 components with the sign –. The matrix disposition of the components with the sign + fits the disposition of the 32 black triplets. These black triplets encode eight kinds of high-degeneracy amino acids (Ala, Arg, Gly, Leu, Pro, Ser, Thr, Val); the other 12 amino acids are encoded by the white triplets and they are low-degeneracy acids. In the case of the Vertebrate Mitochondrial Code, the matrix disposition of these two canonical subsets fits the matrix disposition of the YY-coordinates with the signs + and – correspondingly.

Now we present additional phenomenological rules, which were discovered from the viewpoint of the octet bipolar algebra YY_8 and which are additional evidence of the adequacy of this algebra for the genetic code and its evolutionary peculiarities. What are the formal attributes that are utilized by nature in its choice of evolutionary changeable triplets from the set of 64 triplets? How are these triplets and their appropriate amino acids disposed in the genomatrix $[C\ A;\ U\ G]^{(3)}$ (Figures 8.25 and 8.26)? Has the matrix disposition of these variable triplets any relation to the YY-coordinates $x_0, x_1, \ldots, x_7$ and to their disposition in the genomatrix? Can these variable triplets be associated naturally with the groups of the purine triplets, pyrimidine triplets, and YY-coordinates? Or do the YY-coordinates have no relation to evolution of the genetic code and to a systemic disposition of the variable triplets in the genomatrix $[C\ A;\ U\ G]^{(3)}$? In this section we continue the comparison analysis to answer such questions.

Table 8.1 includes data for analyzing these questions. The Vertebrate Mitochondrial Code (code 1) is utilized as the standard for comparison of code meanings of triplets in different dialects. The second tabular column shows those changeable triplets, which possess another code meaning (relative to their meaning in dialect 1) in the dialect named in the first column. The name of the encoded amino acid or stop codon is given near each triplet in the second column in connection with the appropriate dialect named in the first column. Brackets in the second column contain the amino acid or stop codon that is encoded by this triplet in dialect 1. Each row of the second column is finished by the YY-coordinate, which is disposed together with this triplet in the same cell of the genomatrix in Figure 8.26. The third column displays data about start codons, which define the beginning of protein synthesis in the dialect considered. An appropriate YY-coordinate is shown for each start codon as well.

TABLE 8.1   Changeable Triplets and Start Codons in the Dialects of the Genetic Code

Dialect of the Genetic Code	Changeable Triplets	Start Codons
1. The Vertebrate Mitochondrial Code		AUU, $-x_6$ AUC, $-x_6$ AUA, $-x_7$ AUG, $-x_7$ GUG, x_3
2. The Standard Code	UGA, Stop (Trp), $-x_5$ AGG, Arg (Stop), $-x_5$ AGA, Arg (Stop), $-x_5$ AUA, Ile (Met), $-x_7$	UUG, $-x_7$ CUG, x_3 AUG, $-x_7$
3. The Mold, Protozoan, and Coelenterate Mitochondrial Code and the Mycoplasma/ Spiroplasma Code	AGG, Arg (Stop), $-x_5$ AGA, Arg (Stop), $-x_5$ AUA, Ile (Met), $-x_7$	UUG, $-x_7$ UUA, $-x_7$ CUG, x_3 AUC, $-x_6$ AUU, $-x_6$ AUG, $-x_7$ AUA, $-x_7$ GUG, x_3
4. The Invertebrate Mitochondrial Code	AGG, Ser (Stop), $-x_5$ AGA, Ser (Stop), $-x_5$	UUG, $-x_7$ AUU, $-x_6$ AUC, $-x_6$ AUA, $-x_7$ AUG, $-x_7$ GUG, x_3
5. The Echinoderm and Flatworm Mitochondrial Code	AGG, Ser (Stop), $-x_5$ AGA, Ser (Stop), $-x_5$ AUA, Ile (Met), $-x_7$ AAA, Asn (Lys), $-x_7$	AUG, $-x_7$ GUG, x_3
6. The Euplotid Nuclear Code	UGA, Cys (Trp), $-x_5$ AGG, Arg (Stop), $-x_5$ AGA, Arg (Stop), $-x_5$ AUA, Ile (Met), $-x_7$	AUG, $-x_7$
7. The Bacterial and Plant Plastid Code	UGA, Stop (Trp), $-x_5$ AGG, Arg (Stop), $-x_5$ AGA, Arg (Stop), $-x_5$ AUA, Ile (Met), $-x_7$	UUG, $-x_7$ CUG, x_3 AUC, $-x_6$ AUU, $-x_6$ AUA, $-x_7$ AUG, $-x_7$
8. The Ascidian Mitochondrial Code	AGG, Gly (Stop), $-x_5$ AGA, Gly (Stop), $-x_5$	UUG, $-x_7$ AUA, $-x_7$ AUG, $-x_7$ GUG, x_3
9. The Alternative Flatworm Mitochondrial Code	UAA, Tyr (Stop), $-x_7$ AGG, Ser (Stop), $-x_5$ AGA, Ser (Stop), $-x_5$ AUA, Ile (Met), $-x_7$ AAA, Asn (Lys), $-x_7$	AUG, $-x_7$

TABLE 8.1 *Continued*

Dialect of the Genetic Code	Changeable Triplets	Start Codons
10. The Blepharisma Nuclear Code	UGA, Stop (Trp), $-x_5$ UAG, Gln (Stop), $-x_7$ AGG, Arg (Stop), $-x_5$ AGA, Arg (Stop), $-x_5$ AUA, Ile (Met), $-x_7$	AUG, $-x_7$
11. The Chlorophycean Mitochondrial Code	UGA, Stop (Trp), $-x_5$ UAG, Leu (Stop), $-x_7$ AGG, Arg (Stop), $-x_5$ AGA, Arg (Stop), $-x_5$ AUA, Ile (Met), $-x_7$	AUG, $-x_7$
12. The Trematode Mitochondrial Code	AGG, Ser (Stop), $-x_5$ AGA, Ser (Stop), $-x_5$ AAA, Asn (Lys), $-x_7$	AUG, $-x_7$ GUG, x_3
13. The Scenedesmus obliquus Mitochondrial Code	UGA, Stop (Trp), $-x_5$ UAG, Leu (Stop), $-x_7$ UCA, Stop (Ser), x_5 AGG, Arg (Stop), $-x_5$ AGA, Arg (Stop), $-x_5$ AUA, Ile (Met), $-x_7$	AUG, $-x_7$
14. The Thraustochytrium Mitochondrial Code	UGA, Stop (Trp), $-x_5$ UUA, Stop (Leu), $-x_7$ AGG, Arg (Stop), $-x_5$ AGA, Arg (Stop), $-x_5$ AUA, Ile (Met), $-x_7$	AUU, $-x_6$ AUG, $-x_7$ GUG, x_3
15. The Alternative Yeast Nuclear Code	UGA, Stop (Trp), $-x_5$ AGG, Arg (Stop), $-x_5$ AGA, Arg (Stop), $-x_5$ AUA, Ile (Met), $-x_7$ CUG, Ser (Leu), x_3	CUG, x_3 AUG, $-x_7$
16. The Yeast Mitochondrial Code	AGG, Arg (Stop), $-x_5$ AGA, Arg (Stop), $-x_5$ CUG, Thr (Leu), x_3 CUU, Thr (Leu), x_2 CUA, Thr (Leu), x_3 CUC, Thr (Leu), x_2	AUA, $-x_7$ AUG, $-x_7$
17. The Ciliate, Dasycladacean and Hexamita Nuclear Code	UGA, Stop (Trp), $-x_5$ UAG, Gln (Stop), $-x_7$ UAA, Gln (Stop), $-x_7$ AGG, Arg (Stop), $-x_5$ AGA, Arg (Stop), $-x_5$ AUA, Ile (Met), $-x_7$	AUG, $-x_7$

Source: Initial data from http://www.ncbi.nlm.nih.gov/Taxonomy/Utils/wprintgc.cgi.

Triplets that Change Their Code Meaning   Let us analyze the data from the second column of Table 8.1. This column shows 14 types of changeable triplets that possess different code meanings in different dialects: AAA, AGA, AGG, AUA, CUA, CUC, CUG, CUG, CUU, UAA, UAG, UCA, UGA, and UUA. Some of these triplets have several meanings. For example, the triplet AGA encodes the stop signal in dialect 1, the amino acid Arg in dialect 4, and the amino acid Gly in dialect 8. Or the triplet UAA encodes the stop signal in dialect 1, the amino acid Tyr in dialect 9, and the amino acid Gln in dialect 17.

All kinds of changeable triplets are encountered 69 times in the second column. But only two types of male (or purine) YY-coordinates, $-x_5$ and $-x_7$ with the sign $-$, correspond to these triplets in all dialects in practice. Specifically, the male coordinate $-x_5$ is encountered 41 times (59.4% of all cases), and the male coordinate $-x_7$ is encountered 22 times (31.9% of all cases), a total of more than 90% of all cases. The male coordinate $+x_5$ is encountered once in dialect 13 but with the sign $+$. One can name the male YY-coordinates $-x_5, -x_7$, and $+x_5$ as canonical bipolar coordinates for the changeable triplets (Table 8.1). The statistics described allow one to formulate the following rule.

Phenomenological Rule 3, Connected with Octet Bipolar Algebra   Those triplets possess different code meanings in the various dialects of the genetic code, which correspond to the canonical male coordinates $-x_5, -x_7$, and $+x_5$ of the matrix YY_8.

This rule holds true precisely for all the dialects except for the case of yeast, with its two dialects: dialect 15, where the noncanonical male coordinate $+x_3$ appears (for the triplet CUG), and dialect 16, which has a unique feature. In dialect 16 the four triplets CUA, CUG, CUC, and CUU, which begin with the same pair of letters (CU), change their code meanings in an identical way; all of them encode the acid Thr instead of the acid Leu. (It is an unusual case because, if any other four triplets are begun with the same pair of any letters, they do not change their code meanings jointly in other dialects.) These four triplets correspond to the noncanonical YY-coordinates $+x_2$ and $+x_3$.

Yeasts are unicellular mushrooms, chemoorganoheterotrophs, which reproduce by vegetative cloning (asexual reproduction). Probably the genetic-code deviation of yeast from rule 3 is connected with their asexual reproduction and heterotrophy. The additional evidence of molecular-genetic singularity of yeast is the fact that no histone H_1 is discovered in their genetic system (http://drosophila.narod.ru/Review/histone.html).

One can make one more remark about the male coordinates $-x_5$ and $-x_7$, which are connected to more than 90% of all changeable triplets, as mentioned above. All triplets that correspond to these coordinates, change their code meanings except for the four invariable triplets: UGG with the coordinate $-x_5$, and AAG, AUG, and UUG with the coordinate $-x_7$. Perhaps new dialects of the genetic code will be discovered in the future in which these triplets change their code meanings as well.

Phenomenological Rule 4, Connected with Genetic Octet Bipolar Numbers
All 16 triplets which correspond to the YY-coordinate x_0 and x_1 never change
their code meanings in the dialects of the genetic code (including the case of
yeast).

One can see that coordinates x_0 and x_1 are absent in Figure 8.1 together
with their 16 triplets: CCC, CCA, CCU, CCG, CGC, CGA, CGU, CGG, GCC,
GCA, GCU, GCG, GGC, GGA, GGU, and GGG. One can interpret coordinates x_0 and x_1 as scalar parts of the yin and yang genoquaternions correspondingly (see above) and other yin and yang coordinates (x_2, x_4, x_6 and x_3, x_5, x_7
correspondingly) as vector parts of the yin and yang genoquaternions by
analogy with Hamilton quaternions; this approach leads to an idea about the
anosotropic character of YY_8-space (Petoukhov, 2008a,d,e; Petoukhov and He,
2009). From a mathematical point of view, rule 3 concerns the anisotropic
vector parts of yang genoquaternions, and rule 4 concerns the scalar parts of
the yin and yang genoquaternions.

Stop Codons   Encoding of stop signals of protein synthesis turns on a special
interest. Stop signals are encoded by different triplets (stop codons) in different dialects of the genetic code. The seven types of triplets play the role of
stop codons in these dialects. Three of them (UUU, UAG, UUA) fit the YY-
coordinate $-x_7$. The other three triplets (AGA, AGG, UGA) fit the coordinate
$-x_5$. The seventh triplet (UCA) fits the coordinate $+x_5$. All these coordinates
are the anisotropic yang coordinates. Consequently, the function of stop codons
is closely connected with the anisotropy of YY_8-space. The results of the investigation of stop codons in the genetic dialects from the viewpoint of YY_8-
algebra allow one to formulate the following rule.

**Phenomenological Rule 5, Connected with Octet Bipolar Algebra and the
Anisotropy of YY_8-Space**   Those triplets serve as stop codons in the dialects
of the genetic code, which correspond to the anisotropic yang coordinates $-x_5$,
$-x_7$, and $+x_5$.

This rule holds true, without exception, for all 17 dialects. It draws attention
to the fact that the function of stop codons is always the yang function (or
male function) from the viewpoint of YY_8 algebra because stop codons are
connected with the yang coordinates. A few triplets exist (e.g., UUA and
UGG), which correspond to the same coordinates, $-x_5$, $-x_7$, and $+x_5$, but which
are not stop codons in known dialects of the genetic code. Will such a dialect
of the genetic code be discovered in the future, where these triplets play the
role of stop codons? Time will tell.

Start Codons   Until now we have not analyzed start codons (the function of
start codons is the additional function of some triplets which they execute
besides their basic function of coding of amino acids). The third column of

Table 8.1 shows the start codons of the 17 dialects of the genetic code, which are presented in basic sets of code meanings of 64 triplets of the considered 17 dialects at http://www.ncbi.nlm.nih.gov/Taxonomy/Utils/wprintgc.cgi. Eight triplets play the role of start codons in these 17 cases. Four of them (AUA, AUG, UUA, UUG) correspond to the YY-coordinate $-x_7$. The two triplets AUC and AUU correspond to the coordinate $-x_6$. The other two triplets, CUG and GUG, correspond to the coordinate $+x_3$. The set of start codons of dialect 1 corresponds to all these coordinates $-x_7$, $-x_6$, and $+x_3$. These data allow one to formulate an additional rule about start codons.

Phenomenological Rule 6, Connected with Octet Bipolar Algebra All start codons in the dialects of the genetic code correspond to YY-coordinates $-x_7$, $-x_6$, and $+x_3$.

This rule holds true, without exception, for all 17 dialects of the genetic code. One can add that the start codon AUG, which corresponds to the YY-coordinate $-x_7$, is included in all 17 dialects. All start codons in Table 8.1 have the letter U in the second position and should remind one of the U-algorithm connection between genomatrices and Hadamard matrices.

8.6 CHALLENGES AND PERSPECTIVES

Matrix genetics can be interpreted as a part of an algebraic biology on genetic systems by means of their matrix forms of presentation. Matrix genetics has been developed intensively by the authors during the past decade (He, 2001, 2003a,b; He and Petoukhov, 2007; Kappraff and Petoukhov, 2009; Petoukhov, 2001a,b, 2005a,b, 2008a–e; Petoukhov and He, 2009). Let us list some of the main results that were obtained in these works:

- New phenomenological rules of evolution of the genetic code
- Connections of matrix structures of the genetic code with Rademacher functions, Walsh functions, and Hadamard matrices
- Multidimensional algebras for modeling and for analyzing the genetic code systems
- Hidden interrelations between the golden section and parameters of genetic multiplets
- Relations between the Pythagorean musical scale and an important class of quint genetic matrices which show a molecular genetic basis with a sense of musical harmony and of aesthetics of proportions
- Cyclic algebraic principles in the structure of matrices of the genetic code
- Materials for a chronocyclic conception, which connects structures of the genetic system with chrono-medicine and a problem of an internal clock of organisms

- Connections of the genetic code with the famous Gray code
- A conception of matrix operators and vector presentations of genetic sequences to use in bioinformatics effective methods of digital communication

Spectral methods of decomposition of signals on orthogonal systems of functions have long shown themselves as especially important in the theory of signals and informatics in general. Researchers on genetic informatics attempt to address them already [see, e.g., the work of Kargupta, (2001) and of Lobzin and Chechetkin (2000), which draw attention to the importance of spectral methods in this field]. But an infinite quantity of orthogonal systems of functions exists. It is difficult for researchers of molecular-genetic systems to make a choice in one of an infinite number of possible orthogonal systems as adequate for spectral methods in the field of genetic informatics. Here they should make rather a volitional choice, risking the waste of many years of work in the case of the failure of such a choice. They usually make this choice proceeding from secondary reasons that do not have a direct connection to genetic systems. For example, they choose the system of orthogonal harmonious functions, which is applied in classical frequency Fourier analysis, because reason that system has extensive applications in technical fields.

The results described in this chapter show the relation of the genetic code to the orthogonal systems of Rademacher functions and Walsh functions, which are connected with Hadamard matrices and Gray code. These systems possess a special meaning for genetic informatics and its spectral methods. The orthogonal systems of functions connected with Hadamard matrices are picked out by nature from the infinite set of basic systems for their deep connection with an essence of molecular-genetic coding. A consistent investigation of bioinformatics systems should be done from the viewpoint of the theory of Hadamard matrices and their applications. In particular, the comparative analysis of various genetic sequences on their Hadamard spectrums is interesting. The results described give important help in the choice of a research tool from an infinite set of orthogonal systems of functions and from a set of variants of noise-immunity codes.

In the spectral analysis of genetic sequences (e.g., their correlation functions), it is meaningful to spend their decomposition on orthogonal vector rows of Hadamard genomatrices, instead of on trigonometric functions of the frequency Fourier analysis. Investigations of Hadamard spectrums in mathematical genetics are prospective and well founded, especially since some works are already known as applications of Walsh functions (alongside with other systems of basic functions) to the spectral analysis of various aspects of genetic algorithms and sequences (Forrest and Mitchell, 1991; Geadah and Corinthios 1977; Goldberg, 1989; Lee and Kaveh, 1986; Shiozaki, 1980; Vose and Wright, 1998; Waterman, 1999). The book by Zalmanzon (1989, p. 416) contains a review of works about applications of Walsh orthogonal functions in some other fields of physiology.

The discovery of connections of the genetic matrices with Hadamard matrices leads to many new possible investigations using the methods of symmetry, spectral analysis, and so on. One can expect that those Walsh functions, which are related to the genetic Hadamard matrices described, will be used effectively in the spectral analysis of genetic sequences. It seems that investigations of structural and functional principles of bioinformation systems from the viewpoint of quantum computers and of unitary Hadamard operators are very promising. A comparison of orthogonal systems of Walsh functions in molecular-genetic structures and in genetically inherited macrophysiological systems can give new understanding to the interrelation of various levels in biological organisms. Data about the genetic Hadamard matrices, together with data about algebras of the genetic code, can lead to new understanding of genetic code systems, to new effective algorithms of information processing, and perhaps, to new directions in the field of quantum computers. Matrix genetics has also given some impetus for developing new mathematical researches (see, e.g., Adamson, 2009; Kappraff and Adamson, 2009).

REFERENCES

Adamson, G. (2009). Articles A164575, A164557, A164522, A164516, A164309, A164308, A164281, A164279, A164092, A164057. On-Line Encyclopedia of Integer Sequences. http://www.tinyurl.com/4zq4q.

Ahmed, N., and Rao, K. (1975). *Orthogonal Transforms for Digital Signal Processing*. New York: Springer-Verlag.

Chapeville, F., and Haenni, A.-L. (1974). *Biosynthèse des proteins*. Paris: Hermann.

Forrest, S., and Mitchell, M. (1991). The performance of genetic algorithms on Walsh polynomials: some anomalous results and their explanation. In: R. K. Belew and L. B. Booker (Eds.), *Proceedings of the Fourth International Conference on Genetic Algorithms*. San Mateo, CA: Morgan Kaufmann, pp. 182–189.

Frank-Kamenetskiy, M. D. (1988). *The Most Principal Molecule*. Moscow: Nauka (in Russian).

Geadah, Y. A., and Corinthios, M. J. (1977). Natural, dyadic and sequency order algorithms and processors for the Walsh–Hadamard transform. *IEEE Trans. Comput.*, **C-26**, 435–442.

Geramita, A. V. (1979). *Orthogonal Designs: Quadratic Forms and Hadamard Matrices*. London: Dekker.

Gierer, A., and Mundry, K. W. (1958). Production of mutants of tobacco mosaic virus by chemical alteration of its ribonucleic acid in vitro. *Nature (London)*, **182**, 1457–1458.

Goldberg, D. E. (1989). Genetic algorithms and Walsh functions. *Complex Syst.*, **3**(2), 129–171.

He, M. (2001). Double helical sequences and doubly stochastic matrices. In: S. Petoukhov (Ed.), *Symmetry in Genetic Information*. Budapest, Hangary: International Symmetry Foundation, pp. 307–330.

He, M. (2003a). Symmetry in structure of genetic code. In: *Proceedings of the 3rd All-Russian Interdisciplinary Scientific Conference: Ethics and the Science of Future—Unity in Diversity.* Moscow, Feb. 12–14, pp. 80–85.

He, M. (2003b). Genetic code, attributive mappings and stochastic matrices. *Bull. Math. Biol.*, **66**(5), 965–973.

He, M., and Petoukhov, S. (2007). Harmony of living nature, symmetries of genetic systems and matrix genetics. *Int. J. Integr. Med.*, **1**(1), 41–43.

He, M., and Petoukhov, S. (2009). Symmetries in matrix genetics and Hadamard matrices of the genetic code. *Symmetry: Cult. Sci.*, **20**(1–4), 77–98.

He, M., Petoukhov, S. V., and Ricci, P. E. (2004). Genetic code, Hamming distance and stochastic matrices. *Bull. Math. Biol.*, **66**(5), 965–973.

Kappraff, J., and Adamson G. (2009). Generalized DNA matrices, silver means, and Pythagorean triples. *FORMA*, **24**(2), 45–59.

Kappraff, J., and Petoukhov, S. V. (2009). Symmetries, generalized numbers and harmonic laws in matrix genetics. *Symmetry: Cult. Sci.*, **20**(1–4), 23–50.

Kargupta, H. (2001). A striking property of genetic code-like transformations. *Complex Syst.*, **11**, 57–70.

Konopelchenko, B. G., and Rumer, Y. B. (1975). Classification of the codons in the genetic code. *Dokl. Akad. Nauk SSSR*, **223**(2), 145–153 (in Russian).

Lee, M. H., and Kaveh, M. (1986). Fast Hadamard transform based on a simple matrix factorization. *IEEE Trans. Acoust. Speech Signal Process.*, **ASSSP-34**(6), 1666–1667.

Lobzin, V. V., and Chechetkin, V. P. (2000). The order and correlations in genome sequences of DNK. *Usp. Fizi. Nauk*, **170**(1), 57–81 (in Russian).

Nielsen, M. A., and Chuang, I. L. (2001). *Quantum Computation and Quantum Information.* Cambridge, UK: Cambridge University Press.

Pan, C. (2007). *Applications of Hadamard Transform in Analytical Chemistry.* Birmingham, AL: University of Alabama, Department of Chemistry. Graduate Students Seminar Series. http://www.bama.ua.edu/~chem/seminars/student_seminars/spring07/s07-papers/pan-sem.pdf.

Peterson, W. W., and Weldon, E. J. (1972). *Error-Correcting Codes.* Cambridge, MA: MIT Press.

Petoukhov, S. V. (2001a). Genetic codes I: binary sub-alphabets, bisymmetric matrices and golden section. *Symmetry: Cult. Sci.*, **12**(3–4), 255–274.

Petoukhov, S. V. (2001b). Genetic codes II: numeric rules of degeneracy and a chronocyclic theory. *Symmetry: Cult. Sci.*, **12**(3–4), 275–306.

Petoukhov, S. V. (2005a). The rules of degeneracy and segregations in genetic codes: the chronocyclic conception and parallels with Mendel's laws. In: M. He, G. Narasimhan, S. Petoukhov (Eds.), *Advances in Bioinformatics and Its Applications.* Series in Mathematical Biology and Medicine, Vol. **8**. Hackensack, NJ: World Scientific, pp. 512–532.

Petoukhov, S. V. (2005b). Hadamard matrices and quint matrices in matrix presentations of molecular genetic systems. *Symmetry: Cult. Sci.*, **16**(3), 247–266.

Petoukhov, S. V. (2006). Bioinformatics: matrix genetics, algebras of the genetic code and biological harmony. *Symmetry: Cult. Sci.*, **17**(1–4), 253–291.

Petoukhov, S. V. (2008a). *Matrix Genetics, Algebras of the Genetic Code, Noise-Immunity.* Moscow: RCD (in Russian).

Petoukhov, S. V. (2008b). The degeneracy of the genetic code and Hadamard matrices. 1–8. Retrieved Feb. 22, 2008, from http://arXiv:0802.3366.

Petoukhov, S. V. (2008c). Matrix genetics: 1. Permutations of positions in triplets and symmetries of genetic matrices. 1–12. Retrieved Mar. 6, 2008, from http://arXiv:0803.0888.

Petoukhov, S. V. (2008d). Matrix genetics: 2. The degeneracy of the genetic code and the octave algebra with two quasi-real units (the "yin–yang octave algebra"). 1–27. Retrieved Mar. 8, 2008, from http://arXiv:0803.3330.

Petoukhov, S. V. (2008e). Matrix genetics: 4. Cyclic changes of the genetic 8-dimensional yin–yang-algebras and the algebraic models of physiological cycles. 1–22. Retrieved Sept. 17, 2008, from http://arXiv:0809.2714.

Petoukhov, S. V., and He, M. (2009). *Symmetrical Analysis Techniques for Genetic Systems and Bioinformatics: Advanced Patterns and Applications.* Hershey, PA: IGI Global.

Rumer, Y. B. (1968). Systematization of the codons of the genetic code. *Dokl. Akad. Nauk SSSR,* **183**(1), 225–226 (in Russian).

Schrödinger, E. (1955). *What Is Life? The Physical Aspect of the Living Cell.* Cambridge, UK: Cambridge University Press.

Schuster, H., and Schramm, G. (1958). Bestimmung der biologisch wirksamen Einheit in der RNS des TMV auf chemischen Wege. *Z. Naturforsch.,* **13b**, 697–704.

Shiozaki, A. (1980). A model of distributed type associated memory with quantized Hadamard transform. *Biol. Cybern.,* **38**(1), 19–22.

Sklar, B. (2001). *Digital Communication: Fundamentals and Applications.* Upper Saddle River, NJ: Prentice Hall.

Stewart, I. (1999). *Life's Other Secret: The New Mathematics of the Living World.* New York: Penguin.

Tolmachev, Y. A. (1976). *New Optic Spectrometers.* Leningrad: Leningrad University (in Russian).

Trahtman, A. M., and Trahtman, V. A. (1975). *The Foundations of the Theory of Discrete Signals on Finite Intervals.* Moscow: Sovetskoie Radio (in Russian).

Vose, M., and Wright, A. (1998). The simple genetic algorithm and the Walsh transform: I. Theory. *J. Evol. Comput.,* **6**(3), 253–274.

Waterman, M. S. (Ed.) (1999). *Mathematical Methods for DNA Sequences.* Boca Raton, FL: CRC Press.

Yarlagadda, R., and Hershey, J. (1997). *Hadamard Matrix Analysis and Synthesis with Applications to Communications and Signal/Image Processing.* London: Kluwer Academic.

Zalmanzon, L. A. (1989). *Fourier, Walsh and Haar Transformations and Their Application in Control, Communication and Other Systems.* Moscow: Nauka (in Russian).

9 Bioinformatics, Denotational Mathematics, and Cognitive Informatics

Bioinformatics is the comprehensive application of mathematics, science, and a core set of problem-solving methods to an understanding of living systems. It will have profound effects on all fields of biological and medical sciences. Cognition is viewed as a process of living systems. Cognition is an abstract property of advanced living organisms. It is studied as a direct property of a brain or of an abstract mind on subsymbolic and symbolic levels. Cognitive informatics studies cognition and information sciences that investigates the processes of the natural intelligence. As both fields continue their rapid development and progress, it is a central challenge to understand the biological basis of cognition, perception, learning, memory, thought, and mind.

The time seems ripe to bring these varied topics together to focus on our understanding of the emerging patterns, dissipative structures, and evolving cognition of living systems through a process of experimental application, scientific computation, and theoretical abstraction.

In this chapter we review briefly the intersections and connections between these two emerging fields of bioinformatics and cognitive informatics through a systems view of emerging pattern, dissipative structure, and evolving cognition of living systems. A new kind of math-denotational mathematics (Wang, 2008) for cognitive informatics is introduced. It is hoped that this brief review will encourage further exploration of our understanding of the biological basis of cognition, perception, learning, memory, thought, and mind.

9.1 INTRODUCTION

Patterns, structures, and rules arise and play an important role in living systems and nearly all branches of science. This is particularly true in mathematics, physics, theoretical biology, and neurosciences. It is remarkable that aspects of pattern discovery have only recently been explored in the field of genetics and

Mathematics of Bioinformatics: Theory, Practice, and Applications, By Matthew He and Sergey Petoukhov
Copyright © 2011 John Wiley & Sons, Inc.

bioinformatics. Bioinformatics is a new scientific discipline that merges biology, computer science, mathematics, and other subjects into a broad-based field that will have a profound impact on all fields of biology. Bioinformatics is the comprehensive applications of mathematics, science, and a core set of problem-solving methods to an understanding of living systems. Living systems are open self-organizing systems that have the special characteristics of life and interact with their environment. This takes place by means of information and material-energy exchanges. We summarize living systems broadly in Table 9.1.

These systems are based on nucleic acids that self-replicate, mutate, and compete. There is now a growing collection of investigations in bioinformatics

TABLE 9.1   Overview of Living Systems

Living System	Description	Distinctive Properties
Viroids	Plant pathogens that consist of a short stretch (a few hundred nucleobases) of highly complementary, circular, single-stranded RNA without the protein coat that is typical of viruses.	Self-replication by use of host enzymes, mutation Specificity to host Harmful but not destructive to host Individuality given by self-replication only, without compartmentalization
Plasmids	Extrachromosomal DNA molecules separate from chromosomal DNA; capable of replicating independent of chromosomal DNA. In many cases, it is circular and double-stranded.	Self-replication by use of bacterial enzymes, mutation Autonomous control of self-replication and distribution of copies Nonspecific propagation within hosts Harmless or advantageous symbiont for host Individuality given by autonomy, functions without compartmentalization
Viruses	Microscopic infectious agent that can reproduce only inside a host cell. Viruses infect all types of organisms: from animals and plants, to bacteria and archaea.	Self-reproduction by use of whole host translation and replication machinery, mutation Individuality given also by compartmentalization Variety of shapes Specific recognition and ultimately destructive attack of host Latency by invasion of host genetic material

TABLE 9.1 *Continued*

Living System	Description	Distinctive Properties
Bacteria	Large group of unicellular microorganisms.	Self-reproduction by individual translation and replication machinery, mutation Compartmentalization in cells Motility and response to external stimuli Sexual mating
Protozoa	Unicellular heterotrophic protist, such as an amoeba or a ciliate.	Self-reproduction by individual machinery mutation Compartments inside cell with different functions Motility and response to environmental stimuli Aggregation in colonies
Higher organisms	Any living system (such as animal, plant, fungus, or microorganism). In at least some form, all organisms are capable of response to stimuli, reproduction, growth and development, and maintenance of homeostasis as a stable whole. An organism may be either unicellular (single-celled) or composed of, as in humans, many billions of cells grouped into specialized tissues and organs.	Reproduction, sexual, germination, partenogenetic Multicellular organization with cell differentiation for multiplicity of functions Growth and morphogenesis Motility in response to environmental stimuli Storage and elaboration of information about environment Behavior Social behavior Self-consciousness Cultural evolution

attempting to investigate patterns, structures, and processes at every level of form, pattern, structure, function, interaction, and evolution through biological data objects. The potential data objects in bioinformatics are illustrated in Figure 9.1.

The general biology-driven problems in bioinformatics include:

- Finding functionally significant motifs in a family of protein sequences.
- Developing techniques to detect alternative genetic codes.
- Developing techniques to identify the extent of horizontal gene and intron transfer.

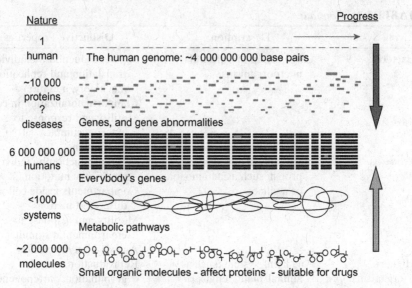

FIGURE 9.1   Potential data objects in bioinformatics.

- Developing techniques to help understand the role of DNA repeats in genome evolution.

Over the past few decades, major advances in the field of molecular biology, coupled with advances in genomic technologies, have led to an explosive growth in the biological data generated by the scientific community. This deluge of genomic information has, in turn, led to an absolute requirement for computerized databases to store, organize, and index the data and for specialized tools to view, analyze, and interpret the data. Bioinformatics is an emerging field of science in which biology, computer science, and information technology merge to form an emerging discipline. The ultimate goal of the field is to enable the discovery of new biological insights and hidden patterns of living systems at every level. At the beginning of the genomic revolution, a bioinformatics concern was the creation and maintenance of a database to store biological information, such as nucleotide, amino acid, and protein sequences. Development of this type of database involved not only design issues but the development of complex interfaces whereby researchers could both access existing data as well as submit new or revised data. Ultimately, all of this information must be combined to form a comprehensive picture of normal cellular activities. Therefore, the field of bioinformatics has evolved such that the most pressing task now involves the analysis and interpretation of various types of data, including nucleotide, amino acid sequences, protein domains, and protein structures and interactions. Important research branches within bioinformatics include the development and implementation of tools (e.g., biolanguages; see Table 1.2) that enable efficient access to, and use and management of, various types of information and new algorithms and statistics with which to assess relationships among members of large data sets, such as methods to locate a gene within a sequence, predict protein structure and/or function, and cluster protein sequences into families of related sequences.

Given a sequence of data such as a DNA or amino acid sequence, a motif or a pattern is a repeating subsequence. Such repeated subsequences often have important biological significance, and hence discovering such motifs in various biological databases turns out to be a very important problem in computational biology. Of course, in biological applications the various occurrences of a pattern in the given sequence may not be exact, and hence it is important to be able to discover motifs even in the presence of small errors. Various tools are now available for carrying out automatic pattern discovery. This is usually the first step toward a more sophisticated task such as gene finding in DNA or secondary structure prediction in protein sequences at the system level.

Systems biology is an emergent field that aims at system-level understanding of biological systems. It focuses on systems that are composed of molecular components. Since the days of cybernetics, system-level understanding has been a long-standing goal of biological sciences. It was only recently that system-level analysis can be grounded on discoveries at the molecular level. With the progress of the genome sequence project and range of other molecular biology projects that accumulate in-depth knowledge of the molecular nature of biological system, we are now at the stage to look into the possibility of a system-level understanding solidly grounded in molecular-level understanding. Although systems are composed of matter, the essence of a system lies in dynamics and it cannot be described merely by enumerating the components of the system. Both the structure of the system and components plays an indispensable role in forming the symbiotic state of the system as a whole. This may include the understanding of the structure of the system, such as gene regulatory and biochemical networks, and an understanding of the system dynamics, both quantitative and qualitative analysis. There are numbers of exciting and profound issues that are actively investigated, such as the robustness of biological systems, network structures and dynamics, and applications to drug discovery. Systems biology and network biology are in their infancy, but these are the areas that have to be explored and the areas that demonstrate the mainstream of the biological sciences in this century (Kitano, 2002a,b).

In summary, to understand biology at the system level, we must examine the structure and dynamics of cellular function rather than the characteristics of isolated parts of a cell or organism. Properties of systems, such as robustness, emerge as central issues, and understanding these properties may have an effect on the future of medicine. However, many breakthroughs in experimental devices, advanced software, and analytical methods are required before the achievements of systems biology can live up to their much-touted potential.

A key feature of the biological organization in all organisms is the tendency of proteins with a common function to associate physically via stable protein-to-protein interactions (PPIs) to form larger macromolecular assemblies. These protein complexes are often linked together by extended networks of weaker, transient PPIs, to form interaction networks that integrate pathways mediating the major cellular processes. Consequently, the cell is viewed increasingly as an assembly of interconnected functional modules that integrate and coordinate a cell's major biochemical activities and responses to external and intrinsic signals. Given their broad significance, systematic analyses of PPI networks have become a major experimental focus. One of the ultimate goals of biological networks is to improve our understanding of the processes and events that lead to pathologies and diseases. The analysis of biological pathways can provide a more efficient way of browsing through biologically relevant information and offer a quick overview of underlying biological processes. Protein interactions help put biological processes in context, allowing researchers to characterize specific pathway biology. Hence, an analysis of biological networks is crucial for an understanding of complex biological systems and diseases. The analysis of protein interaction networks is an important and very active research area in bioinformatics and computational biology (Dyke, 1988).

9.2 EMERGING PATTERN, DISSIPATIVE STRUCTURE, AND EVOLVING COGNITION

The understanding of patterns, system biology, and network biology is of crucial importance to a scientific understanding of living systems. However, a full understanding of a living system requires further understanding of the system's pattern, structure, and process. A new synthesis of living systems was introduced by Capra (1997). The key idea of his synthesis is to express the key criteria of a living system in terms of three conceptual dimensions: pattern (autopoiesis), structure (dissipative structure), and process (cognition) (He, 2008).

Autopoiesis: The Pattern of Life

Autopoiesis literally means "auto (self)-creation" and expresses a fundamental interaction between structure and function. The term was introduced by Humberto Maturana and Francisco Varela in 1973 (Maturana and Varela, 1973, 1980). According to Maturana and Varela, a living system produces itself continuously. Autopoiesis is a network pattern in which the function of each component involves the production or transformation of other components in the network. The simplest living system we know is the biological cell. The eukaryotic cell, for example, is made of various biochemical components, such as nucleic acids and proteins, and is organized into bounded structures such as the cell nucleus, various organelles, a cell membrane, and a cytoskeleton. These structures, based on an external flow of molecules and energy, produce the components which, in turn, continue to maintain the organized bounded structure that gives rise to these components. An autopoietic system is to be contrasted with an allopoietic system, such as a car factory, which uses raw materials (components) to generate a car (an organized structure), which is something other than itself (a factory). More generally, the term *autopoiesis* resembles the dynamics of a nonequilibrium system; that is, organized states that remain stable for long periods of time despite matter and energy continually flowing through them. From a very general point of view, the notion of autopoiesis is often associated with that of self-organization. However, an autopoietic system is autonomous and operationally closed, in the sense that every process within it helps directly in maintaining the whole. Autopoietic systems are structurally coupled with their medium in a dialect dynamics of changes that can be called *sensory-motor coupling*. This continuous dynamics is considered as knowledge and can be observed throughout life-forms (Luisi, 1993; Mingers, 1994; Varela et al., 1974). Mathematical models of self-organizing networks were known as *cellular automata*, a powerful tool for simulating autopoiesis networks. A cellular automaton is a collection of "colored" cells on a grid of specified shape that evolves through a number of discrete time steps according to a set of rules based on the states of neighboring cells. The rules are then applied iteratively for as many time steps as desired. Von Neumann was one of the first people to consider such a model and incorporated a cellular model into his "universal constructor." Cellular automata were studied in the early 1950s as a possible model for biological systems (Wolfram, 2002). The simplest type of cellular automaton is a binary, nearest-neighbor, one-dimensional automaton. Such automata were called *elementary cellular automata* by S. Wolfram, who has studied their amazing properties extensively (Wolfram, 2002). The theory of cellular automata is immensely rich, with simple rules and structures capable of producing a great variety of unexpected behaviors.

Dissipative Structure: The Structure of Living Systems

The term *dissipative structure* of a living system was coined by Ilya Prigogine, who pioneered research in the field of thermodynamics (Mingers, 1994). A dissipative structure is a system thermodynamically open to the flow of energy and matter. A dissipative structure operates far from thermodynamic equilibrium in an environment with which it exchanges energy and matter. Prigogine describes a living system as a dissipative structure that is both structurally open and organizationally closed. Matter flows through it continually, but the system maintains a stable form, and it does so autonomously through self-organization. Simple examples of dissipative structure include convection, cyclones and hurricanes. More complex examples include lasers, Bénard cells, the Belousov–Zhabotinsky reaction, and at the most sophisticated level, life itself. The vast network of metabolic processes keeps the system in a state far from equilibrium and gives rise to bifurcations through its inherent feedback loops.

According to Prigogine, dissipative structures are islands of order in a sea of disorder, maintaining and even increasing their order at the expense of greater order in their environment. The dissipative structure is sensitive to small fluctuations in its environment at the bifurcation point. A bifurcation point represents a dramatic change in the system's trajectory in phase space. A new attractor may suddenly appear, so that the system's behavior as a whole branches off in a new direction and thus leads to development and evolution. Exactly what happens at the bifurcation point depends on the system's previous history. A living system is a record of previous development. A tiny fluctuation in the environment will lead to the choice of the branch and lead to the emergence of new forms of order. Prigogine has coined the phrase *order through fluctuations* to describe the situation. One way of modeling a dissipative structure mathematically involves the action of a group on a measurable set (Prigogine, 1967). Dissipative structures are dynamical systems described by a state $x(t)$, inputs $u(t)$, and outputs $y(t)$ at time t such that there exist a function of x and t, $V(x, t)$ (storage functions), and a function of u and y, $w(u, y)$ (supply rates), such that

$$V(x, t) \geq 0 \quad \text{and} \quad \frac{dV(x(t), t)}{dt} < u(t) \cdot y(t) \quad \text{for any time } t \qquad (9.1)$$

where $\cdot$ is the scalar product.

The physical interpretation is that $V(x, t)$ is the energy in the system, whereas $u(t) \cdot y(t)$ is the energy that is supplied to the system. Dissipative systems are still an active field of research in systems and control, due to their important applications. Prigogine's mathematical techniques (Prigogine, 1967) were applied by Brian Goodwin to model the stages of development of a single-celled alga. By setting up differential equations that interrelate patterns of calcium concentration in the alga's cell fluid with the mechanical properties of the cell walls, the feedback loops in self-organizing processes were identified, and structures of increasing order emerge as successive bifurcation points. As described earlier, a bifurcation point is a threshold of stability. The dissipative structure may branch to new states of order or may break down. Prigogine has observed that even in chemical oscillations, the history of a dissipative structure at bifurcation points seems to be the physical origin of the intersection between structure and history that is characteristic of all living systems. Living structure is always a record of previous development.

Cognition: The Process of Life

The concept of cognition is closely related to such abstract concepts as mind, reasoning, perception, intelligence, learning, and many others that describe numerous capabilities of the human mind and expected properties of artificial or synthetic intelligence. Cognition or cognitive processes can be natural and artificial, conscious and not conscious; therefore, they are analyzed from different perspectives and in different contexts, in neurology, psychology, philosophy, and computer science. Cognition, according to Maturana and Varela, is the activity involved in the self-generation and self-perpetuation of living systems. In other words, cognition is the very process of life. In this new view, cognition involves the entire process of life—including perception, emotion, and behavior—and does not necessarily require a brain and a nervous system. At the human level, however, cognition includes language, conceptual thought, and all the other attributes of human consciousness. Mind is not a thing but a process—the process of cognition, which is identified with the process of life. The brain is a specific structure through which this process operates. The relationship between mind and brain is therefore one between process and structure. The brain is, moreover, by no means the only structure involved in the process of cognition. In the human organism, as in the organisms of all vertebrates, the immune system is increasingly being recognized as a network that is as complex and interconnected as the nervous system and serves equally important coordinating functions (Capra, 1997).

Neuroscience

Neuroscience studies the structure, function, evolutionary history, development, genetics, biochemistry, physiology, pharmacology, informatics, computational neuroscience, and pathology of the nervous system. The nervous system is composed of a network of neurons and other supportive cells (functional circuits). Each neuron is responsible for specific tasks of behavior at the organism level. Therefore, neuroscience can be studied at many different levels, ranging from the molecular level to the cellular level to the systems level to the cognitive level.

At the molecular level, the basic questions addressed in molecular neuroscience include the mechanisms by which neurons express and respond to molecular signals and how axons form complex connectivity patterns. At this level, tools from molecular biology and genetics are used to understand how neurons develop and die, and how genetic changes affect biological functions.

At the cellular level, the fundamental questions addressed in cellular neuroscience are the mechanisms of how neurons process signals physiologically and electrochemically. They address how signals are processed by the dendrites, somas, and axons, and how neurotransmitters and electrical signals are used to process signals in a neuron.

At the systems level, the questions addressed in systems neuroscience include how the circuits are formed and used anatomically and physiologically to produce the physiological functions, such as reflexes, sensory integration, motor coordination, circadian rhythms, emotional responses, learning, and memory. In other words, they address how these neural circuits function and the mechanisms through which behaviors are generated.

At the cognitive level, cognitive neuroscience addresses the questions of how psychological/cognitive functions are produced by the neural circuitry. The emergence of powerful new measurement techniques such as neuro-imaging, electrophysiology, and human genetic analysis, combined with sophisticated experimental techniques from cognitive psychology, allow neuroscientists and psychologists to address abstract questions such as how human cognition and emotion are mapped to specific neural circuitries.

9.3 DENOTATIONAL MATHEMATICS AND COGNITIVE COMPUTING

Denotational mathematics is a category of expressive mathematical structures that deals with high-level mathematical entities beyond numbers and sets, such as abstract objects, complex relations, behavioral information, concepts, knowledge, processes, and systems. Denotational mathematics is usually in the form of abstract algebra, a branch of mathematics in which a system of abstract notations is adopted to denote relations of abstract mathematical entities and their algebraic operations based on given axioms and laws.

Typical paradigms of denotational mathematics are concept algebra, system algebra, real-time process algebra (RTPA), visual semantic algebra (VSA), fuzzy logic, and rough sets. A wide range of applications of denotational mathematics has been identified in many modern science and engineering disciplines that deal with complex and intricate mathematical entities and structures beyond numbers, Boolean variables, and traditional sets (Wang, 2008). Wang defined the basic expressive power and mathematical means in system modeling as outlined in Table 9.2.

Within the new forms of descriptive mathematics, *concept algebra* is designed to deal with the new abstract mathematical structure of concepts and their representation and manipulation. Concept algebra provides a denotational mathematical means for algebraic manipulations of abstract concepts. Concept algebra can be used to model, specify, and manipulate generic *to be*–type problems, particularly system architectures, knowledge bases, and detail-level system designs, in cognitive informatics, computational intelligence, computing science, software engineering, and knowledge engineering.

System algebra is created for the rigorous treatment of abstract systems and their algebraic operations. System algebra provides a denotational mathematical means for algebraic manipulations of all forms of abstract systems. System algebra can be used to model, specify, and manipulate generic *to be* and *to*

TABLE 9.2   Denotational Mathematics

Basic Power Expressive in System Modeling	Classic Mathematics	Denotational Mathematics	Use
To *be*	Logic	Concept algebra	To identify objects and attributes
To *have*	Set theory	System algebra	To describe relations and procession
To *do*	Functions	Real-time process algebra	To describe status and behavior

have problems, particularly system architectures and high-level system designs, in cognitive informatics, computational intelligence, computing science, software engineering, and system engineering.

RTPA is developed to deal with a series of behavioral processes and architectures of software and intelligent systems. RTPA provides a coherent notation system and a formal engineering methodology for modeling both software and intelligent systems. RTPA can be used to describe both *logical* and *physical* models of systems, where logic views of the architecture of a software system and its operational platform can be described using the same set of notations.

A wide range of applications of denotational mathematics have been identified, which encompass concept algebra for knowledge manipulations, system algebra for system architectural manipulations, and RTPA for system behavioral manipulations (Wang, 2008).

Cognitive informatics studies intelligent behavior and cognition. Cognition includes mental states and processes, such as thinking, reasoning, learning, perception, emotion, consciousness, remembering, language understanding, and generation. In the emerging theory of living systems, mind is not a thing but a process. It is cognition, the process of knowing, and it is identified with the process of life itself. Cybernetics provided cognitive science with the first model of cognition: that is, as the manipulation of symbols based on a set of rules. The main themes of cognitive informatics encompass three categories of topics: cognitive computing, computational intelligence, and neural informatics, outlined as the theoretical framework of cognitive informatics by Wang et al. (2009) (Table 9.3). Across the three themes of cognitive informatics, their denotational and expressive needs lead to new forms of mathematics collectively known as *denotational mathematics*.

Neural Networks   The concept of a neural network appears to have first been proposed by Alan Turing in his 1948 paper "Intelligent Machinery." Historically, computers evolved from the von Neumann architecture, which is

TABLE 9.3   Cognitive Informatics

Cognitive Computing	Computational Intelligence	Neural Informatics
Informatics models of the brain	Imperative vs. autonomous computing	Neuroscience foundations of information processing
Cognitive processes of the brain	Reasoning and inferences	Cognitive models of the brain
Internal information processing mechanisms	Cognitive informatics foundations	Functional modes of the brain
Theories of natural intelligence	Robotics	Neural models of memory
Intelligent foundations of computing	Informatics foundations of software engineering	Neural networks
Denotational mathematics	Fuzzy/rough sets/logic	Neural computation
Abstraction and means	Knowledge engineering	Cognitive linguistics
Ergonomics	Pattern and signal recognitions	Neuropsychology
Informatics laws of software	Autonomic agent technologies	Bioinformatics
Knowledge representation	Memory models	Biosignal processing
Models of knowledge and skills	Software agent systems	Cognitive signal processing
Formal linguistics	Decision theories	Gene analysis and expression
Cognitive complexity and metrics	Problem-solving theories	Cognitive metrics
Distributed intelligence	Machine learning systems	Neural signal interpretation
Semantic computing	Distributed objects/granules	Visual information representation
Emotions/motivations/attitudes	Web-contents cognition	Visual semantics
Perception and consciousness	Nature of software	Sensational cognitive processes
Hybrid (AI/NI) intelligence	Granular computing	Human factors in systems

based on sequential processing and execution of explicit instructions. On the other hand, the origins of neural networks are based on efforts to model information processing in biological systems, which may rely largely on parallel processing as well as implicit instructions based on the recognition of patterns of sensory input from external sources. In other words, at its very heart a neural network is a complex statistical processor. Artificial neural networks are made up of interconnecting artificial neurons. Artificial neural networks may either be used to gain an understanding of biological neural networks, or for solving artificial intelligence problems without necessarily creating a model of a real biological system. Biological neural networks are made up of real biological neurons that are connected or functionally related in the peripheral nervous system or the central nervous system. A biological neuron may have as many as 10,000 different inputs and may send its output to many other neurons. A single neuron may be connected to many other neurons and the total number of neurons and connections in a network may be extensive. In the field of neuroscience, they are often identified as groups of neurons that perform a specific physiological function in laboratory analysis. The cognitive modeling field involves the physical or mathematical modeling of the behavior of neural systems, ranging from the individual neural level, such as modeling the spike response curves of neurons to a stimulus, through the neural cluster level, such as modeling the release and effects of dopamine in the basal ganglia, to the complete organism on behavioral modeling of the organism's response to stimuli. In more practical terms, neural networks are nonlinear statistical data modeling or decision-making tools. They can be used to model complex relationships between inputs and outputs or to find patterns in data. Although a detailed description of neural systems is nebulous, progress is being charted toward a better understanding of basic biological mechanisms.

Evolving Cognition   Recently, biologists and philosophers have been attracted by an evolutionary epistemology. It was argued that our cognitive abilities are the outcome of organic evolution and that, conversely, evolution itself may be described as a cognition process. Furthermore, it is argued that the key to an adequate evolutionary epistemology lies in a system-theoretical approach to evolution which grows from, but goes beyond, Darwin's theory of natural selection. Although random mutation and natural selection are all still acknowledged as important aspects of biological evolution, the central focus is shifting from evolution to co-evolution. This is an ongoing dance that proceeds through a subtle interplay of competition and cooperation, creation and mutual adaptation. In other words, proper understanding of human evolution is impossible without understanding the evolution of language, art, and culture. We must turn our attention to the mind process of life.

Biological Peptides and Psychosomatic Network   Research in the 1980s described by Capra (1997) uncovered ubiquitous neuron-peptide-receptor distribution in brain structures associated with emotional processing and throughout many organ systems. This finding supported neuron peptides as biochemical substrates of emotion, and the neuron-peptide-receptor network as a parasynaptic system crossing traditional brain–body boundaries. The medical relevance of these findings was affirmed by psychoneuroimmunology research. Neuropeptides help to regulate immunocyte trafficking. There is bidirectional communication between nervous and immune system components, immunocytes produce neuron-peptides, and nerve cells produce immune-associated cytokines. In the past decade, the concept of a unified psychosomatic network has been strengthened by animal and human research demonstrating relationships between behavior and neuron-peptide-mediated regulation of immune functions.

The discovery of this psychosomatic network implies that the nervous system is not hierarchically structured, and ultimately this implies that cognition is a phenomenon that expands throughout an organism, operating through an intricate chemical network of peptides that integrates our mental, emotional, and biological activities.

9.4 CHALLENGES AND PERSPECTIVES

From a scientific perspective, discovering how the brain thinks is a major undertaking in the history of humankind. Bioinformatics provides computational and experimental tools to study biological patterns, structures, and functions. Cognitive informatics investigates the internal information-processing mechanisms and process of life cognition. According to Kandel (2006), "understanding the human mind in biological terms has emerged as the central challenge for science in the twenty-first century. We want to understand the biological nature of perception, learning, memory, thought, consciousness, and the limits of free will. Thus, we gain from the new science of mind not only insights into ourselves—how we perceive, learn, remember, feel, and act—but also a new perspective of ourselves in the context of biological evolution. The task of neural science is to explain behavior in terms of the activities of the brain. How does the brain marshal its millions of individual nerve cells to produce behavior, and how are these cells influenced by the environment ...? The last frontier of the biological sciences—their ultimate challenge—is to understand the biological basis of consciousness and the mental processes by which we perceive, act, learn, and remember."

Mathematical modeling has had an enormous impact on cognition and neuroscience. The Hodgkin–Huxley format for describing membrane ionic currents has been extended and applied to a variety of neuronal excitable membranes. The significance of dendrites for the input–output properties of neurons was not understood before the development of Rall's cable theory (Rall, 1962, 1964). Hartline and Ratliff (1972) were pioneers in developing quantitative and predictive network models. In addition, Fitzhugh's work (1960, 1969) demonstrated the value of simplified nonlinear models and of qualitative mathematical analysis. The success of these theoretical contributions, and the high degree of quantification in neurobiology, ensures continued opportunities for mathematical work.

Recent advances in experimentation, such as patch clamp recording, voltage- and ion-specific dyes, and confocal microscopy, are providing data to facilitate further theoretical development for addressing fundamental issues ranging from the subcellular to cell-ensemble to whole-system levels. We must synthesize information and mechanisms across these different levels for a thorough understanding from molecule to ecosystem. This is perhaps the fundamental challenge facing mathematical and theoretical biology. How do we relate phenomena at different levels of organization? How are small-scale processes to be integrated and related to higher-level phenomena? For example, in modeling neuronal networks, what are the crucial properties of individual cells that must be retained in order to address a particular set of questions? Most network formulations use highly idealized *neural units*, which ignore much of what is known about cellular biophysics. We need to develop systematic procedures to derive, in a biophysically meaningful way, descriptions of ensemble behavior.

Correspondingly, we seek to identify low-level mechanisms from data at higher levels. The Hodgkin–Huxley theory hypothesized that macroscopic currents might be generated by molecular "pores"; only much later were these individual channels discovered. Another set of common modeling needs are methods for dealing reasonably with the wide range of time and space scales involved with different intracellular domains and processes, with short- and long-distance interactions between cells, and among different cell assemblies. At the lowest level, we need improved biophysical understanding of the mechanisms for ion transport through membrane channels. How does the voltage dependence of opening and closing rates arise? What accounts for ion selectivity by which, for example, channels discriminate among ions of the same charge and similar properties? Theories at this level are beginning to involve stochastic descriptions for fluxes and simulation methods for molecular structure and dynamics. Kinetic modeling of single channel data is being debated hotly with regard to whether a finite or infinite number of open/closed/inactivated states are appropriate.

One of the most active pursuits in neuroscience research is to discover the mechanisms for plasticity and learning at the cellular–molecular level. The foregoing techniques, together with state-of-the-art biochemical methodologies, are beginning to yield information for feasible detailed biophysical modeling. Dendritic spines, NMDA receptor channels, spatiotemporal dynamics of calcium, and other intracellular second messengers are focal points for these explorations. Such studies are bringing together theoreticians, neuroscientists, and biochemists. Although theorizing about mechanisms for synaptic plasticity is proceeding, disagreement remains about the basic mechanism of chemical synaptic transmission. Two competing hypotheses (one involving calcium alone, and the other including voltage effects as well) are being explored with fervor, and mathematical modeling is a key ingredient in arguments for each case.

Models of neural interactions lead to many interesting mathematical questions for which appropriate tools must be developed. Typically, networks are modeled by (possibly stochastic) systems of differential equations. In some simplified limits, these become nonlinear integro-differential equations. The question now becomes one of proving or otherwise demonstrating that the simplified models have the desired behavior. Furthermore, one must characterize this behavior as parameters in the model vary (i.e., understand the bifurcations in the dynamics). Another important point that mathematicians must address is the extraction of the underlying geometric and analytic ideas from detailed biophysical models and simulations.

The next level of neuronal complexity beyond the single cell is the small network with on the order of tens to hundreds of neurons. Such networks have been studied most extensively in invertebrates and the sensory or motor systems of vertebrates, in which the function of small groups of neurons can be related to specific behaviors of the animal (Kandel, 1984; Lockery et al., 1989; Selverston and Moulins, 1985). These "simple systems" are also attractive because one can expect to characterize their cellular and intercellular properties more completely than in vertebrates. Much research on their structural features has been based on the explicit assumption that once network structure was understood, functional understanding would follow. Recently, however, many workers have come to realize that even with a great deal of structural information, the understanding of functional mechanisms will require the development of sound, structurally based theoretical models.

A principal challenge for modeling at this level is the development of more biologically realistic computational models and mathematical analyses that can provide insight into how these networks function. Although these networks involve relatively small numbers of neurons, their complexity will require increasingly powerful mathematical tools. At the same time, modeling at this level is likely to be especially valuable for neurobiology. In few other neural systems is the link between neural structure and behavior more direct. Thus, it is already possible to see in the structure of the nervous system its functional correlates. Also, few other systems currently provide the anatomical and physiological parameters essential for realistic modeling. As models for understanding the general dynamical properties of such neural networks or for understanding the way in which feedback modifies neuronal behavior, small neural systems represent a gold mine for computational and mathematical neurobiology.

Coherent brain areas dedicated to particular functions, such as primary sensory cortical areas, provide complex challenges for computational and mathematical models (Sereno et al., 1988). Such areas typically contain multiple types of cells, receive inputs from multiple distinct sources, and often are heavily interconnected with their links to interarea recurrent or reentrant loops. Large bodies of anatomical and physiological data are available, but the integrative capabilities are poorly understood, and modeling techniques will almost surely be needed to unravel them.

Developmental neurobiology is a source of biologically important and mathematically interesting questions. Modeling at the large network level has played an important role in this field, with much collaboration between mathematicians and experimental biologists. Among the important questions arising in this field are the topography of connections from one part of the brain to another and how these maps might form spontaneously. Many examples exist of such maps in the central nervous system; the best characterized are in the vertebrate visual system. The earliest theoretical models and experiments concerned the wiring from the retina to the optic tectum. Many models have been proposed and analyzed (von der Malsburg, 1973; Whitelaw and Cowan, 1981; see Linsker, 1990, for a review), but as new experimental results have become available, many of the models must be altered or eliminated.

Several new technologies, such as voltage-sensitive dyes and deoxyglucose injection, have led to the discovery of beautiful regular maps in the visual cortex of mammals. The patterns include stripes of ocularity and twists and singularities of orientation preference. Models proposed for these patterns (Durbin and Mitchison, 1990; Miller et al., 1989) involve mechanisms ranging from bandpass-filtered noise, to competitive interactions, to Hebbian rules with lateral inhibition. What must be done is to decide what the common idea is that underlies these models and how these mechanisms might possibly be realized in the nervous system.

As we begin to understand the mechanisms of synaptic plasticity, it is natural to ask about the consequences of this for the behavior of large networks involving plastic elements. Only in this way will we understand the relation between synaptic plasticity and learning at the organismic level. This has been a major focus in the study of computational properties of large-scale neural networks across a number of disciplines, including physics, biology, psychology, and mathematics (Hopfield, 1984; Rumelhart et al., 1986). Mathematical analysis promises to provide an important bridge between computational and behavioral studies and the empirical results of neurobiology (Poggio and Girosi, 1990). An excellent survey is given by Koch and Segev (1989).

Models at the level of the complete organism provide an opportunity to make real progress on the long-sought unification of the behavioral sciences with neurobiology. Models intended to explain behavioral observations (e.g., from psychology and ethology) can be cast in terms of underlying neural mechanisms rather than at the phenomenological or control theory level, as before. Such models can bring about a new understanding of such phenomena as visual illusions (e.g., Treisman et al., 1990), the relation between long- and short-term memory, and category formation. They will provide significant constraints on psychological explanations that have not in the past been easy to correlate with the nervous system. To carry out this analysis, one must eventually couple models of the nervous system with those of the environment in which the whole system exists (Kersten, 1990).

REFERENCES

Capra, F. (1997). *The Web of Life*. New York: Random House.

Durbin, R., and Mitchison, G. (1990). A dimension reduction framework for understanding cortical maps. *Nature*, **343**, 644–647.

Dyke, C. (1988). *The Evolutionary Dynamics of Complex Systems: A Study in Biosocial Complexity*. New York: Oxford University Press.

Fitzhugh, R. (1960). Thresholds and plateaus in the Hodgkin–Huxley nerve equations. *J. Gen. Physiol.*, **43**, 867–896.

Fitzhugh, R. (1969). Mathematical models of excitation and propagation in nerve. In: H. P. Schwan (Ed.), *Biological Engineering*. New York: McGraw-Hill, pp. 1–85.

Hartline, H. K., and Ratliff, F. (1972). Inhibitory interaction in the retina of *Limulus*. In: M. G. F. Fuortes (Ed.), *Handbook of Sensory Physiology*, Vol. **VII/2**. Berlin: Springer-Verlag, pp. 381–448.

He, M. (2008). On bioinformatics and cognitive informatics: emerging pattern, dissipative structure, and evolving cognition. In: Y. Wang and W. Kinsner (Eds.), *Proceedings of the 8th IEEE International Conference on Cognitive Informatics* (ICCI'08), Stanford University, Aug. 14–16, pp. 40–49.

Hopfield, J. J. (1984). Neurons with graded response have collective computational properties like those of two-state neurons. *Proc. Natl. Acad. Sci. USA*, **81**, 3088–3092.

Kandel, E. R. (1984). Steps toward a molecular grammar for learning: explorations into the nature of memory. In: K. J. Isselbacher (Ed.), *Medicine, Science and Society. Symposia Celebrating the Harvard Medical School Bicentennial*. New York: Wiley, pp. 555–604.

Kandel, E. R. (2006). *In Search of Memory: The Emergence of a New Science of Mind*. New York: W. W. Norton.

Kersten, D. (1990). Statistical limits to image understanding. In: C. Blakemore (Ed.), *Vision: Coding and Efficiency*. Cambridge, UK: Cambridge University Press.

Kitano, H. (2002a). Systems biology: a brief overview. *Science*, **295**, 1662–1664.

Kitano, H. (2002b). Computational systems biology. *Nature*, **420**, 206–210.

Koch, C., and Segev, I. (Eds.) (1989). *Methods in Neuronal Modeling: From Synapses to Networks*. Cambridge, MA: MIT Press.

Linsker, R. (1990). Perceptual neural organization: some approaches based on network models and information theory. *Annu. Rev. Neurosci.*, **13**, 257–281.

Lockery, S. K., Wittenberg, G., Kristan, W. B. J., and Cottrell, G. W. (1989). Function of identified interneurons in the leech elucidated using neural network trained by back-propagation. *Nature*, **340**, 468–471.

Luisi, P. L. (1993). Defining the transition to life: self-replicating bounded structures and chemical autopoiesis. In: W. Stein and F. J. Varela (Eds.), *Thinking About Biology*. SFI Studies in the Sciences of Complexity, Lecture Notes, Vol. **III**. Reading, MA: Addison-Wesley, pp. 3–23.

Maturana, H., and Varela, F. (1973). Autopoiesis and cognition: the realization of the living. In: R. S. Cohen and M. W. Wartofsky (Eds.), *Boston Studies in the Philosophy of Science*, Vol. **42**. Dordecht, The Netherlands: D. Reidel.

Maturana, H., and Varela, F. (1980). *Biology of Cognition*, published originally in 1970. Urbana, IL: University of Illinois. Reprinted in 1980. Dordecht, The Netherlands: D. Reidel.

Miller, K. D., Keller, J. B., and Stryker, M. P. (1989). Ocular dominance column development: analysis and simulations. *Science*, **245**, 605–615.

Mingers, J. (1994). *Self-Producing Systems*. New York: Kluwer Academic/Plenum.

Poggio, T., and Girosi, F. (1990). Regularization algorithms for learning that are equivalent to multilayer networks. *Science*, **247**, 978–982.

Prigogine, I. (1967). Dissipative structures in chemical systems. In: S. Claesson (Ed.), *Fast Reactions and Primary Processes in Chemical Kinetics*. New York: Interscience.

Rall, W. (1962). Theory of physiological properties of dendrites. *Ann. N.Y. Acad. Sci.*, **96**, 1071–1092.

Rall, W. (1964). Theoretical significance of dendritic trees for neuronal input–output relations. In: R. F. Reiss (Ed.), *Neural Theory and Modeling*. Stanford, CA: Stanford University Press, pp. 73–97.

Rumelhart, D. E., McClelland, J. L., and the PDP Group (1986). *Parallel Distributed Processing: Explorations in the Microstructure of Cognition*. Cambridge, MA: MIT Press.

Selverston, A. I., and Moulins, M. (1985). Oscillating neural networks. *Ann. Rev. Neurophysiol.*, **47**, 29–48.

Sereno, M. E., Kersten, D. J., and Anderson, J. A. (1988). A neural network model of an aspect of motion perception. In: *Science at the John von Neumann National Supercomputer Center*: Consortium for Scientific Computing, Princeton, NJ, pp. 173–178.

Treisman, A., Cavanagh, P., Fischer, B., Ramachandran, V. S., and von der Heydt, R. (1990). Form perception and attention. In: L. Spillman and J. S. Werner (Eds.), *Visual Perception: The Neurophysiological Foundations*. San Diego, CA: Academic Press, pp. 273–316.

Varela, F., Maturana, H., and Uribe, R. (1974). Autopoiesis: the organization of living systems, its characterization and a model. *Biosystems*, **5**, 187–196.

von der Malsburg, C. (1973). Self-organization of orientation sensitive cells in the striate cortex. *Kybernetik*, **14**, 85–100.

Wang, Y. (2008). On contemporary denotational mathematics for computational intelligence. In: M. L. Gavrilova et al. (Eds.), *Transactions on Computational Science*, Vol. **II**. Lecture Notes in Computer Science, Vol. 5150. Berlin: Springer-Verlag, pp. 6–29.

Wang, Y., Zhang, D., and Tsumoto, S. (2009). Preface: cognitive informatics, cognitive computing, and their denotational mathematical foundations: I. *Fundamenta Informaticae*, Vol. **90**. Amsterdam: IOS Press, pp. i–viii.

Whitelaw, V. A., and Cowan, J. D. (1981). Specificity and plasticity of retinotectal connections: a computational model. *J. Neurosci.*, **1**, 1369–1387.

Wolfram, S. (2002). *A New Kind of Science*. Champaign, IL: Wolfram Media.

10 Evolutionary Trends and Central Dogma of Informatics

Life consists of matter and energy, but it is not just matter and energy. Life is also information. Life has three fundamental dimensions. The life of an individual comes from the DNA of its parents. DNA is insignificant in terms of its elemental composition. It is composed of nitrogen, oxygen, sulfur, and so on. DNA as a source of energy is composed of the similar level of chemical energy that can be produced by experiments. The characteristic of DNA is an informational molecule, a molecule containing a large amount of information.

Informatics is evolving and being transformed. Many boundaries among science, engineering, and social systems are cross-linked in the face of combinations of knowledge and tools. It is the time when the physical, biological, and social sciences are joining forces with information sciences and technology. It is the time when we will make extraordinary advances in the history of humankind through information sciences. However, throughout the history of information science, many definitions of information, knowledge, and data have been suggested, and other definitions of them may continue to merge.

In this chapter we return to the big picture of informatics introduced in Chapter 1. We propose a general concept of data, information, and knowledge and then place the main focus on the process and transition from data to information and then to knowledge. We present the concept of the central dogma of informatics, in analogy to the central dogma of molecular biology.

10.1 INTRODUCTION

Informatics studies the foundation, representation, processing, and communication of information in natural and artificial systems. The central notion is the transformation of data to information and information to knowledge—whether by computation or communication, whether by organisms or artifacts. It deals with the structure, function, behavior, and interactions of natural and artificial computational systems. It has computational, experimental, theoretical, cognitive, and social aspects.

Mathematics of Bioinformatics: Theory, Practice, and Applications, By Matthew He and Sergey Petoukhov
Copyright © 2011 John Wiley & Sons, Inc.

Understanding informational phenomena such as computation, cognition, and communication enables scientific, engineering, and technological advances and promotes scientific enquiry. The science of information and the engineering of information systems are interdependent and develop hand-in-hand. Informatics is the emerging discipline that combines the two. In natural and artificial systems, information is carried at many levels, ranging, for example, from biological molecules and electronic devices through nervous systems and computers and on to societies and large-scale distributed systems. It is characteristic that information carried at higher levels is represented by informational processes at lower levels. Each of these levels is the proper object of study for some discipline of science or engineering. Informatics aims to develop and apply firm theoretical and mathematical foundations for the features that are common to all complex systems. In its attempts to account for phenomena, science progresses by defining, developing, criticizing, and refining new concepts. Informatics is developing its own fundamental concepts of data, information, knowledge, communication, and interaction, and relating them to such phenomena as computation, thought, and language (Belkin and Robertson, 1976; Wersig and Neveling, 1975).

Informatics has many aspects, and encompasses a number of existing academic disciplines: artificial intelligence, cognitive science, and computer science. Each takes part of informatics as its natural domain: In broad terms, cognitive science concerns the study of natural systems; computer science concerns the analysis of computation and the design of computing systems; and artificial intelligence plays a connecting role, designing systems that emulate those found in nature. Informatics also informs and is informed by other disciplines, such as mathematics, electronics, biology, linguistics, and psychology. Thus, informatics provides a link between disciplines with their own methodologies and perspectives, bringing together a common scientific paradigm, common engineering methods, and a pervasive stimulus from technological development and practical application.

Three of the truly fundamental questions of science are: What is matter?, What is life?, and What is mind? The physical and biological sciences concern the first two. The emerging science of informatics contributes to our understanding of the latter two by providing a basis for the study of organization and process in biological and cognitive systems. Progress can best be made by means of strong links with the existing disciplines devoted to particular aspects of these questions.

Informatics provides an enormous range of problems and opportunities. One challenge is to determine how far, and in what circumstances, theories of information processing in artificial devices can be applied to natural systems. A second challenge is to determine how far principles derived from natural systems are applicable to the development of new types of artificial systems. A third challenge is to explore the many ways in which artificial information systems can help to solve problems facing humankind and help to improve the quality of life for all living things. One can also consider systems of mixed character; a question of longer-term interest may be to what extent it is helpful to maintain the distinction between natural and artificial systems. Throughout the history of information science, many definitions of data, information, and knowledge have been suggested, and other definitions of them may continue to merge. We propose a general concept of data, information, and knowledge and then place the focus on the process and transition from data to information and from information to knowledge. We introduce the concept of central dogma of informatics in analogy to the central dogma of molecular biology.

10.2 EVOLUTIONARY TRENDS OF INFORMATION SCIENCES

Recently, a systems view of technologies has been emerging. General systems theory was originally proposed by Hungarian biologist Ludwig von Bertalanffy in 1928 (von Bertalanffy, 1976). It studies the nature of complex systems in nature, society, and science. The emergence of systems thinking was a profound revolution in the history of Western scientific thought in terms of connectedness, relationships, and context. Various technological systems, such as manufacturing systems, construction systems, transportation systems, and communication systems, are emerging. Subsystems of the communication system, such as people-to-people communication, people-to-machine communication, machine-to-people communication, and machine-to-machine communication, are evolving. These technological systems reflect interactions between human and physical devices. These interactions, together with recent advances in biological and social systems, lead us to the systems view of technology and information sciences. We classify technology and information sciences into three principal phases of evolution, as illustrated in Figure 10.1:

1. Physical information science and technology (nonorganic/nonliving material-based)
2. Biological information science and technology (organic/living material-based)
3. Societal information science and technology (language/mind-based)

Physical information science and technology constitute an original system science that exists in the physical world. They consist of physical materials with

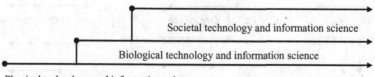

FIGURE 10.1 Three phases of technology and information science (the PBS model).

informational instructions. A voluminous literature on physical science and technology is documented throughout history (Meyers, 2001).

Biological technology involves biological means embedded in living systems. It is made of biological matter and naturally evolved "machines" that perform molecular calculations and complex functions. The biological or natural technology is a major and most effective technology for ensuring life on our planet, and acquirement of this technology, occurring in modern time, is a major movement in the evolution of humankind.

Societal technology, the technological or engineering counterpart to the social sciences, emphasizes genuine solutions to social problems and social life, treating their underlying causes. It is a science that answers questions about "what" and "why"; as technology is a collection of the study, invention, and refinement of tools and techniques, it also answers "how" questions. Law, government, business, finance, research, development, education, and other activities within human society constitute a collection of tools/rules and techniques applied for societal purposes, and thus societal technology. These three phases of technologies are well connected with the process of universal evolution. Evolution is the primary cosmic force that creates order and makes it visible in different categories of nature. Evolution arises from the interaction of mutation and selection: mutation occurring by chance and selection by necessity for survival. In the categorization of nature, Salk divided universal evolution into three main eras in which different types of matter have emerged. The universal growth of complexity as part of this evolution is demonstrated in Table 10.1 (He, 2009; Salk, 1983).

Technology evolves. Physical, biological, and societal technologies interact and grow into a complex network system. We illustrate their interactions by the physical–biological–societal (PBS) technology triangle model (He, 2009) shown in Figure 10.2. The interactions among these physical, biological, and

TABLE 10.1   Salk's Model: Universal Evolution

Physical Sphere	Biosphere	Metabiosphere
Physical matter	Living matter	Human matter
Elementary particles	Replicating molecules	Human mind

Atoms	Cells	Human culture
Molecules	Organisms	Human morality

Prebiological evolution	Biological evolution	Metabiological evolution

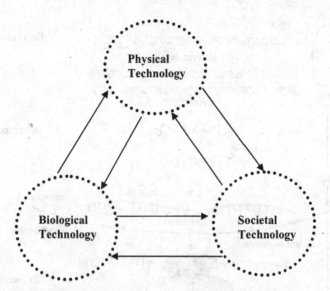

FIGURE 10.2   PBS technology triangle model.

societal technologies are connected and interdependent, and the technologies are the driving force of life. They are connected through a central unit: *information*. Information is everything; and everything is connected to everything else. Information exits, mutates, and evolves. Rules, patterns, and blueprints are embedded in information. Technology is a natural reflection, configuration, and innovation of physical matter, biological materials, and the human mind. The simple PBS triangle rotates around a central information point. The evolution of technology and information sciences causes social, biological, and environmental changes.

There is a direct correlation between the development of technology and changes in history. Physical technology allows human beings to change their world, including societal and biological technologies. At the same time, technological advances allow people to thrive and become more successful within their own society.

10.3   CENTRAL DOGMA OF INFORMATICS

The central dogma of molecular biology was first enunciated by Francis Crick in 1958 and restated in an article in *Nature* in 1970 (Crick, 1970). It states the conversion of the genetic message in DNA to a functional mRNA (transcription) and subsequent conversion of the genotype that was copied, to a phenotype in the form of proteins. The process of conversion of a mRNA to a functional protein, known as *translation*, is illustrated in Figure 10.3 by three major stages. This central dogma forms the backbone of molecular biology.

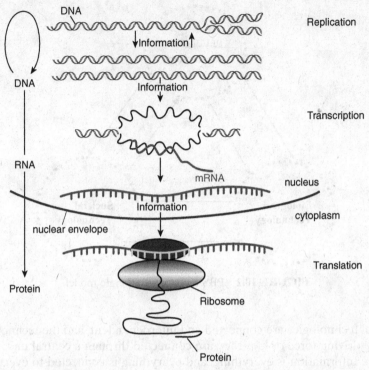

FIGURE 10.3 Central dogma of molecular biology.

Stage 1 (Replication) The DNA replicates its information in a process that involves many enzymes. It is a fundamental process occurring in all living organisms to copy their DNA. Each strand of the original double-stranded DNA molecule serves as a template for reproduction of the complementary strand. Hence, following DNA replication, two identical DNA molecules have been produced from a single double-stranded DNA molecule. Cellular proof-reading and error-checking mechanisms ensure nearly perfect fidelity for DNA replication (Berg et al., 2002).

Stage 2 (Transcription) The DNA codes for the production of messenger RNA (mRNA) during transcription. In eucaryotic cells, the mRNA migrates from the nucleus to the cytoplasm. Transcription is the synthesis of RNA under the direction of DNA. RNA synthesis, or transcription, is the process of transcribing DNA nucleotide sequence information into RNA sequence information. The nucleic acid sequences use complementary language, and the information is simply transcribed, or copied, from one molecule to the other. DNA sequence is copied enzymatically by RNA polymerase to produce a complementary nucleotide RNA strand, called messenger RNA (mRNA) because it carries a genetic message from the DNA to the protein-synthesizing machinery of the cell. One significant difference between the RNA and DNA sequences is the presence of U, or uracil, in RNA instead of the T, or thymine, of DNA. In the case of protein-encoding DNA, transcription is the first step and usually leads to the expression of the genes by the production of the mRNA intermediate, which is a faithful transcript of a gene's protein-building instruction. The stretch of DNA that is transcribed into an RNA molecule is called a *transcription unit*. A DNA transcription unit that is translated into protein contains sequences that direct and regulate protein synthesis in addition to coding the sequence that is translated into protein. The regulatory sequence that is before [upstream (−), toward the 5′ DNA end] the coding sequence is called the 5′ *untranslated region* (5′UTR), and the sequence found following [downstream (+), toward the 3′ DNA end] the coding sequence is called the 3′ *untranslated region* (3′UTR). Transcription has some proofreading mechanisms, but they are fewer and less effective than the controls for copying DNA; therefore, transcription has a lower copying fidelity than DNA replication (Berg et al., 2006).

Stage 3 (Translation)   Messenger RNA carries coded information to ribosomes. The ribosomes "read" this information and use it for protein synthesis. Translation is the first stage of protein biosynthesis (part of the overall process of gene expression). Translation is the production of proteins by decoding mRNA produced in transcription. Translation occurs in the cytoplasm, where the ribosomes are located. Ribosomes are made of a small and a large subunit, which surround the mRNA. In translation, messenger RNA (mRNA) is decoded to produce a specific polypeptide according to the rules specified by the genetic code. This uses an mRNA sequence as a template to guide the synthesis of a chain of amino acids that form a protein. Many types of transcribed RNA, such as transfer RNA, ribosomal RNA, and small nuclear RNA, are not necessarily translated into an amino acid sequence. Translation proceeds in four phases: activation, initiation, elongation, and termination (all describing the growth of the amino acid chain, or polypeptide, which is the product of translation). Amino acids are brought to ribosomes and assembled into proteins. Proteins do not code for the production of protein, RNA or DNA. They are involved in almost all biological activities, structural or enzymatic.

The central dogma of molecular biology has paved a revolutionary road for further investigations in great details of the process of replication, transcription, and translation. Furthermore, this central dogma has provided a great impact on the study of informatics. The process of conversion from data to information and to knowledge has a much broader and fundamental impact on many domains, as information is an intrinsic property of the universe: the intricate organization of matter and energy.

As the philosopher Paul Churchland (1989) notes, humans have been trying to understand the world throughout most of recorded history; in just the past

200 years, our curiosity has revealed much of what nature had kept hidden from us: the fabric of space–time, the constitution of matter, the many forms of energy, the origins of the universe, the nature of life itself with the discovery of DNA, and the completion of the mapping of the human genome in 2001. But one mystery has not been solved: the mystery of the human brain and how it gives rise to thoughts and feeling, hopes and desires, love, and the experience of beauty, not to mention dance, visual art, literature, and information (Freeman, 2000a,b).

Interaction among matter, energy, and information is the root of evolution. Information is distributed throughout the brain (Allman, 2000). Animals evolve certain physical forms as a response to their environment, and the characteristics that conferred an advantage for mating were passed down to the next generation through the genes. A subtle point in Darwinian theory is that living organisms—whether plants, viruses, insects, or animals—coevolved with the physical world. In other words, the world is also changing in response to them. If one species develops a mechanism to keep away a particular predator, that predator's species is then under evolutionary pressure either to develop a means to overcome that defense or to find another food source. Natural selection is an arms race of physical morphologies changing to catch up with one another. Our minds are the product of millions of years of evolution. Our thought patterns, our predispositions to solve problems in certain ways, and our sensory systems are all products of evolution. Our minds coevolved with the physical world, changing in response to ever-changing conditions (La Cerra and Bingham, 2002; Madden, 2004). A combinatorial mind has opened up a world of words and sentences, of theories and equations, of poem and melodies, of jokes and sorties (Bates, 2005; Cooper, 2001; Durham, 1991; Goonatilake, 1991).

Darwin's theory of natural selection was revolutionized by the discovery of the gene, specifically Watson and Crick's discovery of the structure of DNA. Perhaps we are witnessing another revolution in the aspect of evolution that depends on social behavior, on culture (Madden, 2004).

The term *information* includes data on the one hand, and knowledge on the other. In the following, we briefly review the key definitions of data, information, and knowledge from various aspects and then introduce a general definition of data, information, and knowledge. In analogy with the central dogma of molecular biology, we establish the central dogma of informatics. Each concept of data, information, and knowledge carries its own entity with arrays of spectrum that can be investigated. Most important, the process of transforming data to information and converting information to knowledge continue to be the central theme of informatics.

A datum is a small chunk of information. Data are commonly seen as something raw. Data are symbols without relationships and may be seen as a portion of the entire information without being processed. Data may be referred to information selected or generated by human beings for social purposes (Bates, 2005).

Here we define *data* as a collection of symbols, images, or other outputs from devices on source to represent the qualitative or quantitative attributes of a variable or set of variables that are unprocessed and for which no relationships have been established. *Data* is a multidimensional abstract concept on a path to being fully distilled (Hammarberg, 1981), that is, in a sequence that goes from data to information to knowledge.

The term *information* is thought of as organized data, or "facts," organized into a coherent pattern. According to Peirce (Short, 2007), information was embedded in his wider theory of symbolic communication, which he called the *semeiotic*, now a major part of semiotics. For Peirce, information integrates the aspects of signs and expressions covered separately by the concepts of denotation and extension, on the one hand, and by connotation and comprehension, on the other.

Information is also viewed as a form of mass–energy system (Stonier, 1990, 1997). Information is an implicit component (the hidden dimension) of virtually every single equation governing the laws of nature. Information is the core ingredient of all communication and control processes in living and nonliving systems (Young, 1987).

Claude E. Shannon, for his part, was very cautious: "The word *information* has been given different meanings by various writers in the general field of information theory" (Shannon and Weaver, 1975, Wiener, 1961). Gregory Bateson defined *information* as "a difference that makes a difference" (Bateson, 1979).

According to Floridi, four types of mutually compatible phenomena are commonly referred to as information (Floridi, 2002):

1. Information about something (e.g., a train timetable)
2. Information as something (e.g., DNA or fingerprints)
3. Information for something (e.g., algorithms or instructions)
4. Information in something (e.g., a pattern or a constraint)

Here we define *information* as a multidimensional organized entity derived from data source through a process of transformation. The information entity has many attributes or patterns with relationships. It has its own structure and can be converted to knowledge through a process of transformation.

The term *knowledge* is thought of as organized and internalized information and the ability to utilize the information. Knowledge was viewed as information given meaning and integrated with other contents of understanding (Bates, 2005; Davenport and Prusak, 1998). It simply defines knowledge as information given meaning. Knowledge represents the intellectual constructs of human beings organizing human information. Knowledge may be defined as organized information in people's heads.

Here we define *knowledge* as a multidimensional functional entity derived from information through a process of transformation. Knowledge has its own structure and function. Knowledge about primitive organisms provides much

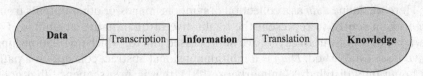

FIGURE 10.4   Central dogma of informatics.

TABLE 10.2   Central Dogma of Informatics

Data (Replication)	Information (Transcription)	Knowledge (Translation)
A datum is a small chunk of information.	Information is thought of as organized data, or "facts" organized into coherent patterns	Knowledge is thought of as organized and internalized information and ability to utilize the information
	Information = data + meaning	Knowledge = internalized information + ability to utilize the information

Associated areas:
  Data structure
  Data mining
  Data analysis
  Data integration
  Data replication
  Databases
	Associated areas:
	  Pattern discovery
	  Information processing
	  Information storage
	  Information retrieval
	  Information flow
	  Information control
		Associated areas:
		  Knowledge discovery
		  Knowledge management
		  Knowledge transfer

information about shared metabolic features and hints at diseases that affect humans in an economical and ethically acceptable manner. Knowledge from many scientific disciplines and their subfields has to be integrated to achieve the goals of informatics. Applying knowledge can lead to new scientific methods, to new diagnostics, and to new discoveries.

We now propose the *central dogma of informatics*, as illustrated in Figure 10.4 and described in Table 10.2.

Data and knowledge are connected through a central unit: *information*. All living systems are dependent on an environment with which they can exchange matter, energy, and information. The evolution of information causes social, biological, and environmental changes.

10.4   CHALLENGES AND PERSPECTIVES

Historically, tools and weapons made of stone were the technologies in the Stone Age. Tools and weapons made of bronze were the technologies in the

Bronze Age. The Iron Age marks the period of development of technology, when the working of iron came into general use, replacing bronze as the basic material for implements and applications.

During certain periods in history, innovations in technology have grown at such a rapid pace that they have produced what has become known as an industrial revolution. Nineteenth- and twentieth-century inventions such as the telephone, phonograph, wireless radio, motion picture, automobile, airplane, computer, Internet, and wireless devices have added nearly universal technological complexity to modern daily life. Biotechnology, nanotechnology, and emerging technologies are rapidly becoming embedded in every sector of our lives. While technology, tools, and applications are being developed and evolved, the newly developed information sciences study the collection, classification, manipulation, storage, retrieval, and dissemination of information. By the nineteenth century the first signs of information science emerged as separate and distinct from other sciences and social sciences but in conjunction with communication and computation. In 1854, George Boole published *An Investigation into Laws of Thought* ... , which lays the foundations for Boolean algebra, used later for information retrieval.

Today, a device for data and information is booming in society in general. With the development of assembly-line mass production of automobiles, household appliances, and the building of ever-taller skyscrapers, technology became not only a fact of everyday life, but also a way of life in itself. Society is being transformed rapidly by increased mobility, rapid communication, and a deluge of information available from mass media and the World Wide Web. What is information? What are the structures of data? What are the topological and geometrical properties of information? What are the functional features of knowledge? How are data transcribed into information? How are information sets translated into knowledge? These are fundamental questions that require further investigation. Data mining is an active field that examines the process of extracting hidden patterns from data. Knowledge discovery is a growing field that examines the process of converting the information into knowledge. Knowledge tends to travel from descriptive to qualitative to quantitative. During the process of this transition, numerical, graphical, and mathematical aspects emerge to explore the issues of data, knowledge, intelligence, noise, and meaning. This new kind of mathematics may be called the mathematics of knowledge and intelligence.

REFERENCES

Allman, J. M. (2000). *Evolving Brains*. New York: Scientific American Library.

Bates, M. J. (2005). Information and knowledge: an evolutionary framework for information science. *Inf. Res.*, **10**(4).

Bateson, G. (1979). *Mind and Nature: A Necessary Unity*. Advances in Systems Theory, Complexity, and the Human Sciences. Cresskill, NJ: Hampton Press.

Belkin, N. J., and Robertson, S. E. (1976). Information science and the phenomenon of information. *J. Am. Soci. Inf. Sci.*, **27**(4), 197–204.

Berg, J. M., Tymoczko, J. L., Stryer, L., and Clarke, N. D. (2002). *Biochemistry.* New York: W.H. Freeman.

Berg, J., Tymoczko, J. L., and Stryer, L. (2006). *Biochemistry*, 6th ed. New York: W.H. Freeman.

Churchland, P. (1989). *A Neurocomputational Perspective: The Nature of Mind and the Structure of Science.* Cambridge, MA: MIT Press.

Cooper, W. S. (2001). *The Evolution of Reason: Logic as a Branch of Biology.* Cambridge, MA: Cambridge University Press.

Crick, F. (1970). Central dogma of molecular biology. *Nature*, **227**, 561–563.

Davenport, T., and Prusak, L. (1998). *Working Knowledge.* Cambridge, MA: Harvard University Press.

Durham, W. H. (1991). *Coevolution: Genes, Culture and Human Diversity.* Stanford, CA: Stanford University Press.

Floridi, L. (2002). What is the philosophy of information? *Metaphilosophy*, **33**(1–2), 123–145.

Freeman, W. J. (2000a). *How Brains Make Up Their Minds.* New York: Columbia University Press.

Freeman, W. J. (2000b). A neurobiological interpretation of semiotics: meaning, representation and information. *Inf. Sci.*, **124**(1–4), 93–102.

Goonatilake, S. (1991). *The Evolution of Information: Lineages in Gene, Culture and Artifact.* London: Pinter.

Hammarberg, R. (1981). The cooked and the raw. *J. Inf. Sci.*, **3**(6), 261–267.

He, M., (2009). The evolution and future trends of technology and information sciences. *2009 WASE International Conference on Information Engineering*, Vol. 1, pp. 11–15.

La Cerra, P., and Bingham, R. (2002). *The Origin of Minds: Evolution, Uniqueness and the New Science of the Self.* New York: Harmony Books.

Madden, A. D. (2004). Evolution and information. *J. Document.*, **60**(1), 9–23.

Meyers, R. (Ed.) (2001). *Encyclopedia of Physical Science and Technology*, 3rd ed. New York: Elsevier.

Salk, J. E. (1983). *Anatomy of Reality.* Westport, CT: Greenwood Publishing Group.

Shannon, C. E., and Weaver, W. (1975). *Mathematical Theory of Communication.* Urbana, IL: University of Illinois Press.

Short, T. L. (2007). *Peirce's Theory of Signs.* New York: Cambridge University Press.

Stonier, T. (1990). *Information and the Internal Structure of the Universe.* Berlin: Springer-Verlag.

Stonier, T. (1997). *Information and Meaning: An Evolutionary Perspective.* Berlin: Springer-Verlag.

von Bertalanffy, L. (1976). *General System Theory: Foundations, Development, Applications.* New York: George Braziller.

Wersig, G., and Neveling, U. (1975). The phenomena of interest to information science. *Inf. Sci.*, **9**(4), 127–140.

Wiener, N. (1961). *Cybernetics: or Control and Communication in the Animal and the Machine*, 2nd ed. Cambridge, MA: MIT Press.

Young, P. (1987). *The Nature of Information*. New York: Praeger.

APPENDIX A
Bioinformatics Notation and Databases

In this appendix we list the universal or standard genetic code, general mathematical notation, physical units, chemical notation, molecular biological databases, and the abbreviations and linear, chemical, and three-dimensional structures of the 20 naturally occurring amino acids. These notations and units have appeared in the bioinformatics literature and are used throughout the book. We collect them here for use as a general reference.

A.1 STANDARD GENETIC CODE

		Second Position of Codon				
First Position		U	C	A	G	Third Position
	U	UUU Phe [F]	UCU Ser [S]	UAU Tyr [Y]	UGU Cys [C]	U
		UUC Phe [F]	UCC Ser [S]	UAC Tyr [Y]	UGC Cys [C]	C
		UUA Leu [L]	UCA Ser [S]	UAA *Ter* [end]	UGA *Ter* [end]	A
		UUG Leu [L]	UCG Ser [S]	UAG *Ter* [end]	UGG Trp [W]	G
	C	CUU Leu [L]	CCU Pro [P]	CAU His [H]	CGU Arg [R]	U
		CUC Leu [L]	CCC Pro [P]	CAC His [H]	CGC Arg [R]	C
		CUA Leu [L]	CCA Pro [P]	CAA Gln [Q]	CGA Arg [R]	A
		CUG Leu [L]	CCG Pro [P]	CAG Gln [Q]	CGG Arg [R]	G
	A	AUU Ile [I]	ACU Thr [T]	AAU Asn [N]	AGU Ser [S]	U
		AUC Ile [I]	ACC Thr [T]	AAC Asn [N]	AGC Ser [S]	C
		AUA Ile [I]	ACA Thr [T]	AAA Lys [K]	AGA Arg [R]	A
		AUG Met [M]	ACG Thr [T]	AAG Lys [K]	AGG Arg [R]	G
	G	GUU Val [V]	GCU Ala [A]	GAU Asp [D]	GGU Gly [G]	U
		GUC Val [V]	GCC Ala [A]	GAC Asp [D]	GGC Gly [G]	C
		GUA Val [V]	GCA Ala [A]	GAA Glu [E]	GGA Gly [G]	A
		GUG Val [V]	GCG Ala [A]	GAG Glu [E]	GGG Gly [G]	G

Mathematics of Bioinformatics: Theory, Practice, and Applications, By Matthew He and Sergey Petoukhov

A.2   MATHEMATICAL NOTATION

$N = \{1, 2, 3, \ldots\}$	set of natural numbers
$N_0 = \{0, 1, 2, 3, \ldots\}$	set of nonnegative integers
$Z = \{\ldots, -3, -2, -1, 0, 1, 2, 3, \ldots\}$	set of integers
$Q = \{p/q \mid p, q \neq 0 \text{ are integers}\}$	set of rational numbers
$R = \{x \mid x \text{ repeating and nonrepeating decimals}\}$	set of real numbers
$R^n = \{(x_1, x_2, \ldots, x_n) \mid x_i \text{ is a real number}\}$	n-dimensional vector space
$\|u\| = \sqrt{u_1^2 + u_2^2 + \cdots u_n^2}$	norm of a vector $\boldsymbol{u}$
$\boldsymbol{u} \cdot \boldsymbol{\upsilon} = u_1\upsilon_1 + u_2\upsilon_2 + \cdots + u_n\upsilon_n$	standard inner product of $\boldsymbol{u}$ and $\boldsymbol{\upsilon}$

$$\boldsymbol{u} \times \boldsymbol{\upsilon} = \begin{pmatrix} u_2\upsilon_3 - u_3\upsilon_2 \\ u_3\upsilon_1 - u_1\upsilon_3 \\ u_1\upsilon_2 - u_2\upsilon_1 \end{pmatrix}$$ cross product of $\boldsymbol{u}$ and $\boldsymbol{\upsilon}$

$A_{n \times n}$	square matrix of dimension n
I_n	unit matrix of dimension n
$\mathrm{Tr}(A)$	trace of a matrix A
A^{T}	transpose of matrix A

A.3   PHYSICAL UNITS

Angstrom	$1\,\text{Å} = 10^{-10}\,\text{m}$
Atomic mass	$1\,\text{Da} = 1.661 \times 10^{-27}\,\text{kg}$
Avogadro's number	$N_A = 6.022 \times 10^{23}\,\text{L/mol}$
Boltzmann constant	$k_B = 1.38 \times 10^{-23}\,\text{J/K}$
Electron charge	$e = 1.602 \times 10^{-19}\,\text{C}$
Electron mass	$m_e = 9.109 \times 10^{-31}\,\text{kg}$
Energy (joule, J)	$\text{kg}\,\text{m}^2\text{s}^{-2} = \text{N}\,\text{m}$
Force (newton, N)	$\text{kg}\,\text{m}\,\text{s}^{-2} = \text{J}\,\text{m}^{-1}$
Planck constant	$h = 6.626 \times 10^{-34}\,\text{J}\,\text{s}$
Reduced Planck constant	$\hbar = h/(2\pi)\,\text{J}\,\text{s}$

A.4   CHEMICAL NOTATION

H	hydrogen atom
O	oxygen atom
C	carbon atom
N	nitrogen atom
R	side chain of amino acid
S	sulfur atom
CA	alpha-carbon amino acid
CB	beta-carbon amino acid

Φ	dihedral backbone angle
Ψ	dihedral backbone angle
Ω	dihedral backbone angle
χ	dihedral side-chain angle
A	ademine
C	cytosine
G	guanine
T	thymine
U	uracil
5'-----3'	single DNA strand
3'-----5'	single DNA strand

A.5 PUBLIC MOLECULAR BIOLOGICAL DATABASES

The following table lists all major public bioinformatics databases. Detailed information is given in a book by M. Kanehisa, *Post-Genome Bioinformatics*, Oxford University Press, New York, 2000.

Database	Primary Function	URL	Organization
GenBank	Nucleotide sequences	http://www.ncbi.nlm.nih.gov	National Center for Biotechnology Information (NCBI)
EMBL	Nucleotide sequences	http://www.ebi.ac.uk	European Bioinformatics Institute (EBI)
DDBJ	Nucleotide sequences	http://www.ddbj.nig.ac.jp	National Institute of Genetics, Japan (NIG)
SWISS-PROT	Amino acid sequences	http://www.expasy.ch	Swiss Institute of Bioinformatics (SIB)
PIR	Amino acid sequences	http://www.nbrf.georgetown.edu	National Biomedical Research Foundation (NBRF)
PRF	Amino acid sequences	http://www.prf.or.jp	Protein Research Foundation, Japan (PRF)
PDB	Protein structures	http://www.rcsb.org	Research Collaboratory for Structural Bioinformatics (RCSB)
CSD	Protein structures	http://www.ccdc.cam.ac.uk	Cambridge Crystallographic Data Center (CCDC)
MEDLINE	Bibliographic	http://www.nlm.nih.gov	National Library of Medicine (NLM)

A.6 20 AMINO ACIDS: ABBREVIATIONS, LINEAR, CHEMICAL, AND THREE-DIMENSIONAL STRUCTURES

Amino Acid Abbreviations and Linear Structure

Name	Abbreviation	Linear Structure Formula
Alanine	ala, a	$CH_3-CH(NH_2)-COOH$
Arginine	arg, r	$HN=C(NH_2)-NH-(CH_2)_3-CH(NH_2)-COOH$
Asparagine	asn, n	$H_2N-CO-CH_2-CH(NH_2)-COOH$
Aspartic acid	asp, d	$HOOC-CH_2-CH(NH_2)-COOH$
Cysteine	cys, c	$HS-CH_2-CH(NH_2)-COOH$
Glutamine	gln, q	$H_2N-CO-(CH_2)_2-CH(NH_2)-COOH$
Glutamic acid	glu, e	$HOOC-(CH_2)_2-CH(NH_2)-COOH$
Glycine	gly, g	NH_2-CH_2-COOH
Histidine	his, h	$NH-CH=N-CH=C-CH_2-CH(NH_2)-COOH$
Isoleucine	ile, i ·	$CH_3-CH_2-CH(CH_3)-CH(NH_2)-COOH$
Leucine	leu, l	$(CH_3)_2-CH-CH_2-CH(NH_2)-COOH$
Lysine	lys, k	$H_2N-(CH_2)_4-CH(NH_2)-COOH$
Methionine	met, m	$CH_3-S-(CH_2)_2-CH(NH_2)-COOH$
Phenylalanine	phe, f	$Ph-CH_2-CH(NH_2)-COOH$
Proline	pro, p	$NH-(CH_2)_3-CH-COOH$
Serine	ser, s	$HO-CH_2-CH(NH_2)-COOH$
Threonine	thr, t	$CH_3-CH(OH)-CH(NH_2)-COOH$
Tryptophan	trp, w	$Ph-NH-CH=C-CH_2-CH(NH_2)-COOH$
Tyrosine	tyr, y	$HO-p-Ph-CH_2-CH(NH_2)-COOH$
Valine	val, v	$(CH_3)_2-CH-CH(NH_2)-COOH$

Source: National Center for Biotechnology Information (NCBI), http://www.ncbi.nlm.nih.gov/Class/Structure/aa/aa_explore.cgi.

Chemical Structure of the 20 Natural Amino Acids

gly g Glycin

ala a Alanin

arg r Arginin

asn n Asparagin

asp d Asparaginsaeure

cys c Cystein

gln q Glutarnin

glu e Glutaminsaeure

his h Histidin

ile l Isoleucin

leu l Leucin

lys k Lysin

met m Methionin

phe f Phenylalanin

pro p Prolin

ser s Serin

thrt Threonin

trp w Tryptophan

tyr y Tyrosin

val v Valin

Three-Dimensional Shapes of the 20 Amino Acids (Molmasse and pH Value)

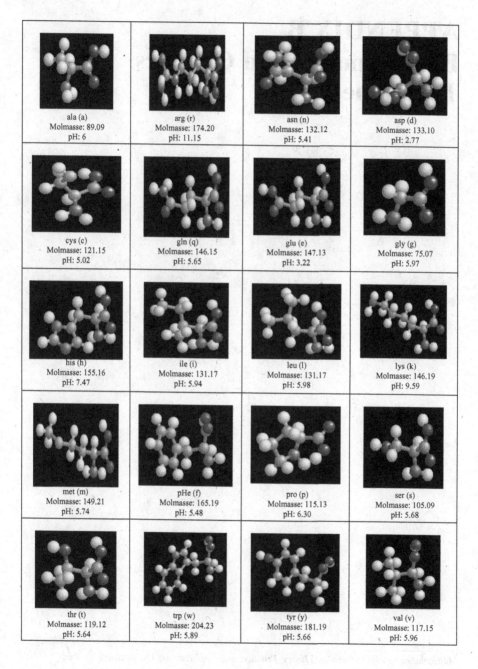

ala (a) Molmasse: 89.09 pH: 6	arg (r) Molmasse: 174.20 pH: 11.15	asn (n) Molmasse: 132.12 pH: 5.41	asp (d) Molmasse: 133.10 pH: 2.77
cys (c) Molmasse: 121.15 pH: 5.02	gln (q) Molmasse: 146.15 pH: 5.65	glu (e) Molmasse: 147.13 pH: 3.22	gly (g) Molmasse: 75.07 pH: 5.97
his (h) Molmasse: 155.16 pH: 7.47	ile (i) Molmasse: 131.17 pH: 5.94	leu (l) Molmasse: 131.17 pH: 5.98	lys (k) Molmasse: 146.19 pH: 9.59
met (m) Molmasse: 149.21 pH: 5.74	pHe (f) Molmasse: 165.19 pH: 5.48	pro (p) Molmasse: 115.13 pH: 6.30	ser (s) Molmasse: 105.09 pH: 5.68
thr (t) Molmasse: 119.12 pH: 5.64	trp (w) Molmasse: 204.23 pH: 5.89	tyr (y) Molmasse: 181.19 pH: 5.66	val (v) Molmasse: 117.15 pH: 5.96

APPENDIX B
Bioinformatics and Genetics Time Line

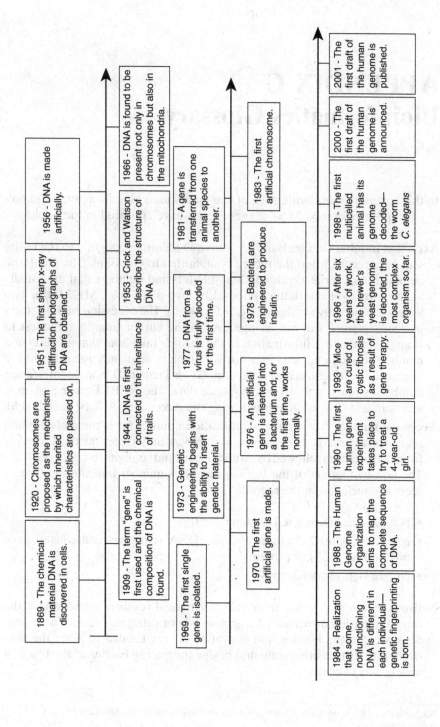

1869 - The chemical material DNA is discovered in cells.

1909 - The term "gene" is first used and the chemical composition of DNA is found.

1920 - Chromosomes are proposed as the mechanism by which inherited characteristics are passed on.

1944 - DNA is first connected to the inheritance of traits.

1951 - The first sharp x-ray diffraction photographs of DNA are obtained.

1953 - Crick and Watson describe the structure of DNA

1956 - DNA is made artificially.

1966 - DNA is found to be present not only in chromosomes but also in the mitochondria.

1969 - The first single gene is isolated.

1970 - The first artificial gene is made.

1973 - Genetic engineering begins with the ability to insert genetic material.

1976 - An artificial gene is inserted into a bacterium and, for the first time, works normally.

1977 - DNA from a virus is fully decoded for the first time.

1978 - Bacteria are engineered to produce insulin.

1981 - A gene is transferred from one animal species to another.

1983 - The first artificial chromosome.

1984 - Realization that some, nonfunctioning DNA is different in each individual—genetic fingerprinting is born.

1988 - The Human Genome Organization aims to map the complete sequence of DNA.

1990 - The first human gene experiment takes place to try to treat a 4-year-old girl.

1993 - Mice are cured of cystic fibrosis as a result of gene therapy.

1996 - After six years of work, the brewer's yeast genome is decoded, the most complex organism so far.

1998 - The first multicelled animal has its genome decoded—the worm *C. elegans*

2000 - The first draft of the human genome is announced.

2001 - The first draft of the human genome is published.

APPENDIX C
Bioinformatics Glossary

In this appendix we provide a list of commonly used bioinformatics terminology for quick reference. Most of these terms have appeared in the book.

Accession number (in GenBank)[1,2]: a unique identifier assigned to the entire sequence record when the record is submitted to GenBank. The GenBank accession number is a combination of letters and numbers that are usually in the format of one letter followed by five digits (e.g., M12345) or two letters followed by six digits (e.g., AC123456). The accession number for a particular record will not change even if the author submits a request to change some of the information in the record. Take note that an accession number is a unique identifier for a complete sequence record, while a sequence identifier, such as a Version, GI, or ProteinID, is an identification number assigned only to the sequence data. The NCBI Entrez System is searchable by accession number using the Accession [ACCN] search field.

Accession number[1,2]: a unique identification number for a complete RefSeq sequence record. RefSeq accession numbers are written in the following format: two letters followed by an underscore and six digits (e.g., NT_123456). The first two letters of the RefSeq accession number indicate the type of sequence included in the record:

- NT_123456: constructed genomic contigs
- NM_123456: mRNAs (actually, the cDNA sequences constructed from mRNA) NP_123456: proteins
- NC_123456: chromosomes

Active site: a region made of certain amino acid residues found within the three-dimensional surface of a protein where catalysis occurs. These residues provide the binding and activation energy needed to place the substrate into its transition state and bridge the energy barrier of the reaction undergoing catalysis.

Mathematics of Bioinformatics: Theory, Practice, and Applications, By Matthew He and Sergey Petoukhov
Copyright © 2011 John Wiley & Sons, Inc.

Adenine: one of the nitrogenous bases that has a double-ring structure, classified as a purine, found in DNA and RNA.

A DNA: a more dehydrated form of DNA than the typical, B form. It is more compact, with 11 nitrogen bases per turn of the helix. RNA–DNA and RNA–RNA helices typically exist in this form.

Agents: software modules that can search the Internet for data. These modules are independent and autonomous.

Algorithm[1,2]**:** a series of steps defining a procedure or formula for solving a problem that can be coded into a programming language and executed. Bioinformatics algorithms typically are used to process, store, analyze, visualize, and make predictions from biological data.

Alignment: the result of a comparison of two or more gene or protein sequences in order to determine their degree of nitrogen base or amino acid similarity or dissimilarity. Sequence alignments are used to determine the similarity, homology, function, or other degree of relatedness between two or more genes or gene products.

Allele: a given form of a gene that occupies a specific position or locus on a chromosome.

Alpha carbon: the central carbon atom in an amino acid to which side chains (R groups) are bound.

Alpha helix[1,2]**:** one of two types of protein secondary structure. An α-helix is a tight helix that results from the hydrogen bonding of the carboxyl (CO) group of one amino acid to the amino (NH) group of another amino acid, four residues away (toward the carboxyl terminus).

Alternative splicing: the production of two or more mRNA molecules from a single hnRNA by using different splice junctions.

Amino acid: one of the 20 chemical building blocks that are joined by amide (peptide) linkages to form a polypeptide chain of a protein.

Amphipathic: a molecule that has hydrophilic and hydrophobic characteristics simultaneously. This term is often used to describe large proteins with several domains of composed of different types of amino acid residues.

Annotation: a collection of comments, notations, references, and citations, either in free format or utilizing a controlled vocabulary, that together describe all the experimental and inferred information about a gene or protein. Annotations can also be applied to the description of other biological systems. Batch, automated annotation of bulk biological sequence is one of the key uses of bioinformatics tools.

Anticodon: the triplet of contiguous bases on tRNA that binds to the codon sequence of nucleotides on mRNA (e.g., the codon for glycine is GGG, on mRNA; the anticodon for glycine is CCC, on tRNA).

Antigen: any foreign molecule that stimulates an immune response in a vertebrate organism. Many antigens are proteins, such as the surface proteins of foreign organisms. Antigens bind to antibodies.

Antisense: DNA or RNA composed of the sequence complementary to the target DNA or RNA.

Array: a group of variables that can store multiple values. Each value is retrieved using an integer index.

Assembly: a compilation of overlapping sequences from one or more related genes that have been clustered together based on their degree of sequence identity or similarity. Sequence assembly may be used to piece together "shotgun" sequencing fragments based upon overlapping restriction enzyme digests, or may be used to identify and index novel genes from single-pass cDNA sequencing efforts.

Backbone (of an amino acid): consists of an amide, an alpha carbon, and a carboxylic acid or carboxylate group.

Base pair: a pair of nitrogenous bases (a purine and a pyrimidine), held together by hydrogen bonds, that form the core of DNA and RNA (i.e., the A–T, G–C, and A–U interactions).

B DNA: the typical form of DNA, which has 10 nitrogen bases per turn of the helix. Stacked bases are regularly spaced 0.34 nm apart and the helix makes a complete turn every 3.4 nm.

Beta sheet: a three-dimensional arrangement taken up by polypeptide chains that consists of alternating strands linked by hydrogen bonds between a carboxyl group's oxygen on one strand and the amide group's hydrogen from another strand. The alternating strands together form a sheet that is frequently twisted. Beta sheets may be parallel (both strands oriented the same direction, amino to carboxyl terimus) or antiparallel (both strands running in opposite directions; for example, if one is oriented amino to carboxyl, the other would be running carboxyl to amino).

Bifurcation: a point in a phylogenetic tree in which an ancestral taxon splits into two independent lineages.

BLAST[1,2] (Basic Local Alignment Search Tool): a fast technique for detecting ungapped subsequences that match a given query sequence.

Bootstrap test: a test that allows for a rough quantification of confidence levels.

Carboxyl group: the –COOH functional group, acidic in nature, found in all amino acids.

cDNA (complementary DNA): a DNA strand copied from mRNA using reverse transcriptase.

cDNA library: a set of DNA fragments prepared from the total mRNA obtained from a selected cell, tissue, or organism. It represents all the DNA expressed in a cell.

CDS[1,2]**:** the coding sequence or the portion of a nucleotide sequence that makes up the triplet codons that actually code for amino acids.

Chromosome: the structure in the cell nucleus that contains all of the cellular DNA together with a number of proteins that compact and package the DNA.

Clone: a population of genetically identical cells or DNA molecules.

Cloning: the formation of clones or exact genetic replicas.

Cluster: the grouping of similar objects in a multidimensional space. Clustering is used for constructing new features which are abstractions of the existing features of those objects. The quality of the clustering depends crucially on the distance metric in the space. In bioinformatics, clustering is performed on sequences, high-throughput expression (microarray data), and other experimental data.

Coding regions (CDS): the portion of a genomic sequence bounded by start and stop codons that identifies the sequence of the protein being coded for by a particular gene.

Codon: a sequence of three adjacent nucleotides (on mRNA) that designates a specific amino acid or start/stop site for transcription.

Compiler: a computer program that translates a symbolic programming language into machine language so that the instructions can be executed by a computer.

Conformation: the precise three-dimensional arrangement (structure) of atoms and bonds in a molecule describing its geometry and hence its molecular function.

Consensus sequence: a sequence that represents the most common nucleotide or amino acid at each position in two or more homologous sequences.

Conservation[1,2]: substitution of one amino for another to preserve the physicochemical properties of the original residue: for example, when a hydrophobic amino acid residue is replaced by another hydrophobic residue.

Convergence: the endpoint of any algorithm that uses iteration or recursion to guide a series of data-processing steps. An algorithm is usually said to have reached convergence when the difference between the steps computed and those observed falls below a predefined threshold.

Crossing over: the situation that usually occurs during prophase I of meiosis, where homologous chromosomes may exchange pieces of genetic information, leading to increased genetic variation among the possible resulting gametes.

Crystal structure: a high-resolution molecular structure derived by x-ray crystallographic analysis of protein or other biomolecular crystals.

C-value: the measure of a cell's total DNA content.

Cytoplasm (also referred to as **cytoskeleton**): the medium, including structural proteins such as actin and tubukin) making up the cellular space between the nucleus and the cell membrane.

Cytosine: one of the nitrogenous bases that has a single-ring structure, classified as a pyrimidine, found in DNA and RNA.

Data mining: the ability to query very large databases in order to satisfy a hypothesis ("top-down" data mining); or to interrogate a database in order to generate new hypotheses based on rigorous statistical correlations ("bottom-up" data mining).

Data processing: the systematic performance on data of such operations as handling, merging, sorting, and computing. The semantic content of the original data should not be changed, but the semantic content of the processed data may be changed.

Data warehouses: vast arrays of heterogeneous (biological) data, stored within a single logical data repository, that are accessible to different querying and manipulation methods.

Database: any file system by which data get stored following a logical process. (*See also* Relational database.)

Deconvolution: a mathematical procedure to separate out the overlapping effects of molecules, such as mixtures of compounds in a high-throughput screen or mixtures of cDNAs in a high-density array.

Degeneracy: the ability of some amino acids to be coded for by more than one triplet codon (a type of system redundancy).

Deletion: a chromosomal alteration in which a portion of the chromosome or the underlying DNA segment is lost; can be a chromosomal or point deletion.

DNA (deoxyribonucleic acid): the chemical that forms the basis of the genetic material in virtually all organisms. DNA is composed of the four nitrogenous bases adenine, cytosine, guanine, and thymine, which are covalently bonded to a backbone of deoxyribose-phosphate to form a DNA strand. Two complementary strands (where all G's pair with C's and A's with T's) form a double-helical structure which is held together by hydrogen bonding between the cognate bases.

DNA fingerprinting: a technique for identifying human individuals (may also be applied to domesticated pets) based on a restriction enzyme digest of tandemly repeated DNA sequences that are scattered throughout the human genome but are unique to each individual.

DNA microarrays: the deposition of oligonucleotides or cDNAs onto an inert substrate such as glass or silicon. Thousands of molecules may be organized spatially into a high-density matrix. These DNA chips may be probed to allow expression monitoring of many thousands of genes simultaneously. Uses include study of polymorphisms in genes, de novo sequencing, or molecular diagnosis of disease.

DNA polymerase: an enzyme that catalyzes the synthesis of DNA from a DNA template given the deoxyribonucleotide precursors.

DNA probes: short single-stranded DNA molecules of specific base sequence, labeled either radioactively or immunologically, that are used to detect and identify the complementary base sequence in a gene or genome by hybridizing specifically to that gene or sequence.

DNA sequencing: the technique by which the specific sequence of bases forming a particular DNA region is determined, usually as the result of an automated process.

Domain[1,2]: a discrete portion of a protein assumed to fold independent of the rest of the protein and possessing its own function.

Domain (protein): a region of special biological interest within a single protein sequence. However, a domain may also be defined as a region within the three-dimensional structure of a protein (tertiary structure) that may encompass regions of several distinct protein sequences that accomplishes a specific function. A domain class is a group of domains that share a common set of well-defined properties or characteristics.

Dot plot: a graphical method of comparing two sequences corresponding to regions of sequence similarity.

Dynamic programming: a program that allows a computer to explore efficiently all possible solutions to certain types of complex problems; it divides a problem into reasonably sized subproblems and uses parts to compute the final answer.

Electrophoresis: the use of an external electric field to separate large biomolecules on the basis of their charge by running them through acrylamide or agarose gels.

Enhancers: DNA sequences that can greatly increase the transcription rates of genes even though they may be far upstream or downstream from the promoter they stimulate.

Entrez[1,2]: an online resource provided by the National Center for Biotechnology Information (NCBI). It organizes GenBank sequences and links them to the literature sources in which they originally appeared.

Enzyme: a class of proteins that is capable of catalyzing chemical reactions (the making or breaking of chemical bonds). They do so by orienting their substrates into a suitable geometry in a particular location (the active site) where electrophilic or nucleophilic amino acid residues can participate in the reaction. Enzymes are protein catalysts that speed up chemical reactions that would otherwise be prohibitively slow under physiological conditions.

Equilibrium constant: a value that describes the equilibrium state of the reversible reaction between two molecular species.

Eukaryote: a cell or organism with a distinct membrane-bound nucleus as well as specialized membrane-based organelles. (*See also* Prokaryote.)

Exon: the region of DNA within a gene that codes for a polypeptide chain or domain. Typically, a mature protein is composed of several domains coded by different exons within a single gene.

Expression (gene or **protein):** a measure of the presence, amount, and time course of one or more gene products in a particular cell or tissue. Gene chips and proteomics now allow the study of expression profiles of sets of genes or even entire genomes.

Expression profile: the level and duration of expression of one or more genes, selected from a particular cell or tissue type, generally obtained by a variety of high-throughput methods, such as sample sequencing, serial analysis, or microarray-based detection.

Expression vector: a cloning vector that is engineered to allow the expression of protein from a cDNA. The expression vector provides appropriate promoter and restriction sites that allow insertion of cDNA.

FASTA format[1,2]: a sequence in FASTA format begins with a single-line description, followed by lines of sequence data. The description line is distinguished from the sequence data by a greater-than symbol (>) in the first column. It is recommended that all lines of text be shorter than 80 characters in length. An example sequence in FASTA format is

```
>gi|532319|pir|TVFV2E|TVFV2E    envelope protein
ELRLRYCAPAGFALLKCNDADYDGFKTNCSNVSVVHCTNLMNTTVTTGLLLNGS
YSENRT
QIWQKHRTSNDSALILLNKHYNLTVTCKRPGNKTVLPVTIMAGLVFHSQKYNLR
LRQAWC
HFPSNWKGAWKEVKEEIVNLPKERYRGTNDPKRIFFQRQWGDPETANLWFNCHG
EFFYCK
MDWFLNYLNNLTVDADHNECKNTSGTKSGNKRAPGPCVQRTYVACHIRSVIIWL
ETISKK
TYAPPREGHLECTSTVTGMTVELNYIPKNRTNVTLSPQIESIWAAELDRYKLVE
ITPIGF
APTEVRRYTGGHERQKRVPFVXXXXXXXXXXXXXXXXXXXXXXXXXVQSQHLLAGIL
QQQKNL
LAAVEAQQQMLKLTIWGVK
```

A FASTA file can also contain multiple sequences:

```
>VECTOR32    synthetic vector sequence 32
ATGAGCGGCGGCCCCATGGGCGGCAGGCCCGGCGGCAGGGGCGCCCCCGCCGTG
CAGCAG
AACATCCCCAGCACCCTGCTGCAGGACCACGAGAACCAGAGGCTGTTCGAGATG
CTGGGC
>VECTOR33    synthetic vector sequence 33

ACGAGCGGCGGTCCCATGGGCGCCAGGCCCGGCGGCAGGGGCGCTGCCGCCGTG
CAGCAC
ATCATCCCCAGCACCCTGCAGCAGGACCACGAGTACCAGAGGCTGTTCGAGATG
CTGGGC
>VECTOR34    synthetic vector sequence 34

GTGAGCGGCGGCTACTTGGGCGGCAGGCCCGGCGGCAGGGGCGCCCACGCCGTG
CAGCAG
```

Sequences are expected to be represented in the standard IUB/IUPAC amino acid and nucleic acid codes, with these exceptions: lowercase letters are accepted and are mapped into uppercase letters; a single hyphen or dash can be used to represent a gap of indeterminate length; and in amino acid sequences, U and * are acceptable letters. Invalid characters (digits, blanks) are removed automatically.

Frame shift: a deletion, substitution, or duplication of one or more bases that causes the reading frame of a structural gene to shift from the normal series of triplets.

Function: a subroutine that returns a value.

Functional genomics: the use of genomic information to delineate protein structure, function, pathways, and networks.

Gap (affine gap): any maximal, consecutive run of spaces in a single string of a given alignment.

Gap penalty: the penalty applied to a similarity score for the introduction of an insertion or deletion gap, the extension of a gap, or both. Gap penalties are usually subtracted from a cumulative score being determined for a comparison of two or more sequences via an optimization algorithm that attempts to maximize that score.

GC content: the measure of the abundance of G and C nucleotides relative to A and T nucleotides within DNA sequences.

GenBank: a data bank of genetic sequences operated by a division of the National Institutes of Health.

Gene: classically, a unit of inheritance. In practice, a gene is a segment of DNA on a chromosome that encodes a protein and all the regulatory sequences (promoter) required to control expression of that protein.

Gene chips (also known as **gene arrays**): oligonucleotides or cDNA covalently attached directly onto a small glass or silicon chip in organized arrays. Over 50,000 different DNA fragments can be presented on a single chip, providing a high-throughput parallel method of probing gene expression, genotype, or gene function.

Gene expression: the conversion of information from gene to protein via transcription and translation.

Gene families: subsets of genes containing homologous sequences which usually correlate with a common function.

Gene index: a listing of the number, type, label, and sequence of all the genes identified within the genome of a given organism. Gene indices are usually created by assembling overlapping EST (expressed sequence tag) sequences into clusters and determining if each cluster corresponds to a unique gene. Methods by which a cluster can be identified as representing a unique gene include identification of long open reading frames, comparison to genomic sequence, and detection of single nucleotide polymorphisms or other features in the cluster that are known to exist in the gene.

Gene library: a collection of cloned DNA fragments created by restriction endonuclease digestion that represent part or all of an organism's genome.

Gene locus (pl. **loci**)[1,2]**:** a gene's position on a chromosome or other chromosome marker; also, the DNA at that position. The use of *locus* is sometimes restricted to mean expressed DNA regions.

Gene name[1,2]**:** the official name assigned to a gene. According to the Guidelines for Human Gene Nomenclature developed by the HUGO Gene Nomenclature Committee, it should be brief and describe the function of the gene.

Gene ontology[1,2]**:** a controlled vocabulary of terms relating to molecular function, biological process, or cellular components developed by the Gene Ontology Consortium. A controlled vocabulary allows scientists to use consistent terminology when describing the roles of genes and proteins in cells.

Gene product: the product, either RNA or protein, that results from expression of a gene. The amount of gene product reflects the activity of the gene.

Gene symbol[1,2]**:** symbols for human genes, usually designated by scientists who discover the genes. The symbols are created using the Guidelines for Human Gene Nomenclature developed by the HUGO Gene Nomenclature Committee. Gene symbols usually consist of no more than six uppercase letters or a combination of uppercase letters and Arabic numbers. Gene symbols should start with the first letters of the gene name. For example, the gene symbol for insulin is "INS." A gene symbol must be submitted to HUGO for approval before it can be considered an official gene symbol.

Genetic code: the mapping of all possible codons into the 20 amino acids, including the start and stop codons.

Genetic engineering (in recombinant DNA technology): the procedures used to isolate, splice, and manipulate DNA outside the cell. Genetic engineering allows a recombinantly engineered DNA segment to be introduced into a foreign cell or organism and to be able to replicate and function normally.

Genetic marker: any gene that can be recognized readily by its phenotypic effect and which can be used as a marker for a cell, chromosome, or individual carrying that gene. Also, any detectable polymorphism used to identify a specific gene or DNA sequence (used in genealogical studies).

Genome: the complete genetic content of an organism.

Genomic DNA (sequence): a DNA sequence typically obtained from mammalian or other higher-order species, which includes both an intron and an exon sequence (a coding sequence), as well as noncoding regulatory sequences such as promoter and enhancer sequences.

Genomics: the analysis of the entire genome of a chosen organism.

Genotype: strictly, all of the genes possessed by an individual; in practice, the particular alleles present in a specific genetic locus.

GI (in GenBank)[1,2]: a GI (GenInfo identifier) is a sequence identifier that can be assigned to a nucleotide sequence or protein translation. Each GI is a numerical value of one or more digits. The protein translation and the nucleotide sequence contained in the same record will be assigned different GI numbers. Every time the sequence data for a particular record is changed, its version number increases and it receives a new GI. However, although each new version number is based on the previous version number, a new GI for an altered sequence may be completely different from the previous GI. For example, in the GenBank record M12345, the original GI might be 7654321, but after a change in the sequence is submitted, the new GI for the changed sequence could be 10529376. Individuals can search for nucleotide sequences and protein translations by GI using the UID search field in the NCBI sequence databases. NCBI's Sequence Revision History page can be used to view the various GI numbers, version numbers, or update dates associated with a particular GenBank record.

Global alignment[1,2]: two nucleic acid or amino acid sequences lined up along their entire length. (*See also* Local alignment.)

Guanine (G): one of the nitrogenous bases that has a double-ring structure, classified as a purine, found in DNA and RNA.

Hairpin: a double-helical region in a single DNA or RNA strand formed by hydrogen bonding between adjacent inverse complementary sequences to form a hairpin-shaped structure.

Heteroduplex: a hybrid structure formed by the annealing of two DNA strands (or an RNA strand and a DNA strand) that have sufficient complementarity in their sequence to allow hydrogen bonding between their separate strands.

Heuristic methods: trial-and-error, self-educating techniques for parsing a tree.

Hidden Markov model (HMM): a joint statistical model for an ordered sequence of variables. The result of stochastically perturbing the variables in a Markov chain (the original variables are thus "hidden"), where the Markov chain has discrete variables that select the "state" of the HMM at each step. The perturbed values can be continuous and are the "outputs" of the HMM. A hidden Markov model is equivalently a coupled mixture model where the joint distribution over states is a Markov chain. Hidden Markov models are valuable in bioinformatics because they allow a search or alignment algorithm to be trained using unaligned or unweighted input sequences, and because they allow position-dependent scoring parameters such as gap penalties, thus more accurately modeling the consequences of evolutionary events on sequence families.

High-throughput screening: the method by which very large numbers of compounds are screened against a putative drug target in either cell-free or whole-cell assays. Typically, these screenings are carried out in 96-well plates using automated, robotic station-based technologies or in higher-density array (chip) formats.

hnRNA (heterogeneous RNA): primary RNA polymerase II transcripts in eukaryotes, converted to mRNAs after capping, splicing, and polyadenylation.

Homology: (*strict*) two or more biological species, systems, or molecules that share a common evolutionary ancestor; (*general*) two or more gene or protein sequences that share a significant degree of similarity, typically measured by the amount of identity (in the case of DNA), or conservative replacements (in the case of protein) that they register along their lengths. Sequence homology searches are typically performed with a query DNA or protein sequence to identify known genes or gene products that share significant similarity and hence might inform on the ancestry, heritage, and possible function of the query gene.

Homologous chromosomes: chromosomes of the same size and shape that contain alternate forms of the same genes (alleles). For example, a human being should have two copies of chromosome 1. These copies are the homologous chromosomes. (*See also* Nonhomologous chromosomes.)

Housekeeping genes: genes that are always expressed (i.e., they are said to be *constitutively expressed*), due to their constant requirement by the cell.

Human antimurine antibody response (HAMA): an immune response generated in humans to antibodies raised in murine (e.g., mouse or rat) cells.

Hybridization: the interaction of complementary nucleic acid strands. This can occur between two DNA strands or between DNA and RNA strands, and is the basis of many techniques, such as Southern and Northern blots and microarray.

Hydrogen bond: a weak chemical interaction between an electronegative atom (e.g., nitrogen or oxygen) and a hydrogen atom that is covalently attached to another atom. This bond keeps the two helices of DNA together, maintains the secondary structure (α-helices and β-sheets) of proteins, and is also the primary interaction between water molecules.

Hydrophilicity (literally, water-loving): the degree to which a molecule is soluble in water. Hydrophilicity depends to a large degree on the charge and polarizability of the molecule and its ability to form transient hydrogen bonds with (polar) water molecules.

Hydrophobicity (literally, water-hating): the degree to which a molecule is insoluble in water and hence is soluble in lipids. If a molecule lacking polar groups is placed in water, it will be driven to find a hyrdophobic environment (such as the interior of a protein or a membrane).

Identity[1,2]**:** the extent to which two sequences are invariant.

Immunoglobulin: a member of the globulin protein family, consisting of two light and two heavy chains linked by disulfide bonds. All antibodies are immunoglobulins.

In silico (in biology): the use of computers to simulate, process, or analyze a biological experiment.

In situ hybridization: A variation of the DNA/RNA hybridization procedure in which the denatured DNA is in place in the cell and is then challenged with RNA or DNA extracted from another source.

Integration: the physical insertion of DNA into the host cell genome. The process is used by retroviruses where a specific enzyme catalyzes the process or can occur at random sites with other DNA (e.g., transposons).

Intracellular signaling: the communication of a molecular message from the surface of a cell to the nucleus via the participation of a series of molecules, including receptors, enzymes, proteins, and small molecules. The end result of the signaling process is the up- or down-regulation of a particular series of genes that may be involved in cell growth, division, or differentiation.

Introns: nucleotide sequences found in the structural genes of eukaryotes that are noncoding and interrupt the sequences containing information that codes for polypeptide chains. Intron sequences are spliced out of their RNA transcripts before maturation and protein synthesis. (*See also* Exons.)

Iteration: a series of steps in an algorithm whereby the processing of data is performed repetitively until the result exceeds a particular threshold. Iteration is often used in multiple sequence alignments whereby each set of pairwise alignments is compared with every other set, starting with the most similar pairs and progressing to the least similar, until there are no longer any sequence pairs remaining to be aligned.

Junk DNA: the excess DNA that is present in the genome beyond that required to encode proteins. Disposable DNA sequences in which no function is currently known.

Karyotype: the constitution (typically, number and size) of chromosomes in a cell or individual organism.

Knockout mice: mice that have been engineered to lack a chosen gene. The gene is inactivated in embryonic stem cells using the technique of homologous recombination. These cells are then introduced into an early-stage embryo (blastocyst), which is then transplanted into a recipient mouse. The subsequent progeny lack the targeted gene in some cells. This technique is used to determine the function of the chosen gene.

Lab on a chip: a microdevice that allows rapid microanalytical analysis of DNA or protein in a single fully integrated system. Typically, these devices are miniature surfaces, made of silicon, glass, or plastic, which carry the necessary microdevices (pumps, valves, microfluidic controllers, and detectors) that allow sample separation and analysis. These devices are used in drug discovery, genetic testing, and separation science.

Lead compound: a candidate compound identified as the best "hit" (tight binder) after screening of a combinatorial (or other) compound library, which is then taken into further rounds of screening to determine its suitability as a drug.

Lead optimization: the process of converting a putative lead compound ("hit") into a therapeutic drug with maximal activity and minimal side effects, typically using a combination of computer-based drug design, medicinal chemistry, and pharmacology.

Library: a large collection of compounds, peptides, cDNAs, or genes which may be screened to isolate cognate molecules.

Ligand: any small molecule that binds to a protein or receptor; the cognate partner of many cellular proteins, enzymes, and receptors.

Linkage: the association of genes (or genetic loci) on the same chromosome. Genes that are linked together tend to be transmitted together.

Linkage map: a genetic map of a chromosome or genome delineated by mapping the positions of genes to their chromosomes by their linkage to readily identifiable genetic loci.

Local alignment[1,2]**:** the alignment of portions (rather than the entire sequence length) of two nucleic acid or amino acid sequences.

Locus: the specific position occupied by a gene on a chromosome. At a given locus, any one of the variant forms of a gene may be present. The variants are said to be *alleles* of that gene.

Markov chain: any multivariate probability density whose independence diagram is a chain. The variables are ordered, and each variable "depends" on its neighbors only in the sense of being conditionally independent of the others. Markov chains are an integral component of hidden Markov models.

Masking[1,2]**:** the removal of repeated or low-complexity regions from a sequence so that sequences are compared.

Match score: the amount of credit given by an algorithm to an alignment for each aligned pair of identical residues.

Matrix genetics: a branch of bioinformatics and mathematical biology that studies the matrix forms of presentations of the genetic code.

Maximum likelihood approach: a phylogenetic approach in which probabilities are considered for individual nucleotide substitution in a set of sequence alignments; a purely statistically based method of phylogenetic reconstruction.

Meiosis: a process within a cell nucleus that results in the reduction of the chromosome number from diploid (two copies of each chromosome) to haploid (a single copy) through two reductive divisions in germ cells.

Messenger RNA (mRNA): the complementary RNA copy of DNA formed from a single-stranded DNA template during transcription that migrates from the nucleus to the cytoplasm, where it is processed into a sequence carrying the information to code for a polypeptide domain.

Microarray: a two-dimensional array, typically on a glass, filter, or silicon wafer, upon which genes or gene fragments are deposited or synthesized in a predetermined spatial order, allowing them to be made available as probes in a high-throughput, parallel manner.

MIM number (also known as **MIM#, OMIM number**, or **McKusick code**)[1,2]: a unique six-digit number assigned to each entry listed in the catalog of human genes and genetic disorders, "Online Mendelian Inheritance in Man" (OMIM). The first digit of a MIM number describes a gene's mode of inheritance as outlined below.

First Digit	Format[a]	Mode of Inheritance
1	1XXXXX	Autosomal dominant (for entries created before May 15, 1994)
2	2XXXXX	Autosomal recessive (for entries created before May 15, 1994)
3	3XXXXX	X-linked loci or phenotypes
4	4XXXXX	Y-linked loci or phenotypes
5	5XXXXX	Mitochondrial loci or phenotypes
6	6XXXXX	Autosomal loci or phenotypes (for entries created after May 15, 1994)

[a]X is any digit.

Mismatch score: the penalty assigned by an algorithm when nonidentical restudies are aligned in an alignment.

Missense mutation: a point mutation in which one codon (triplet of bases) is changed into another, designating a different amino acid.

Mitochondiral signal sequence: a string of amino acids that causes a eukaryotic protein to be delivered to a cell's mitochondria.

Modeling: (*in bioinformatics*) refers to molecular modeling, a process whereby the three-dimensional architecture of biological molecules is interpreted (or predicted), visually represented, and manipulated in order to determine their molecular properties. (*general*) a series of mathematical equations or procedures that simulate a real-life process given a set of assumptions, boundary parameters, and initial conditions.

Monomer: a single unit of any biological molecule or macromolecule, such as an amino acid, nucleic acid, polypeptide domain, or protein.

Motif: a conserved element of a protein sequence alignment that usually correlates with a particular function. Motifs are generated from a local multiple protein sequence alignment corresponding to a region whose function or structure is known. It is sufficient that it is conserved, and is hence likely to be predictive of any subsequent occurrence of such a structural or functional region in any other novel protein sequence. A motif is built from particular combinations of secondary structures (typically, α-helices and β-sheets).

Multiple (sequence) alignment: a multiple alignment of k sequences is a rectangular array, consisting of characters taken from the alphabet A that satisfies the following conditions: There are exactly k rows; ignoring the gap character, row i is exactly the sequence sI; and each column contains at least one character different from –. In practice, multiple sequence alignments include a cost/weight function, which defines the penalty for the insertion of gaps (the – character) and weights identities and conservative substitutions accordingly. Multiple alignment algorithms attempt to create the optimal alignment, defined as the one with the lowest cost/weight score.

Multiplex sequencing: an approach to high-throughput sequencing that uses several pooled DNA samples run through gels simultaneously and then separated and analyzed.

Mutation: an inheritable alteration to the genome that includes genetic (point or single base) changes, or larger-scale alterations such as chromosomal deletions or rearrangements.

Naked DNA: pure, isolated DNA devoid of any proteins that may bind to it.

Native structure (conformation): unique structure into which a particular protein is usually folded within a living cell.

Nested PCR: the second round amplification of an already PCR-amplified sequence using a new pair of primers which are internal to the original primers, typically done when a single PCR reaction generates insufficient amounts of product.

Neural net: an interconnected assembly of simple processing elements, units, or nodes whose functionality is based loosely on the animal brain. The processing ability of the network is stored in the interunit connection strengths, or weights, obtained by a process of adaptation to, or learning from, a set of training patterns. Neural nets are used in bioinformatics to map data and make predictions, such as taking a multiple alignment of a protein family as a training set in order to identify novel members of the family from their sequence data alone.

Neutral mutation: a mutation that has no effect on the fitness of an organism.

NMR (nuclear magnetic resonance): a technique for resolving protein structures.

Nonhomologous chromosomes: chromosomes that are not of the same size and shape and contain different genes. For example, a typical human being has 23 different types of nonhomologous chromosomes.

Nonsense mutation: a point mutation in which a codon specific for an amino acid is converted into a stop codon.

Nuclease: any enzyme that can cleave the phosphodiester bonds of nucleic acid backbones.

Nucleoside: a five-carbon sugar covalently attached to a nitrogen base (a nucleotide without the phosphate group added).

Nucleotide: a nucleic acid unit composed of a five-carbon sugar joined to a phosphate group and a nitrogen base.

Object-relational database: databases that combine the elements of object orientation and object-oriented programming languages with database capabilities. They provide more than persistent storage of programming language objects. Object databases extend the functionality of object programming languages (e.g., C++, Smalltalk, Java) to provide full-featured database programming capability. The result is a high level of congruence between the data model for the application and the data model of the database. Object-relational databases are used in bioinformatics to map molecular biological objects (such as sequences, structures, maps, and pathways) to their underlying representations (typically, within the rows and columns of relational database tables). This enables users to deal with the biological objects in a more intuitive manner, as they would in the laboratory, without having to worry about the underlying data model of their representation.

Oligonucleotide: a short molecule consisting of several linked nucleotides (typically, between 10 and 60) attached covalently by phosphodiester bonds.

Open reading frame (ORF): any stretch of DNA that potentially encodes a protein. Open reading frames start with an initiation (or start) codon and end with a termination (or stop) codon. No termination codons may be present internally. The identification of an ORF is the first indication that a segment of DNA may be part of a functional gene.

Operator: a segment of DNA that interacts with the products of regulatory genes and facilitates the transcription of one or more structural genes.

Operon: in prokaryotes, a unit of transcription consisting of one or more structural genes, an operator, and a promoter.

Orthologs: genes in different species that evolved from a common ancestral gene by speciation. Normally, orthologs retain the same function in the course of evolution. Identification of orthologs is critical for reliable prediction of gene function in newly sequenced genomes.

Orthologous genes[1,2]**:** homologous sequences in different species that result from a common ancestral gene during speciation. Orthologous genes may or may not have similar functions.

Overlapping clones: a collection of cloned sequences made by generating randomly overlapping DNA fragments with infrequently cutting restriction enzymes.

Palindrome: a region of DNA with a symmetrical arrangement of bases occurring about a single point such that the base sequences on either side of that point are identical (if the strands are both read in the same direction; e.g., 5'-GAATTC-3', whose complementary sequence is 3'-CTTAAG-5').

Paralogous genes[1,2]**:** homologous sequences within a single species that are the result of gene duplication.

Parameters: user-selectable values, typically determined experimentally, that govern the boundaries of an algorithm or program. For example, selection of the appropriate input parameters governs the success of a search algorithm. Some of the most common search parameters in bioinformatics tools include the stringency of an alignment search tool and the weights (penalties) provided for mismatches and gaps.

Pathways: bioinformatics strives to define representations of key biological datatypes, algorithms, and inference procedures, including sequences, structures, biological pathways, and reactions. Representing and computing with biological pathways requires ontologies for representing pathway knowledge, user interfaces to these databases, physicochemical properties of enzymes and their substrates in pathways, and pathway analysis of whole genomes, including identifying common patterns across species and species differences.

Pattern: a molecular biological pattern usually occurs at the level of the characters making up a gene or protein sequence. A pattern language must be defined in order to apply different criteria to different positions of a sequence. In enable a computer to carry out position-specific comparisons, a pattern-matching algorithm must allow alternative residues at a given position, repetitions of a residue, exclusion of alternative residues, weighting, and ideally, combinatorial representation.

Peptide: a short stretch of amino acids each covalently coupled by a peptide (amide) bond.

Peptide bond (amide bond): a covalent bond formed between two amino acids when the amino group of one is linked to the carboxy group of another (resulting in the elimination of one water molecule).

pH: a unit of measure used to indicate the concentration of hydrogen ions in a solution; specifically, the negative log of the molar concentration of H^+. The greater the concentration of H^+, the lower the pH.

Phenotype: any observable feature of an organism that is the result of one or more genes.

Physical map: a linearly ordered set of DNA fragments encompassing the genome or region of interest. Physical maps are of two types. A *macrorestriction map* consists of an ordered set of large DNA fragments generated using restriction enzymes whose recognition sequences are represented infrequently in the genome. An *ordered clone map* consists of an overlapping collection of cloned DNA fragments.

Plasmid: any replicating DNA element that can exist in the cell independent of the chromosomes. Synthetic plasmids are used for DNA cloning. Most commonly found naturally in bacterial cells as a ring of DNA.

Point mutation: a mutation in which a single nucleotide in a DNA sequence is substituted for another nucleotide.

Poly(A) tail: the stretch of adenine (A) residues at the 3′ end of eukaryotic mRNA that is added to the pre-mRNA as it is processed, before its transport from the nucleus to the cytoplasm and subsequent translation at the ribosome.

Polyadenylation site: a site on the 3′ end of messenger RNA (mRNA) that signals the addition of a series of adenines during the RNA processing step and before the mRNA migrates to the cytoplasm. These poly(A) "tails" increase mRNA stability and allow one to isolate mRNA from cells by reverse transcriptase PCR amplification using poly(T) primers.

Polygenic inheritance: inheritance involving alleles at many genetic loci.

Polymerase chain reaction (PCR): a technique used to amplify or generate large amounts of replicated DNA of a segment of any DNA whose "flanking" sequences are known.

Polymorphism: the existence of a gene in a population in at least two different forms at a frequency far higher than that attributable to recurrent mutation alone. Variations in a population may be measured by determining the rate of mutation in polymorphic genes.

Polypeptide (chain)[1,2]**:** a single chain of covalently attached amino acids joined by peptide bonds. A polypeptide chain usually consists of 100 or fewer amino acids. Polypeptide chains usually fold into a compact, stable form (a domain) that is part (or all) of the final protein. A protein is made up of one or several polypeptide chains.

Primary structure[1,2]**:** the amino acid sequence of a polypeptide chain. Of the four levels of protein structure, this is the most basic protein structure.

Primer: a short oligonucleotide that provides a free 3′ hydroxyl for DNA or RNA synthesis by the appropriate polymerase (DNA polymerase or RNA polymerase).

Probe: any biochemical that is labeled or tagged in some way so that it can be used to identify or isolate a gene, RNA, or protein.

Profile: a sequence profile is usually derived from multiple alignments of sequences with a known relationship, and consists of a table of position-specific scores and gap penalties. Each position in a profile contains scores for all possible amino acids, as well as one penalty score for opening and one for continuing a gap at the position specified. Attempts have been made to further improve the sensitivity of a profile by refining the procedures to construct the profile, starting from a given multiple alignment. Other representations for sequence domains or motifs do not necessarily require the presence of a correct and complete multiple alignment, such as hidden Markov models.

Prokaryote: an organism or cell that lacks a membrane-bound nucleus. Bacteria and blue-green algae are the only surviving prokaryotes. (*See also* Eukaryote.)

Promoter site: defined by its recognition of eukaryotic RNA polymerase II; its activity in a higher eukaryote; by experimental evidence, or homology and sufficient similarity to an experimentally defined promoter; and by observed biological function.

Protein families: sets of proteins that share a common evolutionary origin reflected by their relatedness in function, which is usually reflected by similarities in sequence or in primary, secondary, or tertiary structure. Families are subsets of proteins with related structure and function.

Protein ID (in GenBank)[1,2]: an identification number assigned to the amino acid sequence data included within a sequence record. This sequence identifier uses the accession.version format. Each protein ID is made up of three letters, followed by five digits, a period, and a version number. For example, in sequence record M12345, the Protein ID for the sequence translation could be AAA35650.1. If the protein sequence data change in any way (even by only one amino acid), the version number in the Protein ID will be increased by an increment of one while the accession number base remains constant; for example, AAA12345.1 would become AAA12345.2. Each amino acid sequence change also results in the assignment of a new GI number to the altered protein translation.

Proteome: the entire protein complement of a given organism.

Proteomics: the study of a proteome. Typically, the cataloging of all the expressed proteins in a particular cell or tissue type, obtained by identifying the proteins from cell extracts using a combination of two-dimensional gel electrophoresis and mass spectrometry. Proteomics includes the large-scale analysis of the amassed protein composition and function. (*See also* Genomics.)

Purine: a nitrogen-containing compound with a double-ring structure. The parent compound of adenine and guanine.

Pyrimidine: a nitrogen-containing compound with a single six-membered ring structure. The parent compound of thymidine (uracil in RNA) and cytosine.

Quaternary structure[1,2]: the interconnection and arrangement of polypeptide chains within a protein. Only proteins with more than one polypeptide chain can have quaternary structure.

Query (sequence): a DNA, RNA of protein sequence used to search a sequence database in order to identify close or remote family members (homologs) of known function, or sequences with similar active sites or regions (analogs), from whom the function of the query may be deduced.

Reading frame: a sequence of codons beginning with an intiation (or start) codon and ending with a termination (or stop) codon, typically of at least 150 bases (50 amino acids), coding for a polypeptide or protein chain.

Recombinant DNA (rDNA): DNA molecules resulting from the fusion of DNA from different sources. The technology employed for splicing DNA from different sources and for amplifying the resulting heterogeneous DNA.

Recombination: a new combination of alleles resulting from the rearrangement occuring by crossing over or by independent assortment. (*See also* Crossing over.)

Recursion: an algorithmic procedure whereby an algorithm calls on itself to perform a calculation until the result exceeds a threshold, in which case the algorithm exits. Recursion is a powerful procedure with which to process data and is computationally quite efficient.

Regulatory gene: a DNA sequence that functions to control the expression of other genes by producing a protein that modulates the synthesis of their products (typically by binding to the gene promoter). (*See also* Structural gene.)

Relational database: a database that follows E. F. Codd's 11 rules, a series of mathematical and logical steps for the organization and systemization of data into a software system that allows easy retrieval, updating, and expansion.

Relational database management systems (RDBMS): a software system that includes a database architecture, query language, and data loading and updating tools and other ancillary software that together allow the creation of a relational database application. An RDBMS stores data in a database consisting of one or more tables of rows and columns. The rows correspond to a record (tuple); the columns correspond to attributes (fields) in the record. In an RDBMS, a view, defined as a subset of the database that is the result of the evaluation of a query, is a table. RDBMSs use Structured Query Language (SQL) for data definition, data management, and data access and retrieval. Relational and object-relational databases are used extensively in bioinformatics to store sequences and other biological data.

Repeats (repeat sequences): repeat sequences and approximate repeats occur throughout the DNA of higher organisms (mammals). For example, Alu sequences of about 300 characters in length appear hundreds of thousands of times in human DNA, with about 87% homology to a consensus Alu string. Some short substrings, such as TATA-boxes, poly-A, and (TG)*, also appear more often than would be expected by chance. Repeat sequences may also occur within genes, as mutations or alterations to those genes. Repetitive sequences, especially mobile elements, have many applications in genetic research. DNA transposons and retroposons are used routinely for insertional mutagenesis, gene mapping, gene tagging, and gene transfer in several model systems.

Repetitive elements: elements that provide important clues about chromosome dynamics, evolutionary forces, and mechanisms for exchange of genetic information between organisms. The most ubiquitous class of repetitive elements in the DNA sequence in primate genomes is the Alu family of interspersed repeats, which have arisen in the last 65 million years of evolution. Alu repeats belong to a class of sequences defined as short interspersed elements (SINEs). Approximately 500,000 Alu SINEs exist within the human genome, representing about 5% of the genome by mass. The pattern of these repeats in the human population can be used to address questions of large-scale genealogy.

Replication: the synthesis of an informationally identical macromolecule (e.g., DNA) from a template molecule.

Repressor: the protein product of a regulatory gene that combines with a specific operator (regulatory DNA sequence) and hence blocks the transcription of genes in an operon.

Residue: the portion of an amino acid that remains a part of a polypeptide chain. In the context of a peptide or protein, amino acids are generally referred to as residues.

Restriction enzyme (restriction endonuclease): a type of enzyme that recognizes specific DNA sequences (usually, palindromic sequences 4, 6, 8, or 16 base pairs in length) and produces cuts on both strands of DNA containing those sequences only.

Restriction map: a physical map or depiction of a gene (or genome) derived by ordering overlapping restriction fragments produced by digestion of the DNA with a number of restriction enzymes.

Retroposons: mobile DNA segments that insert into chromosomes after they have been reverse-transcribed from an RNA molecule.

Reverse genetics: the use of protein information to elucidate the genetic sequence encoding that protein.

Reverse transcriptase: a DNA polymerase that can synthesize a complementary DNA (cDNA) strand using RNA as a template; called RNA-dependent DNA polymerase.

Ribosomal RNA (rRNA): a type of rRNA that plays a large structural role in determining the structure and function of the ribosome (cellular structure on which proteins are assembled).

RNA (ribonucleic acid): a category of nucleic acids in which the component sugar is ribose and consisting of the four nucleotides: thymidine, uracil, guanine, and adenine. The three types of RNA are messenger RNA (mRNA), transfer RNA (tRNA), and ribosomal RNA (rRNA).

Secondary structure[1,2]**:** the folded, coiled, or twisted shape of a polypeptide that results from hydrogen bonding between parts of a molecule. There are two main types of secondary structure: an α-helix and a β-pleated sheet.

Selectivity: the selectivity of bioinformatics similarity search algorithms is defined as the significance threshold for reporting database sequence matches. For example, in BLAST searches, the parameter E is interpreted as the upper bound on the expected frequency of chance occurrence of a match within the context of the entire database search. E may be thought of as the number of matches that one expects to observe by chance alone during a database search.

Sensitivity: the sensitivity of bioinformatics similarity search algorithms centers around two areas: how well the method can detect biologically meaningful relationships between two related sequences in the presence of mutations and sequencing errors; and how the heuristic nature of the algorithm affects the probability that a matching sequence will not be detected. At the user's discretion, the speed of most similarity search programs can be sacrificed in exchange for greater sensitivity—with an emphasis on detecting lower-scoring matches.

Sequence tagged site (STS)[1,2]**:** a short (200 to 500 base pairs) DNA sequence that has a single occurrence in the human genome and whose location and base sequence are known. Detectable by polymerase chain reaction, STSs are useful for localizing and orienting the mapping and sequence data reported from many different laboratories and serve as landmarks for developing physical maps of the human genome. Expressed sequence tags (ESTs) are STSs derived from cDNAs.

Shotgun cloning: the cloning of an entire gene segment or genome by generating a random set of fragments using restriction endonucleases to create a gene library that can subsequently be mapped and sequenced to reconstruct the entire genome.

Signal sequence (leader sequence): a short sequence added to the amino-terminal end of a polypeptide chain that forms an amphipathic helix allowing the nascent polypeptide to migrate through membranes such as the endoplasmic reticulum or the cell membrane. It is cleaved from the polypeptide after the protein has crossed the membrane.

Similarity (homology) search: given a newly sequenced gene, there are two main approaches to the prediction of structure and function from the amino acid sequence. Homology methods are the most powerful and are based on the detection of significant extended sequence similarity to a protein of known structure, or of a sequence pattern characteristic of a protein family. Statistical methods are less successful but more general and are based on the derivation of structural preference values for single residues, pairs of residues, short oligopeptides, or short sequence patterns. The transfer of structure and function information to a potentially homologous protein is straightforward when the sequence similarity is high and extended in length, but the assessment of the structural significance of sequence similarity can be difficult when sequence similarity is weak or restricted to a short region.

Single nucleotide polymorphisms (SNPs): variations of single base pairs scattered throughout the human genome that serve as measures of genetic diversity in humans. About 1 million SNPs are estimated to be present in the human genome, and SNPs are useful markers for gene mapping studies.

Single-pass sequencing: rapid sequencing of large segments of the genome of an organism by isolating as many expressed (cDNA) sequences as possible and performing single sequencer runs on their 5′ or 3′ ends. Single-pass sequencing typically results in individual, error-prone sequencing reads of 400 to 700 bases, depending on the type of sequencer used. However, if many of these are generated from numerous clones from different tissues, they may be overlapped and assembled to remove the errors and generate a contiguous sequence for the entire expressed gene.

Site(s): sites in sequences can be located either in DNA (e.g., binding sites, cleavage sites) or in proteins. To identify a site in DNA, ambiguity symbols are used to allow several different symbols at one position. Proteins need a different mechanism, however (*see* Pattern). Restriction enzyme cleavage sites, for example, have the following properties: limited length (typically, fewer than 20 base pairs); definition of the cleavage site and its appearance (3′, 5′ overhang or blunt); definition of the binding site.

Splicing: the joining together of separate DNA or RNA component parts. For example, RNA splicing in eukaryotes involves the removal of introns and the stitching together of the exons from the pre-mRNA transcript before maturation.

Start codon: a triplet codon (i.e., AUG) at which both prokaryotic and eukaryotic ribosomes begin to translate the mRNA.

Stop codon: one of three triplet codons (UGA, UAG, and UAA) that does not instruct the ribosome to insert a specific amino acid and thereby causes translation of an mRNA to stop. Instead, a termination factor is typically inserted, causing the ribosome to be disassembled and the completed protein to be released.

Structural gene: a gene that encodes a structural protein.

Structure prediction: algorithms that predict the secondary, tertiary, and sometimes even quarternary structure of proteins from their sequences. Determining protein structure from a sequence has been dubbed "the second half of the genetic code" since it is the higher-level folded structure of a protein that governs how it functions as a gene product. As yet, most structure prediction methods have been only partially successful and typically work best for certain well-defined classes of proteins.

Substitution matrix: a model of protein evolution at the sequence level, resulting in the development of a set of widely used substitution matrices. These are frequently called Dayhoff, MDM (mutation data matrix), BLOSUM, or PAM (percent accepted mutation) matrices. They are derived from global alignments of closely related sequences. Matrices for greater evolutionary distances are extrapolated from those for lesser distances.

Substrate: a specialized type of ligand that binds specifically to an enzyme.

Tertiary structure: folding of a protein chain via interactions of its side-chain molecules, including formation of disulfide bonds between cysteine residues.

Thymine: one of the nitrogenous bases that has a single-ring structure, classified as a pyrimidine, found in DNA but not in RNA.

Tissue: a section of an organ that consists of a largely homogeneous population of cell types. Since many organs are multifunctional, they have developed highly specialized cell types to perform different functions. Identifying the section of an organ that is homogeneous for a particular cell type ensures that the gene expression profiles extracted from those cells will accurately resemble the class of cells that make up the tissue.

Toxicology: the science of the harmful effects of chemicals (including drugs) on living biological systems. It seeks to determine the mechanisms by which chemicals produce adverse effects in cells and organisms.

Transcript: the single-stranded mRNA chain that is assembled from a gene template.

Transcription: the assembly of complementary single-stranded RNA on a DNA template.

Transcription factors: a group of regulatory proteins that are required for transcription in eukaryotes. Transcription factors bind to the promoter region of a gene and facilitate transcription by RNA polymerase.

Transfer RNA (tRNA): a small RNA molecule that recognizes a specific amino acid, transports it to a specific codon in the mRNA, and positions it properly in the nascent polypeptide chain.

Transformation: a genetic alteration to a cell as a result of the incorporation of DNA from a genetically diferent cell or virus; can also refer to the introduction of DNA into bacterial cells for genetic manipulation.

Translation: the process of converting RNA to protein by the assembly of a polypeptide chain from an mRNA molecule at the ribosome.

Transposons: mobile DNA elements that insert into other chromosomal elements (also referred to as "jumping genes.")

Triple helical DNA: a mostly synthetic form of DNA; it may exist during recombination and DNA repair.

Unidentified reading frame (URF): an open reading frame encoding a protein of undefined function.

UniGene database[1,2]**:** a public database, maintained by NCBI, which brings together sets of GenBank sequences that represent the transcription products of distinct genes.

Unique clone[1,2]**:** an Incyte sequence that has no match in GenBank or other public database.

Uracil: one of the nitrogenous bases that has a single-ring structure, classified as a pyrimidine, found in RNA but not in DNA.

Variable numbers of tandem repeats (VNTRs): DNA sequence blocks of 2 to 60 base pairs which are repeated from two to more than 20 times in different individuals. This polymorphism makes VNTRs very useful DNA markers used in genomic mapping, linkage analysis, and DNA fingerprinting.

Variations (genetic): variations in genetic sequences and the detection of DNA sequence variants genome-wide allow studies relating the distribution of sequence variation to a population history. This, in turn, makes possible a determination of the density of SNPs or other markers needed for gene mapping studies. Quantitation of these variations, together with analytical tools for studying sequence variation, also relates genetic variations to phenotype.

Vector: any agent that transfers material (typically, DNA) from one host to another. Typically, DNA vectors are autonomous DNA elements (such as plasmids) that can be manipulated and integrated into a host's DNA or recombinant viruses.

Version (in GenBank)[1,2]: similar to the Protein ID for protein sequences, the version is a nucleotide sequence identification number assigned to each GenBank sequence. The format for this sequence identifier is accession. version (e.g., M12345.1). Whenever the author of a particular sequence record changes the sequence data in any way (even if just a single nucleotide is altered), the version number will be increased by an increment of one while the accession number base remains constant. For example, M12345.1 would become M12345.2. Each sequence change also results in the assignment of a new GI number (link to GI entry). Whenever an NCBI sequence database is searched, only the most recent version of a record is retrieved. NCBI's Sequence Revision History page is used to view the various GI numbers, version numbers, or update dates associated with a particular GenBank record.

Virtual libraries: the creation and storage of vast collections of molecular structures in an electronic database. These databases may be queried for subsets that exhibit specific physicochemical features, or may be "virtually screened" for their ability to bind a drug target. This process may be performed prior to the synthesis and testing of the molecules themselves.

Visualization: a process of representing abstract scientific data as images that can aid in understanding the meaning of the data.

Weight matrix: the density of binding sites in a gene or sequence can be used to derive a ratio of density for each element in a pattern of interest. The combined individual density ratios of all elements are then used collectively to build a scoring profile known as a weight matrix. This profile can be used to test the prediction of the identification of the pattern selected and the ability of the algorithm to discriminate it from a nonpattern sequences.

X chromosome: in mammals, the sex chromosome that is found in two copies in the homogametic sex (female in humans) and one copy in the heterogametic sex (male in humans).

Y chromosome: in mammals, the sex chromosome that is found in one copy in males and not at all in females.

Yeast two-hybrid system: a yeast-based method used to simultaneously identify, and clone the gene for, proteins interacting with a known protein.

Z DNA: a conformation of DNA existing as a left-handed double helix (the phosphate-sugar backbone forms a left-handed zigzag course), which may play a role in gene regulation.

REFERENCES

1. The Department of Energy (DOE) Human Genome Program. http://www.ornl.gov/sci/techresources/Human_Genome/glossary/.
2. National Center for Biotechnology Information (NCBI).http://www.ncbi.nlm.nih.gov/Education/BLASTinfo/glossary2.html.

INDEX

Mathematics of Bioinformatics: Theory, Practice, and Applications, By Matthew He and
Sergey Petoukhov
Copyright © 2011 John Wiley & Sons, Inc.

Wiley Series on

Bioinformatics: Computational Techniques and Engineering

Bioinformatics and computational biology involve the comprehensive application of mathematics, statistics, science, and computer science to the understanding of living systems. Research and development in these areas require cooperation among specialists from the fields of biology, computer science, mathematics, statistics, physics, and related sciences. The objective of this book series is to provide timely treatments of the different aspects of bioinformatics spanning theory, new and established techniques, technologies and tools, and application domains. This series emphasizes algorithmic, mathematical, statistical, and computational methods that are central in bioinformatics and computational biology.

Series Editors: **Professor Yi Pan** and **Professor Albert Y. Zomaya**
                  pan@cs.gsu.edu   zomaya@it.usyd.edu.au
